Working for Social Justice
Inside & Outside the Classroom

sj Miller & Leslie David Burns
GENERAL EDITORS

Vol. 2

The Social Justice Across Contexts in Education series is
part of the Peter Lang Education list.
Every volume is peer reviewed and meets
the highest quality standards for content and production.

PETER LANG
New York • Bern • Frankfurt • Berlin
Brussels • Vienna • Oxford • Warsaw

Working for Social Justice Inside and Outside the Classroom

A Community of Students, Teachers, Researchers, and Activists

Nancye E. McCrary and E. Wayne Ross, Editors

PETER LANG
New York • Bern • Frankfurt • Berlin
Brussels • Vienna • Oxford • Warsaw

Library of Congress Cataloging-in-Publication Data
Names: McCrary, Nancye E. | Ross, E. Wayne.
Title: Working for Social Justice Inside and Outside the Classroom:
A Community of Students, Teachers, Researchers, and Activists /
edited by Nancye E. McCrary, E. Wayne Ross.
Description: New York: Peter Lang, [2016] | Series: Social justice across
contexts in education, ISSN 2372-6849 (print), ISSN 2372-6857 (online); vol. 2 |
Includes bibliographical references.
Identifiers: LCCN 2015024540 | ISBN 9781433129469 (hardcover: alkaline paper) |
ISBN 9781433129452 (paperback: alkaline paper) | ISBN 9781453917046 (e-book)
Subjects: LCSH: Social justice—Study and teaching. | Teaching—Social aspects. |
Social action. | Critical pedagogy.
Classification: LCC LC192.2 .S65 2016 | DDC 370.115—dc23
LC record available at http://lccn.loc.gov/2015024540

Bibliographic information published by **Die Deutsche Nationalbibliothek**.
Die Deutsche Nationalbibliothek lists this publication in the "Deutsche
Nationalbibliografie"; detailed bibliographic data are available
on the Internet at http://dnb.d-nb.de/.

Cover art by Nancye E. McCrary, 2014.

© 2016 Peter Lang Publishing, Inc., New York
29 Broadway, 18th floor, New York, NY 10006
www.peterlang.com

All rights reserved.
Reprint or reproduction, even partially, in all forms such as microfilm,
xerography, microfiche, microcard, and offset strictly prohibited.

In memory of our friend
Adam Renner
1970–2010

Contents

Preface..xi
Acknowledgments...xiii

Working for Social Justice Inside and Outside the Classroom: A Community of Teachers, Researchers, and Activists... 1
    Nancye McCrary and E. Wayne Ross

Part I: What's Going On?

Chapter One: The Last Teacher... 9
    Nancye McCrary

Chapter Two: What Is to Be done?... 21
    Staughton Lynd

Chapter Three: Against Obedience... 29
    Susan Ohanian

Chapter Four: Pearson, Inc.: Slashing Away at Hercules' Hydra............................... 47
    Alan Singer and Eustace Thompson

Part II: Relation of Theory and Research to Practice in Social Justice Education

Chapter Five: On the Urgency and Relevance of Research for Marxists......................... 61
    Faith Agostinone-Wilson

Chapter Six: Reclaiming Our Indigenous Worldview: A More Authentic Baseline
for Social/Ecological Justice Work in Education 93
    Four Arrows and Darcia Narvaez

Chapter Seven: Why It Is Possible and Imperative to Teach Capital,
Empire, and Revolution—and How 113
    Rich Gibson

Chapter Eight: Class Struggle and Education: Neoliberalism, (Neo)conservatism,
and the Capitalist Assault on Public Education 139
    Dave Hill

Part III: Social Justice Education in the Classroom

Chapter Nine: Social Justice in the Classroom? It Would Be a Good Idea 159
    Doug Selwyn

Chapter Ten: Poverty, Politics, and Reading Education in the United States 179
    Patrick Shannon

Chapter Eleven: Counter-Narratives in State History: The 100 Years of State and
Federal Policy Curriculum Project Educational Thought and Sociocultural Studies..........193
    Glenabah Martinez

Chapter Twelve: Broadening the Circle of Critical Pedagogy 209
    E. Wayne Ross

Part IV: Social Justice Education Outside the Classroom

Chapter Thirteen: "Putting First Things First": Obligation and Affection
in Ecological Agrarian Education 221
    Leah Bayens

Chapter Fourteen: "Barely in the Front Door" but Beyond the Ivory Tower:
Women's and Gender Studies Pedagogy Outside the Classroom 231
    Tara M. Tuttle

Chapter Fifteen: Our Pass-Fail Moment: Livable Ecology, Capitalism, Occupy,
and What Is to Be Done 239
    Paul Street

Chapter Sixteen: Youth-Led Organizations, the Arts, and the 411 Initiative
for Change in Canada: Critical Pedagogy for the 21st Century 247
    Brad J. Porfilio and Michael Watz

Editors 263

Contributors 265

Preface

What were once distinct professions for serving others and building knowledge are now communities of workers struggling against the tide of increasingly unregulated capitalism fed by human greed. Teachers have become education workers, joining a working class that is rapidly falling behind, increasingly silenced and becoming part of an underclass working for the benefit of a power elite who control nearly all the wealth that once supported a thriving middle class. Yet, many continue to resist and work for a just and sustainable world.

One such community that has endured for 20 years is the Rouge Forum, a group of educators, students, parents, organizers, and activists who persist in working for social justice, democratic education, and a common good. Founded by social education teachers, scholars, and activists, the Rouge Forum moves like waves that, once set in motion, are unstoppable. This remarkably inclusive group exemplifies the power of community and the urgency for dialogue among us. It prevails with hundreds of thousands of visitors to the Rouge Forum website, annual conferences held throughout the United States and Canada, and many of the original founders continuing to ride the waves of change.

This book is written in memory of Adam Renner and dedicated to hopeful communities exemplified by the people of the Rouge Forum who fight for democratic ideals and work against perpetual war, the destruction of our natural environment, and increasing poverty and social inequalities. These people who have been part of the conversation that is the Rouge have long stood together to deliver important counter-narratives to resist the insatiable greed of a few and support a common good for most.

The Rouge Forum is uniquely inclusive. Educators, scholars, students, writers, union organizers, artists, and many more gather each year for dialogic interaction and learning together. Membership crosses cultural, national, racial, and class boundaries in the struggle for a just and sustainable world. Conferences aim to foster dialogue among participants rather than stand-and-deliver speeches. Panel and roundtable discussions are encouraged. As one student said after presenting with a panel of college students at the 2014 Denver Conference, "As we went one by one, you could tell that our confidence continued to rise. When we completed our panel, the crowd kept the conversation going with questions…*about our ideas*…on how to have dialogic discussions and [build] communities." She continued, saying that the participants were not asking questions about what they knew or how well-prepared they were. Instead, they wanted to hear their ideas. She ended by saying "…this experience was one for the books."

We want to thank *all* of the contributors to this book for sharing their ideas and building community inside and outside the **Rouge Forum**. We also want to thank all the people who, over many years, have made the **Rouge Forum** what it is. What follows is an incomplete list of those who have made extraordinary contributions to the cause.

Thanks to all the members of the Rouge Forum Steering Committee; these are the folks who make our conferences, special events, websites, and publications happen, especially: Amber Goslee, Greg Queen, Gina Steins, Doug Morris (Rouge Forum Music Director), Doug Selwyn, Joe Cronin, Bryan Reinholdt (Financial Manager), Joe Wegwert, Joe Bishop, Travis Barrett, Marc Pruyn, Gregg Jorgensen, and William Boyer (Rouge Forum Resident Peformance Artist), and Elishia Smith.

Thanks to all who have directed Rouge Forum meetings and events: Greg Queen, Amber Goslee, Bill Boyer, Michael Peterson, and Rich Gibson have directed many of our Detroit events; David Hursh (Rochester); Stephen C. Fleury (Syracuse); the late Adam Renner (Louisville); J. Joe Bishop (Ypsilanti, MI); Faith Agostinone-Wilson (Williams Bay, WI); Brad J. Porfilio (Chicago); Stephen Petrina (Vancouver); the late Dennis Carlson (Oxford, OH); and C. Gregg Jorgensen (Denver).

We appreciate our collaborators and conference cosponsors over the years including the Whole School Consortium, the Whole Language Umbrella of the National Council of Teachers of English, Syracuse Center for Urban Education (at Le Moyne College), PrESS Network, the journal *Cultural Logic*, Institute for Critical Education Studies at the University of British Columbia and its journals *Critical Education* (criticaleducation.org) and *Workplace: A Journal for Academic Labor* (workplace-gsc.com).

Thanks to the universities and departments that have helped make our conferences possible including Wayne State University, Warner Graduate School of Education at the University of Rochester, SUNY Albany (and United University Professions), University of Louisville, Syracuse University, Bellarmine University, Eastern Michigan University, Aurora University, University of British Columbia, Lewis University, Miami University, and Metropolitan State University of Denver.

We have been honored to have a long list of keynote speakers and other special guests at Rouge Forum meetings including, Josh White, Jr., Ed Sanders, M. L. Leiber, Detroit Storyliving, The Uprising, The Movement, Billy X. Curmano, Sandra Mathison, Susan Ohanian, Richard Brosio, Cate Fosl, Kenneth J. Saltman, Kevin D. Vinson, Dave Hill, George Schmidt, Michael Peterson, Rich Gibson, Milton Brown, Staughton Lynd, Dennis Carlson, Gustavo Fischman, Stephen Petrina, Jill Pinkney-Pastrana, Alan Spector, Brad Porfilio, Vincent Emanuele, Julie Herrada, Mike Prysner, Paul Street, Monty Neil, and Roy Rosenzweig to name a few. Since 2011, the Rouge Forum has presented the Adam Renner Education for Social Justice Lecture, which has been delivered by Peter McLaren, Susan Ohanian, Patrick Shannon, and David Barsamian.

Acknowledgments

Chapters 2, 3, 6, and 14 were originally delivered as keynote addresses at the Rouge Forum. Chapters 3, 8, 14, and 15 appeared in different forms in the journal *Critical Education* and are republished here with permission.

Working for Social Justice Inside and Outside the Classroom: A Community of Teachers, Researchers, and Activists

Nancye McCrary and E. Wayne Ross

This book represents a tapestry of social justice issues woven in and out of formal and informal educations and written by some of the most influential contemporary thinkers. While such a text might or should begin with a clear and singular definition of social justice, it is not possible because there is such a wide array of understandings of what it means to be just and socially responsible. In speaking about education in large research universities, Wendell Berry (2012) said, "…we are promoting a debased commodity paid for by the people, sanctioned by the government, for the benefit of the corporations" (para. 5). As you will see, the contributors to this book take aim at social justice and education in varied ways, yet intersect by articulating ideals worth weaving into the fabric of our collective consciousness.

This book is organized in four sections. In Part I, What's Going On?, Nancye McCrary sets the stage by discussing the education and the day-to-day work of teachers, examining some of the reasons teachers, as we know them, are rapidly becoming extinct. Staughton Lynd, a well-known leader of the Freedom Schools during the Civil Rights Movement, provides an historical perspective that informs much of what is happening today and "What is to be done." Susan Ohanian writes "Against Obedience," explaining that teachers are being pushed to prepare their "students to be commodities in the Global Economy." Ohanian insists "Either you join the revolution or you stand against the needs of children, and you aid the destruction of your own profession, not to mention democracy." And finally, Alan Singer and Eustace Thompson conclude Part I with "Pearson, Inc.: Slashing Away at Hercules' Hydra," in which they deconstruct the means and ends of the corporate education reform. Pearson, the multi-headed mega-publisher, has inordinate influence over education in the United States and around the world, yet it also has serious vulnerabilities.

Singer and Thompson argue that: "For all its claims about valuing education, the only thing Pearson appears to value is profit."

In Part II, Relation of Theory and Research to Practice in Social Justice Education, Faith Agostinone-Wilson writes her chapter "On the Urgency and Relevance of Research for Marxists," providing an eloquent analysis of the politics of research methodology, arguing that class must be the central unit of analysis in a capitalist society because Marxist research aims, not only to document the world, but to change it. In Chapter 6, "Reclaiming Our Indigenous Worldview: A More Authentic Baseline for Social/Ecological Justice Work in Education," Four Arrows and Darcia Narvaez offer a hopeful paradigm for reclaiming indigenous perspectives to guide our work toward social and ecological justice. Rich Gibson, a cofounder of the Rouge Forum, follows with, "Why It Is Possible and Imperative to Teach Revolution—and How," using the analogy of the *Spider and the Fly* in urging revolution that interrupts the trend toward educating for war and detaches public education from the production of capital. Dave Hill, in "Class Struggle and Education: Neoliberalism, Neo-Conservativism, and the Capitalist Assault on Public Education," provides a more global perspective on education, in which he examines the neoliberal alliance with conservative forces in Turkey. He says the Erdogan government is pushing forward with Islamicization of society using the repressive apparatuses of the state, reminding us that the takeover of public education in the United States is not unique.

Parts III and IV, Social Justice Education in the Classroom and Social Justice Education Outside the Classroom, converge on teaching and learning formally and informally. Doug Selwyn, in Chapter 9, "Social Justice in the Classroom? It Would Be a Good Idea," examines the terrible toll of stress and poverty on public school students, insisting that teachers cannot be held accountable for the injustices in our society. In "Poverty, Politics, and Reading Education in the United States," Patrick Shannon details the catastrophic consequences of poverty on the learning lives of children. He says, "Neoliberals' promotion of innovation [in education] contradicts their enthusiasm for a single testing regime." Following Shannon, Glenabah Martinez examines the deculturalization of Indigenous Peoples in the state of New Mexico in her chapter: "Teaching Counter-Narratives: Indigenous Peoples, History, and Critical Consciousness." She articulates the importance of integrating Pueblo core values and the gifts of the Creator in school curriculum as a means to control the destinies of Pueblo people and preserve their culture. Martinez outlines a framework for curriculum that includes Pueblo core values such as love, respect, compassion, faith, understanding, spirituality, and balance, as well as gifts of the Creator, land, language, way of life, laws and customs, governance, family, community, and natural resources. Part III concludes with "Broadening the Circle of Critical Pedagogy" in which E. Wayne Ross argues for a critical pedagogy that "…is not about showing life to people, but bringing them to life." He notes contradictions in Freire's critical pedagogy, while artfully weaving Dewey's ideas on democracy with John Holt's argument that attempting to change society through schools evades "personal responsibility because authentic meaning cannot be cultivated en masse." Ross asserts that the aim of critical pedagogy should be getting students "…to speak for themselves" in order to reach for "…an equal degree of participation and a better future."

Part IV, Social Justice Education Outside the Classroom, begins with Leah Bayens' chapter "'Putting First Things First': Obligation and Affection in Ecological Agrarian Education." She details an innovative program that she directs at St. Catharine College in Central Kentucky. Working closely with the Wendell Berry Foundation and relying on Berry's work as a fulcrum for the program, Bayens quotes Berry (2010) regarding our current system of postsecondary education as an "instigator of social instability, ecological oblivion, and economic insecurity" (p. 32, 33). This so-called upward mobility major, argues Berry, "has put our schools far too much at the service of what we have been calling overconfidently our economy" (p. 32). It has been preparing graduates for "expert servitude to the corporations" (p. 32) rather than for reciprocal community membership. Tara Tuttle follows with Chapter 14 "'Barely in the Front Door' but Beyond the Ivory Tower: Women's and Gender Studies Pedagogy Outside the Classroom," arguing that Women and Gender Studies is an *interdiscipline* where learning depends on enacting knowledge gained in the classroom. Tuttle makes a strong case that Women and Gender Studies necessarily goes "beyond the ivory tower" as a body of knowledge that requires praxis and interaction to be fully synthesized. In Chapter 15, Paul Street contends that the work of social justice encompasses so much that our energies can be diffuse in struggling against poverty, environmental issues, gender inequities, and so on. He offers the analogy to triage as separating the most urgent issue from those that can be addressed later. The most urgent are examined, giving priority to the ill most likely to cause immediate demise. In doing so, Street suggests environmental sustainability must be addressed first because destruction of the earth will render all other work of equity and justice meaningless. He says: "What good is it to inherit a poisoned Earth from the bourgeoisie? What's the point of more equally sharing out a poison pie?"

And finally, Brad Porfilio and Michael Watz examine "Youth-Led Organizations, the Arts, and the 411 Initiative for Change in Canada" in the context of critical pedagogy for the 21st century. Porfilio and Watz critically examine how our youths' "quality of life has ...been denigrated by the implementation of commercialized and militarized practices in K-12 educational structures." They discuss the fact that many urban schools in the United States and Canada are unsafe, unsanitary, dilapidated, racially segregated, and overcrowded institutions, where ill-equipped educators implement "drill and kill" methods of instruction. This chapter, however, offers hope by highlighting youth-led organizations, the motivation to establish and enact, the methods used to engage peers in social commentary and activism, and how members confront and overcome barriers in schools when implementing their pedagogical initiatives.

In sum, this book crosses intersections of community, place, and time through the environs of home, school, work, and our sacred earth in ways that honor histories, communities, diversities, and human rights. It is a collection of voices speaking from inside and outside classrooms, formal and informal education, the Rouge Forum, and beyond on issues of consciousness and common good. Nearly all of the writers are or have been teachers and, in this book, they *teach* by articulating disturbing practices and offering powerful ideas that can change the world. Indeed, they speak in concert on embracing community, resisting injustice, and protecting inalienable human rights. From the first chapter to the last, this collection of essays poses difficult questions, exposes inequities, and offers ideas for change.

In what follows, we begin in honor of the memory of Adam Renner, who was our friend, a scholar, teacher, musician, and the Community Coordinator of the Rouge Forum until his sudden death in 2010. Once rooted in Liberation Theology, Adam told a story of how he became aware of the complicit connections between his own privileged position and the relative consequences for those less fortunate. It was a summer job during high school when he became friends with a man who was homeless, displaced by the new construction on which Adam was working. It was a simple and familiar yet powerful story, as he told how that connection with just one *different other*, a casualty of his summer work, awakened his own critical thinking, a new kind of knowing, his questioning mind. From his roots in Freirean Liberation Theology, to a real-world human connection, and disillusionment, Adam Renner devoted the rest of his short life to the power of community and the interconnectedness of us all. The year before he died, he wrote an article that contributed in significant ways to the conversation started by Paulo Freire in 1970 with his book *Pedagogy of the Oppressed*.

Teaching Community, Praxis, and Courage

Pointing toward our broken-down sense of community and dis-connectedness, Renner (2009) argued that rekindling concepts of "community, connectedness, and the collective is central to the thesis of social justice." That is, "a hopeful path toward justice depends on the extent to which we can (re)invigorate solidarity and more active, participatory democracy" (p. 59). Using a series of early 21st century "shocks" (e.g., the Iraq War, the genocide in Darfur, Hurricane Katrina, the No Child Left Behind Act, and corporate globalization) as a springboard, Renner develops pedagogical possibilities from which resistance to these shocks might emerge and asks: How can educators use these events as part of an effort to build (or rebuild) community? After describing the background of each event he makes connections to a local context and then explores the event's "pedagogical contexts." Let's take a look at just one of the "shocks" Renner deconstructs.

> **Genocide in Darfur.** As the echoes of "never again" become fainter and fainter; as more and more Darfurians are displaced; as more and more Darfurians are murdered by state sanction; and as the world community drags its feet (and considers who might get Sudan's oil), one already imagines the horrific narratives that will be written about this era—wondering how it could have happened, why no one stopped it, and what the world community will do to make sure that this time it never happens again. This is the (ultimate) breakdown and disconnect of community, indeed—a world in which the relative wealthy receive the technical bread and circus of reality TV and the latest electronic gadgets, yet thousands of their brothers and sisters are murdered by relatively simple and unsophisticated implements: knives, machetes, and rifles.
>
> **Local context.** Locally, like many other places, Save Darfur campaigns continue to pop up, lectures and films (at the Jewish Community Center, by Catholic Relief Services, at the Muhammad Ali Center, etc.) are given and shown, and awareness waxes and wanes. Likewise, many refugees from Sudan and from other African zones of displacement and devastation arrive in Louisville for a fresh start, corralled into the center part of the city and creating an interesting and segregated international camp. Perhaps more interesting, the children of these refugees are educated at a Newcomer's Academy in one of the poorest high schools in Louisville, isolated from the general population by schedule and geography, residing in a formerly abandoned floor of this aging building.
>
> **Pedagogical context.** Questions for teacher candidates and students in P–12 schools who reside in the city alongside these refugees include: Do they understand the context from which these immigrants come? Can the residents connect the holocaust recalled in the history texts to the subsequent genocides that continue to unfold and progress? Do teacher candidates understand anything about the holocaust on their own American soil? What work can be done to integrate students from the Newcomer's Academy into the mainstream of area schools? As many of these teachers and students enjoy the festivities of the Kentucky Derby festival each year, which includes Thunder over Louisville—a fireworks and military exhibition—can they

imagine of what the sound of these exploding munitions and roaring aircraft must remind the traumatized migrants? (Renner, 2009, pp. 64–65)

Where is the hope? Where is the resistance to these shocks; injustices in education? How do we move toward solidarity and more active, participatory democracy in schools and beyond? Renner (2009; Renner & Brown, 2006) offers us a framework that focuses on community, praxis, and courage.

First, he argues we need to connect ourselves, our students, and curriculum to communities. This means putting a human face on issues like war, poverty, and exploitation. Asking questions of and exploring connections and responses to "shocks" and their reverberations globally and particularly in our everyday lives. In short, this implies education conceived as community-building (rather than education for economic development), learning how we can live together in a global democracy, and

> finding ways to connect students' lives together, connecting curriculum with the world outside of school…and connecting students with real lives/stories/faces in local, national, and global communities [so] that teachers and students can both better understand our privileged positions and work for more level, equitable partnerships. (Renner, 2009, p. 72)

Second, along with community we need to work toward more radical (e.g., proceeding from the roots) understanding of class and injustice: "teachers must consistently seek to craft more nuanced lenses, deepen their consciousness, and develop a discourse of social justice," what Renner labels praxis (p. 73). Teachers, for example, can craft these lenses through community activity that resembles critical service learning (e.g., Renner, 2011; Westheimer & Kahne, 2004), which asks questions about why such service may even be necessary and then students have the opportunity to "connect heretofore unseen dots." These activities might lead them toward "noticing the corporatizing trends in education, the privatizing influences in our economy, and threats to democracy" (Renner, 2009, p. 73).

> Teachers can do this through humanizing pedagogical practices which pose problems for their students, making the world a series of issues to be researched, resolved, and improved, rather than one that is given, static, and unchanging. (Renner, 2009, p. 74)

Third, we have to recognize that teaching community, teaching for social justice and/or social change, requires great courage, because it demands a new way of being in the world. Social justice requires a revolution of everyday life, a reversal of perspective (Ross & Vinson, 2006). It takes courage to critically examine our everyday life and how our practical activities in a capitalist society reproduce capitalism and the conditions of our own (and others') oppression, for example, alienation from self, our work, and others (Perlman, 1969). And it takes courage to explore the possibilities of self-realization, communication, and participation as activities that can transcend the threats of capitalism and fragmented disconnection (e.g., alienation, oppression, and exploitation).

The revolution of everyday life comes with our ability to understand and transform our world—the fundamental goal of social justice education (aka critical pedagogy). "To avoid the socially reproductive tendencies of injustice, educators must recognize the tremendous stakes and the pressing nature of the work" (Renner, 2009, p. 75). In sum, it requires teaching community and praxis, while becoming visible in the struggle through courageous action: engaging in passionate acts of refusal and consciousness of the necessity of resistance to trigger stoppages in the factories of collective illusion—whether those factories be schools that only offer students alienation, spectacle, surveillance, and training for consumption or a corporate media that offers us fear and perpetual war; responding to the call for a "militant humanism" (Brown 2008) that interrupts dehumanizing trends in education, politics, and elsewhere, and expands humanizing practices; and developing one's voice (recognizing silence as an act of aggression that denies the disenfranchised their humanity). Wherever these actions are found, the revolution of everyday life is under way. Teaching for community, praxis, and courage is the heart of what working for social justice means to the community of teachers, researchers, and activists that is the Rouge Forum.

References

Berry, W. E. (2010). *A major in homecoming. What matters? Economics for a renewed commonwealth.* Berkeley, CA: Counterpoint Press. (Original work published 2000).

Berry, W. E. (2012, May 14). *Wendell Berry and the meaning of higher education.* Commencement address Bellarmine University, Louisville, KY. Retrieved from http://myunquietheart.blogspot.com/2012/05/wendell-berry-and-meaning-of-higher.html

Brown, M. (2008, March 14). *Dehumanization.* Keynote address delivered at the Rouge Forum Conference, Louisville, KY.

Freire, P. (1970). *The pedagogy of the oppressed.* New York: Continuum.

Perlman, F. (1969). *The reproduction of everyday life.* Detroit: Black & Red. Retrieved from https://libcom.org/library/reproduction-everyday-life-fredy-perlman

Renner, A. (2009). Teaching community, praxis, and courage: A foundations pedagogy of hope and humanization. *Educational Studies, 45,* 59–79.

Renner, A. (2011). To build a sustainable international service learning partnership: Pushing service learning beyond the boundaries toward a revolutionary project of community and consciousness in Jamaica. In B. J. Porfilio & H. Hickman (Eds.), *Critical-service learning as revolutionary pedagogy: An international project of student agency in action.* Charlotte, NC: Information Age Publishing.

Renner, A., & Brown, M. (2006). A hopeful curriculum: Community, praxis, and courage. *Journal of Curriculum Theorizing, 22,* 101–122.

Ross, E. W., & Vinson, K. D. (2006). Social justice requires a revolution of everyday life. In R. L. Allen, M. Pruyn, & C. A. Rossatto (Eds.), *Reinventing critical pedagogy* (pp. 143–186). Lanham, MD: Rowman & Littlefield.

Westheimer, J. & Kahne, J. (2004). What kind of citizen? The politics of educating for democracy. *American Educational Research Journal, 41*(2), 237–269.

PART I
What's Going On?

ONE

The Last Teacher

Nancye McCrary

Public education in the United States is rapidly disappearing, especially since the world economy took a dive. Increasingly louder neoliberal demands for smaller government [shrinking public sector] and deregulation [wider corporate privilege] coincide with seemingly unrelated demands for *re-forming* public education. As the calls to liberate private enterprise become louder, a bizarre contradiction has unfolded in the context of global climate change and increasing poverty in the United States. This push to corporatize nearly everything, while further deregulating corporate practices, seems almost ghostly, a reflection of Ayn Rand's *rational self-interest* at just the wrong time, were there ever a right time for such objectivism. As we watch the ice melt and conclude, through nearly all scientific evidence, that human enterprise is causing earth's demise; those who stand to amass even more capital are calling for maximizing corporate rights to ravage whatever is left. The toll this is taking on the vast majority is enormous, primarily because privileging a few never actually *trickles down* to those who produce the goods and services. In fact, those on the front lines of production are often blamed when profits from their work decline. Such injustice results in decreasing wages, busted unions, and increasing poverty for the majority.

In this context, there is a growing assault on public education in the United States like none we have seen since Sputnik (1957). In complicit ignorance of the art and science of teaching and learning, politicians and their corporate funders continue to claim that public education in the United States is failing when, in fact, all that is failing is corporate takeover and reform of public education. Ill-informed efforts to fix public education have resulted in a cacophony of statistical and political rhetoric in the media that serves to undermine the very foundations of public education in the United States. As economic and cultural inequalities grow, our society pressures the field of education to close the *achievement gap* and guarantee an increasingly unattainable promise of equal opportunity for all (Hayes, 2012). Education is expected to amend the mistakes of our society and is condemned when the task cannot be accomplished by education alone. As the United States frantically tries to hold on to economic and military dominance, dubious results from standardized tests are touted as evidence that our public schools are failing by those who stand to profit from *fixing* education. The more media sound bites claim schools are failing, the more public education in the United States is being ravaged. The effects of such assaults on our students are devastating and concurrent attacks on teachers as the primary cause of the problem are nearly as ghastly. The media, largely controlled by the wealthy class, persists in blaming teachers for the ills of society, not superintendents, state education administrators, or boards of education. As a result, we are losing many of our most effective educators and discouraging college students from becoming teachers through increasingly prohibitive state mandated requirements for entering teacher education programs. Indeed the population of well-trained and knowledgeable educators in the United States is shrinking rapidly and fewer are choosing to become teachers. Once a highly respected service produced and maintained by well-trained professional teachers is rapidly becoming a for-profit corporate enterprise.

This is no requiem, and it is not yet over. Although gravely endangered, teachers who impassion learners because they know them well, understand pedagogical content, encourage self-efficacy, and care deeply about students' achievement are not yet extinct. Like most endangered species, their survival is threatened by loss of habitat, prevailing ignorance, and unfettered greed. Should this continue without collective resistance, we may all live to know the *last teacher* and hear the requiem for public education sung by a chorus of those who will know the enormity of the loss. While attacking teachers may help pave the way for corporate takeover and profit, it has never led to better education. Media assaults on teachers serve to distract the citizenry from critical issues that do impede education, such as widespread poverty, growing inequity, and efforts to control curriculum by those who are shamelessly ignorant of the profession of teaching and learning. Attacking teachers is not about improving education for our children. It is about corporate profit. Those who stand to gain from bogus reform initiatives delight in criticising teachers and ignoring education's successes. This continual denigration of the teaching profession is certainly taking its toll on teachers. "Who would ever want to go into this *now-beleaguered profession?*" asks one teacher, claiming that current education reform is like weeding out teachers by using students as collateral (Retrieved from http://perdidostreetschool.blogspot.com/2012/02/who-would-want-to-become-teacher-these.html).

Indeed the work done in schools is neither responsible for the problems in our society nor can it alleviate them. Schools and teachers cannot change the tragic fact that in 2012, 16 million, or 22%, of all children in the United States under the age of 18 were in families living in poverty (Retrieved from http://nces.ed.gov/programs/coe/indicator_cce.aspover). What is worse, of those living in poverty in the United States in 2012, black and Hispanic children accounted for 73%, while white/non-Hispanic comprised only 12.4 % (Retrieved from http://npc.umich.edu/poverty/). In 2013, according to the Southern Education Foundation, more than half (51%) of U.S. public school students lived in low-income households as determined by data from the National Center for Education Statistics eligibility for free or reduced lunches (Klein, 2015).

Public school teachers are expected to mitigate such disparities. When they don't, they are faced with increasing oppressive accountability, obsession with measurable outcomes, uninformed ideas, and disregard for the emotional well-being of school children. For example, over the past several decades, teachers have been trained to embrace diversity. Diversity has become a standard catch-phrase for instilling a belief that all children can learn. Those of us who know the value of human diversity have jumped on the bandwagon as though the primary problem has been that teachers have not embraced diversity in their classrooms. Examining this seemingly honorable intent a little deeper, however, reveals another more challenging problem in education, overwhelming poverty among families who are black and Hispanic. Avoiding socio-economic inequities in public schools by focusing on racism clearly lays blame on teachers' attitudes about children of color without raising more serious systemic problems. In fact, were disparities among school children due to teachers' ignorance and biases about racial and ethnic diversity, such inequity would no longer exist. That is not to say teachers are less predisposed toward racism than any other group, but to say that poverty claims many more victims in education than race or ethnicity.

Unfettered Greed

In the current climate of unfettered greed by a very small minority of power brokers, addressing issues of poverty is unlikely. Effective teachers are increasingly growing weary of rowing against the tide of corporate reform and face extinction as quick-fix organizations like Teach for America (TFA) have seen enormous profits in the *industry* of teacher education. Investors pour money into the materials of teaching and learning to market for less well-trained education workers. The toll taken by such profit is the loss of teachers as we know them. Indeed, the paradigm is rapidly changing from how best to educate the populace to increasing corporate profit from the state-funded practice of educating them.

As McLaren (2014) asserts, "the United States has become an oligarchy in which the power elite benefit from the consolidation of power, arranged industrial, bureaucratic, and commodity models that have commonly been associated with the military industrial complex…" (para. 5). Such power centers, says McLaren, are connected through "…intersecting social, cultural, and political spheres that can be managed ideologically by means of powerful, all-encompassing corporate media apparatuses and the culture industry in general, including both popular and more traditional forms of religious dogma and practice" (para. 5). As he left office, President Eisenhower warned the American people of the danger of the developing military industrial complex that has since realized enormous profits from continual war. As war has become profitable for private corporations, it is in the interests of their executives, who comprise the power elite, to persist in fueling continual wars across the globe. Those who can control the means of production are determined to maintain their economic prosperity whatever the consequences. In education, though, the causalities are not distant others or soldiers, they are generations of our own children.

The argument that teachers are responsible for so-called failing schools has invited corporate/state takeover of teaching and reduced teachers to workers in service of ever-changing mandates imposed by profiteers and ideologues. "Teachers are easy targets for the state to victimize" (p. 7) say Freeman, Mathison, and Wilcox (2014). "In this process, the dominant ideology, which in this case is a neo-liberal one, succeeds both in laying the blame upon those they wish to control while at the same time effectively silencing them" (p. 7).

Adding insult, the public is being convinced that teachers' complaints are really about not wanting to work harder. Such contemptuous accusations harken back to Fordism, a manufacturing philosophy, initiated by Henry Ford, which aims to increase productivity by standardizing output and segmenting skilled work into smaller deskilled tasks. Produce more material, hire unskilled workers to follow simple instructions and increase profit by getting the job done for less. But teaching our children is not an industry and conflating production for profit with educating a child is preposterous. When we allow such a shift to continue, we are denying our children the right to be educated by expert professionals and complicit in objectifying them as products.

Impressive educators continue to teach in enough schools to offer some hope of restoring the species and reviving a functional public education for all, at least in the United States, where it has long been the hallmark of our democratic dream. These educators suffer terribly under failed corporate re-forming of public education. Those in power have exhausted precious capital and are turning toward the public sector in search of more. American capitalists have consumed nearly all available capital in the United States, moved on to globalization, consumed vast amounts of global resources, and now eagerly eye what can be gained by tapping into the trough of *public* education. For example, there are for-profit corporations that create their own nonprofit intermediary to consume public funding. One of the best examples is Pearson Education Foundation, a philanthropy that has been under investigation for its work as an intermediary on behalf of its for-profit parent corporation, Pearson Education, Inc. In 2011, the Gates Foundation announced a partnership with the Pearson Foundation to produce resources for the Common Core State Standards. Pearson simultaneously announced it was developing a digital curriculum to support the proposed standards. Microsoft then unveiled its own $15 million research and development for Next Generation products, aligned to the new standards. The potential return on such an investment is staggering and on every level appears most favorable for the data industry. Pearson Education is now closing its partner nonprofit Pearson Foundation after having legal problems in New York and California. "In 2013, Pearson Foundation paid $7.7 million in fines in New York State to reach an out-of-court settlement after the Office of the State Attorney General found the Foundation had broken state laws by generating business for the for-profit company" (Singer, 2014, Pearson's Foundation Closing, para. 1). According to the settlement agreement, says Singer, the charitable foundation staff consisted almost entirely of Pearson Education, Inc. employees and nearly all of the foundation's board members were Pearson executives. The language of *failing schools* inspires a kind of Cold War urgency to avoid falling behind. It has opened the door to unscrupulous control and scrutiny that exists in few other public or private professions. With enrollment in K–12 public schools in the United States reaching 49.8 million in 2012 (National Center for Education Statistics, 2012), it is little wonder that corporate control will be highly profitable.

Shrinking Habitat

The most ravaging effect of corporate *re-forming* of public education begins with the loss of skillful teachers and privatization of public education. It may well end with no means to maintain the ideals of democracy. The loss of public habitat, prevailing ignorance of what teachers actually know and do and unfettered greed endanger an entire species of inspired, dedicated, knowledgeable, and effective educators, which in turn sacrifices our most precious common good for the benefit of a hungry market.

Indeed, we are losing the kind of educators who combine passion for and deep knowledge, of content, learners, and learning; those who possess a high level of skill in designing instruction and assessment, and have the abilities to orchestrate meaningful learning activities and think critically about teaching and learning. For example, educators have long embraced assessment as means to determine the effectiveness of instruction. It is an iterative process in which the design of instruction is based on student characteristics, learning objectives guided by curriculum, and classroom affordances, such as learning materials, technologies, and space. The instruction is then implemented, followed by assessments that indicate the extent to which learners have achieved the learning objectives. It is classic instructional design: Who are the learners (target audience), what are they to learn (curriculum), and how will we know if they have learned (assessment)? Most teachers do this quite well. Assessment, however, no longer connotes a method for refining instruction. It has become a way to produce standard scores to use against teachers and schools, a means to determine so-called low-performing schools and the basis for punishing both. High-stakes assessment simply adds risk to job security. Such unreasonable accountability has led to a relatively new phenomenon that is called *teaching to the test*. This shift is no accident—it positions teachers as workers in service of the state or corporation and distances them from their students, the curriculum, and instructional practices that work. No longer is assessment simply a means to continually determine the extent to which students grasp new knowledge and master new skills or refine instruction. Assessment has become a weapon to assert control of curriculum and financial profit for companies that produce and score standardized tests, subsequently producing textbooks and other material purchased with public funds. The barrage of attacks aimed at controlling curriculum to suit particular ideologies, limited resources, and exhausting harassment are reducing instructional time and separating teachers from their students, while insisting it is all about learners and their learning.

Prevailing Ignorance

Those who import terms and assumptions from business (Saltman, 2014), who now call education an industry instead of a profession and aim to market it for profit, continue to call their efforts *reform*. Yet, there is a disturbing dissonance between what we know about teaching and learning and so-called *new* initiatives or *industry standards* for improving public education in the United States. While educators have long understood how learning occurs and how best to orchestrate it, our society persists in failing to provide adequate support for teachers, who continue to work under increasing demands for extraordinary and incoherent accountability. It has been called the "corrosive call for improving teacher quality" (Thomas, 2013, p. 203), which works to replace public education with free-market competition and quality teachers with service workers. Giroux (2011) described it as a corporate business culture masked in generosity and reform that supports a charter school movement aiming to dismantle public education for a business-friendly privatized system.

Reducing teaching to arbitrary measures of student achievement on so-called objective tests is driving the most conscientious away from public education (Strauss, 2014). Carol Burris (2013), an award winning principal of South Side High School in New York, witnessed firsthand how the New York Education Department in partnership with Pearson, Inc. created high-stakes tests that were taken and scored before deciding what score constituted passing. Such misuse of high-stakes tests in the name of accountability is, at best, ignorance of what we know about testing and measurement. At worst, it is abuse of students and teachers for the purpose of controlling the education market. Were teachers to use tests in the same manner, determining the minimum passing score after tests are taken, it would be tantamount to felonious false reporting of students' standardized test scores, a crime for which educators have been prosecuted in the United States.

Yet, such scores are easy to spin in mass media to control the populace. But what do standardized test scores actually tell us about students? As Au (2009) found, such tests do measure important demographic qualities. He calls it the *zip code effect* that can suggest which students will succeed in school and in life according to their relative sociocultural privileges, as evidenced by where they live. Au traces the origins of standardized testing to eugenics and social efficiency initiatives of the late 19th and early 20th centuries. He details how standardized tests are centered on inequality woven with the social inequities that exist outside school. The idea of standardizing education to assure *all students learn* the same content and skills at the same rate has never been a good idea or a practical possibility. Social efficiency to increase profit and preserve existing power structures is contrary to the ideals of democracy. Yet, according to teachers, students are increasingly subjected to extraordinary testing, which dramatically diminishes time for instruction. A teacher posted the following on social media.

> Last spring, you wouldn't find the fifth-graders in my Language Arts class reading as many rich, engaging pieces of literature as they had in the past or huddled over the same number of authentic projects as before. Why? Because I had to stop teaching to give them a Common Core Partnership for Assessment of Readiness for College and Careers (PARCC) online sample test that would prepare them for the upcoming PARCC pilot pre-test which would then prepare them for the PARCC pilot post-test – all while taking the official Ohio Achievement Tests. This amounted to three tests, each 2 ½ hours, in a single week, the scores of which would determine the academic track students would be placed on in middle school the following year. (Strauss, 2014, *Washington Post*, Neely-Randall, para. 3)

The nonsense of this is all too clear when the increasing use of standardized tests is combined with the rhetoric of *all students can learn*. It belies a fundamental ignorance of the field of education, learning theory and years of building knowledge on teaching and learning. We speak on one hand of accommodation for learning differences (as well as cultural differences, etc.) and on the other hand about standardized assessment. Such bizarre inconsistency sounds like: *All learners matter but if they don't attain high scores on the tests, teachers and schools will be punished. All children can learn but they must learn in a standardized language and demonstrate their knowledge on tests geared to a so-called norm.* Why should we care? Because public school students in the United States are scoring lower than those in some other countries on certain standardized tests. One child "sobbed because she cared so much about her test score, and it became blatantly obvious how one high-stakes standardized test had just negated a year worth of reading confidence and motivation she had worked so hard to attain. I can no longer be a teacher who tries to build these 10-year-olds up on one hand, but then throws them to the testing wolves with the other" (Strauss, 2014, Neely-Randall, para. 17).

In urgency to create and capitalize on the needs of public school students, corporate reformers reveal an embarrassingly limited understanding of the field of education and what teachers actually do. It seems as though corporate reformers rely on political notions of how to divert public funds by using whatever language is palatable, giving little attention to clarity and having even less concern for what educators and educational psychologists know about effective teaching. Instead, they promise desperately needed funding in exchange for a privatized educational system.

Sadly this takeover cannot be accomplished completely from the outside and many educators have joined corporate reformers in dismantling public education in the United States. From the United States Department of Education to school superintendents and college and university deans and faculty of education, so-called educational leaders have offered up public education and sacrificed skilled teachers in exchange for Gates Foundation and other private sector funding. Be it ignorance, self-positioning, or simply greed, many of these educational leaders have joined the contemptuous march toward privatization of public schooling. Indeed, they are dismantling the field from within, hoping for a seat at the corporate table and most of them know better. While it is certainly a good bet that some of them will gain from such complicity, it is an unconscionable and self-serving act. It is not, as some school systems claim, *all about kids.*

What Teachers Actually Know and Do

Great teachers choreograph students in the dance of intellectual, physical, moral, and social development. They direct the actors in the classroom; center stage, stage left, and stage right are positions traded among learners at precisely the right moments to promote development and demonstration of growth. The performers write the plays, act in them, and increasingly become directors themselves. Great teachers orchestrate that naturally as their students grow in efficacy and agency.

Year after year P–12 teachers holdon largely because of a shared passion for knowledge, learners, and learning. Such passion is set in motion as they study and practice becoming teachers in educator preparation programs that are intellectually rigorous and inspiring. Yet, over the past 20 years, teaching as a profession, albeit not a financially rewarding one, has been nudged toward teaching as a job, teachers as workers, and learning as a commodity. The autonomy to inspire and relate content to learners has been replaced by so-called *teacher-proof lessons and guidelines.* Indeed, as the middle class shrinks in the United States, so does the space for professions requiring graduate study and extensive internship that offer autonomy to think critically and engage with learners in deeply meaningful ways. As novel events occur regularly in classrooms, well-trained and dedicated teachers are ready to connect, redirect, clarify, and move forward. The value of their preparation, studying content, learning to think deeply, and refining pedagogical and collaborative skills in intensive apprenticeships is immensely important. It sets the stage for the real world of becoming professional educators.

In the real world of public education, passion for learning deepens as new teachers build and orchestrate communities of learners, who begin to understand otherwise challenging content in the contexts of their lived experiences. When high achieving learners begin to soar, teachers' passion for the process deepens. Day after day, year after year, teachers see learning in ways that very few ever witness. It is up close, on the front line, one day struggling, and another knowing. It may be similar to the joy of seeing your own child walk or talk for the first time and it happens almost every day in public school classrooms. When it doesn't happen, teachers rethink what they are doing, consider the pressures on their students, analyze previous efforts, and refine instruction. Conditions change minute-by-minute in classrooms and teachers adapt to those changes in remarkable ways. This does not happen because of *new reforms* in education, the Gates Foundation, and their former partner Pearson Foundation. It happens because well-educated professional experts in teaching and learning ensure the welfare and advancement of their students first, while working to insulate them from endless pressures and distractions propagated by powerful politicians and wealthy investors.

Expert teachers can sift through enormous amounts of information, often delivered in clever and seductive ways, and find truth worth teaching. They recognize untruths that promote corporate, religious, or political agendas in efforts to hijack the minds of children and youth. Good teachers can redirect our children and youth toward thoughtful decision making and away from those who aim to profit from seducing them to think their wants are needs. Even at the expense of unreasonable compensation, those who endure know the importance of their work and are committed to their students beyond imposed standards and test scores.

These professionals have been trained to question what does not make sense or contradicts what they understand. They are experts in the content they teach and in pedagogical approaches to teaching that content. They know how to think about their own thinking and teach metacognitive skills to their students. Teachers command respect and model respectfulness for their students. Most teachers are too smart and well trained to follow blindly. They need to understand what they are being asked or told to do and question the relative benefits for their students.

Teachers are professionals who stand between danger and their students. They are the ones who remain standing and unprotected during emergencies because someone needs to make sure students are safe. Teachers are courageous and not afraid of taking a stand for something or someone they care about. They are the ones children trust and go to when they are in school and the ones who will give their lives to save the lives of other people's children. These are not people who can be forced to do otherwise. Teachers know our schools are not failing and that standardization is incongruent with individual needs of learners. They know all children can learn and that all children learn differently and at varying rates. Teachers take courses in differentiating instruction because students learn best in a variety of individual ways. They take psychology courses in learning theory and human development, philosophy of education, behavior management, and instructional design. They know how to level the playing field for students who are challenged. These well-educated and knowledgeable professionals are difficult to control and not easily fooled.

Teachers are an endangered species, rapidly dying off as they work against ignorance, greed, and diminishing habitat. When forced to repeat sound bites like *all children can learn* or *no child left behind*, while devoting precious instructional time to standardizing curriculum, assessment, and learners, many teachers leave the profession or burn out while trying to make sense of nonsense. Maybe public schools will eventually make money for capitalists. Maybe they already are, but, without qualified and dedicated teachers, they will make little else. The irony, perhaps, is that teachers, as we have known them, will become extinct because of ignorance of a privileged few and the unfettered greed of unbounded capitalism. When we conflate wealth with knowledge, public education with easy money, and learners as commodities, we are complicit in the extinction of teachers as we know them. As they disappear so will a far-reaching common good in a flailing democracy that depends on, at least, a few essential public services like free public education for all. When the value for common good diminishes, so does any hope for the ideals of democracy.

Teachers are initially trained in teacher education programs that include pedagogical content or methods courses, instructional design, curriculum studies, educational psychology, classroom management, assessment, and technology applications. Additionally, teacher education students spend, at minimum, 200 hours working as apprentices *in the field* (public schools) over the course of their studies. One entire semester is devoted to full-time student teaching in P–12 schools. Following initial certification, usually while teaching full time, teachers must also complete an advanced degree within five or so years.

Pre-service teachers are now tested on entry into their undergraduate teacher education programs. They must *pass* a state-mandated norm-referenced standardized test to be admitted to teacher education. The Praxis I Examination is now a five-hour exam that costs approximately $130.00 and is produced, scored, and interpreted by the Educational Testing Service (ETS). Then, as these students near completion of their bachelor's degrees, they are required to pass a criterion reference test, the Praxis II exam, also produced by ETS. The Praxis II exam covers pedagogical content knowledge, as well as literacy, mathematics, science, and/or social studies, depending on the level of certification (early childhood, elementary, middle, or secondary). Finally, in most states, teachers must also complete another one- to two-year supervised internship before being granted a *permanent* license to teach. It is a daunting and expensive undertaking to become a teacher. Coursework is rigorous and proving qualified by the state is a long and arduous process.

Almost no other profession demands so much for so little compensation. Hardly any other profession is so controlled by the corporate state or held as accountable as education. Teachers are increasingly told to follow scripted instruction, post daily instructional plans in their classrooms, and use common assessments, all while enduring constant interruption to monitor their compliance. Many complain about the unreasonable demands of standardized testing on their students. It is no wonder 50% of new teachers leave within five years and 20% leave within the first three years. Recently Teach for America (TFA) boasted that their teachers stay in classrooms longer than most traditional teacher education graduates (Greene, 2014). The extent to which this is true is unclear, but why they might stay longer is a much easier answer. They never were in teacher education to stay and, once they leave, it is on to graduate school and the lucrative professional life they planned all along. In fact, TFA teachers are trained in as little as five weeks for a job that typically requires at least six years of challenging coursework and apprenticeship. Such minimal investment of time affords a kind of ignorant bliss where they are told what to do and how to do it. Why not stay a little longer?

Dwindling numbers of well-prepared teachers, who are knowledgeable and devoted to the art and science of learning, have been under enormous pressure to implement incongruent state and national requirements. The language used to move education toward an industry controlled by mega corporations is muddled and confounded by juxtaposed paradigms. For example, ask teacher education students, faculty, or state education administrators what theoretical stance underpins current practice. Most will respond in constructivist language. As a particular pattern of thinking, educators using a constructivist paradigm look for increasingly deeper understandings constructed by students in social contexts that support learning. Constructivist perspectives underpin a research-supported revolution from teacher to student-centered instruction. Constructivism, as a set of assumptions to guide pedagogical approaches, leads to active classrooms, inquiry-based instruction, and communities of learners working together to solve authentic problems. Assessment of learning, from a constructivist perspective, also requires authentic demonstrations of knowledge and skills. Yet, most assessments that really matter are standardized to produce numerical scores that are easily compared across schools, systems, and countries. In fact, these numerical scores are widely published in aggregate so the *public* can more easily consume whatever interpretation the market desires. Given that the minimum passing score can also be determined after the tests are taken, student, teacher, and school success is a constantly moving target. We need to ask what is missing in assessing the quality of schooling through standardized tests. Do such measures really offer insight to what happens in schools? What is the relationship of skill in taking such tests to creating fulfilling lives?

Conclusion

In sum, corporations in a capitalist country have a single aim that is to amass capital. Public education is vastly more complex, requiring well-trained professionals who understand the nuances of educating and the challenges of assuring common good in a diverse and ever-changing society. In fact, teaching and learning is so complex that corporate moguls struggle to grasp what teachers actually know and do. Profiting from public education, tapping into the public education market, as so many have done, requires a gross simplification and standardization of the process. The Common Core, Next Generation products, and Race to the Top initiatives, are rolled out as quick fixes for a system they have convinced many needs fixing. But where is the evidence that public education is failing? It is a picture, foregrounded by so-called failure and back-grounded by greed, with scant evidence that re-forming is necessary. Is it really as simple as quantitative results of multiple choice tests that convince us to abandon a free public education for all? Are teachers to blame? Can the data industry effectively replace teachers? Should educating our children be given over to corporations whose primary aim is profit? Will the last teacher *lie in state* in our nation's capital to be mourned by all who still care more about the ideal of democracy than satisfying corporate greed?

References

Au, W. (2009). *Unequal by design: High-stakes testing and the standardization of inequality.* New York: Routledge.
Burris, C. (2013). *How come officials could predict new test score results?* Retrieved from http://www.washingtonpost.com/blogs/answer-sheet/wp/2013/08/12/how-come-officials-could-predict-results-on-new-test-scores/
Freeman, M., Mathison, S., & Wilcox, K. (2012). 'Critical thinking' and state-mandated testing: The collision of state rhetoric and teacher beliefs. *Critical Education, 3*(5). Retrieved from http://ojs.library.ubc.ca/index.php/criticaled/article/view/182342
Giroux, H. A. (2011). Education and the crisis of public values: Challenging the assault on teachers, students, and public education. *Counterpoints: Studies in the Postmodern Theory of Education.* New York: Peter Lang.
Greene, P. (2014). Let's talk about teacher retention, not tenure. *The Huffington Post.* Retrieved from http://www.huffingtonpost.com/peter-greene/lets-talk-about-teacher-r_b_6079712.html?utm_hp_ref=teachers
Hayes, C. (2012). *Twilight of the Elites: America After Meritocracy.* New York: Broadway Paperbacks.
Klein, R. (2015, January 20). More than half of American public school children now live in poverty. *The Huffington Post.* Retrieved from http://www.huffingtonpost.com/2015/01/16/southern-education-foundation-children-poverty_n_6489970.html
McLaren, P. (2014). The death rattle of the American mind: A call for pedagogical outlawry. *Cultural Studies—Critical Methodologies, 11*(4), 373–385.
National Center for Education Statistics. (2102). *Digest of Education Statistics.* Retrieved from http://nces.ed.gov/programs/digest/d12/
Saltman, K. J. (2014). Neoliberalism and corporate school reform: "Failure" and "Creative Destruction." *Review of Education, Pedagogy & Cultural Studies, 36*(4), 249–259.
Singer, A. (2014, December 15). Pearson Education can run, but it cannot hide. *The Huffington Post.* Retrieved from http://www.huffingtonpost.com/alan-singer/pearson-education-can-run_b_6327566.html

Strauss, V. (2014, September 5). Teacher: No longer can I throw my students to the 'testing wolves.' *Wall Street Journal*. Retrieved from http://www.washingtonpost.com/blogs/answer-sheet/wp/2014/09/05/teacher-no-longer-can-i-throw-my-students-to-the-testing-wolves/

Thomas, P. L. (2013). Corporate education reform and the rise of state schools. *Journal for Critical Education Policy Studies, 11*(2), 203–238.

TWO

What Is to Be Done?

Staughton Lynd

Greetings, fellow teachers.

What I plan to do in the next little while is to tell you about my experience in the Mississippi Freedom Schools in summer 1964 and to offer my thoughts about how that experience might relate to the question, What is to be done?

In my remarks, I shall try to convince you of three things:

First, everything we know about learning instructs that people do not learn by reading Left wing newspapers, or by attending lectures like this one at which some learned person offers correct theory. People learn by experience. And that is especially true if the learning we have in mind is glimpsing the hope that another world is possible. People must touch and taste an alternative way of doing things; they must however briefly live inside that hope, in order to come to believe that an alternative might really come true.

Second, capitalist society in the United States offers very few opportunities to experience another world, another way of doing things. During the transition from feudalism to capitalism in Europe it was possible to create the institutions of a new society in the interstices of feudal society: thus there came into existence free cities, guilds, Protestant congregations, banks and corporations, new styles of painting and making music. By the time an emerging bourgeoisie created parliaments, and sought to take over state power, a network of new institutions had come into being within the shell of the old. This does not seem to be possible within capitalism as the sad history of trade unions teaches us.

Third, how then, are we to help young people to imagine what a new society might be like? As educators we know that we can't do it just by talking, it has to happen through experience. As organizers we know that it is very difficult to provide such experiences in these United States.

So, first, everything we know about learning instructs that people learn by experience.

I assume that this is a topic about which we are in agreement, and so I can be brief. Let me tell a couple of my favorite stories about Myles Horton and the Highlander Folk School. The Highlander Folk School in Tennessee was created in the 1930s. During its early years Highlander supported the creation of trade unions and then, in the 1960s, assisted the Civil Rights Movement. The Civil Rights version of "We Shall Overcome" was put together by Guy Carawan and others at Highlander; thereafter they taught it to Civil Rights workers who came to Highlander for retreats. Myles Horton, the principal founder of Highlander, was the Paulo Freire of the United States, and there is a wonderful book entitled *We Make the Road by Walking* in which Freire and Horton as two old men share their experiences.

One summer in the early 1930s, when Horton was more of a Christian than in his later years, he taught Bible school for the YMCA in a remote Appalachian hamlet named Ozone. Midway through the summer the young teacher concluded that this impoverished community in the midst of the Depression needed something more than the Bible. He let it be known that on a certain evening there would be a meeting to address the question of what was to be done. People walked across the mountains barefoot to get to that meeting. As the meeting was about to begin, Horton realized that he had nothing consequential to suggest. In panic and desperation he said, "Let's go around the circle and see what ideas people brought with them." They did so. A program materialized. The Highlander style of education emerged from this experience.

A second story concerns how Horton dealt with race. When the CIO began organizing in 1935, segregation, disfranchisement, and racism pervaded the South, including its fragile labor movement. As individual union organizers, black and white, arrived at Highlander for a retreat, they would be assigned to cabins in order of their arrival. Sleeping, eating, and discussing were integrated throughout the week of the retreat, but nothing was said about race. Participants experienced the overcoming of racism. At week's end, as folks made ready to disperse, Horton would say something like: "Now, we all know how silly these racial customs are. How are we going to get that across to workers we organize?" Second, and again to repeat: capitalist society in the United States offers very few opportunities to experience another way of doing things.

When I was a teenager in New York City I rode the subway for half an hour to get to school. I gave myself a radical education. One of the books I read, by an ex-Trotskyist named James Burnham entitled *The Managerial Revolution*, laid out the way in which the rising middle class in medieval Europe created, first, new institutions, and only second, a revolution, and concluded that nothing like this was possible in a capitalist society. Burnham particularly insisted that trade unions were not pre-figurative institutions, that they would never challenge the capitalist economy comprehensively. Their role, Burnham argued, was at best to smooth a few of the rough edges and make capitalism tolerable for those it exploited. When I got off the subway I hurried to my parents' bookshelves to find the answer to Burnham. I looked, for example, at Emile Burns' *Handbook of Marxism*. I couldn't find an answer then or for decades afterwards.

I tried to respond to Burnham's thesis in a different way at the end of the 1960s. Those of you old enough to have lived through that time will recall that in those years there again came to the fore the Marxist idea that the working class would lead the way in creating a new society. So I briefly considered looking for a job in a steel mill. A young friend employed at U.S. Steel

Gary Works told me that if I did so, after 20 years workers would still say to each other about me, "Let's see what the Professor thinks." I decided that I might do better seeking to assist those same workers by offering a needed skill. I became a lawyer. I was a Legal Services lawyer for almost 20 years, confronting as best I could the layoffs, plant closings, and bankruptcies of that time. Unfortunately my experience confirmed rather than rebutted Burnham's conclusion that unions were not a force for fundamental social change. I often represented local unions as well as individual workers in trouble. It was the larger structures, the national unions, which repeatedly let down the rank-and-file workers they represented. Bureaucrats at some national headquarters far distant from the shop or school floor drafted contracts that gave the employer the unilateral right to make the big decisions, like closing a facility or cancelling health benefits for retirees. At the same time, national unions acquiesced in a no-strike clause that took away from local unions and their members the only effective way to resist. Critical as I am of national unions, I do not wish to romanticize the ordinary rank-and-file worker. Much depends on whether people are encouraged to stand beside their brothers and sisters, risking personal sacrifice on behalf of a shared vision, or instead to base decisions on a calculus of individual self-interest.

At the end of the 1800s and the beginning of the 20th century, the Knights of Labor and the Industrial Workers of the World popularized the phrase, "An injury to one is an injury to all." Ralph Chaplin, a member of the IWW, while imprisoned during World War I took the old tune to the Battle Hymn of the Republic and wrote the words of "Solidarity Forever." But how many fellow workers do any of us know who still believe that "In our hands there is a power greater than their hoarded gold" so that "We can bring to birth a new world from the ashes of the old"? I don't mean to issue iron pronouncements of doom for union effort at all times and in all places. I tried for 20 years. In the end I found more solidarity among the prisoners locked in Youngstown's many new prisons than I had experienced in the steel mills that the prisons replaced.

That leaves, brothers and sisters, schools. If we calculate 7 hours to the school day, 18 days to the school month, 10 months to the school year, and 12.5 years in school, that comes to 15,750 hours in which a young person who graduates from high school has been in the presence of another human being called a teacher. I know a man sentenced to death who is writing his autobiography. He figures that despite a miserable, heart-breaking childhood, he kept it together as a youngster who got good grades and had hope for the future until his early teens. His first encounter with the criminal injustice system came when he went joy-riding in a stolen car with several older friends. The judge took note of the fact that Keith had no criminal record and asked his stepfather and mother if they wished to take him home or have him assigned to the juvenile detention facility. Keith's stepfather told the judge, "You take him." Later, after shooting a best friend in a dispute over drugs and brief participation in a major prison riot, Keith Lamar was sentenced to death. He decided that something out of the ordinary was required and took the name Bomani Shakur, Swahili for "Thankful Mighty Warrior." He asks himself the question I am asking, when a young person experiences next to no support, encouragement, or recognition from everyday life in his community, how can we expect that young person to become anything other than a candidate for life behind bars? And I am answering, maybe, just maybe, in a place called "school."

You may be skeptical and, if so, I think I know how you feel. I lost my opportunity to make a living as a teacher when I tried to go all-out to stop the Vietnam War. I took account of all the rules and requirements. I went to Hanoi during Christmas vacation, and practically overturned the world Communist bureaucracy to be back in the States in time for my first scheduled class in the New Year. It didn't make any difference. The president of Yale said I had "given aid and comfort to the enemy," a phrase from the law of treason. But I don't want to exchange war stories, or display our respective scars. I don't want to have an abstract debate about education as a social force. I want to tell you about the Mississippi Freedom Schools, which I had the honor of helping to create, and which I coordinated in the summer of 1964.

Freedom Schools were improvised summer high schools. They did not offer academic credit. For the most part the schools were located in church basements, and in more than one instance the church was bombed or burned to the ground. The students were African American teenagers. The teachers were mostly from the North, mostly white, and mostly women, who lived with African American families brave enough to take them in. By attending Freedom School the youngsters deprived their families of days of much needed labor in the fields. As I assume you can understand, statistical exactness wasn't possible in these circumstances. All studies agree that more than 2,000 youngsters attended more than forty Freedom Schools. The summer project began with a two-week orientation at the College for Women in Oxford, Ohio. Voter registration volunteers attended during the first week. They left as we who would try to create Freedom.

Schools arrived. I drove from Atlanta with three students from Spelman College who were summer volunteers like me. The trunk of my Rambler was packed with copies of the Freedom School curriculum, laboriously reproduced on an ancient hectograph machine in the Lynd's apartment on the Spelman campus.

The day after we arrived at Oxford there came the news that Meridian project director Michael Schwerner, summer volunteer Andrew Goodman, and Mississippi resident James Chaney, had disappeared. They had driven from Ohio, had snatched a few hours' sleep, and then had set out for nearby Philadelphia, Mississippi. There the deacons of a local African American church, after lengthy discussion, had voted to let the church be used for a Freedom School. Soon after, the church was burned down. Schwerner, Goodman, and Chaney went to Philadelphia to find a new location for a Freedom School. Their station wagon got a flat tire. I assume you know the rest of the story. The bodies were discovered the first week of August. Back at Oxford, everyone was making long distance telephone calls: to Mississippi, to the Department of Justice in Washington, DC, to parents. I was invited to a small meeting of staff for the Student Nonviolent Coordinating Committee or SNCC. Bob Zellner and others volunteered to travel to Philadelphia and go through the woods at night to see if there was underground knowledge in the black community about what had happened to the missing men. I was in and out of larger meetings, talking with volunteers for the Freedom Schools about whether to go home or go to Mississippi. I don't remember anyone going home. During that week I made an arrangement with a volunteer named Tom Wahman. Tom's wife Sue was a member of the cast of Martin Duberman's play "In White America." They were going to be rehearsing in Jackson, the state capitol. Tom wondered if he too could be assigned to Jackson. I said, "Sure: you go to headquarters every day and answer telephone calls about the Freedom Schools, and I will spend the summer traveling through Mississippi, visiting the schools."

I remember going to McComb, Mississippi. It was just after the Freedom House where summer volunteers had been sleeping, and where the Freedom School had been meeting, was bombed. We gathered on the lawn next to the Freedom House. We sang "I'm on my way to the freedom land," and Bob Moses suggested the verse, "If you can't go let your children go."

One of the summer volunteers, Wally Roberts, was having a hard time getting the Freedom School started in Shaw, in the Mississippi Delta. We talked. The solution turned out to be for the youngsters to do voter registration every morning. Then in the afternoon, at Freedom School, it took on more meaning to learn that in the Reconstruction period after the Civil War there had been black representatives in the Mississippi state legislature. Alongside my fragmentary impressions the best way I can convey what happened in those schools that summer is to read some of the letters to home written by teachers, and some of the prose and poetry by Freedom School students, and a recollection of one of my students at Spelman who went to Mississippi.

Some teachers were welcomed as heroes. Geoff wrote home:

Batesville welcomed us triumphantly—at least Black Batesville did. Children and adults waved from their porches and shouted hello as we walked along the labyrinth of dirt paths and small wooden houses…In a few days scores of children knew us and called us by name. Similarly in Ruleville, in the Delta, the summer volunteers…were given the best of everything, and housing was found for all of us. Two people have already lost their jobs for housing us, and yet in each case half a dozen families begged us to stay with them.

My student Gwen Robinson was welcomed just as warmly, but much less obtrusively, in Laurel, Mississippi. She recalled:

One of the few things that I was trying to hold onto in terms of thinking maybe I will survive this [was] the fact that there were all these white young people going…So when I was told I was being assigned to Laurel with two other people only and both of them were black men and the three of us were going to Laurel because it was too dangerous for white people, I was like, "Well, wait a minute…" We went and we did have some names of people. One of them was…Mrs. Euberta Sphinks. When I got to Mrs. Sphinks' door, I knocked on her door. I introduced myself.…She looked at me and said, "Girl, I've been waiting [for] you all my life. Come on in."

Freedom School students in Hattiesburg wrote a Declaration of Independence that said in part:

In this course of human events, it has become necessary for the Negro people to break away from the customs which have made it very difficult for the Negro to get his God-given rights. We, as citizens of Mississippi, do hereby state that all people should have the right to petition, to assemble, and to use public places. We also have the right to life, liberty, and to seek happiness…We do hereby declare independence from the unjust laws of Mississippi which conflict with the United States constitution.

Naomi Long Nadget, Greenwood Freedom School, wrote a poem:

I've seen daylight breaking high above the bough,
I've found my destination and I've made my vow;
So whether you abhor me or deride me or ignore me,
Mighty mountains loom before me and I won't stop now.

You recall that in McComb the Freedom House had been bombed and the Freedom School had to meet on the grass outside. No local black institution dared offer facilities for a school. Joyce Brown, 16, addressed the problem in a poem in which she said in part:

> I asked for your churches, and you turned me down,
> But I'll do my work if I have to do it on the ground.
> You will not speak for fear of being heard,
> So crawl in your shell and say, "Do not disturb."
> You think because you've turned me away
> You've protected yourself for another day.

According to Professor Dittmer, author of a splendid book on the Mississippi Movement, "moved – and shamed – by Joyce Brown's poem, local people soon made church facilities available for the Freedom School."

At the end of the first week in August, the same week that the three bodies were discovered and the Mississippi Freedom Democratic Party held its state convention, there took place a so-called Freedom School Convention. Sandra Adickes, a professional teacher from New York, says that I suggested it. I have only a visual memory of the meeting of Freedom School coordinators where we decided to do it. The idea was for each Freedom School to send a couple of delegates, accompanied by a teacher, to a ramshackle Baptist seminary on the outskirts of Meridian, and for the assembled delegates to debate and adopt resolutions about the future of Mississippi as they envisioned it. The "1964 Platform of the Mississippi Freedom School Convention," adopted that weekend, includes resolutions on Public Accommodations, Housing, Education, Health, Foreign Affairs, Federal Aid, Job Discrimination, the Plantation System, Civil Liberties, Law Enforcement, City Improvements, Voting, and Direct Action.

The most consequential discussion concerned whether, at summer's end, the Mississippi Movement should attempt to extrapolate the summer Freedom Schools into a comprehensive alternative school system, or whether, instead, these young people should return to their segregated schools with used textbooks handed down from the white schools, inadequately prepared teachers, not enough money, and a curriculum that prohibited African American history. They decided that individual communities might experiment with Freedom Schools or school boycotts as desired, but as a statewide movement they would go back to their old schools. I believed then, and I believe now, that it was the correct decision. We did not have the resources to create a permanent parallel school system. Had we tried to do so, the effort would predictably have collapsed and students might have had to face the world without even a high school diploma. But that was not quite the end of the story. To begin with, there was the experience that Freedom School students carried into the rest of their lives. John Dittmer says that he could always tell which of his students had been in Freedom Schools: they did not hesitate to challenge the professor and ask questions, they were comfortable in discussions, and they were not intimidated by white teachers. Dittmer tells the story of one such alumnus, Wayne Saddler. Saddler attended the Freedom School in Gluckstadt, Mississippi. Saddler recalled the night that the school was burned to the ground and how, after the summer ended, he continued to attend a Freedom School in nearby Canton. Little more than a decade later, Wayne Saddler was the anchor of the state's most widely watched TV news program.

The Freedom Schools also laid the basis for the Mississippi Headstart program, which in summer 1965 served 6,000 children through 84 centers in 24 counties. I believe that many of the church basements in which the pre-school children gathered had previously been used for Freedom Schools and that many of the African American women who staffed the Headstart program had previously welcomed 1964 summer volunteers into their homes. And there was also the following. Years later I was making my way through law school. I read the decision of the United States Supreme Court in Tinker v. Des Moines, the case of a high school student in Iowa who wore a black arm band to school to protest the Vietnam War, and was sent home. The high Court held that what she did was protected by the First Amendment. I noticed that the Supreme Court, in its opinion, repeatedly cited a case called Burnside v. Byars decided by an appeals court in the South. I looked it up. It seems that on the first day of school in fall 1964, African American students in Philadelphia—that same Philadelphia where Schwerner, Goodman, and Chaney had been murdered a few months earlier—went to school wearing buttons that said "SNCC" and "One Man One Vote." They were sent home, but the federal appeals court held that what they did was not so disruptive as to outweigh their right to free speech. Thus the action of these black students—the single most courageous action I remember from that summer of bravery—protected the right of a young white student in a Northern state to protest the Vietnam War a few years later. So my proposed solution to the dilemma I posed at the outset is, let's try to make every school a Freedom School. Fifteen thousand seven hundred fifty hours in which a young person who makes it through high school has been in the presence of someone called a teacher is a fair chunk of time within which to try to offer young people a glimpse of the dawning of a new day. Am I saying, because we did it in Mississippi under these dangerous and difficult conditions, you should be able to do it? No, I'm not saying that. Danger and difficulty gave rise to opportunities as well as obstacles. Who among us would not wish to teach with a program for first-time voter registration, or any other kind of popular liberation, going on—so to speak—next door? But I am saying: we did do it. And hopefully, knowing that may make it a little easier for you when next you confront the teacher who teaches out of last year's notes but has more seniority; the Neanderthal principal and school board; or indeed, hostile parents and students who seemingly don't give a damn. In the face of all that, I say, let's make every school a Freedom School.

Every school a Freedom School, because how else will young people have the experience of putting the chairs in a circle and sharing as equals?

Every school a Freedom School, because this may be the one time and place, the one island of experience when youngsters experience the possibility of taking seriously ideas and ideals.

Every school a Freedom School, because the military is raiding inner city public schools to recruit for its imperialist wars and we have a duty to help our students resist.

Every school a Freedom School, because this may be a young person's one chance to meet a person whose example will reverberate for the rest of that student's life, namely, yourself.

Every school a Freedom School, because even for those who make it through high school it is very difficult to find a decent job and young people will need whatever inner resources we can help them to develop before graduation.

Every school a Freedom School, because if that aspiration will create risks for teachers, it is a greater risk for our students to grow up in inner city America.

Every school a Freedom School because: If not now, then when? If not here, then where? If not ourselves, then who?

THREE

Against Obedience

Susan Ohanian

It's rather mind-boggling to find myself in McGuffey Hall—to find myself, the only teacher in my school who refused to use a basal reader, in such close proximity to William Holmes McGuffey. With the publication in 1836 of the most famous school textbook of all time, *The McGuffey Reader*, McGuffey, a professor at Miami University in Oxford, Ohio, planted a strong seed for a national curriculum. Estimates posit the sales of McGuffey Readers sold between 1836 and 1960 at 122 million copies, putting it in a category with the Bible and *Webster's Dictionary*.

The McGuffey Reader was used in 37 states. Forty-six states have accepted the Common Core bribe, that is, 46 states plus Mariana Islands. I'd like to see Common Core consigned to the Mariana Trench. I admit I didn't know what that was until, when writing a review of E. D. Hirsh's *Cultural Literacy: What Every American Needs to Know*, I carried the book on my travels and amazed and alarmed strangers on airplanes, in hospital waiting rooms, and in hotel lobbies about items on the list: What do you know about Leyden jars and when did you know it? How are your Mach numbers? Is your *amicus curiae* in working order? My husband was the only person who could identify the Mariana Trench, and he was quick to admit he acquired this arcane bit of information from *The Guinness Book of World Records*, and not from his university education, which includes a PhD in physics. When I asked him—in a long distance phone call—about "throw weight," he laughed for ten minutes before starting a lecture on naval engineering. I wonder if my complaint in the pages of *Education Week* about the presence of Onan and the absence of Ruth, Naomi, Esther, and Anne Frank might have inspired the changes in the second edition.

Being here in Oxford, Ohio also puts me uncomfortably close to the site of that blood-sucking education law No Child Left Behind, which was signed in Hamilton, Ohio in 2002. Soon after that event, I started a website in opposition to NCLB. It has since morphed into opposing just about everything the state does in education. I started the site because I thought it was important to document what was happening to public education. I saw myself as a sort of Madame Defarge, chronicling the day's bloody events. In the ensuing 10 years the site has gradually moved from *what's* happening into *why* it's happening. Until teachers understand the reasons they're being beaten up, they'll never revolt, and the thing I can't forgive the unions for is that besides avoiding any explanations, they perpetuate the reform myths.

Very early in my teaching career I was involved in a federal effort to contribute to teachers' professional knowledge. After teaching for a year in New York City, I received a National Defense Education Act grant for a six-week summer program at Princeton University. Topic: Educating urban youth. Although there is some irony in holding a course on the problems of urban youth in bucolic Princeton (they bused in kids from Trenton every day), I'll be forever grateful to the federal government for introducing me to Daniel Fader and his *Hooked on Books*. These days, federal reformers would denounce the Princeton course as anarchistic. Today the feds offer a carefully controlled, scripted message—with templates paid for by the Bill and Melinda Gates Foundation and distributed by the James B. Hunt, Jr. Institute for Educational Leadership and Policy.

Becoming Political

Through my website, for the past 10 years I've worked at getting teachers to become more political. I've abetted a number of grassroots efforts—from the easy stuff such as buttons and T-shirts and petitions to the more difficult test refusal. I'm talking teacher refusal. If we could ever get a school to refuse to give the test, the refusal would spread like wildfire. But I know firsthand that most teachers feel that their work is with kids and most decidedly *not* with political action. Years ago, Patrick Shannon asked me if I'd participate in the political caucus he was organizing for an upcoming NCTE convention. A great admirer of Pat's work, I wanted to say yes, but, as I confessed to him, "I'm not political."

Pat reassured me. "All you have to do is tell your toilet paper story." Ohmygoodness. I can't tell you how shocked I was to hear this. First shocked and then relieved. If my four-year chase after toilet paper to fit the dispensers in the women's lavatory is all it takes to be political, I could do it. I had, in fact, already done it. I'd actually been political without knowing it.

In 1987, I published an article in *Phi Delta Kappan* called "The Paper Chase. "It was named the best education article of the year, beating out mass media finalists such as *Newsweek*. The whole thing started out by my trying to persuade the principal in my middle school to order toilet paper for the ladies room that fit the dispensers. By the time I'd talked to the janitor, the principal, the union rep, the Teachers and Administrators Liaison Committee, I'd learned a lot about how bureaucracies function and about where teachers fit into the scheme of things. And that was just the beginning.

When I organized the Women's March—we walked in a line carrying toilet paper rolls on broomsticks–the principal confiscated my roll of toilet paper, saying that the sight of "you women carrying rolls of toilet paper in the hallway— in full view of the students—is one of the most disgusting sights imaginable." I could easily have pointed out two dozen more disgusting sights in our school. He said that if I didn't like the toilet paper supplied by the district I certainly could bring my own, but he insisted that I keep it out of the sight of innocent children. After this Women's March, some colleagues announced loudly that there was no problem with the tissue.

People familiar with my writing find this hard to believe, but I am a shy person. Writing allows my other self to surface. But even this other self avoids making phone calls. For two years working in Manhattan and another two in Princeton, I didn't even own a phone. I mention this to illustrate how difficult I found it to make that first phone call about toilet paper. First I called four different offices at the County Health Department—in search of someone willing to discuss public school lavatory requirements. Each time my call was transferred, I heard the incredulous question, "You say your tissue is in a shoe box? On the floor?"

Finally, I was transferred to someone in the Environmental Protection Unit. He told me that there is no question that "rolls are more sanitary than single sheets and are recommended for toilets in public buildings."

"Would you write a letter to that effect to my principal?" I asked; long silence.

"Actually," I offered, "it would be fine if you wrote the letter to me. I could pass it on."

Suddenly, the fellow who had been so forthright about the preferred installation of tissue in public buildings became cautious in the extreme. It is one thing to make statements over the phone; recommendations in writing are apparently an entirely different kettle of fish. He told me that he did not have the authority to write letters. I asked to be transferred to someone who *did* have letter-writing authority, and then the bureaucratic waffling began in earnest. I talked to three more people. But, after agreeing that roll dispensers are preferable to single-tissue dispensers, each one clammed up when I asked for a letter to that effect.

A public-health nurse was sympathetic. Drawing on her experience in fieldwork in Appalachia, she gave me directions for making a toilet paper roll out of a coat hanger. But she wouldn't write a letter either, pointing out that that was not her area of responsibility. The Senior Public Health Sanitation Officer informed me that "all standards for the maintenance of health in public schools are the responsibility of the New York State Education Department." He further informed me that the County Department of Health cannot enter a school unless invited by school officials. He agreed that if we had an outbreak of bubonic plague, the health department would not wait for an official invitation to investigate. But he suggested that the dispensing of toilet paper fell short of such an emergency. He would not write a letter either, because he did not want to infringe on someone else's responsibilities. Everybody at the Department of Health asserted that someone there *did* have the authority to write letters, but I finally gave up trying to find that someone.

There were more phone calls: Three transfers at the New York State Education Department, more at the Occupational Safety and Health Administration (OSHA), the agency of the U. S. Department of Labor that is ostensibly the guardian of the health and safety of workers—mine workers, steelworkers, and cotton pickers, maybe. Not teachers, who are referred back to the local parent-teacher association.

I spoke to administrators at New York State Department of Labor, Division of Safety and Health. In both New York City and in Albany, their line was pretty much the same: "There are no restroom standards for schools." One told me that if I had complaints about toilet paper dispensers I could write my congressional representative about getting provisions added to the Public Employee Health and Safety codes.

You can see that by now I was far beyond the tissue issue. I was a resident of Kafka's *Castle*. I had discovered that, despite a myriad government agencies, teachers live on a plantation ruled by the whim of a few people whose best talent seems to be passing the buck. Teachers have no inherent right to decent working conditions.

I gave up. I conceded that there was no way that I was going to get working toilet paper dispensers in the lavatories.

Then a new school year brought a contract dispute with the board of education, and I was officially reprimanded by the principal for wearing a T-shirt (on which I'd sewed lace trim to make it look snazzy) that said "Support Troy Teachers." He ordered me to take off the T-shirt. I pointed out that P. E. teachers in the school wore T-shirts with letters, and asked which specific letters in my shirt were offensive. Unable to deal with complexity, the principal issued a fiat that the wearing of any T-shirt with letters was forbidden. The union then asked me to take off the T-shirt as my wearing it might interfere with "sensitive negotiations." The principal and I were standing in the hallway outside the lavatories when he informed me that my "dress attire" was not up to professional standards and that an official document from the superintendent would follow.

I asked, "Is the toilet paper in there of professional standards?" He smirked and said, "I don't know. I don't use the ladies' room." Whereupon I went a bit berserk. For *four years* I'd been trying to effect a reasonable change through regular channels: the custodian, the principal, the union, the county health department, the state department of education, OSHA, and so on. And this guy could win every battle; he could smile and tell me that the ladies didn't know how to pull the paper, that storing tissue in a shoebox was reasonable…I threw a minor fit and told him I was going to phone the local media and tell them that he said he didn't know whether we had suitable toilet paper in the ladies' room because he didn't use the ladies room. Toilet paper rolls were installed in all faculty lavatories the following day.

Now I know what Edmund Burke meant when he said, "There is, however, a limit at which forbearance ceases to be a virtue." Simply put this means that teachers should not wait for years to throw a fit. It took more years for me to learn that all this was political. In this, I'm typical of most teachers—so immersed in the daily intricacies of teaching—or securing toilet paper—that we don't see the political forest for the trees. This is why I push so hard at my website. As Robert Frost once asked, "How many things have to happen to you before something occurs to you?" It takes some of us longer than others.

Great Moments at the *New York Times*

It was only because my principal never read anything but the sport section that he didn't realize my threat to "inform the media" wasn't worth a hill of beans. If I hear one more person talk about the "liberal media" in America, I will probably vomit on them. Truth is, 97.63% of the media are stenographers for power. My recent encounter with *The New York Times* illustrates this. Picking up my account from my website, Sam Smith at *Progressive Review* called it "Great moments at *The New York Times*." I admit to being excited when I received an e-mail from a *New York Times* editor addressing me as an education expert and inviting me to submit a short opinion piece, using the film *Race to Nowhere* as a departure point for writing about student stress. When I wouldn't delete criticism of Thomas Friedman, they wouldn't publish it. I say "they" because the editor with whom I corresponded referred to her edits in the plural: "Our feeling…" Here's what I wrote, carefully expurgating the original student text:

> "Race to Nowhere" accurately portrays the heartbreaking stress schools place on children. The fear of "not being good enough" now begins with standardized requirements for Pre-K.

Although the *Times* review emphasized the pressure felt by suburban students preparing their resumes for the Ivy League, a Vermont high schooler with an Individualized Education Plan (IEP) wrote six pages of expletives on his federally-required test.

"You f_ _ _ ing a_ _holes. I have been taking these f_ _ _ing tests since first grade and I am f_ _ _ing sick of it. I know I can't spell. You know I can't spell. I have more important things to do than this bulls_ _ _ test.... This is a f_ _ _ing waste of time. You could spend this time teaching me something."

Suspended for inappropriate behavior, this youth missed out on the lumberjack test he'd planned to take the next day. The state of Vermont owes him an apology for going along with federal mandates insisting that one size fits all.

The pressure will get worse. The US Department of Education bribed states to accept Common Core Standards and has dished out over $300 million for tests to accompany these standards. Wordsworth and Jane Austen for all.

Parents and teachers must fight for childhood. Say "No!" to Barack Obama, to Thomas Friedman, to Ben Bernanke, to Oprah, and to everybody else who mouths nonsense about educating workers for the global economy, trying to put the blame for our economic woes on the backs of schoolchildren.

We need artists, bakers, lumberjacks, manicurists, welders, and yurt builders, as well as people who study math and science in college. Let's respect the variety of skills needed in our communities—and make sure everyone receives a decent wage. Talking about "Race to Nowhere" is a good place to start.

The New York Times **to Susan:** Unfortunately, I can't use your anecdote about the Vermont kid, so I've tried to rework the piece to make your point.

Susan to *The New York Times***:** I "fixed" the expletive problem. I guess I can understand that a family newspaper has certain issues, though I know that the student's words pull at heartstrings. I read them at my Bank Street College Biber Lecture this fall (They bill this talk as the annual lecture *that sets the tone for the year*).

There was more back and forth, and then we got to "The Thomas Friedman Problem."

Original Text: Parents and teachers must fight for childhood. Say "No!" to Barack Obama, to Thomas Friedman, to Ben Bernanke, to Oprah, and to everybody else who mouths nonsense about educating workers for the global economy, trying to put the blame for our economic woes on the backs of schoolchildren.

The New York Times **Edit:** Parents and teachers must fight for childhood. Say "No!" to everybody who mouths this nonsense about educating workers for the global economy, trying to put the blame for our economic woes on the backs of schoolchildren.

Susan to *The New York Times***:** Why has this paragraph been stripped of content? Saying "everybody" doesn't hold *anyone* responsible. Is one not allowed to criticize the influential people who mouth the global economy nonsense? I want the original paragraph back.

The New York Times **to Susan:** Regarding your penultimate paragraph, our feeling is that it seems odd to blame such a large audience—celebrities, etc.—when the fault lies with the policymakers and education experts, so hopefully you're okay with that tweak, which goes back to most of your original wording.

The New York Times Edit: Parents and teachers must fight for childhood. Say "No!" to political leaders and education policy experts who mouth this nonsense about educating workers for the global economy, trying to put the blame for our economic woes on the backs of schoolchildren.

Susan to The New York Times: I co-wrote a book called *Why Is Corporate America Bashing Our Public Schools,* detailing why the fault most definitely does NOT lie with education experts. The current education policy was planned by the Business Roundtable with help from politicos like Gov. Bill Clinton and IBM chief Lou Gerstner. Obama has come late to the party, but he's there. Thomas Friedman, for one, frequently orates about our economy depending on schoolchildren taking college prep curriculum. And his words are quoted by CEOs and politicos. I'm willing to take out Oprah, though every teacher would know why her name is there.

That was the end of our exchange. I did not hear from anyone at *The New York Times* again. If you want to read about poverty's effect on public school attendees, then you'll have to read Professor P. L. Thomas, not Thomas Friedman (Matt Taibbi asked the right question: "What the fuck is he talking about?…makes me wonder if the editors over at *The New York Times* editorial page spend their afternoons dropping acid or drinking rubbing alcohol"). People who say that Twitter is a waste of time aren't following the right people. I pass on more of P. L. Thomas's Tweets than those of anybody else.

The course of the edits is interesting and even significant. *The New York Times* removed the suggestion that the State of Vermont should apologize to the high school student and I okayed it. When they substituted "truck drivers" for "yurt builders," I pointed out that in that sentence yurt builders represent a whole group of people who don't want to be standardized, but I agreed to the change. When I stood firm on laying blame for student anxiety at the feet of Obama, Friedman, and Bernanke (offering, as a gesture of compromise, to remove Oprah), suddenly the *New York Times* reinstated the State of Vermont apology and the yurt builders. I interpreted this as an attempt to get me to yield on Obama, Friedman, and Bernanke: "Give her back the yurt builders, so she'll shut up about Friedman!" Although *The New York Times* initially addressed me as an expert, in the end my experience, my research, and my opinion added up to a goose egg. Five people contributed to "Room for Debate" on December 13, 2010, blaming student stress on a variety of things including AP classes, homework, too many after-school activities. Of course, nobody blamed Thomas Friedman. Most will think *The New York Times* won. Maybe so. But I think their victory would have been bigger had I gone along with the demand to remove that one sentence. It would have been worse than taking off the T-shirt, which I've regretted for decades.

> I don't think I'm over reading things to note Noam Chomsky's observation:
> The smart way to keep people passive and obedient is to strictly limit the spectrum of acceptable opinion, but allow very lively debate within that spectrum—even encourage the more critical and dissident views. That gives people the sense that there's freethinking going on, while all the time the presuppositions of the system are being reinforced by the limits put on the range of the debate.

As we will see, this is a strategy used by the press, by the unions, by the professional organizations.

Experts Quoted in the Media

When *Extra*, the publication of FAIR (Fairness and Accuracy in Reporting), invited me to contribute to the September 2010 education issue, I decided to read all the articles on Race to the Top and Common Core appearing in the print media between mid-May 2009 and mid-July 2010—to see who gets quoted—and who doesn't. Interested in which "independent experts" reporters called upon to offer wisdom about these programs, I eliminated cites from state education officials, union officials, and elected politicos. This left me with 152 outside experts quoted in 414 articles—pared down from over 700 articles.

Early on it became clear that the problem lies not just in who gets quoted but also in how they are identified. For example, Chester Finn, Mike Petrilli, and Andy Smarick at the Thomas B. Fordham Institute were cited 49 times. *Education Week* wants you to know that Smarick is a "prolific writer on Race to the Top." Might there be more telling information here? When citing Finn, Sam Dillon and Tamar Lewin at *The New York Times* identify him simply as "president of an education research group in Washington." Sometimes, *Education Week* quoted Fordham Institute people in three articles in the same issue. Never giving a hint about their bias, where they get their money, and so on.

Of the 152 experts cited in the 414 articles under review, 24 were associated with universities, but you won't find academics elucidating pedagogy. Instead, we get mostly economists and statisticians supporting market-based education policies. Take your pick whether it's deviousness or just sloppiness when the *Washington Post* (January 2, 2010) and *The New York Times Magazine* (March 7, 2010) refer to Eric Hanushek as a "Stanford economist." Hanushek is a fellow at the Hoover Institution, a conservative think tank on the Stanford campus. Carlo Rotella at least gets the descriptor right in the *New Yorker* (February 1, 2010) when he pegs Hanushek as "one of the most outspoken senior academics in the market-forces camp."

Certainly, "market forces" are the unacknowledged elephant in the room of the Obama/Duncan/Gates school reform policy. But it's up to the reader to figure this out when the press quotes experts associated with groups like New America Foundation, NewSchools Venture Fund, New Leaders for New Schools, Mass Insight, and on and on—without a hint about their pro-market agenda. Reporters often don't even identify the Cato Institute as libertarian, never mind reveal the ties of the charter-advocate New Schools Venture Fund to the Broad and Gates Foundations and to the Obama administration. How many education reporters, citing Fred M. Hess (14 times in this time period), director of education policy studies at the American Enterprise Institute, could even name a scholar who represents a view from the left, never mind phone one and ask for a sound bite? Maybe more shameful than who's quoted over and over is who's missing. Reports can't find anybody to comment on the relationship of capital, democracy, and schooling. Or call Richard Rothstein, research associate and respected author of numerous books, briefs, studies, and reports, including the Economic Policy Institute Briefing Paper he wrote with William Peterson, "Let's Do the Numbers: Department of Education's 'Race to the Top' Program Offers Only a Muddled Path to the Finish Line" (April 20, 2010). Wouldn't you think a single reporter churning out the 600+ articles on Race to the Top might ask him about *that?* Maybe the problem is that, for years, Rothstein has been reminding people that no matter how many fourth graders pass the test, it won't raise the minimum wage. The education press seem incapable of hearing this message—or sharing it with the public.

I keep thinking about who else is missing. Although I put blogs beyond the purview of my study, this bit from David Berliner's commentary on Valerie Strauss' *Washington Post Answer Sheet* blog nicely shows the kind of analysis that seems to scare reporters off:

> We create through our housing, school attendance and school districting policies a system designed to encourage castes–a system promoting a greater likelihood of a privileged class and an underclass. These are, of course, harbingers of demise for our fragile democracy.

Berliner was not cited once in the print media during the time period studied. Why would the press shut out an expert, the coauthor of the acclaimed *Manufactured Crisis* and *Collateral Damage: How High-Stakes Testing Corrupts America's Schools*—while calling up Joe Williams and his cohort Charles Barone of the Democrats for Education Reform, a political action committee (PAC) tied to hedge fund interests, for 40 citations? Forty. Williams and Barone, of course, can be depended on to trumpet market-based policies and smear public schools.

The *New York Times* has a "Wealth Matters" column but no "Poverty Matters" column, a Business Section but no Labor Section. And their education coverage reflects this.

Unions and Professional Organizations

If our unions and professional unions worked for the interests of their dues-paying members they would explain what former research analyst at the Arizona School Boards Association Michael Martin put so succinctly: "Public schools *have* to fail in order to crack open this egg and give these financiers access to the $360 billion they are after (estimates are that it is around $700 billion today). No matter what logic you use to explain the problems or successes of public education, it will be of no avail: public schools *have* to fail. Whatever it takes."

Not only do unions ignore this hard fact about market-driven education policy, they attack those who resist federal reform. I worked hard for the Educator Roundtable petition launched by Professor Philip Kovacs calling for the abolition of NCLB. NEA headquarters sent out urgent messages to their locals, denouncing my website and telling members *not* to sign because any anti-NCLB activity jeopardized their "seat at the table." The reality is that the only way teachers appear at education reform tables is when they're served up as the main course—to be eaten alive. I suggested to *Phi Delta Kappan* editors that it would be interesting to see publish point/counterpoint articles. In the December 2007 issue then-NEA director of education policy and practice Joel Packer wrote a defense of their position. Kovacs and I wrote why NCLB needs to be repealed.

My association with the AFT is more direct, and it did not get off to an auspicious start. My first teaching day in New York City was on a Wednesday in October. Hired to replace a teacher who went to work for the UFT, I learned that he'd left the day before parent conferences. So my first day on the job I met the parents, never having laid eyes on the kids. Decades later, I'm still shocked that a teacher would pull such a stunt. And that the UFT would abet him. Decades later, I was sitting in the second row, an on-the-spot witness to the standing ovation given to presidential candidate Barack Obama at the 2008 AFT convention in Chicago—right after he delivered, by video (even though George Schmidt proved he was in Chicago at the time), his education platform that included more testing, merit pay, and so forth. As Joanne Barkin has observed, "[T]he federal drive to use student test scores to grade teachers–came exclusively from the Obama administration." And now Obama has hyped up his agenda, and both the

AFT and the NEA continue to applaud, endorse, and contribute to his campaign. The NEA gave its automatic endorsement many months before the 2012 Democratic convention, and their 2012 Representative Assembly refused to consider a dump Duncan resolution.

AFT president Randi Weingarten's gushing praise of the Common Core in an AFT press release—"I am a zealot about the Common Core"—has its roots in Al Shanker's 1987 dust jacket exaltation over E. D. Hirsch's *Cultural Literacy: What Every American Needs to Know.* On Twitter, Weingarten pronounced, "AFT supported common core well before it was in vogue–there is a knowledge base kids need to know." When I posted this on my website, I added this note:

Bill and Melinda Gates Foundation Grants

2011 American Federation of Teachers Educational Foundation $1,000,000
2011 American Federation of Teachers Educational Foundation $230,000
2010 American Federation of Teachers Educational Foundation $3,421,725
2010 American Federation of Teachers Educational Foundation $217,200
2009 American Federation of Teachers Educational Foundation $250,000
2009 American Federation of Teachers Educational Foundation $1,000,000

In 2011, the AFT sent money to their Chicago affiliate to design instructional units that include curriculum, instruction, and performance assessments aligned to the Common Core State [sic] Standards. Other monies for embedding the Common Core went to Albuquerque. There, the union is working with the local PBS station. Subsequent AFT press releases claim these materials are well received. Albuquerque and Chicago teachers tell me a different story. At a critical moment when teachers need a union to explain why they are under assault, their union offers Common Core piffle, what longtime educator Marion Brady calls "a pig in a poke." Brady points out that this pig is "a freak, shaped by naiveté, political ideology, unexamined assumptions, ignorance of history, and myths." Of course the Council of Chief State School Officers and the National Governors Association received a ton of Gates money to promote the Common Core. Gates shipped off $100 million to Hillsborough and $90 million and then, acting in concert, the U.S. Department of Education sent them Race to the Top lucre. Arne Duncan's spokesman Peter Cunningham told Daniel Goldman, one of the very few reporters to write about Bill Gates' moneyed influence on national education policy, that the Bill and Melinda Gates Foundation agenda "is very much aligned with the Obama Administration agenda. We partner with them on a whole host of things."

Writing in *The Nation*, Jane McAlevey warns,

> "As long as the labor movement (what is left of a labor movement) continues to support 'Democrats' who stab them in the back, the future for the labor movement is nonexistent. And since the Democratic Party cannot exist without union financial support, the Party itself, under Obama and the phonies, is committing suicide."

Rich Gibson helps us to get to the root of the problem:

> It is Not Just Bankers. It is Capitalism. The core issue of our time is the potential of a mass, activist, class conscious movement to transcend capitalism met by the reality of a corporate state, fascism, conducting perpetual war on workers world-wide. "We Say Fight Back!"

Save Our Schools: SOS

I went to the SOS rally in Washington, DC in July 2011—just to be a body there—to help the count. On the way to the airport, my husband asked me how many people would be there and I replied, "100,000." That just shows what a cockeyed optimist I am. Among the 5,000 or so people there, I met wonderful, earnest teachers who had journeyed from Oregon, from Oklahoma, and so on. I marched with New York's Grassroots Education Movement (GEM), the people who made "The Inconvenient Truth Behind Waiting for Superman." When you talk to young activist teachers like this, you begin to think there might be hope.

For over a year, I asked SOS leaders why SOS doesn't oppose Common Core. Finally, the answer came: *because it would upset the unions*, the same unions that wouldn't denounce NCLB. This was no surprise. After all, Lily Eskelsen Garcia, NEA base salary of $248,349 and allowances of $54,285 for a total of $302,634, was a featured speaker at the SOS rally podium. But off the podium, union presence at the rally was only token. I was startled so see that the DC union, which provided water for the event, couldn't even get out local teachers who were only a subway ride away. The Chicago union was well represented, as was Wisconsin, but otherwise? No. So with so little presence at the event, one has to ask why the unions have so much influence on the agenda. The solution seems to be to act on the original good impulses and return to the grassroots impulses for change.

National Council of Teachers of English

I was a member of National Council of Teachers of English (NCTE) for decades, finding great guidance and community there. So you will know how thrilled I was by this announcement:

> "Susan Ohanian, creator of www.susanohanian.org, has won the 2003 National Council of Teachers of English (NCTE) Orwell Award. The award recognizes writers who have made outstanding contributions to the critical analysis of public discourse and is given by the NCTE Committee on Public Doublespeak." The announcement said the Web site was selected "for its clarity, honesty, and eloquence...dedicated to social and educational justice...with little sympathy for those who view children as things, as commodities." (NCTE press release, Dec. 4, 2003)

Fame is fleeting. These days I'm censored from posting on the NCTE online Connected Community. I received this message:

> NCTE has received your post. We will not be publishing the post because it violates the Code of Conduct for the community, specifically the sections noted below: All defamatory, abusive, profane, threatening, offensive, or illegal materials are strictly prohibited.

I wrote the executive director, asking what on earth I had written that was "defamatory, abusive, profane, threatening, offensive, or illegal." I am still waiting for a reply—and won't be sending any more membership dues until I get one.

Here is the message I attempted to post—in response to the NCTE decision to split their online Connected Community into two groups—"The NCTE Members Open Forum is now the Teaching and Learning Forum; it will focus predominantly on the daily challenges of classroom teaching and planning. We've also created a discussion area just for those important education policy conversations: the Education Policy Forum."

> I'd say that the teacher who expresses concern about having to enter 27,000+ assessment marks for her kindergartners IS talking about daily challenges of classroom teaching and planning *as well as* about important education policy.
>
> A professional organization claiming that daily challenges of classroom teaching and planning can be separated from important education policy conversations:
>
> a) is ignorant.
> b) is hiding something.
> c) doesn't want to be forced into taking a stand on the Common Core Curriculum Standards.
> d) just got big money from a foundation with a history of strong support of charter schools.
> e) all of the above.
>
> My website was awarded the 2003 NCTE George Orwell Award for Distinguished Contribution for Honesty and Clarity in Public Language. The award hangs on my wall.
>
> I nominate NCTE for the 2011 Doublespeak Award.

This is my personal story. The bigger story is that the NCTE continues to ignore a Sense of the House Motion condemning the Common Core State (*sic*) Standards. Instead, they publish books, advertise consultants, and set up (for-pay) Internet professional development courses—to reap profits from teachers' worry about the Common Core. The role of courtiers is to parrot the official propaganda. When the September 2011 NCTE *Council Chronicle* ran an interview with Arne Duncan and he claimed, "My wife and I just did Huck Finn and Tom Sawyer with our two children [first grader and third grader]," it did not seem to occur to the interviewer to express astonishment or to ask, "What's next? *War and Peace?* The for-members-only publication no longer accepts letters—or articles. Everything is scripted by Central Office.

The Professor Problem

I can't resist pointing out that according to the story I heard, before he became a professor, John Dewey was a failed teacher. He taught elementary school for one year in the village where I live, Charlotte, Vermont. His ashes are buried 13 miles from there at the University of Vermont, where he earned his undergraduate degree. The story goes that this Charlotte elementary school experience convinced John Dewey that he was unsuited to the task of teaching young children, and so he lit out for Johns Hopkins to get his doctorate. After writing a dissertation on the psychology of Kant, he moved on to the newly-founded University of Chicago. In our current climate of so many people in power insisting that anybody can teach elementary school, I like to tell this story. I use it to assert my authority as a longtime elementary teacher.

> Open Letter on my Website by Omaha lawyer, Rob Bligh
>
> I think that I understand the political malice that guides the Republicans.
> I think that I understand the political correctness that guides the Democrats.
> I think that I understand the arrogant ignorance that guides the Gates crowd.
>
> What I do not understand is the deafening silence of nearly all of the teacher-training faculty employed by America's colleges and universities. They are allowing their graduates to be roasted slowly over a flame of lies and they are doing nothing about it. Perhaps the professors think that they will escape to early retirement before Gates and the politicians come for them. Some profession!

After I posted this on my website, I received a long letter of complaint from a professor who took offense. He explained his dilemma, ending with, "I don't think many of us believe in the Common Core, but at the same time we feel a responsibility to ensure that our students are prepared for this new environment." This reflects what I read on listservs populated by professors and by the professional organizations they lead. Gotta prepare those teachers to prepare students to be commodities in the global economy.

I replied, "I know a lot of good people will be upset by Rob Bligh's letter but I think maybe it's past time for a "J'accuse" statement. I admit to despair at the National Writing Project accepting $2,645,593 from the Gates Foundation to promote Common Core (ASCD got $3,024,695, AFT $1,000,000)." Since my site doesn't have the facility for discussion, I offered to post Rob Bligh's accusation and the professor's response over at Jim Horn's *Schools Matter* (www.schoolsmatter.info), noting that people can discuss the issue there. The professor declined, citing "political tetchiness" and not wanting to be seen as critical of his education department or the National Writing Project.

In a *Texas Observer* op-ed, Robert Jensen introduces himself thusly: "Hi, I'm Robert Jensen, a provider of educational products to consumers at the University of Texas at Austin. I used to introduce myself as a UT professor…" Jensen reveals how distant he is from the current marketplace view of education as an economic exchange and students as consumers of the education product when he says his teaching "focuses on how citizens should understand concentrations of power in government and corporations and how journalists should respond." For years, Glen Ford at *The Black Agenda Report* has been warning that the goal of corporate education reform is to turn teaching into a service industry.

> "Teachers are the biggest obstacle in the way of the corporate educational coup, which is why the billionaires, eagerly assisted by their servants in the Obama administration, have made demonization and eventual destruction of teacher unions their top priority."

So the National Writing Project has joined the professorial parade in becoming a participant in the economic exchange. If they want to promote writing, they could take a page from Professor Stephen Krashen, author of hundreds of letters to the editor. Krashen doesn't let a bogus education claim in the media go unanswered.

Of course some professors are leading the resistance. Rich Gibson and E. Wayne Ross have shown me that "The Education Agenda Is a War Agenda." I have their book and stacks of others sitting at my elbow and piled at my ankles—books I referred to when writing this piece, books with titles like *Neoliberalism and Education Reform* (Ross & Gibson, 2007); *Hopeless: Barack Obama and the Politics of Illusion* (St. Clair & Frank, 2012); *The Phenomenon of Obama and the Agenda for Education* (Carr & Porfilio, 2011); *Reading Wide Awake: Politics, Pedagogies, & Possibilities* (Shannon, 2011); *Power, Resistance, and Literacy: Writing for Social Justice* (Gorlewski, 2011); *Ignoring Poverty in the U.S.: The Corporate Takeover of Public Education* (Thomas, 2012); *Free Voluntary Reading* (Krashen, 2011); *Digital Diploma Mills: The Automation of Higher Education* (Noble, 2003); *Terminator Planet: The First History of Drone Warfare* (Turse, 2012); *The Operators: The Wild and Terrifying Inside Story of America's War in Afghanistan* (Hastings, 2012); *The Imperial Messenger: Thomas Friedman at Work* (Fernández, 2011). And I know I'll buy more—probably tomorrow. But if my own royalty statements are any gauge, not many people are buying these books. I once told a Heinemann editor about my theory: "There are roughly only 3,000 teachers who buy books. They buy *a lot* of books. But they are the only ones buying." The editor did not reply, but she got a very funny look on her face. I think my one good seller sold about 15,000 copies. Clearly not enough to spark a revolution.

Whining and Doing

Yes, the complicity of our professional organizations plus the complicity of the unions has made the Common Core a done deal. But if you believe in heaven and hell, you know where the Standardistos who rob children of imagination and dreams will end up. But we can't wait for their damnation. As civil rights litigator and blogger Glenn Greenwald warns, "If a population becomes bullied or intimidated out of exercising rights offered on paper, those rights effectively cease to exist." This is what's at stake. There are no excuses left. Either you join the revolt against corporate power or you lose your profession. And yourself. Mississippi novelist and short story writer Barry Hannah wrote, "The point is to strip down, get protestant, then even more naked. Walk over scorched bricks to find your own soul." Maybe this is why the feds and Bill Gates want us to stop reading fiction. I watch literacy stalwarts exhibit classic revisionary tactics, pretending this is a fight about how to teach spelling and grammar and what kids should be reading. I admit that Common Core impresario David Coleman's arguments against fiction are so loony and so offensive, I easily fall into *that* diversion. But all these detours just mean we're fiddling while Rome burns.

When teachers stoically keep their silence while corporate politicos shovel shit on them, they really can't expect that tomorrow they'll get roses. Or even less shit. I'm thinking of getting cards printed so I can distribute this message: **You deserve what you accept.** We can see the stages of teacher reaction to Common Core Standards: Denial, Anger, Bargaining, Depression....But please, please, we need to skip Acceptance and move to resistance. Real resistance, not just Twitter/Facebook/blog complaint.

Whining is not the same thing as doing something. Whining is whining. Action is something else.

When I think of *doing*. I think of Don Perl, teacher activist in Greeley, Colorado. To the best of my knowledge, and I watch these things closely, Don was the first teacher to refuse to give the state tests. And he not only lived to tell about it but became the activists' activist. Don leads a group at the Coalition for Better Education that, right before testing season every year, erects billboards urging parents to opt their children out.

I can't catalogue all the grassroots things Don does. I just know that whenever I come up with one campaign or another, Don will join in. For example, when, inspired by Hans Fallada's account in *Every Man Dies Alone* of Otto and Elise Hampel, a working class couple who scattered postcards advocating civil disobedience throughout war-time Nazi-controlled Berlin, I came up with an anti-Common Core postcard, Don joined me in card distribution. The idea was to anonymously leave these postcards in bookstores, coffee shops, libraries, post offices, laundromats—wherever people gather. Whether it's a CD of protest songs (*No Child Left Behind? Bring Back the Joy* https://www.cdbaby.com/cd/dhbdrake4…still available by the way), or a book donation for Oglala College Library on the Pine Ridge Reservation in South Dakota, I know Don will be there.

I've sold buttons, T-shirts, bumper stickers, a 94-page book, *When Childhood Collides with NCLB* (self-published so it would be cheap), thinking each campaign would spark a deluge of activism. When resolute activist teacher Elizabeth Jaeger wrote—and paid for the publication of—10,000 copies of her concise report "What Every Parent, Teacher, and Community Member Needs to Know About No Child Left Behind," I stored the booklets in my garage. We hoped we could cover costs *and* start a revolution by asking people to buy in bulk—100 copies for $50. The idea was that each buyer would distribute the booklet to 100 people, and the revolution would start. I advertised the booklet and took orders, hand-shipping around 9,000 booklets. That meant writing labels and taking packages to post office (not to mention buying the mailers). I began to understand those publisher handling fees. I have to admit I'm still smarting from being stung by the professor who enthusiastically ordered 200 copies but never paid me a dime. Despite dunning. Elizabeth and I did not break even financially on this venture. But the emotional toll was much worse. When we started I thought we'd have to get 100,000 more printed. But what I learned is that there are not even 100 education activists in this country willing to pass out informational booklets.

There is a very good reason *Neoliberalism and Education Reform,* edited by E. Wayne Ross and Rich Gibson, is dedicated to George Schmidt. George, a longtime Chicago English teacher, is also the longtime publisher of *Substance*, the only education newspaper of dissent. In 1999, *Substance* published six of the widely criticized CASE tests (Chicago Academic Standards Examination). The Chicago Public Schools fired George, making sure he was blackballed in the entire area, and sued him for $1.4 million. As George points out,

> The issue was making all test content public after the tests have been given so that the public—not just 'test experts'—can judge whether these tests actually measure and do what they are claimed to be doing by the experts and the media. It was a challenge in democracy when we published six of the CASE tests verbatim in *Substance* in January 1999, and by the time it was all over five years later, democracy had largely lost. The Board of Education had been awarded the right to fire me from a teaching job for work I had done at another job (editing *Substance*), the U.S. Supreme Court had refused to hear the case as a First Amendment case (thereby leaving a toxic Seventh Circuit Court of Appeals decision written by that reactionary icon, Richard Posner, as the last judicial word on the question), and the public was denied the right to examine every test that is used to bash teachers, ruin the lives of students, and mislead the world about the way public schools are working.

George has observed that, "Secret tests are more damaging to democracy than most secret things." Certainly the Obama education policy is showing us how true this is. *Substance* persists, the only newspaper of education resistance in the country. Everyone who cares about the survival of public education should subscribe, sending along an extra contribution to keep this publication alive.

Being Faithful

"You have to pedal and keep pedaling," said *The New York Times* reporter Bruce Weber of his 4,199-mile bike trip across the USA. Mother Teresa put it another way. Cormac McCarthy tells this story. When a reporter said, "You must get very discouraged,"—because she's dealing with dying people—Mother Teresa said, "Well, he didn't call upon me to be successful, he just called upon me to be faithful."

As I look at all my unsuccessful campaigns to try to stir people up, I've decided to re-label. They aren't failures; they are examples of my faithfulness to the cause. And I can report that when, at 11:52 a.m., June 19, 2012, I get an unexpected, unsigned e-mail, it sustains me. All it says is "Bless you." I don't even know who sent it.

Petitions don't work. Do you really think that dumping Arne Duncan will change one whit of education policy? Voting doesn't work (My bumper sticker reads "Republicans/Democrats: Same Shit, Different Piles"). If this testing mania were all about Pearson and McGraw-Hill and profits, why is the rest of the Business Roundtable so enthusiastic? I started writing about the need to create a scared, obedient workforce in the late 1990s when I discovered what a dog Bill Clinton was (*One Size Fits Few: The Folly of Educational Standards*). But few people get it. So-called Progressives still whine about the Conservative agenda. We need to heed Thomas Pynchon's advice: "If they can get you asking the wrong questions, they don't have to worry about the answers." Writing at Rouge Forum, Rich Gibson concedes that we are currently "poorly positioned in this real train wreck"—in part because our union leaders betrayed us—but also because "unionism, even at its best, cannot answer this international crisis."

> What can we do? We can start with what we have, our own critical abilities and the limited organizations that exist that could create the solidarity necessary to build a resistance rooted in the reality of class struggle and the need for direct, on-the-job, action. The Rouge Forum would be one of a very few examples of groups that could do that. Justice demands organization.
>
> Justice also demands a sense of moral right. Ethics. It is wrong to conduct venally graded racist high stakes exams without complaint. It is wrong to fail to say, "appearance is not essence, which is what you claim these exams measure," if for no other reason than if appearance always matched essence, there would be no science, but more importantly, to not resist is to become what you do.

Not to resist is to become what you do.

Being teachers, we are too polite. I think we need to take a cue from bad boy celebrity chef Anthony Bourdain, who called Paula Deen "greedy" and "cynical" for creating a brand based around "excess without guilt" and then, when diagnosed with Type 2 diabetes, transmogrified into the spokesperson for the diabetes drug Victoza. Let's start calling out the gurus of Balanced Literacy, the former presidents of NCTE and IRA, the deans of education, et al. who are now selling books and offering professional development videos and courses on how to embrace the Common Core. Greedy and cynical.

But revolution starts out closer to home. Revolution starts with the poet Mary Oliver's advice to refuse cooperation with the death of the heart.

Refuse.

Walt Whitman was a bit more long-winded in the Preface *to Leaves of Grass:*

This is what you shall do; Love the earth and sun and the animals, despise riches, give alms to every one that asks, stand up for the stupid and crazy, devote your income and labor to others, hate tyrants, argue not concerning God, have patience and indulgence toward the people, take off your hat to nothing known or unknown or to any man or number of men, go freely with powerful uneducated persons and with the young and with the mothers of families, read these leaves in the open air every season of every year of your life, re-examine all you have been told at school or church or in any book, dismiss whatever insults your own soul, and your very flesh shall be a great poem and have the richest fluency not only in its words but in the silent lines of its lips and face and between the lashes of your eyes and in every motion and joint of your body. (Whitman, 1855, para. 6)

There are no excuses left. Either you join the revolution or you stand against the needs of children, and you aid the destruction of your own profession, not to mention democracy. We MUST build a mass movement. Revolution is the only answer[1].

Note

1. This chapter was originally delivered as the Second Annual Adam Renner Education for Social Justice Lecture at the Rouge Forum's Occupy Education! Class Conscious Pedagogies and Social Change Conference held at Miami University in Oxford, OH, June 22–24, 2012.

References

American Federation of Teachers. (2012, July 3). *Common Core workshops promote collaboration*. Retrieved from http://www.aft.org/newspubs/news/2012/070312commoncore.cfm

Barkin, J. (2011, June 29). Firing line: The grand coalition against teachers. *Dissent*. Retrieved from http://www.dissentmagazine.org/online.php?id=504

Berliner, D. (2010, June 29). New analysis of achievement gap: ½ x ½ = 1½. *Washington Post: The Answer Sheet*. Retrieved from http://voices.washingtonpost.com/answer-sheet/guest-bloggers/new-analysis-of-achievement-ga.html

Brady, M. (2011, April 26). Unanswered questions about standardized tests. *Washington Post Answer Sheet*. Retrieved from http://www.washingtonpost.com/blogs/answer-sheet/post/unanswered-questions-about-standardized-tests/2011/04/26/AFNRPlmE_blog.html

Carr, D. (2011, February 11). 'Tis nobler to dive in front of a train? A word with: Tommy Lee Jones, Samuel L. Jackson and Cormac McCarthy, *New York Times*. Retrieved from http://www.nytimes.com/2011/02/11/arts/television/11sunset.html?_r=1&pagewanted=all

Carr, P. D., & Porfilio, B. J. (2011). *The phenomenon of Obama and the agenda for education*. Charlotte, NC: Information Age Publishers.

Fernández, B. (2011). *The imperial messenger: Thomas Friedman at work*. New York: Verso.

Ford, Glen. (2011, May 25). The corporate dream: Teachers as temps. *The Black Agenda Report*. Retrieved from http://blackagendareport.com/print/content/corporate-dream-teachers-temps

Frost, R. (1985, Spring). In E. Hirsch, William Meredith, The Art of Poetry No. 34, *The Paris Review*. Retrieved from http://www.theparisreview.org/interviews/2911/the-art-of-poetry-no-34-william-meredith

Gibson, R. (2008, November 14). *Optimism and Obamagogue*. Retrieved from http://www.susanohanian.org/show_commentary.php?id=635

Gibson, R. (2011, October 11). We say fight back. *Rouge Forum Dispatch*. Retrieved from http://www.richgibson.com/blog/?p=4706

Gibson, R., & Ross, E. W. (2011). The education agenda is a war agenda. In P. R. Carr & B. J. Porfilio (Eds.), *The phenomenon of Obama and the agenda for education* (pp. 227–248). Charlotte, NC: Information Age Publishers.

Goldman, D. (2010, July 15). Bill Gates' school crusade. *Bloomberg Businessweek Magazine*. Retrieved from http://www.businessweek.com/magazine/content/10_30/b4188058281758.htm?chan=magazine+channel_top+stories

Gorlewski, J. (2011). *Power, resistance, and literacy: Writing for social justice.* Charlotte, NC: Information Age Publishers.

Greenwald, G. (2011, November 20). The roots of the UC-Davis pepper-spraying. Salon.com. Retrieved from http://www.salon.com/2011/11/20/the_roots_of_the_uc_davis_pepper_spraying

Hannah, B. (2010). Sick soldier at your door. In *Long, last, happy: New and collected stories.* New York: Grove Press.

Hastings, M. (2012). *The operators: The wild and terrifying inside story of America's war in Afghanistan.* New York: Blue Rider Press.

Jensen, R. (2011. May 2). Delivering educational products: The job formerly known as teaching. *Texas Observer.* Retrieved from http://www.texasobserver.org/oped/delivering-educational-products-the-job-formerly-known-as-teaching

Krashen, S. D. (2011). *Free voluntary reading.* Santa Barbara, CA: Libraries Unlimited.

Martin, M. (2010, March 22). Waiting for SuperFraud. *Kennewick School District Citizens.* Retrieved from http://ksdcitizens.org/2010/12/22/waiting-for-superfraud

McAlevey, J. (2011, February 16). Labor's last stand. *The Nation.* Retrieved from http://www.thenation.com/article/158640/labors-last-stand

Noble, D. F. (2003). *Digital diploma mills: The automation of higher education.* New York: Monthly Review Press.

Ohanian, S. (1987). The paper chase. *Phi Delta Kappan, 69*(2), 153–155. Retrieved from http://susanohanian.org/show_commentary.php?id=721

Ohanian, S. (1987, May 6). Finding a loony list while searching for literacy. *Education Week.* Retrieved from http://susanohanian.org/core.php?id=16

Ohanian, S. (1999). *One size fits few: The folly of educational standards.* Portsmouth, NH: Heinemann.

Ohanian, S. (2010, September). 'Race to the Top' and the Bill Gates connection. *Extra!* Retrieved from http://www.fair.org/index.php?page=4147

Ohanian, S. (2010, September 8). Who gets to speak about what schools need? Race to the Top and the Bill Gates connection. Retrieved from http://susanohanian.org/show_research.php?id=366

Ohanian, S. (2012, June 19). Business Week revealed why Common Core disdains fiction in 2000" *Daily Censored.* Retrieved from http://www.dailycensored.com/2012/06/19/in-20002-business-week-revealed-why-common-core-disdains-fiction/

Ohanian, S., & Kovacs, P. (2007). Make room at the table for teachers. *Phi Delta Kappan, 89*(4), 270–274. Retrieved from http://www.pdkmembers.org/members_online/publications/archive/pdf/k0712oha.pdf

Packer, J. The NEA is fighting for NCLB overhaul, *Phi Delta Kappan, 89*(4), 275–277. Retrieved from http://www.pdkmembers.org/members_online/publications/Archive/pdf/k0712pa1.pdf

Pynchon, T. (1973). *Gravity's rainbow.* New York: Viking Press.

Ross, E. W., & Gibson, R. (Eds.). (2007). *Neoliberalism and education reform.* Cresskill, NJ: Hampton Press.

Rothstein, R., & Peterson, W. (2010). Let's do the numbers: Department of Education's 'Race to the Top' program offers only a muddled path to the finish line. Economic Policy Institute Briefing Paper #263. Retrieved from http://www.epi.org/publication/bp263/

Shannon, P. (2011). *Reading wide awake: Politics, pedagogies, & possibilities.* New York: Teachers College Press.

St. Clair, J., & Frank, J. (Eds.). (2012). *Hopeless: Barack Obama and the politics of illusion.* Oakland, CA: AK Press.

Substance News. (n.d.). Retrieved from http://www.substancenews.net

Taibbi, M. (2009, January 14). Flat n all that. *New York Press.* Retrieved from http://nypress.com/flat-n-all-that/

Turse, N. (2012). Terminator Planet: The first history of drone warfare. Charleston, SC: CreateSpace.

Thomas, P. L. (2012). *Ignoring poverty in the U.S.: The corporate takeover of public education.* Charlotte, NC: Information Age Publishing.

Whitman, W. (1855). Preface to "Leaves of Grass." Retrieved from http://www.bartleby.com/109/15.html

Zimmer, B. (2010, October 1). We. *The New York Times.* Retrieved from http://www.nytimes.com/2010/10/03/magazine/03FOB-onlanguage-t.html

FOUR

Pearson, Inc.: Slashing Away at Hercules' Hydra[1]

Alan Singer and Eustace Thompson

The Hydra Hercules defied
Its nine diminished heads must hide
Before the baneful modern beast
Who has a thousand heads at least.

From "The Hydra" by Oliver Herford, *The Mythological Zoo*
(New York: Charles Scribner's Sons, 1912).

On November 18, 2014, the Pearson Charitable Foundation's Board of Directors publically announced the intent to cease Foundation operations and close the Pearson Foundation at the end of the year. This follows a decision by Pearson plc to integrate all of its corporate responsibility activities and functions into its business as a way to maximize social impact and to no longer fund the Foundation as the primary vehicle for its philanthropic and community activities." (http://www.pearsonfoundation.org/ accessed November 21, 2014)

This announcement, probably unintentionally, makes clear the connection between the ersatz not-for profit foundation and the business end of Pearson. In 2013, Pearson agreed to pay New York State $7.7 million in fines to halt an investigation by the State Attorney General that found

> "Pearson and the Foundation have a close working relationship. The Foundation's staff has consisted of Pearson employees; the Foundation's board was comprised entirely of Pearson executives until 2012; select Foundation programs have been conducted with the advice and participation of senior Pearson executives; and the Foundation continues to rely heavily upon Pearson Inc. for administrative support."

While agreeing to the settlement, Pearson Foundation representatives claimed, "We have always acted with the best intentions and complied with the law. However, we recognize there were times when the governance of the Foundation and its relationship with Pearson could have been clearer and more transparent." (Office of the Attorney General of New York State, 2013: 3). One of the modern-day hydra's heads severed, but there are a lot more to cut off.

According to Reuters,

> "investors of all stripes are beginning to sense big profit potential in public education. The K-12 market is tantalizing huge: The U.S. spends more than $500 billion a year to educate kids from ages five through 18. The entire education sector, including college and mid-career training, represents nearly 9 percent of U.S. gross domestic product, more than the energy or technology sectors" (Simon, 2012).

Pearson, the British multinational conglomerate, is one of the largest and most aggressive private companies profiting from what they and major media outlets euphemistically call educational reform (Rich, 2014), but which teachers from groups like Rethinking Schools (Karp, 2010) and the National Center for Fair and Open Testing (FairTest, n.d.) see as an effort to sell substandard remedial education programs seamlessly aligned with the high-stakes standardized tests for students and teacher assessments they are also selling.

Between 2007 and 2012, Pearson purchased 25 education and publishing companies valued at $5 billion. They include Schoolnet, EDI, America's Choice, eCollege.com, and Harcourt Assessment. If it has its way, Pearson will soon be determining what gets taught in schools across the United States with little or no parental or educational oversight (Singer, 2013a, p. 211).

Pearson standardized exams assess how well teachers implement Pearson instruction modules and Pearson's Common Core Standards, but not what students really learn or whether students are actually learning things that are important to know. Pearson is already creating teacher certification exams for 18 states, organizing staff development workshops to promote Pearson products, and providing school districts with Pearson assessment tools. In New York, Pearson Education has a five-year, $32 million contract to administer state test and provides other "testing services" to the State Education Department. It also received a share of a federal Race to the Top grant to create what the company calls the "next-generation" of online assessments (Hu, 2012).

The Pearson hydra operates in more than 60 countries, although 60% of its sales are in the United States. Under the names Scott Foresman, Prentice Hall, Addison-Wesley, Allyn and Bacon, Benjamin Cummings, and Longman, Pearson markets material for use in classrooms from "pre-school to high school, early learning to professional certification" that "help to educate more than 100 million people worldwide – more than any other private enterprise." In 2010, Pearson's U.S. sales were $4 billion with an operating profit of $733 million (Singer, 2013a, pp. 211–212).

Pearson is in the process of designing mind-numbing "multimedia textbooks…designed for preschoolers, school students and learners of all ages" for use on Apple's iPad so school systems will have more products to purchase instead of investing in quality teaching and instruction. In case you are not already worried about children sitting dazed in front of computer screens for hours on end, Pearson promises its "respected learning content" will be "brought to life with video, audio, assessment, interactive images and 3D animations" (Singer, 2013a, p. 211).

The Pearson footprint is everywhere and taints academic research as well as government policy. The Education Development Center, based in Waltham, Massachusetts, is involved in curriculum and materials development, research and evaluation, publication and distribution, online learning, professional development, and public policy development. Its funders include Cisco Systems, IBM, Intel, the Gates Foundation, and of course, Pearson Education, companies or groups that will benefit from its policy recommendations (Singer, 2013a, 2012).

EDC sponsored a study on the effectiveness of new teacher evaluation systems that Pearson promotes and that have two very big flaws. First, of the five states included in the study—Delaware, Georgia, Tennessee, North Carolina, and Texas—four (Georgia, Tennessee, North Carolina, and Texas) are notorious anti-union states where teachers have virtually no job security or union protection, and Delaware used the imposition of new teacher assessments to make it more difficult for teachers to acquire tenure. In Texas, North Carolina, and Georgia collective bargaining by teachers is illegal. Tennessee, Texas, and North Carolina used the new assessments to make it easier to fire teachers and Georgia used the assessments to determine teacher pay. It is not clear how this model will be transferable to states where teachers have legal rights. The second flaw is that the study draws no connection between the evaluation system and improved student learning (Singer, 2013a: 2012).

The agents of the Pearson hydra are everywhere. A 2014 NCTQ Teacher Prep Review blamed Schools of Education and professors of education for the failure of American schools and teachers (NCTQ, 2014; Singer, 2013b). Members of the NCTQ advisory board include Sir Michael Barber, Chief Education Advisor to Pearson in the UK as well as representatives of Teach for America and the charter school companies (NCTQ, n.d.). Susan Fuhrman, the president of Teachers College at Columbia University, was a "Non-Executive Independent Director of Pearson PLC" from 2004 to 2014 and a major stockholder in the company. As of June 6, 2013, she held over 15,000 shares of Pearson stock valued at $280,000. As a non-executive director she also received an annual fee of £65,000 or almost $100,000. Fuhrman was also president of the National Academy of Education, which received a $140,000 grant from the Pearson Foundation in 2010. The Academy is a major supporter of educational research in the United States with ties to literally thousands of potential academic allies for the Pearson Company (Singer, 2012). The Pearson Foundation's generosity serves to temper criticism of the Pearson Company because people dependent on grants and other forms of financial support do not want to be publicly perceived as a corporate enemy.

There has been resistance to Pearson's influence over American education. In May 2012, students and teachers in the University of Massachusetts, Amherst Campus, School of Education launched a national campaign challenging the forced implementation of Teacher Performance Assessment (Winerip, 2012). In April 2014, thousands of New York City parents, teachers, and students protested against Pearson-designed reading tests that included irrelevant reading passages and meaningless choices and the parents of between 55,000 and 65,000 thousand students had them "opt-out" of the tests (Phillips, 2014; Kirp, 2014). One Westchester county school district, upon learning that many of the questions on the Pearson-designed reading test were considered experimental in nature announced plans to bill Pearson $20,000 for the time the students and teachers missed from class (Christ, 2012; Weiner, 2012).

Key players in Pearson's move to take over the education universe include Glen Moreno, chairman of the Pearson Board of Directors, Dame Marjorie Morris Scardino, formerly the overall chief executive for Pearson, John Fallon, the current CEO, William Ethridge, chief executive for North American Education, and Sir Michael Barber (Singer, 2013a, pp. 214–215).

Glen Moreno became chairman of Pearson in October 2005. Moreno was chairman of UK Financial Investments, the group set up by the British government to protect public funds used to bail out banks after the 2008 global economic collapse. He was forced to resign in 2009 when it was revealed that he was a trustee of a private bank accused of aiding tax evasion. Moreno was also deputy chairman of Lloyds Banking Group, Great Britain's largest mortgage lender, but stepped down there in May 2012.

Dame Marjorie became CEO of Pearson in 1997 and was there until 2012. In 2007, Forbes magazine placed her seventeenth on its list of the 100 most powerful women in the world. Her income in 2011 was $2.5 million but that represents a tiny fraction of wealth that includes 1.5 million shares of Pearson stock.

William Ethridge became chief executive of Pearson's North American Education division in 2008. He has what Pearson considers educational experience because he previously worked for Prentice Hall and Addison Wesley. His total compensation in 2011 was $1.4 million and he holds a half million shares of Pearson stock.

Sir Michael Barber is the Pearson hydra's chief education strategist. He previously was a partner at McKinsey & Company, a global management consulting firm and advisor to some of the world's leading businesses, governments, and institutions where he developed close ties with the Pakistani and Indian governments, areas where Pearson is trying to expand its operations (Pearson a, n.d.). Unlike Barber, John Fallon is a more home-grown executive (Pearson b, n.d). He joined Pearson in 1997 as director of communication and became president of Pearson Inc. in 2000. He has headed the company's non–North America educational activities in 2008 and became Pearson's chief executive officer in 2013. According to *Bloomberg Businessweek* (2014), Fallon has done quite well working at Pearson. His annual salary is £750,000 or approximately $1.1 million, but his total compensation package with stock options is probably over £1.7 million or $2.65 million. Fallon is the key player behind the push for "efficacy" in education, the corporate buzzword, which in practical terms translates into the constant assessing of students', who are using Pearson products, performance. Efficacy is supposed to be about what works in education based on research done at research centers, but everything is actually organized around the Pearson goal of "finding business models for affordable schools" that they will be selling, especially in "developing areas of the world."

Barber; Saad Rizvi, who is Pearson's Senior Vice President for Efficacy and head of its Catalyst for Education team; and Fallon call the hydra's global marketing strategy "The Incomplete Guide to Delivering Learning Outcomes" (Barber and Rizvi, 2013). Rizvi, like Barber, came to Pearson from McKinsey & Company. McKinsey's clients include 100 of the top 150 companies in the world. It has advised the Bank of England, the Roman Catholic Church in the United States, and the German government. The main job of McKinsey is to help companies maintain profitability by closing subsidies, selling assets, shifting production, and laying off workers. McKinsey has had its share of mishaps. Former employees include Jeff Skilling, the disgraced chief executive of Enron and Rajat K. Gupta, who was convicted of insider trading. Other disasters include advising Time Warner on its ill-fated merger with AOL, advising General Motors on how to compete with Japanese automakers, and advising AT&T not to be concerned about cell phones. A top McKinsey partner dismissed these failures saying "We are advisers, and it is management's job to take all the advice they receive and make their own decisions. Not to say that McKinsey told me to do this" (Sorkin, 2013).

Pearson's Affordable Learning division currently focuses on emerging markets in Africa and India, but it is the model for Pearson business worldwide. It includes eAdvance (South Africa), which sponsors a blended learning chain called Spark Schools; Omega, a chain of 38 private schools in Ghana; Bridge International Academies in Kenya; and Zaya, an educational technology and service company contracted to operate 27 schools; Suiksha, a chain of pre-schools; Experifun, which markets science learning products; Avanti, after-school test prep; and Village Capital (Edupreneurs), promoting private education start-up companies, all based in India.

The blurb for eAdvance's SPARK Schools give some sense of what Pearson is trying to do in Africa, India, and worldwide—underprice the market to disrupt existing educational institutions so Pearson companies can move in, take over, and gobble up profits (Pearson c, n.d.). SPARK Schools has bold aspirations to disrupt the South African education system through introducing an innovative learning methodology to the African continent. In the SPARK Schools model, students split their time between digital content that adapts in difficulty to their learning and classroom interaction based on best practice pedagogy. Importantly, the blended model also allows eAdvance to deliver high quality education at an affordable price.

The Pearson hydra uses the desperation of Third World countries to modernize to get its foot in the door and to act without regulation or oversight. SPARK plans to "build eight low-cost blended learning schools over the next three years, and more than 60 in the next ten." Pearson is also using mergers to expand its markets and influence. In December 2013, Pearson agreed to purchase Grupo Multi, an English-language training company in Brazil, to accelerate growth in Latin America (Singer, 2014a).

Up until now, about 60% of Pearson's sales were in the United States, however expansion stalled in this country because of lower freshman enrollments in U.S. colleges and a slowdown in textbook markets. Sales also suffered in Great Britain because of curriculum changes and the company spent about $200 million organizing its push into foreign digital markets. In the first half of 2014, Pearson sales were down 7% from the first half of 2013; Pearson's adjusted operating profit was down 45%; and its adjusted earnings per share were down 53%. Its school sales were down 14% and its North American sales, which account for 57% of its overall business, was down 6%. As we read these figures, Pearson is in trouble (Schweizer, 2014).

In 2014, Moody's Investors Service, a ratings agency, lowered its evaluation of Pearson from stable to negative. "We are changing the outlook to negative as Pearson's debt protection metrics for fiscal year 2013 are likely to weaken considerably." According to Gunjan Dixit, a Moody's assistant vice president-analyst, "This view reflects Pearson's tough trading conditions, particularly in North America and the UK; the greater-than-originally-anticipated spending on restructuring; and certain start-up costs for new contracts in higher education and increased provisions for returns." According to Moody's, key challenges for Pearson in the future include: (1) the fiscal health of U.S. states and international government funding bodies, in its schools and higher education businesses; (2) difficult market conditions in the U.S. education market; (3) the vulnerability of its Financial Times group; and (4) the accelerating transition of trade book publishing to electronic formats. Pearson stockholders were so disappointed in the company's financial performance that in April 2014, shareholders protested against excessive executive bonuses (Pearson d, n.d.; Moody's, 2014).

In the United States, the Pearson hydra faces other problems that may be related to over-expansion, the inability to deliver what was promised and possible under-the-table agreements on contracts. In Florida, state officials blamed Pearson Education when at least a dozen Florida school districts were forced to suspend online testing this April because students had trouble signing in for the test. Other problems included slowness when students tried to download test questions or submit answers and an inexplicable warning message that students should notify their teacher or proctor about a problem that did not exist. State Education Commissioner Pam Stewart complained to Pearson that the "failure is inexcusable, Florida's students and teachers work too hard on learning to be distracted by these needless and avoidable technological issues" (Solochek, 2014).

Pearson blamed the test problems on a third-party hosting service provider. However, in recent years Pearson has had similar problems with computerized tests in Florida before as well as in other states. In 2011, Wyoming fined Pearson $5.1 million because of software problems and then switched back to paper tests. In April, Pearson was also forced to acknowledge and apologize for "intermittent disruptions to some of our online testing services." This time they blamed a different sub-contractor (Singer, 2014a).

In the meantime, the American Institutes for Research is challenging the awarding of a lucrative Common Core test development contract to Pearson. While the complaint is being brought in New Mexico, it has national ramification. The contract is for developing test-items, test delivery, reporting results, and analysis of student performance for states that are part of the Partnership for Assessment of Readiness for College and Careers, or PARCC, one of two main consortia designing tests linked to the CommonCore Standards. The plaintiff claims the process for awarding the contract was designed to specifically benefit Pearson, which ended up being the only bidder, and was therefore illegal (Cavanagh, 2014).

In New York State, parents and teachers are outraged because teachers and building administrators are forced to sign statements promising not to discuss or release questions about new Pearson "Common Core" aligned high-stakes tests. In the past, questions from past state high school "Regents" exams were posted on the State Education website. Now Pearson, which is paid $32 million by New York State to create the tests, is demanding a payment of an additional $8 million to permit the state to post the questions (Strauss, 2014). Meanwhile college faculty rallied on the steps of the state capitol in Albany demanding that the State Education Department "stop sabotaging student teachers" and cancel contracts with Pearson. Pearson designs, administers, and grades the state's teacher certification exams including the video and portfolio assessment of student teachers. Karen Magee, President of New York State United Teachers, "shook a copy of the state's contract with Pearson in the air before tearing out a page and running it through a paper shredder." Magee and other speakers accused Pearson of being a "privateer" making a "buck off of students" (UUP, 2014). The American Federation of Teachers (AFT) passed a resolution supporting the New York state college faculty seriously criticizing the edTPA teacher certification process administered by Pearson. According to the resolution, "The AFT believes that neither edTPA nor any other performance assessment should be tied to a high-stakes testing regime and the outsourcing of evaluation, especially to for-profit corporations such as Pearson, as it is not an appropriate assessment of teacher education programs and teacher performance" (Sawchuk, 2014).

In Atlanta, Georgia, 12 former public school employees are facing trial for conspiring to alter and boost student standardized test scores. The conspiracy accusation is especially serious because it exposes the accused teachers and administrators to racketeering charges that bring sentences of up to 20 years in prison. In 2011, Georgia state investigators concluded that as many as 178 principals and teachers in the Atlanta school district had cheated on the tests. Dozens of district employees have already been fired, forced to resign, or retired and 21 pleaded guilty to lesser crimes like obstruction of justice and making false statements while agreeing to cooperate with investigators in return for probation (Fausset, 2014).

The Pearson hydra has not been implicated in the cheating scandal but it may have some economic vulnerability here. Pearson designs and administers a number of standardized tests in Georgia and ran school improvement programs in Atlanta schools during the years under investigation through its Achievement Solutions division (Pearson, e, n.d.). At least three of the schools where personnel are charged with cheating, Grove Park, East Lake, and Walter White, were named Pearson Achievement Solutions National Demonstration Schools for 2006–2007 (Business Wire, 2007).

Pearson's program in Atlanta was especially important to its marketing efforts because the 51,000 students in the Atlanta public schools are 92% black and Latino and 70% received free or reduced price lunch, a designation for poverty. These are the groups that both the federal No Child Left Behind and Race to the Top programs are targeting for academic improvement. Essentially, Pearson argued that success in Atlanta with these student populations could be translated into success anywhere. Now it appears the success was based on cheating (Singer, 2014b).

In New Zealand, a group called Save Our Schools NZ is protesting the misuse of PISA (Programme of International Student Assessment) tests and rankings by national education departments (Save Our Schools NZ, 2014). They charge "Pisa, with its three-year assessment cycle, has caused a shift of attention to short-term fixes designed to help a country quickly climb the rankings, despite research showing that enduring changes in education practice take decades, not a few years, to come to fruition." Pearson holds the contract to prepare PISA assessments starting in 2015 (Pearson UK, 2011).

The United States Congress has investigated products with a Pearson connection. The Department of Education's research arm "found that students in schools that use Reading First, which provides grants to improve elementary school reading, scored no better on comprehension tests than their peers who attended schools that did not receive program money." A 2006 report from the department's inspector general found that "some program officials steered states to certain tests and textbooks." In addition, Congressional testimony "revealed that some of those officials benefited financially because of ties to companies that produced those products" (Glod, 2008). Pearson's Scott Foresman sub-division developed Reading First instructional material and Pearson marketed a Stanford Reading First assessment package in response to the Reading First initiative of No Child Left Behind (Newman and Jaciw, 2005; SEDL, n.d.).

These problems pale however compared to some more recent Pearson disasters. In August and September 2014, Annie Gilbertson, Education Reporter for 88.3 KPCC, Southern California Public Radio, reported on e-mails that appear to show complicity between officials in LAUSD, Pearson, the Pearson Foundation, representatives of Apple, and America Choice, a Pearson affiliate, to influence a LAUSD contract decision and circumvent the bidding process (Gilbertson, 2014; Blume, 2014; Singer, 2014c).

Three months later, the *Los Angeles Times* reported that the Federal Bureau of Investigation seized 20 boxes of records about the LAUSD's $1.3-billion plan to provide iPads to every student and a federal grand jury is examining the matter (Blume, Kim, & Rainey, 2014).

A subpoena demanded that LAUSD produce documents on deals with Apple, the maker of the iPad, and Pearson, who developed the iPad curriculum material as part of an "official criminal investigation." Marc Harris, the former deputy chief of the public corruption and government fraud unit at the U.S. attorney's office in Los Angeles, said improprieties in the bidding process would be a federal crime if federal funds were involved or if the actions amounted to fraud against taxpayers by public officials. E-mail records show that John Deasy, Superintendent of Los Angeles schools, who resigned under pressure in October 2014, and an assistant superintendent had contacts with Apple and Pearson executives before the bidding process opened and that people connected to Pearson may have actually shaped the final proposal. The LAUSD request for proposals was not issued until six months later in March 2013. However, there are a series of e-mails between Pearson CEO Marjorie Scardino and LAUSD officials starting in May 2012 and September 11, 2012, Sherry King of the Pearson Foundation e-mailed Deasy, setting up a lunch meeting at a restaurant in Santa Monica that included Judy Codding, a Pearson Education corporate field representative (Gilbertson and Keller, 2014; Singer, 2014d).

At the same time disgruntled Pearson employees are lambasting the company online at http://www.glassdoor.com, a website that posts company reviews. Many of their complaints stem from the restructuring Pearson starting in May 2013 to focus on digital services and emerging (Third Word) markets (Gordon, 2013). A former educational specialist at Pearson based in Oregon wrote: "There are still a few decent, intelligent, caring people at Pearson. They're just few and far between and too scared for their own jobs to call attention to themselves....Many, many good people left or were fired and in their place you have lots of managers and executives who have no idea what their jobs entail or what products Pearson sells. It would be comical if it weren't so sad." This employee recommended to anyone working at Pearson, "Don't Let the Door Hit You on Your Way Out" (Glassdoor.com, 2014).

In one case, Pearson is being sued in the United States District Court for the Eastern District of Virginia for wrongful termination and gender and age discrimination (U.S. Federal Court, 2014). According to the complainant's deposition, "From his employment in October 2009 until on or about October 31, 2013" he had "no disciplinary history with Pearson and received positive performance reviews" and for the year 2012, he was awarded "Digital Account Executive of the year as he was the top performer in his position throughout Pearson nationwide." The former employee was even praised on LinkedIn by Pearson supervisors (Baudean, 2014). However, when Pearson announced plans to reorganize the company, the petitioner and other senior employees were dismissed. Pearson claimed their positions were eliminated. The complainant and others claim Pearson just changed job titles. He is suing Pearson for $5 million.

Katrina Bass, a long-time employee in the Pearson hydra's higher education division, contacted me via e-mail and gave me permission to use her name. According to Bass, she was one of a number of over-40 employees eliminated in Pearson's "restructuring." Her story echoes the comments on the "glassdoor" website. Most of these employees had "delivered clean profits for Pearson for decades only to endure several years of harassment leading up to dismissal." Bass believes Pearson's "current state of desperation transitioning to digital was partly a result of their failure to innovate early (especially between 2007- 2012) instead relying on unethical business practices" (Singer, 2014).

Bass reported that "management regularly dumped product into the wholesale channel at year-end which meant shipping new textbooks to wholesale distributors at grossly discounted rates who then resold them as 'used' textbooks. Although representatives were given an annual 'adjustment' for these sales, it undermined field sales efforts and in no way reflected the increasing hours of support needed to train faculty and students on emerging technology."

In addition, Bass believes "managers who were highly skilled at negotiating obscene over-ordering at college bookstores were rewarded and promoted." She claims that Pearson, one of the few (if not only) publishing companies that compensate its sales force on gross sales, "allowed unethical managers to be rewarded for what was ultimately unprofitable activity. Many remained at the helm despite missing their sales targets for up to four years in a row." According to Bass, the "Pearson Solutions Division dedicated a large sales force to poaching existing Pearson business by either customizing a print or web-based product." The Pearson Solution Division has grown rapidly and Bass claims it likes to boast that it is "building an airplane while it is in the air." Bass feels that "Pearson is no longer a content provider." Instead, it has become a "technology company that is heavily invested in data. It is disturbing to consider the amount of data they collect, own, interpret and disseminate that influence policies and practices in education."

Pearson may be banking on new Common Core tests to improve its financial outlook, but given the rising national opposition to Common Core and high-stakes testing in the United States, that may just be wishful thinking (Singer, 2014d). PARCC is one of two federally funded consortia charged with developing high-stakes assessments that are supposedly aligned with national Common Core standards (PARCC, n.d.). In 2011, the PARCC consortium claimed to represent 24 states and the District of Columbia. In May 2014, the PARCC consortium awarded a contract to Pearson to design its math and English language assessments, however only 10 states and Washington, DC are planning to use the PARCC assessments in 2014–2015. That means at this time, PARCC represents only 20% of the states and the number is declining, which is not a good sign for Pearson's bottom line (Schneider, 2014).

For all its claims about efficacy, Pearson, the multi-headed hydra, is not a very efficient company. For all its claims about valuing education, the only thing Pearson appears to value is profit. It may be a Herculean task, but it looks like Pearson's heads are starting to roll.

Note

1. This chapter is based on a presentation at the 2014 Rouge Forum conference in Denver, Colorado and research on Pearson published in the *Huffington Post*.

References

Barber, M., & Rizvi, S. (2013). *The incomplete guide to delivering learning outcomes*. Pearson. Retrieved from http://efficacy.pearson.com/wp-content/uploads/2013/11/The-Incomplete-Guide-to-Delivering-Learning-Outcomes-high-res1.pdf

Baudean, B. (2014). *Linkedin.com*. Retrieved from https://www.linkedin.com/in/bryanbaudean

Bloomberg Businessweek. (2014, December 19). *Pearson PLC (PSON:London)*. Retrieved from http://investing.businessweek.com/research/stocks/people/person.asp?personId=540962&ticker=PSON:LN

Blume, H. (2014, September 3). L.A. schools Supt. Deasy defends his dealings with Apple, Pearson. *Los Angeles Times*. Retrieved from http://touch.latimes.com/#section/-1/article/p2p-81251434/

Blume, H., Kim, V., & Rainey, J. (2014, December 3). FBI seizes LAUSD records related to troubled iPad program. *Los Angeles Times*. Retrieved from http://www.latimes.com/local/education/la-me-lausd-ipads-20141203-story.html#page=1

Business Wire. (2007, January 8). Pearson Achievement Solutions announces National Demonstration School designations. *Boston.com*. Retrieved from http://finance.boston.com/boston/news/read?GUID=828691

Cavanagh, S. (2014, May 6). American Institutes for Research fights Pearson Common-Core testing award. *Education Week*. Retrieved from http://blogs.edweek.org/edweek/marketplacek12/2014/05/american_institutes_for_re search_challenges_pearson_common-core_testing_award_in_court.html

Christ, L. (2012, June 7). Schools boycott latest round of standardized testing. *New York News 1*. Retrieved from http://www.ny1.com/content/162683/schools-boycott-latest-round-of-standardizedtesting

FairTest. (n.d.). *Chicago reforms provide lessons to nation, NCLB*. National Center for Fair and Open Testing. Retrieved from http://fairtest.org/chicago-reforms-provide-lessons-nation-nclb

Fausset, R. (2014, August 11). In Atlanta, jury selection is set to begin in test scandal. *New York Times*, A9.

Gilbertson, A. (2014, August 22). Internal emails show LA school officials started iPad talks with software supplier a year before bids. *89.3 KPCC*. Retrieved from http://www.scpr.org/blogs/education/2014/08/22/17193/internal-emails-show-la-school-officials-started-i/

Gilbertson, A., & Keller, C. (2014, August 29). Search selected LA schools' emails related to the district iPad project. *89.3 KPCC*. Retrieved from http://projects.scpr.org/applications/lausd-ipad-emails/#document/1281201-2012-09-11-email-from-john-deasy-to-sherry-king/

Glassdoor.com. (2014). *Pearson*. http://www.glassdoor.com/Reviews/Employee-Review-Pearson-RVW4750603.htm.

Glod, M. (2008, May 2). Study questions "No Child" Act's reading plan. *Washington Post*. Retrieved from http://www.washingtonpost.com/wp-dyn/content/article/2008/05/01/AR2008050101399.html

Gordon, K. (2013, May 23). Pearson details restructuring. *The Wall Street Journal*. Retrieved from http://online.wsj.com/news/articles/SB10001424127887324659404578500433025096180

Herford, O. (1912). *The mythological zoo*. New York: Charles Scribner's Sons.

Hu, W. (2011, December 21). Testing firm faces inquiry on free trips for officials. *New York Times*. Retrieved from http://www.nytimes.com/2011/12/22/education/new-yorkattorney-general-is-investigating-pearson-education.html

Karp, S. (2010, April 14). School reform we can't believe in. *Common Dreams*. Retrieved from http://www.commondreams.org/views/2010/04/14/school-reform-we-cant-believe

Kirp, D. (2014, December 28). Rage against the Common Core. *New York Times*, SR19. Retrieved from http://www.nytimes.com/2014/12/28/opinion/sunday/rage-against-the-common-core.html?ref=opinion

Moody's. (2014, January 24). Moody's changes outlook on Pearson's Baa1 ratings to negative from stable. *Moody's Investors Service*, https://www.moodys.com/research/Moodys-changes-outlook-on-Pearsons-Baa1-ratings-to-negative-from–PR_291174

NCTQ. (2014, November). *Easy A's and what's behind them*. National Council on Teacher Quality. Retrieved from http://www.nctq.org/dmsStage/EasyAs

NCTQ. (n.d.). Advisory Board, National Council on Teacher Quality. Retrieved from http://www.nctq.org/about/advisoryBoard.jsp#240

Newman, D., & Jaciw, A. (2005). *Effectiveness of Scott Foresman's links to Reading First as an intervention for Struggling Readers*. Evaluation report to Pearson Education. Retrieved from http://assets.pearsonschool.com/asset_mgr/current/201140/Reading%20Street%20ELL%20FINAL%209-26%5B1%5D%5B4%5D.pdf

Office of the Attorney General of New York State. (2013). In the matter of Pearson Charitable Foundation and Pearson Inc. *Assurance of Discontinuance No. 13–487*. http://www.ag.ny.gov/pdfs/Pearson_Executed_AOD.pdf

PARCC. (n.d.) *PARCC: A state look*. Retrieved from http://www.parcconline.org/parcc-states

Pearson. (a, n.d.). *Sir Michael Barber, Office of the Chief Education Advisor*. Retrieved from https://www.pearson.com/michael-barber/bio.html

Pearson. (b, n.d). *John Fallon, Chief executive*. Retrieved from https://www.pearson.com/about-us/board-of-directors/john-fallon.html

Pearson. (c, n.d.). *Affordale learning global portfolio*. Retrieved from http://www.affordable-learning.com/the-fund/investments.html#sthash.USRvYZVP.jhoCzOuU.dpbs

Pearson. (d, n.d.). *Pearson 2014 half-year results*. Retrieved from https://www.pearson.com/news/announcements/2014/july/pearson-2014-halfyearresults.html

Pearson. (e, n.d.). *Pearson Achievement Solutions*. Retrieved from http://www.edweek.org/media/pas%20atlanta_case_study%2012-20-06%20edweek%20wp.doc.pdf

Pearson UK. (2011, September 19). *Pearson to develop frameworks for OECD's PISA student assessment for 2015*. Retrieved from http://uk.pearson.com/home/news/2011/september/pearson-to-develop-frameworks-for-oecds-pisa-student-assessment-for-2015.html

Phillips, E. (2014, April 10). We need to talk about the test. *New York Times*, A25.

Rich, M. (2014, October 17). Deasy resigns as Los Angeles Schools Chief after mounting criticism. *New York Times*, A18.

Save Our Schools NZ. (2014, May 7). *Academics worldwide call for the end of PISA tests.* Retrieved from http://saveourschoolsnz.com/2014/05/07/academics-worldwide-call-for-the-end-to-pisa-tests/

Sawchuk, S. (2014, July 12). *AFT passes resolution blasting the edTPA licensing test. Education Week.* Retrieved from http://blogs.edweek.org/edweek/teacherbeat/2014/07/aft_passes_resolution_knocking.html

Schneider, M. (2014, December 5). PARCC is down to DC plus ten states, and Louisiana isn't one of them. *deutsch29.* Retrieved from https://deutsch29.wordpress.com/2014/12/05/parcc-is-down-to-dc-plus-ten-states-and-louisiana-isnt-one-of-them/

Schweizer, K. (2014, April 25). Pearson confirms guidance with stronger second half. *Bloomberg.* Retrieved from http://www.bloomberg.com/news/2014-04-25/pearson-first-quarter-sales-decline-6-as-pound-strengthens.html

SEDL. (n.d.). *Reading Assessment Database.* http://www.sedl.org/cgi-bin/mysql/rad.cgi?searchid=229

Simon, S. (2012, August 2). Private firms eyeing profits from U.S. public schools. *Reuters.* Retrieved from http://www.reuters.com/article/2012/08/02/usa-education-investment-idUSL2E8J15FR20120802

Singer, A. (2012, November 4). Pearson "Education" – Who are these people? *Huffington Post.* Retrieved from http://www.huffingtonpost.com/alan-singer/pearson-education-new-york-testing-_b_1850169.html

Singer, A. (2013a). Hacking away at the corporate octopus. *Cultural logic: Marxist theory & practice*, pp. 209–223. Retrieved from http://clogic.eserver.org/2013/Singer.pdf

Singer, A. (2013b, September 9). Are schools of education why children don't learn? Reclaiming the conversation on education. *Huffington Post.* Retrieved from http://www.huffingtonpost.com/alan-singer/are-schools-of-education-_b_3563103.html

Singer, A. (2014a). Why Pearson tests our kids. *Huffington Post.* Retrieved from http://www.huffingtonpost.com/alan-singer/why-pearson-tests-our-kid_b_5484257.html

Singer, A. (2014b, September 2). Pearson: Inside the belly of a very troubled beast. *Huffington Post.* Retrieved from http://www.huffingtonpost.com/alan-singer/pearson-inside-the-belly-_b_5749708.html

Singer, A. (2014c, September 10). Pearson and the L.A. school's iPad project – Time to tell the truth. *Huffington Post.* Retrieved from http://www.huffingtonpost.com/alan-singer/pearson-and-the-la-school_b_5796730.html?utm_hp_ref=education&ir=Education

Singer, A. (2014d). Pearson Education can run, but it cannot hide. *Huffington Post.* Retrieved from http://www.huffingtonpost.com/alan-singer/pearson-education-can-run_b_6327566.html

Solochek, J. (2014, April 22). Florida school districts suspend online FCAT after glitches. *Tampa Bay Times.* Retrieved from http://www.tampabay.com/news/education/k12/pasco-hernando-schools-battling-computer-problems-during-fcat/2176268.

Sorkin, A. R. (2013, September 3). McKinsey & Co. isn't all roses in a new book. *New York Times*, B1.

Strauss, V. (2014, April 25). AFT asks Pearson to stop "gag order" barring educators from talking about tests. *The Answer Sheet, The Washington Post.* Retrieved from http://www.washingtonpost.com/blogs/answer-sheet/wp/2014/04/25/aft-asks-pearson-to-stop-gag-order-barring-educators-from-talking-about-tests/

U.S. Federal Court. (2014, October 7). RFC case number 3:2014cv00685. Retrieved from http://www.rfcexpress.com/lawsuits/employment/virginia-eastern-district-court/913286/bryan-m-baudean-v-pearson-education-inc/summary/

UUP. (2014, August 11). *Educators shout, scold, shred in privatization protest.* United University Professions. Retrieved from http://uupinfo.org/communications/uupdate/1314/140812.php

Weiner, R. (2012, June 9). Dozens of Rockland, Westchester pupils boycott company's field tests. *The Journal News.* Retrieved from http://www.lohud.com/apps/pbcs.dll/article?AID=/201206090230/NEWS03/306090048&gcheck=1

Winerip, M. (2012, May 7). Move to outsource teacher licensing process draws protest. *New York Times*, A15.

Part II

Relation of Theory and Research to Practice in Social Justice Education

FIVE

On the Urgency and Relevance of Research for Marxists

Faith Agostinone-Wilson

Overview

Under capitalism, research that reflects the interests of the ruling class is often that which is the most funded, promoted, and easily accessed. Within the field of education, research that uncritically accepts the inevitability of evidentiary tenets of high-stakes, standardized testing such as No Child Left Behind, Race to the Top, Response to Intervention, and Common Core typically receives the most support, along with "school choice" research funded by think tanks (Scott & Jabbar, 2014). For example, the Association for Supervision and Curriculum Development, one of the largest professional organizations for educators, has a "topics" tab on their website where people can access existing resources and research. The totality of the topics listed include: 21st century skills, brain-based learning, building academic vocabulary, character education, classroom management, Common Core, democratic education, differentiated instruction, effective teaching and leading, English language learners, inclusion and special education, multicultural education, multiple intelligences, response to intervention, school culture/climate, school safety, school standards, student assessment, student mentoring, understanding by design, what works in schools, and whole child. Additionally, those studies that use quantitative approaches are also privileged over qualitative, both in terms of funding and prestige of publication (Denzin, 2009; Denzin & Giardina, 2006; Roth, 2002). Analyses that involve a more critical stance, including the use of qualitative methodologies, are marginalized, either by being contained to independent journals or relegated to less attended time slots at major educational conferences.

At the same time, the educational left remains mired in postmodernism and extreme relativism, which has limited the ability to use research for dialectical aims and significant social change. Some examples of this include a resurgence of religious mysticism and what can be best described as a neo-naturalism or faux tribalism that rejects empiricism in favor of alternative approaches of knowledge validation, along with aspects of white supremacy (Gardell, 2003; Hale, 2011). Aspects of this are found within the anti-vaccination and Common Core opposition movements, members of which seek to build coalitions with rightist groups, forsaking sound analysis for sheer numbers of allies (Apple, 2003; de Lange, 2012). Similarly, activist groups such as Occupy utilize consensus decision making, a rejection of notions of party building and leadership, along with other less effective ways to shape and test knowledge (Anarchism, n.d.; Kerl, 2010; Yanowitz, 2007). It is against this backdrop that a strong case will be made for the necessity of dialectical research methodologies grounded in classical Marxism, within the context of social change.

This chapter attempts to make the case for urgency when it comes to opposition to capitalism in the form of dialectical research. While on-the-ground action is essential for revolution, it must be accompanied by the formation of theory through the systematic gathering of evidence and testing of ideas as the working class moves forward. Theories are not just frameworks for planning research; they have real consequences, as Worthen (2014) attests:

> Not all theories are any good. Suppose you follow the steps of Kolb's Learning Cycle and some information is missing, your categories are wrong, and you don't test your ideas enough, and you come up with an analysis that is wrong- what will happen? You've created a bad theory and now you want to act on it. Is anyone going to get hurt? Probably. A bad theory will lead you and everyone around you into all kinds of trouble. (p. 77)

The author will therefore present the case for theory building via dialectical praxis through research throughout the chapter.

First, *Distortions* will deal with the ideological assault on reality, rationality, and critical thought by the right wing and its philosophical arm, postmodernism. Basically what we are seeing is an attack on reality itself, not only represented by the anti-science positions of religion, but by global corporations in an attempt to retain profits in fossil fuels, the military, and health. While it is essential to document the atrocities committed by capitalism worldwide, it is just as important that Marxists understand the ideological role of the "research arm" of the right wing, and how they attempt to legitimize themselves, gaining traction precisely because many people (including leftists) are intimidated by research and/or view it as elitist, or they have bought into the postmodern notion of radical relativism. At the same time, the process of what gets funded and recognized as research is also highly exclusionary, unless one has the power and money to influence the process. The very types of research that would challenge this system are not likely to be promoted, for obvious reasons. This leaves reactionary views unchallenged and only serves to embolden the right wing that relies on common educational tropes such as "culture of poverty."

Second, *Marxian Research Strategies* will outline aspects of Marxist research approaches, such as those used by Engels, Lenin, Luxemburg, Gramsci, and Vygotsky. This will include an overview of the tenets of dialectics and historical materialism, and its applications in the form of scientific socialism and critical realism, including workplace studies. Additionally, examples will be presented of artists who combine research within the visual arts as a potentially vital way to dialectically explore the social world though a unique version of data collection and interpretation. These methodological approaches call for a clearly defined vision backed up with systematic analysis of why things are the way they are. It should be noted that both qualitative and quantitative researchers are able to participate in Marxian analysis and that there is a long history of dialectical approaches used within both camps.

Distortions

A major challenge within research is coming to the realization that the shaping of disciplinary fields and the testing of ideas are no less impacted by capitalism than the ordinary worker's daily movements. This happens despite the efforts of individuals and groups committed to divergent approaches to research. It may take different forms in higher education settings where research is generated, but the concealing function of ideology is ever-present and difficult to confront (sometimes more so), as Tedman (2012) attests:

> In this understanding, bourgeois ideology is never a simple singular proposition that can therefore be simply refuted with its 'opposite,' it always parasitically reflects and warps a material dialectic, and always has at least two (superficially) 'oppositional' sides, so that if you do not fall for one, you become susceptible to the allure of the other. (p. 28)

As long as the superficial façade of "multiple sides" are presented, institutions can pat themselves on the back, believing they have met the basic requirements of academic inquiry. According to Tedman, Philosophy functions as the primary gatekeeper as to what are or aren't acceptable boundaries of knowledge. Disciplinary fields that emerge from Philosophy and distinct philosophical traditions, therefore, are sites of class struggle in the realm of theory. Since all workers live within capitalism, academia is not immune to the influences of the ruling class and in fact serves an important ideological function in promoting the interests of this class, often using elaborate means of justification for all manner of harmful practices.

We know that the media is a multi-billion dollar industry making money off of the creation and distribution of propaganda while delivering customers to an endless stream of products they don't really need or probably even want. Yet it can also be disillusioning to realize how much money and other resources are put into the shaping of ideology through the *academic community*, using research as a legitimizing tool, under the guises of neutrality and following the scientific method. In more extreme past examples, academic research was used during the Bush administration to support medicalized torture, as health care personnel who collected data on the impact of rendition techniques on detainees so as to determine "acceptable" levels of pain that were later written into laws and policies, providing a legal shield to those engaging in these acts (Berkowitz, 2015). Even in less criminal applications, the majority of research practices reflect that:

> Under modern capitalism, the class that runs society relentlessly transforms the material world. It does this in the interest of more intensely exploiting workers and natural resources, producing deadlier weapons, and generating larger profits. As a result, the natural and applied sciences can be made to serve these ends (for example, physics, chemistry, engineering, aerospace, computer science....As a result, mainstream social science—including psychology—

> effectively *obscures* the truth about a social arrangement that benefits the few at the expense of the many, and which uses racism, sexism, and other oppressions to maintain itself. (Sawyer, 2014, para. 5–6)

This section will address current distortions within research, including decentering reality itself, systemic problems within the production of research, and a critique of postmodernism as it applies to research.

Reality Under Attack

Within the right wing, a successful distortion tactic has been to take advantage of the bourgeois expectation of fairness and "open debate" within a democratic society in order to advance their ideology. By using the existing system, the right wing can ride the coat tails of democratic legitimacy, superficial as their efforts may be. This is done through the shallow presentation of point/counterpoint on cable news or the comments sections on Internet news sites (the use of these populist settings is an added bonus to set them apart from those "elitist" academics), to create the image that there is anything remotely controversial about topics like global warming (Creighton, 2014). The manufacturing of controversy is a way to insert just enough doubt into the public's mind, where people are simultaneously taught not to trust research and to see research as synonymous with yet another "opinion." So it's a matter of finding the "right" research to fit one's views. This is part of what Gramsci meant by the formation of common sense, as discussed by Jubas (2010):

> Through [Gramsci's] conceptualizations of hegemony, ideology, and common sense, he developed an extensive theory of the role of civil society as a site of production of ideology and its associated "common sense" through which those in power persuade citizens to consent to hegemony even when it works against their interests, and through which counter-hegemonic forces can articulate challenges and mobilize opposition. (p. 228)

It isn't coincidental that the research fields that the public are taught to not trust are those that have a direct bearing on their daily lives, in the areas of the economy, environment, sexuality, health, and labor.

Eagle (2003) presents an overview of the specific ways that distortions function to shape common sense. A first step is to transform logic (both deductive and inductive) into one of many endless options of rhetorical formation to be consumed—just pick the one you like! It is important to disorient people from central notions of an observable reality. This makes them more open to ruling class ideas that then don't require validation, like supply side economics. Second, a blurring of the differences between what is true and false is critical, except, of course, in matters of religion. With religion, it's important to be narrow minded and singular in focus, especially if one encounters scientific evidence that contradicts religious tenets. Once the blurring occurs, it is then simple to make reality equivalent to whatever version of argument that someone is using, and put the issue to an up or down vote in terms of agreeing or disagreeing. This subverts traditional means of scientific inquiry where the burden of truth is on the one making the claim. When presented with scientific evidence, no matter how well researched, distortions come into play because all someone has to do is "not believe" in things like global climate change. When research is presented this way in a national forum, like Fox News, the effects are immediate and impactful.

In summarizing the concept of motivated reasoning, Mooney (2013) comments that far from being in a separate domain, rational human thought is wrapped up with emotion, or affect: "We push threatening information away; we pull friendly information close. We apply fight-or-flight reflexes not only to predators, but to data itself" (para. 8). The processing of positive and negative feelings about ideas happens so quickly that people are not usually aware of it as it is happening:

> When we think we're reasoning we may instead be rationalizing…we may think we're being scientists, but we're actually being lawyers. Our "reasoning" is a means to a predetermined end—winning our "case"—and is shot through with biases. They include "confirmation bias," in which we give greater heed to evidence and arguments that bolster our beliefs, and "disconfirmation bias," in which we expend disproportionate energy trying to debunk or refute views and arguments that we find uncongenial. (para. 10)

The significance of the theory of motivated reasoning is that people have often convinced themselves that they have weighed the evidence, when in fact they are relying on common sense and other ideological distortions that support the ruling class. Because scientists are careful to outline the limitations, assumptions, and delimitations of their research designs in the spirit of transparency, people can often equate these detailed procedures with "one person's opinion." Add to this the general hostility toward those perceived as "educated elites" and the conditions are ripe for distortion (Williams, 2014). There is a sense of invigorating faux populism to the notion that one can make sweeping judgments without having to do any sort of research or provide sufficient evidence for grandiose claims.

An even scarier aspect of motivated reasoning is that the presentation of facts in the form of research only appears to make the problem *worse*. People cling even more stubbornly to their misconceptions than before the counter-evidence was presented. As Mooney (2013) asserts, "Scientific evidence is highly susceptible to selective reading and misinterpretation. Giving ideologues or partisans scientific data that's relevant to their beliefs is like unleashing them in the motivated-reasoning equivalent of a candy store" (para. 14). So the notion that such people are anti-science is partly a misnomer. More accurately, the distortion positions science as whatever people want it to be, as in pro-"my" science. If "my" science is individualistic and in support of the sale of more guns or fast food, then what possible harm could come from those things that I "feel" or "believe" are good for people, like the free market? For Mooney, a person who buys into hierarchy and the notion of individuals who have free choice "finds it difficult to believe that the things he prizes could lead to outcomes deleterious to society" (para. 17). So it remains important to select the kind of science that will support those things.

Further, the blanket assumption that a low education level automatically makes one susceptible to distortions of research is another fallacy (unfortunately promoted by the left), not entirely supported by evidence. For example, nearly 20% of Republicans with college education disagreed with the concept that humans have contributed to global warming compared to just over 30% of non-college educated Republicans (A Deeper Partisan Divide, 2008). The effect was opposite when it came to level of education among Democrats and Independents. Mooney (2013) explains these contradictions:

> One insidious aspect of motivated reasoning is that political sophisticates are prone to be more biased than those who know less about the issues. People who have a dislike of some policy—for example, abortion—if they're unsophisticated they can just reject it out of hand. But if

they're sophisticated, they can go one step further and start coming up with counterarguments. These individuals are just as emotionally driven and biased as the rest of us, but they're able to generate more and better reasons to explain why they're right—and so their minds become harder to change. (para. 29)

Mooney concludes that the distortion of reality is therefore easier to achieve among those who have been exposed to the lethal combination of higher education and right wing views.

Still another distortion tactic is to label climate change deniers and the like as "skeptics." This is a way to place oneself into the scientifically acceptable category of those who question research while engaging in decidedly un-skeptical practices. Creighton (2014) prefers to call these individuals "deniers" since they produce no evidence of their own, other than corporate-sponsored propaganda, all aimed to create confusion in the general public. In fact, as Mooney (2013) shows, even when evidence is produced, they reject it. This leads Creighton (2014) to the following conclusion:

> Too many people aren't skeptical; they are biased and wrong....Even worse, a number of news sites and science organizations (for one reason or another) refer to science deniers as "skeptics." Skepticism is essentially a quest for evidence and proof....It's not that we can't ever be certain about anything; it's that this certainty needs to be based on research and evidence; it needs to have its foundation in a conversation that extends beyond our own inner thoughts. (Creighton, 2014, para. 2–3)

The harm of misrepresenting the role of the skeptic is that it casts doubt on the entire scientific research process itself and the hope of ever being able to understand the world as it is. If everything is "biased" and "someone's opinion" then one might as well stick with things that confirm one's beliefs, so the logic goes.

Systemic Problems Within Research Production

In addition to the function of distortion, there are systemic aspects of research production that interfere with a dialectical materialist understanding of the world. These include the alignment of certain kinds of theories with ruling class ideology, as in the case of educational research preoccupied with notions of "culture of poverty," "the achievement gap," and the like as well as the more overtly political influences on the research process, such as who does or doesn't obtain grant funding or publication in more prestigious journals. The presentation of ruling class ideologies as being rooted in scientific inquiry only reinforces the distortion and its likelihood of being widely accepted, especially in the absence of alternative findings.

Using the staying power of the children's book *Tarzan* as a metaphor, Worthen (2014) distinguishes between theories in terms of quality, with good theories explaining the world, from the vantage point of the working class engaging in dialectical praxis, and bad theories, which reflect ruling class interests:

> Here is an example of a bad theory. This theory essentially says that if you are white and try hard, you can learn, even if you are completely alone. What matters is willpower, attitude, and "good" genetics. It helps if you are English nobility. This is a good theory if you want to design a school system that sorts out a very few to succeed, and lets most people fail...narratives with this kind of staying power usually reflect some level of popular consensus about reality and how things work. At the very least, they cannot radically diverge from something that people at least hope is possible, no matter whether it seems astonishing or ridiculous. (p. 77)

As Sawyer (2014) notes, these hyper-individualized social theories also penetrate fields such as psychology, where people start to internalize failure early on in school settings. This internalization obviously impacts students identified as "failing" in schools by effectively killing any degree of motivation to learn, but also has a negative impact on those who excel academically in the form of stifled creativity, perfectionism, and taking the low-risk path so they will maintain the image of success.

For Sawyer, much of these distortions originate in the pseudoscientific field of evolutionary psychology (EP). According to the tenets of EP, people's minds contain traits that are resistant to change, holdovers from a prehistoric, evolutionary past. Qualities such as sexism, selfishness, aggression, and even procivility to engage in war are viewed as impenetrable aspects of human existence. It just so happens that these very same traits are also ones that the ruling class benefits from promoting, so EP tends to receive a fair hearing in the media.

Gaspar (2004) connects the success of EP authors such as Wright (1995), Ridley (2003), and Pinker (2003) to promotion via right wing think tanks, which includes the publication of bestseller *The Bell Curve* (Herrnstein & Murray, 1996). While less potent in its distortions than EP, behaviorism also has alliances within the ruling class:

> The behaviorist approach either disavows the existence of consciousness completely, or sees it as beyond the reach of scientific investigation. Behaviorists spend a lot of energy trying to prove empirically that human behavior can be controlled through the selective administration of reinforcement and punishment. This approach has been widely (mis)applied to children's education, and is a favorite of corporate bosses and merit pay enthusiasts. Though behaviorist techniques have proven fairly effective in shaping animal behavior, research has shown that when applied to human beings, these "carrot and stick" tactics cause people to lose intrinsic motivation for discovery and learning, to be less creative, and to generally feel resentful and manipulated. (Sawyer, 2014, para. 12)

What behaviorism does share with EP is a "historically static" conception of human psychology, only impacted by temporal external stimuli. This notion of an unchanging human psyche is essential to ruling class ideology, proponents of which spend an enormous amount of energy getting people to accept things as they are. However, as Sawyer notes, "the good news is that the social internalization process also gives humans the ability to question their society, to direct their own behavior, and to *transform* their society by collaborating with others…to make history within their given conditions" (para. 78). It is this type of emancipatory research that is not likely to be as heavily promoted as derivatives of EP.

Education has long been susceptible to EP and behaviorist influenced research. Ladson-Billings (2006) theorizes that part of this is due to how education in the United States has been positioned as a psychological field, rather than an anthropological one. Teacher candidates receive little to no foundational courses on the history of education, or the cultural role it serves and has served. Distortions of psychology and a lack of anthropological knowledge mean that educators tend to use "culture" as an explanation for everything from students who don't do well in school or those students who act out, particularly African American ones. When it comes to culture, the problem is one of the historical exclusion of people from and within schooling, combined with an over-determining role of culture and just plain bad psychological diagnosing:

> So many of the teachers' interviews and writings identify the so-called self-esteem problem that it has become a commonsense way of speaking and thinking about students who experience academic or discipline problems in schools. The question that this pattern of speaking about students provoked in my mind was how it is that so many teachers have come to make a psychological diagnosis about students who are struggling in schools. Additionally, a growing number of teachers have begun to dump all manner of behavior into a catchall they call "culture." Whenever [teachers] seem not to be able to explain or identify with students, they point to teachers' culture as the culprit. (p. 105)

Ladson-Billings also identifies theories that privilege the individual over the collective as leading to a reliance on culture as an explanatory concept. Because ruling class ideology has distorted the interactions of individual and structural factors surrounding education, students are positioned as being responsible for their own successes and failures. If certain groups of students, such as African Americans, are disproportionally represented in "failing" categories that are not so easily explained away by individual factors, then "culture" becomes a convenient theoretical construct to explain their failing in large groups. As Ladson-Billings notes, culture becomes "a catchall phrase is that it is often a proxy for race" (p. 106). She continues:

> Culture is regularly used as a code word for difference and perhaps deviance in the world of teacher education....Not understanding culture and its role in shaping our thoughts and behavior is not limited to teacher education students. Most members of the dominant society rarely acknowledge themselves as cultural beings. They have no reason to. Culture is that exotic element possessed by "minorities." It is what it means to be nonwhite. It is also the convenient explanation for why some students cannot achieve success in the classroom. (p. 107)

The ideology of "culture of poverty" as a more socially acceptable derivative of early 1900s eugenics thinking derives from two more recent publications: Harrington's (1997) *The Other America* and Payne's (2013) *A Framework for Understanding Poverty*. Though their claims are striking in terms of sheer lack of empirical evidence (see Bomer, Dworin, May, & Semingson, 2008 for a thorough analysis and critique of Payne), both of these authors have achieved massive book sales and their ideas regularly circulate through professional development workshops reaching millions of teachers (most of whom are of the bourgeois demographic already receptive to their writings). In discussing her reaction to *The Other America*, Ehrenreich (2012) remarked, "Harrington did such a good job of making the poor seem "other" that when I read his book in 1963, I did not recognize my own forebears and extended family in it" (para. 4). This speaks to the potential of these theories to break important networks of solidarity among the working class to the point where one wouldn't even recognize one's own family members in their portrayal.

At the same time as ruling class ideology permeates the presentation of what counts as "research," political factors are also a part of the process of the review and publication of research within the academic community itself. Roth's (2002) ethnographic analysis of the research review process in Canada reveals practices by no means unique to the production of research elsewhere. Prior to presenting his own data, Roth provides the example of how the direction of artificial intelligence research was shaped in the United States entirely by a committee responding to a single academic paper that promoted a shift to the approach used in the paper with the result of previous and subsequent approaches not receiving funding. This outcome reveals inherent problems with review committee structures in grant-funding institutions:

> An important "biasing" aspect of the direction a committee will take is the real or perceived expertise of the reader or committee member. In the case of real or perceived expertise, the committee decision will be close to the opinion and assessment of this reader. If real or perceived expertise lies with another committee member who was not the reader, this person, depending on the level of his or her engagement, can change the direction of the discussion to the point of getting a well-rated proposal into the category of un-fundable projects. In some situations, even proposals with high ratings by both readers and the two or three assessors might end up not being funded as a consequence of the influences within the committee. (p. 98)

The peer review process has long been the gold standard of academic research, and seen to be one of the best ways to ensure quality and fairness. However, Roth notes that reviewers, funding agencies, and editors can often engage in attacks on authors. Because the review process is blinded, there is no system of recourse in place:

> The process is inherently biased against the applicant because the very same committee (or parts of it) that made the original decision evaluates the appeal…the funding agency takes appeals to the same committee, which then deliberates whether it erred in the first instance. Curiously, therefore, the committee deliberates whether it has erred though the Council states that it will not accept appeals, even if the committee had erred. This provides opportunities for rejecting appeals based on a factual error in initial deliberations, as long as the committee comes to the conclusion that it "has made a reasonable attempt to judge fairly the merit of an application." (p.103)

In his ethnographic data, Roth found that funding agencies' power was reflected in the way they were referred to by participants as a singular entity, rather than a committee of academics, as in "The National Science Foundation (NSF) accepted my proposal," or "I'm going to Washington" as a reference to their upcoming presentation of a proposal to the NSF.

Roth concludes that when one seeks to research one's own community that possesses a large degree of power, such as grant funding organizations, it is a matter of weighing the risks (to the researcher engaging in such inquiry) and opportunities (to challenge existing structures of research production). He extends his inquiry by posing the following methodological questions:

> What processes can be set in place so that such ethnographies are possible without punitive measures from those at obligatory passage points in power of withholding valued and desirable resources? Do we have to play the game, shut up, and thereby leave unjust practices intact so that we can cull the resources? What is/ought to be the roles of more prominent scholars in changing our practices and communities? (pp. 103–104)

Postmodern Diversions

Immediately after the global recession of 2008, Marxian analysis began to re-enter the mainstream media, with debate about capitalism's viability replacing the usual watered down concepts of "corporate greed" or "corruption." In response to this renewed interest in Marx, the co-opting followed, with the media using Marxian concepts as a way to "save" capitalism (Fuchs & Vincent, 2012). In a similar manner within the academy (where Marx is also being "re-discovered" after decades of postmodernism), Walby (2007) observes how turns in social theory have moved away from dialectical analysis as part of an attempt to disrupt praxis:

> The academicization of sociological critique (and the social sciences) has done much to divorce theory from action and hinder the extent to which sociological critique can inform radical social transformation. The politics of praxical critique have suffered under the modernist/postmodernist dispute, such that the language of transformation in critical social theory is fractured. (p. 908)

Part of this postmodern and neoliberal co-optation involves the presentation of Marxian or critical theory perspectives as potentially non-threatening to capital, as has happened with Gramsci and Freire (Sefla, 2015). In particular, what Gonzalez (2004) identifies as "postmodern ethnicity" is a way for market forces to profit from the co-optation of leftist authors of color who never intended for their work to be utilized to support the postmodern project. Sefla (2015) asserts that Mariategui, a Mexican Marxist writer whose work supported the notion of a revolutionary workers' party, had his work later used in support of postmodern identity and anarcho-syndicalist ends. In a similar manner, Mohanty (2013) speaks to her work being misused in support of localism: "This particular misreading of my work ignored the materialist emphasis on a common context of struggle and undermined the possibility of solidarity across differences" (p. 977).

Walby (2007) conceives of the postmodern critique of capitalism as an unavoidable event (rather than a leftward shift in the field), since the global and impenetrable nature of neoliberalism could no longer be ignored. However, "postmodernists hurriedly negate modern foundationalist claims through deconstruction" and instead critique capitalism's discourses while discounting collective action (p. 898). This fragmentation within the academy has resulted in what Kellner (2014) views as the "trivialization and academicization" of research, where global social concerns are reduced to ineffective commentary and entertainment (para. 62). As part of this process, the chaotic effects of capitalism have become naturalized, and distorted into progressive and liberating aspects of identity (Gonzalez, 2004). "In short, anything goes – except, it appears, actually trying to address the problem" (Mehaffy & Haas, 2012, p. 87).

More disturbingly, the postmodern turn has aligned with neoliberal ideology in its efforts to obscure capitalist social relations. Mohanty (2013) poses the question: "Does postmodernism coupled with neoliberal knowledge economies in effect define a threshold of disappearance where one conceptual frame systemic or intersectional is quietly subsumed under and supplanted by another emerging frame, one that obscures crucial relations of power?" (p. 970). Mehaffy and Haas (2012) do not see the parallel rise of postmodernism and neoliberalism as coincidental:

> At a time when these professions are facing imperatives to develop more sustainable, more resilient, more humanly successful settlements, they are instead offering up, often to naive developing—world clients, a curious mix of ever more exotic visual confections, greenwashing rhetoric and – when rightly criticized – a theoretical apologia of hand—wringing postmodern nihilism. (p. 81)

Therefore, it is not a stretch to conclude that postmodernism has become the ideology, not the critique (Gonzalez, 2004, p. 184).

As part of its ideological operations, postmodernism utilizes the concept of discourse, "that social reality is constituted more by the actor's usage of discourse than shaped by the social structure, which is said to be fixed and static" (Ho, 2012, p. 322). Ho refers to this as "radical constructionism," a form of "non-realism" where *discursive practice* becomes an essential concept inherent in the creation of knowledge" (p. 322). In this conception, experience consists of "the fluid meanings of actors derived from interactions within a specific context" (p. 322). Rather than being theoretically sound, Walby (2007) views this as a form of substitution, where linguistic theories replace Marx's (1867) concept of commodity fetishism, instead of folding discourse into a dialectical materialist analysis, such as Fairclough's (2013) approach to critical discourse analysis.

With everything reduced to discourse, a form of what Gonzalez (2004) calls "ideological ambivalence" has taken hold, where social struggle is reduced to isolated interactions of individuals who are themselves subject to fluid identities in localized, specific contexts. Power is held not by the ruling class, but by those who hold the dominant discourse:

> The critique developed insofar is based on the radical constructionist's relatively lack of concern of the pre-predicative; non-discursive structure of the lifeworld which exerts important patterning effects on the actor's experience....This suggests that those who construct reality and convey it through the "dominant discourse" are often the ones in power. Thus, discursive constructions of the individual are often reflections of the dominant ideology which possesses a privileged and determinative influence on people's language, thought and action. In short, individuals' discursive constructions of reality are directly influenced by the dominant discourse of society. (Ho, 2012, p. 334)

Resistance to a nebulous category of "power" takes the form of playful and rebellious discourses, versus social struggle. People are positioned as eternally existing in various borderlands, without a historically rooted identity or preceding social conditions. Instead, they are shaped by discourses. As Gonzalez (2004) explains, "postmodernist theory misinterprets literary ambivalence as a subversive force in itself, rather than analyzing this ambivalence as the product of capitalist exploitation" (p. 164). Gonzalez concludes that postmodernism cannot account for people's ability to make history, in times not of their choosing, a key dialectical materialist tenet. This has had especially negative consequences for feminist research, already hit by postfeminist ideology that women have already overcome oppression:

> Alongside this postfeminist discourse there has been a shift away from activist feminist movements that seek to bring about political change (and adopt an implicitly anti-capitalist, anti-market stance) to a 'market feminism,' which sees industrialization and the market system as making a large contribution to the growth of feminism. Popularized feminist ideas appear as product images with advertisers repackaging 'feminist quests for freedom, choice and opportunity as images, desires, lifestyles, and emotions that can be attained through consumption.' (Catterall, MacLaran, & Stevens, 2005, p. 490)

Likewise, postmodern feminist analysis has rejected the construct of the family, one of the most essential historical material concepts of socialist feminist inquiry, transforming it into just being one of several competing discourses (Ho, 2012).

The postmodern focus on the local and contextual rather than the collective and historical as sites of research has several aspects that dovetail with the neoliberal project of capitalism. First is the avoidance of any form of what is called "totalizing discourse," such as history and systematic analyses of social processes, which could lead people to understand why things are the way they are (Ho, 2012). This "domesticates power differences, transforming systemic projects of resistance into commodified, private acts of rebellion" (Mohanty, 2013, p. 968). Mohanty continues:

> The complex political economy focus highlighting power and hierarchy of much feminist, antiracist theory, for instance, is either reduced to a politics of representation/presence/multiculturalism or seen as irrelevant in the context of a so-called post-race/postfeminist society. Thus, race and gender justice commitments, among others, are recoded as a politics of presence or benign representation of various differences in neoliberal universities. (p. 972)

Second, concepts such as racism, sexism, and heterosexism are transformed into "privatized notions of individual experience" where even political actions are turned into consumerist ones (Mohanty, 2013, p. 972). Because gender is a modernist, universalizing concept, a holdover from the Enlightenment, it is rejected as a category of analysis, or becomes a fluid, untraceable part of identity that actors can freely shape (Catterall, MacLaran, & Stevens, 2005).

Third, research that is conducted by "insiders," those who are members of the groups being studied, is assumed to be superior by default than research conducted by outsiders. Jubas (2010) asserts that this postmodern assumption is problematic because race, gender, and sexuality are not isolated identities, but are combined with social class or even together. Insider researchers may be operating off of their own assumptions or even ignoring how something like race is socially constructed differently depending on the historical conditions. For example, capitalism has been able to utilize multiculturalism to its benefit, as in corporations touting their tolerant positions about workers of different races and sexual orientations. At the same time as neoliberalism has commodified the public sphere, postmodernism has introduced "an inert theory of identity that emphasizes difference over commonality, coalition, and contestation" (Mohanty, 2013, p. 974). Materialist feminists counter that differences of race and sexuality are utilized by capitalism to further its ends, rather than being forms of discursive categories (Jubas, 2010).

Fourth, localism-through-discourse assumes that people have the same degree of power to resist; it is just a matter of accounting for the differences between discourses and identities: "if all experience is merely individual, and the social is always collapsed into the personal, feminist critique and radical theory appear irrelevant" (Mohanty, 2013, p. 971). However, understanding oppression as a systemic and institutional function under capitalism requires the concept of collective solutions. This is critical for working class women across the globe, who bear the brunt of neoliberal policies—in particular single parents, minimum wage workers, and the elderly. In the absence of alternative research, other distortive projects within academia can more easily assume dominance, such as evolutionary psychology, behaviorism, and management theories (Catterall, MacLaran, & Stevens, 2005). By contrast,

> Materialist feminists see the social as incorporating both cultural aspects of life *and* social structures and systems. Gender, it is argued, is more than just a cultural distinction between men and women; it is sustained through hierarchical social structures that include divisions in labor. (p. 496)

For example, postmodern feminist research might examine multiple identities expressed through fashion, representing consumer culture as a site of liberation for women to transcend social class boundaries. However, this type of research conceals the other side of the garment industry, that of sweatshop labor performed primarily by women, many of whom are children. Where are the "transgressive boundaries" to playfully cross for these individuals?

Finally, postmodern localism has created an overwhelming sense of inertia, that "nothing is to be done, that much greater forces are in control and all we can do is play along, hoping for occasionally brilliant, or at least witty, deconstructions of the truth" (Mehaffy & Haas, 2012, p. 81). This takes aim at "the very possibility of a sharable notion of value" (p. 85). With discourses being individually constructed and the most that can be expected are smaller acts of resistance, larger movements are rendered impossible or structural and imposing. Catterall, MacLaran, and Stevens (2005) note how the postmodern paralysis involves locating resistance to the marketplace, where identities are fluid and represent a range of options, where it ultimately makes no sense to act outside of it. It is interesting how this fits the same neoliberal, capitalist line of thinking of T.I.N.A.: there is no alternative:

> The result has been that our ability to learn from our mistakes, to repeat our successes and to actually solve our urgent problems – that is to say, our collective intelligence – has been the catastrophic casualty. However, this remains a profitable result for some, in the short term. (Mehaffy & Haas, 2012, p. 81)

Mohanty (2013) finds that the neoliberal project of dissolving public spaces fits nicely with the postmodern privatization of resistance by eliminating materialist understanding of how capitalism functions within institutions. This only serves to strengthen the neoliberal project.

Ultimately, postmodernism contributes to the opposition to or de-centering of reality. At the individual level, Eagle (2003) notes that within the field of psychoanalysis, Enlightenment concepts of the ability to know one's self are the foundations of therapy and gaining personal insight into one's thoughts. However, the postmodern turn within psychoanalysis has called into question the ability of the therapist to guide a client through the identification of repressions and other barriers to comprehending reality:

> Disillusionment with or at least skepticism toward the overarching therapeutic value of insight has not only deepened but became transformed into philosophical positions that maintain that there are no truths about the (patients') mind to be discovered and no self-knowledge to be gained. That is, the idea that insight, self-knowledge, and learning truths about oneself may not be as effective as we thought became transformed into a philosophical position that ruled out the very possibility of discovering truths about the mind. (p. 414)

Postmodernists have therefore attacked the essential concepts of there being a real world that exists outside of our understanding of it, and that "our statements are typically true or false depending on whether they correspond to how things are, that is, to facts in the world" (p. 412). By denying empirical reality, the processes of forming the modern subject are rendered irrelevant and become difficult to identify (Walby, 2007).

At the social level, postmodernism responds to what Gonzalez (2004) terms the "cultural schizophrenia" and social fragmentation of society by calling for its acceptance as a welcome respite from the over-determining structures of modern institutions and ideas. Yet cultural schizophrenia has real, material roots within the alienating structure of capitalism. It is a symptom of the historical legacy of capitalism and its attendant oppressions, colonialism, and alienation of labor, not evidence of a postmodern turn, per se. "Cultural schizophrenia becomes a problem only when the conditions of alienation and social fragmentation are misconstrued as politically progressive or as inherently revolutionary" (p. 174). By mystifying the social relations under capitalism and their relationship to labor, the ability of class consciousness to form is truncated, as Mohanty (2013) points out in her discussion of the Occupied Territories:

Back in neoliberal "post-everything" U.S. academic and political culture, I confront discursive shifts that mystify the conditions in Palestine. Postmodernism would suggest a fluidity and mobility of identities and subjects of liberation that obviate systemic critiques of oppression.... None of these "post" frameworks is useful in making sense of the landscape of violence, oppression, and incarceration that constitutes everyday life for Palestinians in the 1948 territories and in the occupied West Bank. (p. 968)

Gonzalez's (2004) critique of Foucault's concept of heterotopia or the coming together of incompatible spaces within a single space also demonstrates how the de-centering of reality has contributed to flawed analyses and approaches to research. According to Gonzalez, Foucault uses this concept to account for the existence of different social classes and groups within public and private spaces while demonstrating "antagonism toward historical consciousness" (p. 175). Walby (2007) compares Foucault's analysis of power as being "distributed across a multiplicity of sites" within a single, surveilled space to Marx locating the source of oppression within the ruling class. Rather than heterotopia, a dialectical materialist would highlight the social limitations (each with a traceable history) that make it difficult for people to achieve mobility between spaces and roles (Gonzalez, 2004). Perhaps Lenin (1902), a modernist, summed it up best in his metaphorical use of the marsh to represent bad theory, though he lived prior to the postmodern turn:

> We have combined, by a freely adopted decision, for the purpose of fighting the enemy, and not of retreating into the neighboring marsh, the inhabitants of which, from the very outset, have reproached us with having separated ourselves into an exclusive group and with having chosen the path of struggle instead of the path of conciliation. And now some among us begin to cry out: "Let us go into the marsh!" And when we begin to shame them, they retort: "What backward people you are! Are you not ashamed to deny us the liberty to invite you to take a better road?" Oh, yes, gentlemen! You are free not only to invite us, but to go yourselves wherever you will, even into the marsh. In fact, we think that the marsh is your proper place, and we are prepared to render you every assistance to get there. Only let go of our hands, don't clutch at us and don't besmirch the grand word freedom, for we too are "free" to go where we please, free to fight not only against the marsh, but also against those who are turning towards the marsh! (para. 8)

Marxian Research Strategies

One of the primary challenges of viewing Marxism as a research methodology is that it has been mostly associated with philosophy and theory versus traditional quantitative and qualitative traditions that outline specific procedures that often contain steps to follow. However, this should not be a barrier for those researchers who seek to interrogate society. As Jubas (2010) points out, theory and methodology are interrelated, particularly when it comes to social inquiry. At the same time, "what society is held to be also affects how it is studied...any given social ontology has implications for the explanatory methodology for which it is endorsed" (Archer, 1995, pp. 2–3). Additionally, the decisions that researchers make about methodology have to do with epistemology, or assumptions about how knowledge is shaped.

Therefore, in order to incorporate Marxian methodologies, it is important to understand the concepts of dialectal and historical materialism, the foundational basis of Marxism. Tedman (2012) defines dialectical materialism as, "the philosophical method by which Marxism has traditionally distinguished between science and ideology" (p. 16). Far from revealing Truth, as a field Philosophy has primarily served to interpret empirical findings in ways that support the ruling class, or at the very least, attempts to stay out of its way: "dialectical materialism, in contrast, understands science according to a 'straight' exploration of its truths and according to the logic inherent in all scientific phenomena: its material dialectics. These material dialectics are in Marxism the *dialectics of contradiction*" (p. 16). Contradiction is ever-present in Marxian research as it seeks to reveal the opposing contentious forces within human society, that of the worker and the capitalist. For Marxists, the struggle will be resolved through the new synthesis brought about by the praxis of the working class becoming a class-for-itself, acting in its own interest:

> The central purpose of praxis is to build understanding of social relations and the capacity to change them among the working class. Research is one part of this process. It helps people in the working class or other subaltern groups comprehend the social ideologies and the structures that characterize their society…research is simply a form of learning…critical research and learning is directed toward social change. (Jubas, 2010, p. 232)

The sections below will first outline key tenets of dialectical and historical materialism, followed by an overview of scientific socialism and its application in workplace studies. Critical realism will then be presented, concluding with arts-based research methodologies that may be of use to researchers.

Dialectics and Historical Materialism

Expanding on Hegelian philosophy that included the master-slave dialectic, Marx and Engels soon turned their interests toward a development of theory that would account for human activity in the material world, known as *historical materialism* (Gredler & Shields, 2008; Walby, 2007). *Dialectical materialism* was a later adaptation to refer to the combination of the empirical study of the real world with the transformation of society by the working class:

> The materialist conception of history starts from the proposition that the production of the means to support human life and, next to production, the exchange of things produced, is the basis of all social structure; that in every society that has appeared in history, the manner in which wealth is distributed and society divided into classes or orders is dependent upon what is produced, how it is produced, and how the products are exchanged. From this point of view, the final causes of all social changes and political revolutions are to be sought, not in men's brains, not in men's better insights into eternal truth and justice, but in changes in the modes of production and exchange. They are to be sought, not in the *philosophy*, but in the *economics* of each particular epoch. (Engels, 1880b, para.1)

For dialectical materialists, capitalism represents a key form of class domination where labor, "a fundamental social activity," is removed from the control of the worker, resulting in alienation (Walby, 2007, p. 892). However, as people come to understand capitalism by seeking to understand the world in a dialectical materialist way, they can *overcome* capitalism by dismantling it.

Gonzalez (2004) presents a helpful way to understand the basic aspects of dialectics and historical materialism applied to research, by outlining five tenets of the philosophy. First, "historical materialism helps to understand the dialectical relation between the particularities of existence and the larger social frameworks that give them meaning" (p. 180). Walby (2007) identifies Marx's concept of *mode of production* as illustrating the dialectical links between an economic system and peoples' lived experiences, which includes the production of ruling class ideologies. Dialectical materialist inquiry is essentially a way of conducting research in order to discern the relationships between individual events and larger, structural factors, part of defining the concrete-real:

> A particular aspect of the concrete-real is individuated on the basis of practical activity that differentiates it from other aspects. However, dialectical cognition can proceed to make explicit the internal connections that obtain between the given aspect and other aspects which have been individuated in the same way, that is, internal relations that are masked in everyday practical activity. (Brien, 2007, p. 18)

Dialectical analysis, then, involves examining the interrelatedness of social factors at a single given moment in time, as well as historically, in order to fully understand these relationships and their impact on human existence.

Second, dialectical historical materialism is a rejection of mysticism and hyper-relativism in favor of the notion that reality has the potential to be grasped (Brien, 2007; Engels, 1880b; Gonzalez, 2004). "Human knowledge flows from the objective world, which determines the categories by which people think" (Gredler & Shields, 2008, p. 5). Part of this involves the acknowledgment that consciousness doesn't necessarily reflect the social world as it exists, because consciousness has been shaped by ruling class ideology:

> Although existence produces necessarily false consciousness, it is only through a critical study of this consciousness that the historical materialist arrives at a greater knowledge of social existence, as if attempting to solve a mystery entirely with clues that are intentionally designed to lead the investigator down a false trail. But even if the clues are false, the truth may be approximated from the formal logic and content of the distortions themselves. (Gonzalez, 2004, pp. 182–183)

Engels (1880b) also asserted that social processes, such as the production of goods, have specific ways of operating outside of people's understanding of those processes. For Lenin, science, as applied to social systems, played an important role in discovering the objective world (Gredler & Shields, 2008). It isn't coincidental that Marx and Engels also found important parallels in Darwin's theory of evolution (Angus, 2009). Just as evolutionary theory had turned formerly religious notions of teleology (that something exists for a purpose) into notions of adaptation (something exists because it has certain characteristics needed for its time), historical materialism overturned Hegel's dialectic to transform it into something grounded in reality and observable by people.

Third, dialectical historical materialism is not hostile to an examination of the interrelatedness of race, sexuality, and gender, but views the current manifestations of these social categories as a function of capitalism rather than being historically stable, independent concepts (Gonzalez, 2004). "A corollary of the role of the social environment is that individuals raised in different cultural environments will differ in both the content of their thinking and the ways that they think" (Gredler & Shields, 2008, p. 5). Part of this is due to capitalism replacing more communal concepts of property and social roles with concepts of race and nationality, making those divisions useful in the transformation of labor power into a commodity (Walby, 2007). Contrary to postmodern notions of social class no longer being a relevant factor, dialectical materialists assert that capitalism is all-encompassing:

> Within that society, and so long as its economic foundations persist, there can be no other culture than a bourgeois culture. Although certain "socialist" professors may acclaim the wearing of neckties, the use of visiting cards, and the riding of bicycles by proletarians as notable instances of participation in cultural progress, the working class as such remains outside contemporary culture. Notwithstanding the fact that the workers create with their own hands the whole social substratum of this culture, they are only admitted to its enjoyment insofar as such admission is requisite to the satisfactory performance of their functions in the economic and social process of capitalist society. (Luxemburg, 1902, para. 20)

Fourth, historical materialism does not view truth as eternal, pre-established, or unchanging (Gonzalez, 2004). As Brien (2007) outlines, "there is no methodological warrant for claims concerning the absolute inevitability of the outcome of a given tendency" (p. 29). We don't really know whether the working class will become a class-for-itself; fascism could also be a potential outcome, or as Brien says, "it all depends on the actual situation" (p. 29):

> Whether counteracting factors in the concrete-real corresponding to those introduced on a given level of analysis will turn out to have sufficient strength to effectively counteract the tendency so as to block its projected outcome is methodologically indeterminate....In some situations it might be possible to specify limiting conditions with respect to some counteracting factors....Even so it is logically possible for new counteracting factors to come into play, in the course of the ongoing development of the concrete-real, which would continue to thwart the development of the tendency and effectively block its projected outcome in the concrete-real. (p. 29)

Part of the job of a dialectical materialist researcher is to locate those specific historical moments where factors come into play to create the conditions for revolution, or at the very least, worker action.

Finally, "the goal of Marxism is not to correct faulty ideas but to negate them — to critique them, to transform them qualitatively" (Gonzalez, 2004, p. 182). As part of the working class, researchers are supposed to test truth claims through the development and refinement of theory in order to meet the material needs of humans (Gredler & Shields, 2008):

> For Marx, humans are active, purposeful creatures and, through their labor, are the prime movers of history. History is produced through production, and bourgeois production creates alienated human beings. Because the relations of production in capitalism are based on exploitative domination, reducing the proletariat to raw materials in the production process, Marx worked for the disappearance of capitalism. (Walby, 2007, p. 892)

Therefore, for dialectical materialists, knowledge alone is insufficient. While it is important to understand how the world works and that knowledge is an essential aspect of that, Marxist researchers want to go further. As Worthen (2014) states, "Knowledge is not power—organizing is power" (p. 110).

Scientific Socialism and Workplace Studies

As historical materialism began to solidify into a theoretical approach and way of outlining not only human activity under capitalism, but how to move past capitalism, *scientific socialism* became a term used to refer to more organized dialectical research inquiry into human society. For scientific socialists, "idealist views generally aim at justification, and are advanced by ruling class ideologues to affirm dominant class interests" while materialist theories set out to explain why the world is the way it is in order to change it (Kellner, 2014, para. 22). In particular, early scientific socialism was interested in "the historical nature of all theories and their subject matter" and to account for such history as social conditions changed by one's theories and research (para. 23). History is also dialectical; as people are acted upon by historical conditions, they also act upon history, shaping and changing their material conditions (Engels, 1880a; Paul, 1918). Distorting notions like human nature and intuition are to be rejected in favor of "changing the concrete conditions under which humans suffer" (Kellner, 2014, para. 28).

According to Sawyer (2014), "it falls to the working class, which has the political power and interest in transforming capitalist society – to take up the revolutionary pursuit of truth about social relations and human nature" (para. 7). Engels (1880a) and Paul (1918) outlined the concept of scientific socialism in their accounts of the development of civilization and the political state, with labor at the center. This contrasted with previous idealistic descriptions of societies where ruling class representations of history made the work of ordinary people merely incidental to the movers and shakers. For Engels, as soon as society became class-based, then history became about the class struggle in economic contexts. This was a new form of sociology meant to sever once and for all human activity from the prison of mystical speculation:

> Socialism was no longer an accidental discovery of this or that ingenious brain, but the necessary outcome of the struggle between two historically developed classes — the proletariat and the bourgeoisie. Its task was no longer to manufacture a system of society as perfect as possible, but to examine the historico-economic succession of events from which these classes and their antagonism had of necessity sprung, and to discover in the economic conditions thus created the means of ending the conflict. (para. 18)

Earlier forms of socialism had been grounded in the accounts of the oppressed and utopian social thought, reflecting more of a general sense of injustice at ruling class excesses (Dietzgen, 1873; Paul, 1918). Instead, scientific socialists were attempting to solidify these earlier forms of socialism into communism by applying empirical methods of research: "just as scientists arrive at their generalizations not by mere speculation, but by observing the phenomena of the material world, so are the socialistic and communistic theories not idle schemes, but generalizations drawn from economic facts" (para. 2).

At the turn of the 20th century, scientific socialism was viewed as a form of defense against the growing encroachment of industrial capitalism on the lives of workers:

> Those who watch carefully the influence exercised by the possessing classes over our universities, churches, political parties, press, and even our literature, and art and drama, can see how this body of social theory is consolidated for its defensive work....The immediate peril which immediately confronts us I cannot forbear to name. It lies in the temptation to rely upon the financial patronage of rich men, millionaire endowments, for the means of establishing universities and colleges for the higher education of the people....Education sustained by such means will never be really free, or fully disinterested. The biology, the economics, the ethics, even the biology taught in these privately bounty-fed institutions, *will carry in various subtle but certain ways the badge of servitude to the special business interests that are their paymasters.* (Hobson, 1909, p. 111)

Paul (1918) concluded that neutrality was not an option when it came to scientific socialism and that revolutionary socialists had to control the direction of their research. He also acknowledged that such research would be met with fierce resistance, especially by liberal elements who were apologists for capital.

Scientific socialist principles were also used in party building, by Lenin (1902) and Luxemburg (1903, 1921). In particular, Lenin's (1902) critique of social democracy as a bourgeois co-optation of socialism reflects his use of dialectical materialist thought:

> Social-Democracy must change from a party of social revolution into a democratic party of social reforms.... Denied was the possibility of putting socialism on a scientific basis and of demonstrating its necessity and inevitability from the point of view of the materialist conception of history. Denied was the fact of growing impoverishment, the process of proletarisation, and the intensification of capitalist contradictions; the very concept, *"ultimate aim"*, was declared to be unsound, and the idea of the dictatorship of the proletariat was completely rejected. Denied was the antithesis in principle between liberalism and socialism. Denied was *the theory of the class struggle*...it was transferred bodily from bourgeois to socialist literature. (para. 3–4)

Another researcher who embodied the scientific socialism of Marx and Engels was Lev Vygotsky, someone whose work figures prominently in the canon of cognitive theory, but whose radical roots are concealed from most who take educational psychology as an undergraduate (Sawyer, 2014). Vygotsky's work reflected four key scientific socialist tenets: human society is the result of evolution and history, society is the major influence on behavior, theories should be tested in practice situations, and humans are not simply reacting to situations, but are conscious planners (Gredler & Shields, 2008; Sawyer, 2014). These tenets were reflected in Vygotsky's thesis of how social interaction develops the human mind in a dynamic process:

> Just as physical tools came to mediate humans' productive relationship with the environment, culturally created *psychological tools* came to mediate human relationships with each other and with themselves. Like tool systems, sign systems (e.g., speech, number systems, writing systems) are created by societies over the course of human history and change with the form of society and its level of cultural development. At this point, *the nature of development itself changes,* from biological to socio-historical. (Sawyer, 2014, para. 40)

Vygotsky's work extended cognitive science's focus on the private, interior world of the individual subject to the possibility of people collaborating with each other to transform society. His science, then, was ultimately one of social struggle, where we could finally "expose the capitalist myth of the lone individual predating society" (para. 8).

Scientific socialism culminated in the creation of The Institute for Social Research at the University of Franfurt am Main in the early 1920s. Research that came out of The Institute addressed four organizing concepts: 1) societies under capitalism are systemically organized, requiring theory to comprehend this organization; 2) capitalism is a totalizing logic, of which no aspect of human life can escape, so theory must likewise deal with total concepts; 3) a global analysis of capitalism is necessary because of its ever-changing nature; and 4) comprehension of history must be a part of the process of transforming society that involves critique and the presentation of alternative visions (Kellner, 2014). The Institute researchers used dialectical materialist methods to address current issues of their time such as tensions between different strata of workers within the working class (i.e., blue and white collar workers). "Their materialist social theory during the early 1930s developed a particular style of 'ideology critique' which analyzes the social interests ideologies serve by exposing their historical roots and assumptions, including the distortions and mystifications which they perpetuate" (para. 19).

As an application of scientific socialism, the existence of workplace studies has its origins in the documentation of revolutionary movements, such as the Paris Commune in 1871, as well as within the emergent field of adult education (Thomas, 2011; Woodcock, 2014). Marx (1880, 1938) himself put out a call for participants (to a decidedly non-random sample of newspaper readers) to answer a questionnaire consisting of 101 items about aspects of working conditions. The results of this data collection effort are not currently known, but the goals were to determine "the exact and positive knowledge of the conditions in which the working class—the class to whom the future belongs—works and moves" (p. 379).

The concept of understanding the workplace from the perspective of workers, not the bosses, was meant to counter the scientific management research of the era, where factory overseers' and owners' perspectives dominated (Woodcock, 2014). Being able to document the world of work as well as the growth of workers' movements was viewed as an accompaniment to worker education through the analysis contained in Marx's (1867) *Capital*, to create a weapon to use against the ruling class (Woodcock, 2014). According to Jubas (2010), Gramsci also viewed workplaces as "model research sites" that "bring individuals into contact with institutional discourses and texts, and allow explorations of the dialectic between ruling relations and experience" (p. 235). Gramsci was also actively involved in workers' education movements, bringing Marxian ideas to these settings (Thomas, 2011).

Worthen's (2014) discussion of work process knowledge provides a useful overview of a key aspect of workplace studies; that of attempting to document the history and current manifestations of how workers function within the workplace, while organizing and managing the conditions of their work. This goes beyond the concept of communities of practice that already assumes knowledge is part of the picture; workplace studies researchers seek to understand how the community *creates* this knowledge as a collective activity, and to uncover its theoretical dimensions. This highlights a key difference between studies where the workplace is a setting and workplace studies:

> The difference is actually access to a whole set of living resources that enables someone to act strategically in a critical moment. Such a moment occurs when there is a balance of power that can tilt one way or the other. At a moment like that, what you add to one end of the scale or the other can make all the difference. This moment itself is a complex product of conditions, constraints, opportunities and talents. In order to make the balance of power tilt your way, you have to be able to work with the whole set of living resources, which means looking at the big picture. The knowledge that matters is more than facts. "What should we do?" and "With whom should we do it?" and "What order should we do it in?" are just as important as "What do we know? (p. 35)

As each of these events accumulate, discussions result, creating theory-in-action and the ability of workers to learn how to control their jobs; though, as Worthen notes, this comes "complete with the risks of betrayal" (p. 85).

Work process knowledge is also an important aspect of historical documentation of what might be considered "obsolete" knowledge (Worthen, 2014). Because capitalism relies on unemployment and redundant workers, the knowledge required for the workplace is constantly being "updated." As Worthen notes, the notion of measuring the worth of human knowledge against the standards set by the ruling class is irrelevant:

> By intentionally studying obsolete knowledge, we repudiate the idea that the only value of knowledge is what you can sell it for.... When we talk about "skills training" we are usually talking about employer-defined knowledge that is needed at a certain moment and at a certain price. By this standard, obsolete knowledge is worthless. By studying obsolete knowledge, however, we confer value on what people have created in order to make a decent life. There is no standard of value that trumps that. (pp. 203–204)

Worthen also identifies yet another type of knowledge that workplace studies can uncover—that of how things could be and *should* be. This type of knowledge is shared, despite the current lack of visible examples, by workers in workplaces and can be accessed through research by dialectical materialist inquiry.

Examples of workplace studies include Romano and Stone's (1946) *The American Worker* pamphlet that arose from a research study of unionized workers at a U.S. car factory. Romano was an employee at the factory and had been a worker in a range of factory settings, giving him an insider perspective (Woodcock, 2014). The pamphlet contained two parts—the data from the workers combined with a second theoretical section, and was distributed to workers in the United States. Woodcock (2014) also presents the work of the *Socialisme ou Barbarie* group who used inquiry as a form of workplace organization as well as a study of FIAT car factory workers where "the interviews with workers would move from criticizing their individual job to broader questions in the factory" (p. 500). In these post-WWII era workplace studies, goals included "gaining contact with workers and attempting to understand the processes taking place, specifically to understand how and why the factory had not seen industrial conflict in the previous wave of struggle" (p. 500). Kolinko's (2002) *Hotlines*, which documented the life of workers in German call centers, is a recent example of a more militant workplace studies approach, where Vitale's (2014) account of faculty activism in the form of resistance to corporate control of curriculum at the City University of New York represents a more toned down application to academic settings.

Researchers can learn much from reviewing workplace studies in terms of methodology and study design. A good starting point is incorporating the concept of representation into the collection of data and analysis plans (Worthen, 2014). Within the workplace, *representation* refers to "the process by which the concerns of one or several people are adopted by someone else for the purpose of addressing them" (p. 156). It can be formal, as in following union procedures for filing grievances, or informal, as experienced workers sharing shortcuts with new workers. Researchers need to be tuned in to these key moments of learning in community contexts, as well as the shaping of knowledge, and can pose the following questions:

> Is the path that takes someone from novice to expert clear, transparent, and known? Does the path they are following have acknowledged legitimacy? Does the newcomer feel he has a right to be there? Is he given real work to do, or is he shunted off into doing something irrelevant or repetitive? Do people who are learning get mentored? Do they get supportive attention of someone who is more expert? (p. 134)

In looking at study design, Kolinko's (2002) *Hotlines* provides an idea for structuring phases of an inquiry. The first, pre-inquiry, involved the gathering of artifacts and information about the workplace. These artifacts were then used in the second phase, theoretical discussions, where they were compared with workers' accounts in group discussions. The third phase utilized interviewing, where employees' views of future workplace resistance were introduced.

Finally, the fourth phase involved study participants encouraging other workers to take part in future research. Additionally, Woodcock (2014) argues that workplace study designs have to allow for people to meet collectively, which is a critical matter for unemployed people, and such studies have to be structured in such a way that they can account for "whether the struggles impact other workers and in doing so interrupt the accumulation of capital" (p. 505). If the political aspects of knowledge construction are not identified, then a study can run the risk of being superficial and reflecting capitalist interests.

Critical Realism

Deriving from the work of Bhaskar (1997, 2008), critical realism is another dialectical option for theoretical framing and methodological construction and is especially compatible with quantitative approaches. Sharing much of the same Marxist tenets as outlined above, critical realism extends the aims of empirical research in order to "examine deeper causal processes at work in the world" (Roberts, 2014, p. 4). To locate these processes critical realists: "first abstract the underlying causal powers of an object under investigation and think conceptually about how they operate" (p. 4). By conceptualizing such processes in the form of theory, such theories can then be empirically tested through further research. Roberts provides the example of education as a site ripe for critical realist analysis:

> The education social structure, for example, exists through a system of human relations based around, in part, its causal power to bestow certain types of knowledge to pupils and articulate a set of values. But these causal powers also create particular social positions—teachers and pupils being the most obvious example. What follows are a number of structured constraints, resources, potentials, and powers associated with the education system. The analytical movement in critical realist research method therefore comprises a movement from a concrete context within which causal mechanisms are abstracted and analyzed and then back to the concrete context to understand how these causal mechanisms operate. (p. 5)

The empirical is what can be directly observed or experienced. However, critical researchers also assert that there "the actual"—that which impacts the empirical (Bhaskar, 1997; Roberts, 2014; Scott, 2007; Walsh & Evans, 2014). It is important to note that even though many of these mechanisms are not visible, they are still real by their effects (Parlour & McCormack, 2012). The critical realist's job is to reveal these mechanisms, which are often "absent" to the naked eye because they have been concealed by ruling class ideology (Bhaskar, 2008). Bhaskar's (1997) concept of emergent properties as entities that arise out of relationships to other entities is an essential aspect of critical realist analysis:

> Emergent properties are relational, arising out of combination (e.g. the division of labor from which high productivity emerges), where the latter is capable of reacting back on the former (e.g. producing monotonous work), has its own causal powers (e.g. the differential wealth of nations), which are causally irreducible to the powers of its components (individual workers). This signals the stratified nature of social reality, where different strata possess different emergent properties and powers. (Archer, 1995, p. 9)

With this in mind, critical realists maintain that traditional sociological categories of macro and micro to refer to size are not as useful and can be misleading for researchers since there are layers of reality (Roberts, 2014; Walsh & Evans, 2004). Instead, they propose *macro* to mean systemic factors while *micro* are those social activities between individuals (Archer, 1995). For social realists, the notion of micro-worlds existing in isolation are an impossibility: "small scale interactions between teachers and pupils do not just happen in classrooms but within educational systems, and those between landlords and tenants are not in-house affairs but take place on the housing market" (Archer, 1995, p. 10).

For critical realists, this means that both strength of feelings of participants and their individual accounts and beliefs should always be viewed as having no guarantee of being a complete explanation of social events or how the world operates (Archer, 1995; Scott, 2007). For Archer (1995), the combination of social reality (being simultaneously free and constrained) with human reflection on that reality can, with appropriate social theorizing, approximate lived social reality. But this has to occur by deeper investigation, as Scott (2007) cautions:

> Self-reports of events and processes cannot provide complete knowledge of relations between different events and states of being, i.e. poverty, homework, school achievement. This is because respondents may not be able to articulate the actual reasons for their actions; or because they may not be aware of other forces or structures that either condition their thinking or their actions; or because most behaviors are routine; or because they may be driven by unconscious desires and impulses; or even because the interview setting may be so structured that the reporting of the chain of reasoning is distorted or inadequate in some way. (p. 151)

This is why it is essential for critical realist researchers to gather information regarding how participants define social phenomena, in order to document how structural properties manifest themselves in particular situations (Parlour & McCormack, 2012). People are shaped by, and consequently shape their environments, regardless of their awareness of this interaction. In this manner, dialectical research differs from traditional positivistic approaches that treats social categories as a given, "rather than being understood as the result of decisions made by individuals and groups of individuals in the present and stretching back in time" (Scott, 2007, p. 153).

Critical realism also corresponds to the historical materialist tenet that society can not only be described, but transformed and that is not a static or eternal concept, but is created and sustained through social and economic relations (Archer, 1995; Parlour & McCormack, 2012; Roberts, 2014): Society, then, "is nothing but itself, and what precisely it is like at any time depends upon human doings and their consequences" (Archer, 1995, p. 1). Critical realists focus on the functional tension between structure at the social level and agency at the individual level, with an interest in locating those "generative mechanisms," (social structures) that reveal ruling class ideologies: "This new knowledge raises consciousness and awareness in those affected so that previous unrecognized needs and wants e.g. self-expression, self-determination, autonomy, become desirable and sought after. The balance shifts from structure to agency and the powerless become empowered" (Walsh & Evans, 2014, p. e4). Yet, a key limitation to being able to do this lies within the inability of many people, subjected to ruling class ideology, to clearly identify how the world external to one's self works, as explained by Scott (2005):

> Those stable and enduring relationships are constituted as stable and enduring relationships because of the historical play of signifiers that constitutes their understanding of the social world, which in turn impacts on historically located but evolving human practices; and this applies equally to the methods that they use to examine the nature of that social world. This position is neither solipsistic nor naively realist, but it does acknowledge the time-specific nature of their deliberations about the world. What it also implies is that, as researchers or observers, they cannot avoid entering into a critical relationship with previous and

current ways of describing the world and, since the way they create knowledge is a part of that social world, entering into a relationship with reality itself and possibly changing it. (pp. 636–637)

Walsh and Evans (2014) applied critical realist tenets to nursing research in order to account for women's experiences of labor during childbirth. In nursing research, the two predominant methodologies are empirical/statistical and phenomenological, which only deals with either the collective (as in clinical trials) or the extreme inter-individual viewpoints of those experiencing the phenomena. Walsh and Evans provide an example of how these approaches to studying dystocia, a specific type of complication in childbirth, have not resulted in a decrease in women experiencing the condition, but just the opposite: "If researchers had grasped the limitations of their research methods by critiquing their ontological and epistemological underpinning, they might have asked different questions about the etiology of dystocia, researched different interventions to manage it and ultimately had a greater impact on women's outcomes and experience" (p. e1). However, when a critical realist framework was used in subsequent research, dystocia was broken into social categories, such as environmental (the setting where maternity care takes place), organizational (discontinuity of care in hospitals), and interpersonal (conflicts between midwives and doctors). This provided a more comprehensive picture than randomized clinical trials because political and social aspects were incorporated into the data. Walsh and Evans found that labor doesn't operate on a simple cause and effect medical model and that it is impacted by larger social and individual factors that can't be captured in a laboratory setting alone.

Critical realism has also been applied to program evaluation research, where the purposes of realistic evaluation are "to establish which contexts are most effective in activating the mechanisms that deliver the intended program outcomes" while also being emancipatory in direction (Parlour & McCormack, 2012, p. 310). For critical realists, context is a significant aspect of comprehending what factors lead to a program being successful for participants. *Context*, in this usage, can refer to both the settings of the program as well as external factors outside of the control of the researcher. The interest is in identifying the mechanisms that result in outcomes, and accounting for the components of those outcomes: "By creating an understanding of why certain conditions prevail and/or why an intervention does or does not work… practice developers can take transformative action based upon emerging evaluation evidence" (p. 310). Rather than expecting results to be applied to all programs of a similar nature, critical evaluation researchers are after gathering evidence of how certain mechanisms create certain tendencies, as part of the overall refinement of theory: "This framework is a conduit for merging emancipatory practice development theory and practice with the theory and practice of realistic evaluation" (p. 318).

There is much that critical realism has to offer for enhancing methodology. First is the manner in which one approaches data collection:

> If objects in the world have potential powers, then at the methodological level, it is appropriate to examine how those powers are manifested; rather than collect information and data about social facts and then attempt to link these social facts together. The reason for doing it in this way is that those social facts may not actually represent what has gone on in the causal sequence that is the object of examination. (Scott, 2007, p. 145)

Second, the researcher needs to pin down the dialectical relationship between "forces of production" and "relations of production" (Roberts, 2014, p. 9). *Forces of production* refer to the ways that human labor (in a variety of forms) creates things and meanings while *relations of production* account for the historical impact on these processes. While something might appear to be one way, as in the case of a worker being "free" to sell her or his labor under capitalism, the historical component reveals this to be untrue: "The ownership-relation is not an interpersonal relationship between an individual worker and an individual capitalist, but is instead a contradictory relationship between free wage labor and capital" (p. 10). Third, with this in mind, methodology needs to account for discovering "how specific causal powers and causal relations associated with these totalities help to generate our knowledge of the world" (p. 16). Roberts provides the example of how capitalism operates at both abstract and concrete levels, as well as systematically and individually.

Finally, prior to being analyzed, data need to attempt to account for how the world operates; if it is not able to do this, there will be an inferior representation of social mechanisms (Scott, 2007). While critical realism does not claim to fully understand the world, it also doesn't offer endless relativism; there is the historical component that needs to be taken into account, which makes the world identifiable to begin with (Scott, 2005). Paolucci (2007) recommends the following research questions within a critical realist framework:

- What are the ongoing empirical regularities within the context in question?
- What are the most essential structural relations in this context?
- What structural relations account for specific empirical regularities?
- What historical events account for the rise of this or that set of relations?
- How have these empirical regularities and structural relations changed over time?
- What are the primary causal forces of this change? (p. 116)

Building on the research questions, in the case of qualitative interviews, the researcher could divide each of multiple sessions into different areas of focus, such as an initial set of interview questions about present-day activities of participants, with a subsequent set examining past events, the creation of the questions being dependent on the analysis of the first transcripts (Roberts, 2014).

Artistic Interrogation
The arts provide yet another accessible option for designing, conducting, and analyzing research using the principles of dialectical materialist inquiry. Although Marx and Engels commented only briefly on the arts, both had an early interest in poetry and literary criticism, which was quickly converted into a focus on revolutionary politics (Solomon, 1979). As Solomon explains, though they did amass a quantity of isolated observations about art and literature, "Marx and Engels left no formal aesthetic system, no single extended work on the theory of art, nor even a major analysis of an individual artist or artwork" (p. 5). However, those who came after Marx and Engels demonstrate that historical materialist ideas can be applied to the use of arts as a *topic* of research (as in the production and role of the arts), a *method* of gathering data (documentation in the form of visual sociology) or even a *methodology* in and of itself (using one's own artwork to conduct dialectical inquiry).

Marxist principles apply to the production of art just as they do to any commodity produced as part of labor:

> The ideology of the market, a place where commodities are bought and sold, is a lived experience in the consciousness of every artist. The mind of the artist is imprinted with History and cannot escape his or her own time. Marxism would oppose the thesis of a transcendent avant-garde that projects to the future and detaches itself from society. From a Marxist point of view, art is always about society and the artist is always a part of the culture, art is never independent or absolute. (Willette, 2010, para. 3)

Indeed, the representation of art production in contemporary capitalist contexts can often be misleading because it appears to be a natural expression of the mind of the artist, in the form of raw inspiration. However, artists, just as with other members of the working class, can be susceptible to confusing the sources of their inspiration with the ideology of the ruling class. Analysis of art therefore involves a deep examination of not only the symbols presented, but the social conditions under which the art (and the artist) is shaped. Willette goes on to note that, "A work of visual culture expresses the prevailing ideology, not just in terms of what a work of art expresses but also what the work of art does not say" (para. 6).

Tedman (2004) made Marx's (1934) *Economic and Philosophic Manuscripts of 1844* a subject of dialectical aesthetic inquiry, using Fay's (1983) analysis of how the physical features of the document reflected the thinking processes of Marx:

> [Fay] demonstrates that, for Marx, the first stage of the dialectical method is the negative side. Its object is not the criticism of the social reality as such (here the production of the nation's wealth), but the hard toil of a human subject attempting to understand and interpret that reality. The 'thought material' that the immanent critic (Marx, here) works on consists of the products of the human mind and the "level of understanding." This involves the "immersion" of the critic in the contents of the object of critical analysis. (Tedman, 2004, p. 431)

Tedman (2012) would later develop his analysis of Marx into the concept of aesthetic level of practice, which "enables us to include and understand the role of form, style, quality, and technique in aesthetic mediations as an historical agency in history and class struggle, and it 'grounds' the role of art and renders artistic phenomena socially accountable" (p. 2). In a similar manner, Fuchs and Vincent (2012) call for a Marxist theory of communication in order to illustrate how the spread of information is tied to social activity and the construction of meaning: "Marxist Media and Communication Studies are not only relevant now, but have been so for a long time because communication has always been embedded into structures of inequality in class societies" (p. 130).

Far from being the romantic (and conventional) bourgeois vision of the rebel bound to no one and having no responsibility, the Marxist artist places the priority of the survival of the working class at the center of her/his work. As Dayna (2012) asserts,

> The creation and existence of art, which in Marxist thought is a manifestation of human desire and imagination, allows for the "base" to be transformed by conscious-altering ideas. Therefore, art is an avenue by which the individual can break through the debilitating fog of "false consciousness." Art can create a state of conscious-altering in a society which can then initiate a revolution. The avant-garde, then, rises to protect culture against capitalist forces. By encouraging individuals to think outside of the limits to which their thoughts are regulated by

the systems of power, art serves to eradicate the "demystification" present in capitalist society. (para. 3)

A contemporary leftist artist who employs art-as-ethnography to interrogate imperialism is New Mexico artist Erin Currier. Her immense body of work uses portraiture of real individuals to represent the larger context of social struggle. The money she raises from the sale of her work funds her travel, not as a tourist-consumer, but for the purpose of "immersing her art in the cultures and political circumstances of ordinary people or activists resisting illegitimate authority in poor or destabilized parts of the word" (Hicks, 2015, p. 45). One of her portraits, Leila: Sphinx Bathroom Attendant, is of a veiled Egyptian woman who cleans the bathrooms of a major tourist attraction. As Hicks explains, the painting, while technically engaging and capturing the individual features of Leila, "is also a representation of and an homage to all Egyptian women, all Muslim women, as well as the women of the world who clean bathrooms, all the world's laborers—and women in general, for that matter" (p. 46).

Currier also periodically inserts herself into these social conditions, through a series of self-portraits that are meant to convey solidarity with the subjects of her artwork. In an interview with Dahr Jamail (2014), she explains the self-reflective component of political action:

> I see our reality as in a state of becoming. I see myself as one of many people working with the skills at hand – be it art-making, planting seeds, penning words, educating, organizing – in a limiting present reality that I am critically objective of, yet that I acknowledge as a historical reality susceptible to transformation. Through reflection and action, human beings can truly transform reality – my partner and I were witness to it in Egypt just weeks after Mubarak was ousted: The people of Cairo were directing traffic, cleaning the streets; young people were gathering mandates in order to draft a new constitution. (para. 20)

Currier intends for her artwork to be utilized as a teaching tool, and a way to visualize a different social reality: "The global economic system, in its capitalist form, purports to be an implacable, unchanging, inevitable reality. Yet, like everything else, it is subject to being overhauled, overthrown, transformed" (para. 22). She refers to three particular paintings of hers—*Attica Schoolboys*, *The Event of Literature*, and *Volver*—as documenting key turning points of revolutionary consciousness, as she calls it, "a window in which an imaginative counter-power prevailed…the moment worth struggling for," which spans all of human history (para. 22).

The work of self-taught folk artist Ralph Fasanella embodies a dialectical historical research methodology. For his series of 18 paintings documenting the violent Bread and Roses strike of 1912, he traveled to Massachusetts to conduct oral history interviews with survivors, gather documentation, and compose sketches of one of the most successful strikes in U.S. history. As May (2014) explains,

> Early on Fasanella realized that art images could be as powerful a means of conveying ideals and promoting working class solidarity as books, photographs, speeches, and songs. He dedicated himself for the rest of his life to creating narrative views advocating social justice for working people and then sought to place them in union halls and meeting rooms to serve as incentives for unity and activism. (p. 43)

It is noteworthy that the styles of Fasanella and Currier emerge from the Social Realist painters of the 19th and 20th century, such as Maxine Albro, Jacob Lawrence, George Bellows, Ben Shahn, and Thomas Hart Benton. Carrying political critique further than the bourgeois

Ashcan School of Painting of the early 1900s (see Zurier, Snyder, & Mecklenburg, 1995), these artists sought to document social life as it existed, from the perspective of the individuals portrayed, so the viewer could see reality as far from idealism as possible. Common subject matter included industrial and agricultural workplaces, cities, portraits of workers, and social conditions. As Willette (2010) observes, "Revelations of the realities of modern times would often be considered political by the forces that functioned best when these "truths" were kept veiled by ideology" (para. 9)

Conclusion—What Makes Marxist Research "Marxist"

Because of its theoretical characteristics, dialectical materialist research can be combined with a range of methodologies, both qualitative and quantitative. This could include basic research, ethnography, grounded theory, critical discourse analysis, oral history, phenomenology, case study, narratology (to name a few), as well as quantitative designs (descriptive, causal-comparative, correlational, and experimental). The following is adapted from Agostinone-Wilson's (2013) discussion of the characteristics of Marxist research and what sets it apart from other liberal-left research traditions.

First, Marxist research rejects capitalism. It does not seek to make capitalism more bearable or to alter its tenets to accommodate it. There is not an interest in "bridging the gaps," "hearing the other side" or other such endeavors. This characteristic alone is perhaps the most challenging to maintain. In a similar manner as the work of Darwin and Freud remain controversial despite being widely accepted, dialectical materialism is not meant to operate seamlessly within capitalism and is bound to butt heads.

> Their sciences conflict with certain ideologies (treating the term 'ideology' as a system of illusionary ideas) of the ruling class; for example, ideologies perhaps justifying exploitation by reference to racial or innate sexual inferiority of a certain category of human being, or ideologies of individual 'responsibility' of 'free subjects.' This latter is a conflict between science and ideology. In the long run, science (which is merely another way of saying the truth) stands opposed to ideology. (Tedman, 2012, p. 15)

Second, Marxist research overtly rejects notions of extreme relativism, as is present in postmodern discourse. Relativism of this nature is highly problematic for dialectical materialists, because of the constant presence of larger systemic and social forces, which reflect the interests of the ruling class. Therefore, a great deal of effort is put into establishing a historical antecedent for phenomena and not overstating the equality of ideas:

> Praxis is anti-philosophy, not in the sense that it refutes the worth of theoretical critique, but in the sense that it asserts that the worth of theoretical critique is measured by the extent to which it is enacted in order to destabilize capitalist production and/or the forms of consciousness that accompany capitalist production." (Walby, 2007, p. 908)

Third, class remains the central unit of analysis. This is not to say that signifiers such as race and gender are secondary; they are the key conduits through which capitalism operates. It just so happens that the exploitation of women, racial minorities, and LGBTQ people are components of capitalism's ability to sustain itself. One of the tasks of dialectical research is to uncover specifically how capitalism has used and still uses these categories in an interrelated manner so that we may be able to more effectively confront these tactics.

Fourth, the aim of Marxist research is not just to document the world, but to change it. This means research must be on the side of workers, not bosses. There is also a difference between research that seeks to better the conditions of the working class, and research that is mere entertainment:

> Topics like the audiences' interpretation of reality TV, popular music, soap operas, sports, movies, quiz shows, or computer games are not so important…in comparison to topics like the exploitation of free labor on the Internet, the commodification of research and education, Internet ideologies, socialist struggles about the role of the media in various countries, the marginalization and discrimination of Marxists and Marxism in Media and Communication Studies, capitalist crisis and the media, communication labor, critical journalism, the socialist open access publishing, or alternative social networking sites.…In the current situation of capitalist crisis and exploding inequality, a focus on political economy topics, class struggle issues, the role of alternatives seems to be more important than the focus on cultural studies topics (like fan culture) that can easily be accommodated into capitalist interests and do not deal with the pressing problems such as precarious living conditions and inequalities in the world. (Fuchs & Vincent, 2012, p. 134)

Fifth, when it comes to materialist analysis, theories that examine structural and collective explanations are more useful than individualistic explanations of human behavior. This does not discount psychology or the thought worlds of people—as we have seen, there are many examples of dialectical psychologists, but they clearly articulate the interrelatedness of one's individual mind and external social factors, such as examining authoritarianism's origin in the patriarchal family. As part of the conceptualizing of the collective, false consciousness must be figured into analysis of data; just because an idea is expressed by workers doesn't make it automatically an authentic representation of reality. A Marxian researcher has to also be ready to document specific moments in the formation of revolutionary consciousness.

> One of the main ways in which these lessons differ from school learning is that they are collective. They are shared, in the sense of "class consciousness," an awareness of and openness to people who understand things from your perspective. This is why they are best learned in classes or informal gatherings where people meet and talk to each other. Another word that captures their character is "readiness": a state of being prepared, awake and aware, fully equipped, in touch with one's allies, ready to go, ready to fight if necessary. Still another word is "forbidden." This word reveals that these lessons are learned in the middle of a fight. In spite of the fact that they can make the difference between an abusive workplace or a decent workplace, a sad life or a decent life, or even life or death, this knowledge is the target of many strategies to make it hard to get, hard to pass on, hard to learn. (Worthen, 2014, p. 16)

The ultimate assertion of Marxist research is that not only is a different world possible, it is necessary. However, "whether it can be created is uncertain and only determined by the outcome of struggles" (Fuchs & Vincent, 2012, p. 129). Likewise, the settings for research are endless and they require documentation within the present set of conditions, which reflect a history and a specific context.

References

A deeper partisan divide over global warming. (2008). *Pew Research Center.* Retrieved from http://www.people-press.org/2008/05/08/a-deeper-partisan-divide-over-global-warming/

Agostinone-Wilson, F. (2013). *Dialectical research methods in the classical Marxist tradition.* New York: Peter Lang.

Anarchism: How not to make a revolution. (n.d.). *International Socialist Review,* 47–53. Retrieved from http://isreview.org/sites/default/files/pdf/03-anarchism.pdf

Angus, I. (2009, May). Marx and Engels…and Darwin? The essential connection between historical materialism and natural selection. *International Socialist Review.* Retrieved from http://isreview.org/issue/65/marx-and-engelsand-darwin

Apple, M. (2003). Strategic alliance or hegemonic strategy? Conservatism among the dispossessed. *London Review of Education, 1*(1), 47–60. doi: 10.1080/1474846032000049125.

Archer, M. (1995). *Realist social theory: The morphogenetic approach.* Cambridge, MA: Cambridge University Press.

Berkowitz, B. (2015, February). The role of health care workers in the Bush torture project. *Z Magazine, 28*(2), 19–20.

Bhaskar, R. (1997). *A realist theory of science.* London: Verso Books.

Bhaskar, R. (2008). *Dialectic: The pulse of freedom.* New York: Routledge.

Bomer, R., Dworin, J., May, L., and Semingson, P. (2008, December). Miseducating teachers about the poor: A critical analysis of Ruby Payne's claims about poverty. *Teachers College Record, 110*(2), 2497–2531. doi: 0161-4681.

Brien, K. (2007, October-December). Marx's dialectical-empirical method of explanation. *Utopia y Praxis Latinoamericana, 12*(29), 9–32.

Catterall, M., MacLaran, P., & Stevens, L. (2005). Postmodern paralysis: The critical impasse in feminist perspectives on consumers. *Journal of Marketing Management, 21,* 489–504.

Creighton, J. (2014, December 8). Deniers are not skeptics: Know the difference. *From Quarks to Quasars.* Retrieved from http://www.fromquarkstoquasars.com/deniers-not-skeptics-difference/

Dayna, L. C. (2012, December 3). A quick discussion of Marxism and art. *An Art Historical Impression.* Retrieved from http://anarthistoricalimpression.blogspot.com/search/label/Marxism

de Lange, S. (2012). New alliances: Why mainstream parties govern with radical right-wing populist parties. *Political Studies, 60*(4), 899–918. doi: 10.111/j.1467.9248.2012.00947.x

Denzin, N. (2009). *Qualitative inquiry under fire: Toward a new paradigm dialogue.* Walnut Creek, CA: Left Coast Press.

Denzin, N., & Giardina, M. (2006). *Qualitative inquiry and the conservative challenge.* Walnut Creek, CA: Left Coast Press.

Dietzgen, J. (1873). *Scientific socialism.* Retrieved from https://www.marxists.org/archive/dietzgen/works/1870s/scientific-socialism.htm

Eagle, M. (2003). The postmodern turn in psychoanalysis: A critique. *Psychoanalytic Psychology, 20*(3), 411–494. doi: 10.1037/0736-9735.20.3.411.

Ehrenreich, B. (2012, March 14). Michael Harrington and the 'culture of poverty.' *The Nation.* Retrieved from http://www.thenation.com/article/166831/michael-harrington-and-culture-poverty#

Engels, F. (1880a). *Part II: Dialectics.* Retrieved from https://www.marxists.org/archive/marx/works/1880/soc-utop/ch02.htm

Engels, F. (1880b). *Part III: Historical materialism.* Retrieved from https://www.marxists.org/archive/marx/works/1880/soc-utop/ch03.htm

Fairclough, N. (2013). *Critical discourse analysis: The critical study of language.* New York: Routledge.

Fay, M. (1983). The influence of Adam Smith on Marx's theory of alienation. *Science and Society, 47*(2), 129–151.

Fuchs, C. & Mosco, V. (2012). Marx is back: The importance of Marxist theory and research for critical communication studies today. *TripleC, 10*(2), 127–140.

Gardell, M. (2003). *Gods of the blood: The pagan revival and white separatism.* Durham, NC: Duke University Press.

Giddens, A. (2013). *The constitution of society.* Malden, MA: Polity Press.

Gonzalez, M. (2004, Summer). Postmodernism, historical materialism, and Chicana/o cultural studies. *Science & Society, 68*(2), 161–186.

Gredler, M., & Shields, C. (2008). *Vygotsky's legacy: A foundation for research and practice.* New York: Guilford Press.

Hale, A. (2011). John Michell, radical traditionalism, and the emerging politics of the pagan new right. *The Pomegranate: The International Journal of Pagan Studies, 13*(1), 77–97. doi: 10.1558/pome.vl3il.77.

Harrington, M. (1997). *The other America: Poverty in the United States.* New York: Touchstone.

Herrnstein, R., & Murray, C. (1996). *The bell curve: Intelligence and class structure in American life.* New York: Free Press.

Hicks, B. (2015, February/March). Making a living creating portraits: The journey of three artists. *Professional Artist Magazine, 29*(1), 42–51.

Ho, W-C. (2012).The limit of the discursive: A critique of the radical constructionist approach to family experience. *The Sociological Quarterly, 53*, 321–340.

Hobson, J. (1909). *The crisis of liberalism: New issues of democracy*. London: P.S. King and Son. Retrieved from https://archive.org/details/crisisofliberali00hobsuoft

Jamail, D. (2014, July 30). Art is a necessary element of every revolution. *Truthout*. Retrieved from http://truth-out.org/news/item/25209-erin-currier-art-is-a-necessary-element-of-every-revolution

Jubas, K. (2010). Reading Antonio Gramsci as a methodologist. *International Journal of Qualitative Methods, 9*(2), 224–239.

Kellner, D. (2014, March 28). *Critical theory and the crisis of social theory*. Heathwood Press. Retrieved from http://www.heathwoodpress.com/critical-theory-and-the-crisis-of-social-theory-douglas-kellner/

Kerl, E. (2010, July). Contemporary anarchism. *International Socialist Review, 72*. Retrieved from http://isreview.org/issue/72/contemporary-anarchism

Kolinko. (2002). *Hotlines: Call centre, inquiry, Communism*. Retrieved from https://libcom.org/library/hotlines-call-centre-inquiry-communism

Ladson-Billings, G. (2006, June). It's not the culture of poverty, it's the poverty of culture: The problem with teacher education. *Anthropology and Education Quarterly, 37*(2), 104–109.

Lenin, V. (1902). Dogmatism and the "freedom of criticism." *What is to be done?* Retrieved from https://www.marxists.org/archive/lenin/works/1901/witbd/i.htm

Luxemburg, R. (1902). *Stagnation and the progress of Marxism*. Retrieved from https://www.marxists.org/archive/luxemburg/1903/misc/stagnation.htm

Luxemburg, R. (1903). *Marxist theory and the proletariat*. Retrieved from https://www.marxists.org/archive/luxemburg/1903/03/14-abs.htm

Luxemburg, R. (1921). *The accumulation of capital: An anti-critique*. Retrieved from https://www.marxists.org/archive/luxemburg/1915/anti-critique/

Marx, K. (1867). Fetishism of commodities and the secret thereof. *Capital, Volume 1*. Retrieved from https://www.marxists.org/archive/marx/works/1867-c1/ch01.htm#S4

Marx, K. (1880; 1938). A workers' inquiry. *New International, 4*(12), 379–381. Retrieved from https://www.marxists.org/history/etol/newspape/ni/vol04/no12/marx.htm

Marx, K. (1932). *Economic and philosophic manuscripts*. Retrieved from https://www.marxists.org/archive/marx/works/1844/manuscripts/preface.htm

May, S. (2014, October). Lest we forget: Ralph Fasanella. *Z Magazine, 27*(10), 41–43.

Mehaffy, M., & Haas, T. (2012). Poststructuralist fiddling while the world burns: Exiting the self-made crisis of "architectural culture." *Urbani Izziv, 23*(1), 80–90. doi: 10.5379/urbani-izziv-en-2012-23-01-001.

Mohanty, C. (2013). Transnational feminist crossings: On neoliberalism and radical critique. *Signs: Journal of Women in Culture and Society, 38*(4), 967–991. doi: 0097-9740/2013/3804-0008.

Mooney, C. (2013, June 18). *The science of why we don't believe science*. Retrieved from https://medium.com/mother-jones/the-science-of-why-we-dont-believe-science-adfa0d026a7e

Paolucci, P. (2007). *Marx's scientific dialectics*. Chicago: Haymarket.

Parlour, R., & McCormack, B. (2012). Blending critical realist and emancipatory practice development methodologies: Making critical realism work in nursing research. *Nursing Inquiry, 19*(4), 308–321. doi: 10.1111/j.1440-1800.2011.00577.x

Paul, W. (1916, 2006). *Scientific socialism: Its revolutionary aims and methods*. Retrieved from https://www.marxists.org/archive/paul-william/pamphlets/1918/scientific_socialism.htm

Payne, R. (2013). *A framework for understanding poverty: A cognitive approach*. Highlands, TX: aha! Process, Inc.

Pinker, S. (2003). *The blank slate: The modern denial of human nature*. New York: Penguin Books.

Porpora, D. (1998). Four concepts of social structure. In M. Archer, R. Bhaskar, A. Collier, T. Lawson, & A. Norrie (Eds.), *Critical realism: Essential Readings*, 339–355. London: Routledge.

Ridley, M. (2003). *The red queen: Sex and evolution of human nature*. New York: Harper Collins.

Roberts, J. M. (2014). Critical realism, dialectics, and qualitative research methods. *Journal for the Theory of Social Behavior, 44*(1), 1–23.

Romano, P., & Stone, R. (1947). *The American worker*. Retrieved from https://libcom.org/history/american-worker-paul-romano-ria-stone

Roth, W-M. (2002). Evaluation and adjudication of research proposals: Vagaries and politics of funding. *Forum: Qualitative Social Research, 3*(3), 84–104.

Sawyer, J. (2014, Summer). Vygotsky's revolutionary theory of psychological development. *International Socialist Review*, 93. Retrieved from http://isreview.org/issue/93/vygotskys-revolutionary-theory-psychological-develpoment

Scott, D. (2005). Critical realism and empirical research methods in education. *Journal of Philosophy of Education, 39*(4), 632–646.

Scott, D. (2007). Critical realism and statistical methods: A response to Nash. *British Educational Research Journal, 33*(2), 141–154.

Scott, J., & Jabbar, H. (2014). The hub and the spokes: Foundations, intermediary organizations, incentivist reforms, and the politics of research evidence. *Educational Policy, 28*(2), 233–257. doi:10.1177/0895904813515327.

Sefla, L. (2015, Spring). Mariategui and Latin American Marxism. *International Socialist Review, 96*, 45–72.

Solomon, M. (1979). *Marxism and art: Essays classic and contemporary*. Detroit, MI: Wayne State University Press.

Tedman, G. (2004, October). Marx's 1844 manuscripts as a work of art: A hypertextual reinterpretation. *Rethinking Marxism, 16*(4), 427–441. doi: 10.1080/0893569042000270906.

Tedman, G. (2012). *Aesthetics and alienation*. London: Zero Books.

Thomas, P. (2011). *The Gramscian moment: Philosophy, hegemony, and Marxism*. Chicago: Haymarket.

Vitale, A. (2014, September-October). The fight against Pathways at CUNY. *Academe, 100*(5), 38–41.

Walby, K. (2007). Mode of production versus mode of information: Marx, Poster, and an argument for anti-capitalist praxis. *Critical Sociology, 33*, 887–912. doi: 10.1163/156916307X230368.

Walsh, D., & Evans, K. (2014). Critical realism: An important theoretical perspective. *Midwifery*, 30, e1-e6. doi: http://dx.doi.org/10.1016/j.midw.2013.09.002.

Willette, J. (2010, June 11). Marxism, art, and the artist. *Art History Unstuffed*. Retrieved from http://www.arthistoryunstuffed.com/marxism-art-artist/

Williams, P. (2014, December 23). America's dangerous turn to anti-intellectualism. *The Guardian*. Retrieved from http://www.alternet.org/education/americas-dangerous-turn-anti-intellectualism

Woodcock, J. (2014). The workers' inquiry from Trotskyism to Operaismo: A political methodology for investigating the workplace. *Ephemera, 14*(3), 489–509.

Worthen, H. (2014). *What did you learn at work today? The forbidden lessons of labor education*. Brooklyn, NY: Hard Ball Press.

Wright, R. (1995). *The moral animal: Why we are the way we are: The new science of evolutionary psychology*. New York: Vintage Books.

Yanowitz, J. (2007, May-June). The Makhno myth. *International Socialist Review, 53*. Retrieved from http://www.isreview.org/issues/53/makhno.shtml

Zurier, R., Snyder, R., & Mecklenberg, M. (1995). *Metropolitan lives: The Ashcan artists and their New York*. Washington, DC: National Museum of American Art.

SIX

Reclaiming Our Indigenous Worldview: A More Authentic Baseline for Social/Ecological Justice Work in Education

Four Arrows and Darcia Narvaez

> *A baseline is a clearly defined starting point (point of departure) from where implementation begins, improvement is judged, or comparison is made.*
> —The Business Dictionary

> *All humans have a two million year-old person inside and if we lose contact with that part of us, we lose our real roots.*
> —Carl Jung[1]

> *...the most practical and important thing about a man is still his view of the universe.... We think the question is not whether the theory of the cosmos affects matters, but whether, in the long run, anything else affects them.*
> —G. K. Chesterton (1986, p. 41)

> *I think we're on the brink of disaster on many fronts. I believe that the Native people can help us out of that, help push us back away from that brink.*
> —N. Scott Momaday (1992, p. 89)

A More Authentic Baseline

We hypothesize that once humans began their anthropocentric journey toward feeling superior to non-human forms of life, we also opened the door for similar attitudes toward nature as a whole and toward other humans as "different" and "lesser" groups of people. This shift from an *Indigenous Worldview* to what has become our *Dominant Worldview* may be the foundation for violence against all forms of diversity. Until we learn to understand, respect, and reclaim the worldview that operated for most of human history, whether comparing levels of warfare or numbers of fish in the ocean, social/ecological injustices and environmental degradation will continue unabated. We need to return to a more authentic baseline so as to better establish our goals.

Unfortunately, most theorists today ignore or keep shifting the baseline used for comparison. Future planners assume that today's human behavior is normative, explaining it as adaptive to current conditions and part of a line of progress from prior Western or Euro-centric existence. There is a lack of awareness of how "worldview" has influenced the state of affairs in the world today. By using "Indigenous Worldview" to describe that which guided human existence for around 99% of human existence, we offer possibilities for achieving relatively peaceful, joyful, and sustainable communities using an authentic model that has for too long been ignored, dismissed, romanticized, or ridiculed.

We refer to such a worldview as "authentic" because it is more true to our human nature. It emerges from deep integration with the Earth and humanity's place in it (all other animals have this perspective and we are related to them all). It may go all the way back, as far as we know, to Homo erectus, referred to by anthropologists as "tall and immensely strong, walking upright, traveling far, with large brains, rich diets, cooking hearths, pair-bonding bands, simple and efficient technology-and nearly two million years of success" (Sale, 2006, p. 112). That is a lot of generations to have produced without destroying Earth's life systems as we have managed in a very short time with the escalating consequences of our Dominant Worldview. The good news is that we are still connected our original ways of understanding the world. Paul Shepard explains, "We are attached to that primitive way of understanding, of double being, in spite of our modern perspective" (1992, p. 45).

Our Neanderthal relatives, who lived from around 40,000 to 350,000 when our own Homo sapiens variety of humans came upon the scene, were also successful. Consider, for example, the Aboriginals who once populated the entire continent of Australia from at least 50,000 or 60,000 years ago with many language and culture groups. In spite of the continuing genocide, ecocide, and culturecide against them since the 19th century, they are still with us. What might we learn from them to help undo the damage our more contemporary selves have done in only a fraction of our time on the planet? Along with those of other indigenous societies, we can examine commonalities in social structures and attitudes as we seek an authentic baseline.

Small-band hunter gatherers (SBHG) managed to maintain societies that kept population in check, avoided hoarding, and maintained respectful relations with human and non-human others. Many American Indian societies fit this category before contact with Europeans. Among small-band hunter-gatherers, hunger and famine do not lead typically lead to environmental destruction or warfare. Some SBHG still survive, refusing to be civilized, giving testimony to such successful living. In fact, 75% of hunter-gatherer cultures have met criteria for being labeled "peaceful societies," and also more than half of Indigenous *agricultural* societies were as well (Leavitts, 1977). Although we can blame overpopulation on moving us away from such values as led SBHG, we feel overpopulation may have been a produce of the shift in worldviews—a shift that was as much a psychological separation from the natural world as a material one. Perhaps a group of humans felt we could do better with more detailed information about the mysteries of life and set out to learn them. Perhaps unaware of the potential risks, we were seduced by our seeming superiority over nature. The law of nature was replaced by the laws of men. Ecological wisdom from more than a million years of observation and implementation all but vanished and the seeds of our current crises were planted.

As a result of the stressful lives that seem to stem from the dominant worldview, things were made worse with resulting child development. We started to neglect a more "evolved developmental niche" (EDN) (Narvaez, 2013). EDN is a form of early caregiving that matches up with the maturational schedule of the young child, including such things as natural childbirth, 2–5 years of breastfeeding, responsiveness to child needs, nearly constant touch, extensive free play, multiple adult caregivers, and positive social support. Early life experience sets the trajectory for multiple systems, including emotion and self-regulatory systems, with epigenetic effects on systems related to social well-being (e.g., vagus nerve) and peaceful capabilities (e.g., stress reactivity can foster aggression).

Since history is largely rewritten by the conquerors and science is filtered by this history, we may never know all the factors that relate to the worldview shift. We do have a solid sense, however, of how life was generally lived during the majority of human history. Noted environmental philosopher, Paul Shepard, describes it in his essay, "Post-historical Primitivism":

> It is not only, or even mainly, a matter of how nature is perceived, but of the whole of personal existence, from birth through death.…In the bosom of family and society, the life cycle is punctuated by formal, social recognition with its metaphors in the terrain and the plant and animal life. Group size is ideal for human relationships, including vernacular roles for men and women without sexual exploitation. The esteem gained in sharing and giving outweighs the vantages of hoarding. Health is good in terms of diet and as well as for social relationships. Organized war and the housing of nature do not exist. Ecological affinities are stable and non-polluting. Humankind is in the humble position of being small in number, sensitive to the seasons, comfortable as one species in many, with an admirable humility toward the universe. (Shepard, 1992, p. 43)

Here we pause to recognize the possibility that you believe that Shepard's positive picturing of the ancient past is merely a romantic notion. We bump into this often in our work and rely here on Shepard's words to counter this notion:

> The legacy of History with respect to primitive peoples is threefold: (1) primitive life is devoid of admirable qualities (2) our circumstances render them inappropriate even if admirable, and (3) the matter is moot as "You cannot go back." This phrase shelters a number of corollaries. Most of these are physical rationalizations- too many people in the world, too much commitment to technology or its social and economic system, ethical and moral ideas that make up civilized sensibilities, and the unwillingness of people to surrender to a less interesting, cruder, or more toilsome life, from which time and progress delivered us. (p. 44)

David Abram's words as offered in his award-winning book *Becoming Animal* offer a similar perspective:

There are many intellectuals today who feel that any respectful reference to indigenous beliefs smacks of romanticism and a kind of backward-looking nostalgia. Oddly, these same persons often have no problem "looking backward" toward ancient Rome or ancient Greece for philosophical insight and guidance in the present day. What upsets these self-styled "defenders of civilization" is the implication that civilization might have something to learn from cultures that operate according to an entirely different set of assumptions, cultures that stand outside of historical time and the thrust of progress. (2010, p. 267)

Being very aware of the problem of "romanticizing the Indigenous," and in spite of likely episodes of violence, greed, or vanity that have likely marked all human beings, there can be little doubt that our ancestors who lived with a nature-based worldview lived more happily, more sanely. Sadly, there are relatively few Indigenous groups left whose cultures have not been largely destroyed. Those still struggling to survive amid the oppression often are unable to live according to them. Indigenous languages are disappearing, and with them goes their associated cultural wisdom. Yet there are many who still do remember the old ways. It is past time for an authentic dialogue to commence between the many cultures under the umbrella of both worldviews before it is too late. Rather than spend time on rebuttals to hundreds of years of anti-Indigenous literature, movies, academic publications, hegemony, and folklore, in this essay we focus more on what may be a healthy baseline with which to plan for the future. We offer three charts to help with this. The first contrasts modern society with that of hunter-gatherers, humanity's 99%, based on anthropological research.

Table 1: Comparison of Two Types of Living (Based on Narvaez, 2014).

	Small-band gatherer-hunters	United States Today
Social embeddedness	High	Low
Social support	High	Low
Socially purposeful living	Normative	Non-normative
Community social enjoyment	Every day	Rare (spectator sports, religious services)
Boundaries	Fluid, companionship/kinship, culture	Rigid kinship culture, social classes
Physical contact with others	Considerable (sleep, rest, dance, song)	Minimal
Relations with other groups	Cooperative	Competitive attitude, cooperative action
Individual freedom	Extensive, no coercion	Free to make consumption choices if adult, coercion
Relationships	Egalitarian (no one bosses anyone)	Hierarchical
Contact with other ages	Multi-age group living day and night	Rare outside of family home
Role models	Virtuous frequently	Vicious within popular media

	Small-band gatherer-hunters	United States Today
Cultural mores	Generosity and cooperation are fostered and expected	Selfishness and stubbornness fostered and expected
Immorality	Cheating, abuse, aggression not tolerated	Cheating, abuse, aggression expected
Natural world	Embeddedness/ in partnership with nature	Detachment from, control and fear of nature

Some readers may feel that we have the same values today as the hunter-gatherers had or have. After all, are not good role models important to us as well? And who likes a cheater? It is true that in the dominant culture, we have a cognitive awareness of such values as honesty. However, unlike indigenous cultures where lying was seen as a form of mental illness (Cooper, 2008), it is woven into the fabric of the dominant cultures on many levels. The realities on the right side of the chart tend to define too much of the thinking and too many of the institutions of modernity. Discovering and using a more authentic baseline may be a key to addressing the contradictions and absurdities that have accompanied the remarkable inventions and technologies of our current paradigm.

Another chart describes two worldviews without assigning the partnership model to our 99% of existence. This has the disadvantage of not giving us an information base to access in the living models of this worldview, but perhaps has the advantage of letting us know the worldview does not belong to any race or culture. We refer to Riane Eisler's work as presented in her book on partnerships (2002).

Table 2: Worldviews (Based on Eisler, 2002).

Domination System	**Partnership System**
Authoritarian and inequitable social and economic structure of rigid hierarchies of domination in *both* family and state.	Democratic and economically equitable structure of linking and hierarchies of actualization in *both* family and state.
High degree of fear, abuse, and violence, ranging from child and wife beating to other forms of abuse by "superiors" in families, workplaces, and society. Children grow up in punitive, authoritarian, male-dominated families where they observe and experience inequality as the accepted norm.	Mutual respect and trust with a low degree of fear, abuse, and violence because they are not required to maintain rigid rankings of domination. Children grow up in families where parenting is authoritative rather than authoritarian and adult relations are egalitarian.
Ranking of the male half of humanity over female half, as well as rigid gender stereotypes, with traits and activities viewed as masculine, such as "toughness" and conquest, ranked over those viewed as feminine, such as "softness" and caregiving.	Equal valuing of the male and female halves of humanity, as well as fluid gender roles with a high valuing of empathy, caring, caregiving, and nonviolence in both women and men, as well as in social and economic policy.
Beliefs and stories justify and idealize domination and violence, which are presented as inevitable, moral, and desirable.	Beliefs and stories recognize and give high value to empathic, mutually beneficial, and caring relations, which are considered moral and desirable.

A third chart comes from a text offering critique of European cultural thought and behavior from the Yurugu's perspective, an Indigenous Peoples of Africa. The author refers to the book in which this graph appears as "an intentionally aggressive polemic" (Ani, 1996, p. 1) in light of the continuing assaults stemming from the dominant worldview. Here she offers a description of the "Indo-European" cultural expressions as being a result of the Yurugu word "Asili," meaning "lacking spirit and seeking power to fill the void" (p. ix). We consider the idea of lacking spirit associated with the separation from nature aspect of worldview that has, does, and may continue to express itself in the negative ways revealed by Ani below.

European cultural thought and behavior:

- **Institutionalized Religion (Christianism):** roselytizing, anti-nature, hierarchical, white supremist, patriarchical, non-spiritual
- **Ideology and Values:** money=symbol of value, materialism, universal dominance, white supremacy, devaluation of spirit
- **Aesthetic:** Artificial, non-spiritual, white pristine, rational
- **Self-Image:** Controlling nature, superior, rational, white
- **Image of Others:** Inferior, natural, object, irrational, black
- **Intercultural Behavior:** No cosmic self, isolated ego, conflicting, competitive, aggressive
- **Behavior Toward Others:** Non-human, exploitive, imperialistic, genocidal

This last list is particularly critical of what many of are immersed in. But it is important to self-reflect on current beliefs and alternative possibilities. The bottom line is that before we can use our baseline for redirecting our beliefs, we have to use it to recognize just how bad things really are as a result of having used a different baseline more recently.

The Importance of Worldview

"Worldview" may not be the best word for describing the source of the Indigenous baseline for cultural development, but comes the closest as a term in the English language for what we intend. In the last chapter of *Unlearning the Language of Conquest*, contributor Bruce Wilshire writes,

> "The first thing to be pointed out is that 'worldview' is a European idea, specifically German (*Weltanschauung*=world looked-at). So we must recognize initially that in speaking of an Indigenous worldview we may have already generated an egregiously distorted account, determined in advance by a European bias that gives priority to seeing and vision…the price paid is that knowers must mask out the whole emotional and cosmological context within which knowing and living occur" (2006, p. 261)

Wilshire later offers an example of this contrast between Western and Indigenous worldviews:

> It is difficult to imagine any of the three great Western religions seconding Black Elk's insight that the roundness of teepees corresponds to the roundness of bird's nets: "Birds build their nests in circles for theirs is the same religion as ours." From this primal original point emanate salient features of the West's worldview. It is hierarchical, dualistic, exclusivist, and divisive (p. 266).

In other words, the deep, compelling conclusions about living life in balance handed down in our 99% did not result from the "viewing" sense alone, but from using all the senses. Indigenous languages even minimize "seeing" applications because they are verb-based rather than noun-based. Nouns tend to describe "seen objects" whereas verbs describe processes that can't be seen with the eyes. Many indigenous languages use active terms (e.g., the equivalent of "tree-being") instead of static ones to describe the world. Indigenous ways of thinking are more concerned with the forces that interact with objects than that which can be seen with the eyes. (Later we propose that this visual and imaging priority as it relates to hypnotic, trance-state "learning or unlearning" is a factor in the sudden emergence and contradictory nature of the Western worldview.)[2]

Because more and more people are blaming the dominant worldview for the violence, inequalities, and ecological disasters of our time, Annick Hedlund-de Witt thought it important for her doctoral studies to research the influence of worldviews on our ecological crises and its possible solutions. She thought the data might contribute to sustainability efforts. Speaking on the importance of her exploration while at the University of Amsterdam, she writes in her 2013 dissertation, *Worldviews and the Transformation to Sustainable Societies*:

> Worldview is a concept 'whose time has come,' and its increasing appearance in the contemporary climate change and global sustainability debates can be understood as both response to, and reflection of, the challenges of our time and the solutions they demand. One of the main arguments and premises of this dissertation is, consequently, that an understanding of worldviews has a major role to play in addressing our highly complex, multifaceted, interwoven, planetary sustainability issues. (p. 3)

Unfortunately, worldview understanding has been stifled in recent years by beliefs among many that there are countless numbers of them. People use "worldview" to describe religious, cultural, and moral beliefs. Some academics and psychologists have viewed humanism, postmodernism, nihilism, existentialism, and many other "isms" as worldviews as well. We think these terms fall short of seeing the word's deeper foundational meaning. Hedlund-de Witt supports a deeper view:

> The concept of worldview may appear to be similar or even interchangeable with concepts such as ideology, paradigm, religion, and discourse, and they indeed possess some degree of referential overlap. However, worldviews can nonetheless be clearly distinguished from these concepts. (p. 19)

She concludes that Koltko-Rivera's definition of worldview[3] comes close to fitting her conclusions when he describes a worldview as a "foundational assumption or perception regarding the underlying nature of reality, 'proper' social relations or guidelines for living and the existence or non-existence of important entities" (2004, p. 5). Robert Redfield, a leader in worldview studies at the University of Chicago in the 1950s, writes "a worldview is the totality of ideas that people within a culture share about self, human society, natural and spiritual worlds" (Wilcox, 2004, p. 146). "It is the organization of ideas which answers the questions: Where am I? Among what do I move? What are my relations to these things?" (Redfield, 1953, p. 30). Thus a worldview goes deeper than a religion, an ideology, a belief, or even a culture. It is the hidden level of culture and controls our thoughts and our behaviors.

When seen in this way, the concept is more useful. Cobern, in his paper "Worldview, Science and the Understanding of Nature," talks about using worldview theory as a framework for "investigating people's understanding and valuation of both science and Nature" (2005, p. 22). For example, without aligning Western civilization's great religions or philosophers with one worldview or the other, we cannot fully evaluate their impact on cultural assumptions. Diversity of cultures is just as vital as biodiversity, but uninvestigated cultural assumptions can rob diverse perspectives of their essence, leaving behind a useless or even dangerous superficiality in its place, what is left after known things are forgotten.

To investigate the source of our beliefs is counter-hegemonic. Our current K–16 curricula socialize us to the more superficial tenants of Eurocentric philosophy. Most students and teachers are unaware of the extent to which they accept them unquestioningly. Imagine how much we might have learned from Greek, Roman, or more contemporary European philosophers if worldview had been incorporated in studying them. We might have better understood inconsistencies and hegemonic influences that are inherent in the philosophies. In the Introduction of his text *100 Essential Thinkers* (2002), Philip Stokes writes, "If there is one thing that characterizes both the method and the results of philosophical inquiry, it must be the general lack of consensus that precedes the whole process, and often remains even after the work is complete" (p. 5). He continues, "The reason these philosophers have trouble agreeing is because philosophy deals in questions that people generally don't agree on and partly because philosophers go about their business by challenging assumptions and concepts in order to generate new perspectives on recalcitrant problems" (p. 6).

We are not advocating, however, challenging assumptions as an academic exercise or to generate new theories. As Wilshire writes, the discussion of worldviews "is no mere matter for the philosophy classroom" (p. 261). We are suggesting the use of our ancient baseline to assess the appropriateness of proffered advice or beliefs. A good life is a wise life that lives within one's means (sustainably). The dominant worldview does not direct us to live good or wise lives in this sense.

"If you see the world in a certain way," says Māori scholar Te Ahukaramū Charles Royal, "this will determine what you value in the world (and what you don't) and how you value it through one's behavior. This statement gives rise to the well-known triumvirate – worldview, values, behavior. In Māori, we use the terms, *aronga, kaupapa and tikanga*" (2002, p. 5).

It is not enough to prepare New York City's buildings for withstanding floods or planting trees in parks to provide shade for the elderly, which was part of the city's response to the White House's long delayed warnings about climate change. Our technologies alone will not save us unless we come to re-member a morality fostered by our ancestors' baseline worldview. Walter Lippmann refers to this "morality" in his classic text *A Preface to Morals,* when he refers to the "dissolution of the ancestral order" and the psychological and philosophical consequences associated with "the modern worldview" (1929:1982, p. 26). The importance of regaining a morality that actually existed in ways to create happy, equal, healthy, system-sustaining societies requires the "real world" realizations that "whitewashed" history lessons and media have hidden from view. From the perspective of most cultures of the world throughout history, we would be considered wicked, immoral, and even stupid in spite of our remarkable technological accomplishments. Modern civilizations seem to have have lost humanity's original moral compass.

What is the solution to the dilemma we face—a culture of denial and despair that undermines human development and our heritage of cooperation and expansive cooperation? We suggest educators and parents engage children in reflection about the two worldviews in every context—from pre-school to graduate school, in every home and community. One of the most important value and behavior differences between the two worldviews we are discussing relates to anthropocentrism. Thomas Berry articulates this particular difference:

> Our secular, rational, industrial society, with its amazing scientific insights and technological skills, has established the first radically anthropocentric society and has thereby broken the primary law of the university, the law of the integrity of the universe, the law that every component member of the universe should be integral with every other member of the universe and that the primary norm of reality and of value is the universe community itself in its various forms of expression, especially as realized on the Earth. (2006, p. 130)

Our indigenous[4] selfhood, shared DNA, and quantum physics all point to how human personhood extends beyond the human world to other entities. A common understanding shared by the great variety of Indigenous cultures around the world, past and present, is the idea that rock people, thunder beings, or lizard grandfathers are persons with agency. In fact, each agent has special teachings for helping humans develop virtues for survival and happiness, from patience and humility to courage and generosity. Of course there are group differences. Not every group considers all rocks, thunder, or lizards to be persons; assignment of personhood varies from tribe to tribe. For example, according to Hallowell (1960), the allocation of sentience or personhood to aspects of the Ojibwa worldview is part of a "culturally constituted cognitive 'set'" (1960, p. 25). Such perspectives contrast with the "inanimate" or "less than persons" perspective that is hammered into children by the dominant worldview. In fact, referring to a rock as a person was once a criterion for diagnosing mental illness. It is common for many scholars to believe that only humans have intrinsic value while everything else on the planet is to be utilized for the benefit of humans alone. For example, Four Arrows's coauthor of *Differing Worldviews in Higher Education: Two Disagreeing Scholars Argue Cooperatively* argued:

> Yes, of course, "everything on Earth should exist solely for human exploitation…" What other reason do the fauna and flora or our planet exist, other than for "human exploitation?" That is, in my view, the earth and its accoutrements exist solely for our sakes, and for no other reason. They do not at all have intrinsic value, only instrumental value, as a means toward *our* ends…if we adopt laissez faire capitalism and free enterprise, where private enterprise and the profit and loss system mitigate against extinctions, via barnyards." (Four Arrows & Block, 2011, p. 62)

With all due respect to Walter, and he is a fine man and a highly respected scholar, it seems to us that such superiority over the other-than-human beings is the beginning of all racism, classism, and other hierarchical structures of inequality. Clearly such a perspective is in part responsible for the devastation of the planet.

Two Worldviews

We are not alone in singling out these two worldviews, in spite of the scholars who continued to believe that each religion and philosophy can be considered a worldview unto itself. For example, Edgar Mitchell, founder of the Institute of Noetic Sciences, sponsor of the IONS

Worldview Exploration Project, also focuses on these two in his speeches. He believes the Indigenous worldview holds keys to solving problems caused by our dominant one. Now in his 80s, Mitchell was the sixth person out of 12 to have walked on the moon, and the sixth person to be inducted into the prestigious Leonardo Da Vinci Society for the "Study of Thinking." Not long ago he wrote on the back cover of *Shapeshifting: Techniques for Global and Personal Transformation* (1997), "Only a handful of visionaries have recognized that Indigenous wisdom can aid the transition to a sustainable world." Similarly, Noam Chomsky wrote a blurb for Four Arrows's book on indigenizing mainstream education: "The grim prognosis for life on this planet is the consequence of a few centuries of forgetting what traditional societies knew and the surviving ones will recognize" (Four Arrows, 2013). It is not Indigenous wisdom and knowledge per se, but the worldviews to which both comments refer. Richard Tarnas is more specific to this point:

> Worldviews create worlds...what sets the modern (worldview) apart is its fundamental tendency to assert and experience a radical separation between subject and object, a distinct division between the human self and the encompassing world. This perspective can be contrasted with what has come to be called the primal worldview, characteristic of traditional indigenous cultures. (2007, p. 16)

In light of so many academics thinking that there are countless ways of seeing the world, how do we explain that in serious scholarship relating to human survival on Earth, most refer only to the dominant and the Indigenous worldview? Robert Redfield, mentioned earlier, led a team of distinguished anthropologists in the 1950s who agreed with his premise that there are essentially only these two worldviews. He valorized, but did not romanticize the Indigenous perspectives, and believed that civilization's radical departure from it was a cultural invention that resulted in "the loss of a unified, sacred and moral cosmos and its replacement by a thoroughly fragmented, disenchanted and amoral one" (Naugle, 2002, p. 248). He saw Indigenous worldview as a constructive basis for a critique of dominant culture, explaining that the latter is always trying to destroy the former. In other words, he saw the Indigenous worldview as a more appropriate baseline.

In the next subsection we offer some thoughts about why we agree with Redfield, and how by making a distinction between these two worldviews and the many cultural manifestations that spring from them as representing different kinds of belief structures, we can engage complementary dualism, as the Indigenous worldview encourages, while at the same time offering the contrasts between the two worldviews, including how the dominant one tends to avoid complementarity. Ultimately we aim for a partnership between dominant and Indigenous paradigms, ideologies, values, cultures, and philosophies that stem from these two worldviews.

Dualism and Complementarity

As we have mentioned previously, symbiosis and complementary relationships are an essential reality in nature and thus a major assumption of the Indigenous worldview. We believe the Indigenous worldview's emphasis on nonduality, with its emphasis on the relational interconnectedness between and among all things, including life and death, is an essentially missing philosophy that has led us to the brink of disaster. Although thinking in terms of opposites seems to be a worldwide practice for all people in all cultures and may be a useful starting place for understandings, relational problems arise when the tension between the opposite remains rigid and polarized where there is no sense of mutual benefit from the two things. Jung writes that Western cultures tend to ignore, repress, or keep separate psychological or relational opposites and thought this practice was dysfunctional for both individuals and societies. (Eastern traditions are better to unify or keep in mind a union of opposites.) "Unfortunately, our Western mind, lacking all culture in this respect, has never yet devised a concept, nor even name, for the union of opposites through the middle path, that most fundamental item of inward experience…" (1966, Volume 7, para. 327.) Instead, the tension of opposites is avoided or even destroyed, not a healthy way to live in a world full of natural dualities that ultimately work together for the greater good.

Galtung (1990) also sees the Western worldview as differing from the Indigenous owing to its inability to unify difference, with an "analytic rather than a holistic conception of epistemology; a human over human conception of human relations and a human over nature conception of relations to nature" (1990, p. 313). In a research paper entitled, "The Distinction Between Humans and Nature," Vining, Merric, and Price (2008) interpreted contradictory participant views about their relationship with nature to reflect a "cognitive dissonance that complicates decision-making and performing environmentally responsible behavior" and that "resolving this conflict in perceptions might lead to greater levels of environmentally responsible behavior" (2008, p. 1). It seems that we are losing cognitive dissonance in modern society, becoming more calloused and cynical about our contradictions. One of the precepts in Indigenous conflict resolution strategies designed to bring people back into community is to respect cognitive dissonance with humor as if to remind the embarrassed party that it is a good thing to have such a feeling.

One of the most important indicators of the worldview difference is found in the twin-hero myths that abound throughout the world that represent the apparent binaries of the sun and the moon. One twin is aggressive, physically strong, and direct like the sun's rays. The other is passive, mentally strong, and reflective or indirect like the dynamics of the moon. In Indigenous stories, twin heroes like the Navajo's "Child Born of the Water" and "Monster Slayer," work together in harmony on the journey to rid the world of its monsters. The emergence of monotheism and patriarchy in Middle Eastern religions muted this type of duality, obscuring the more "feminine" principle.

In fact, this is essentially the position of Shepard (1992), who writes about the great departure from the nature-based Indigenous worldview: "Its true genesis lies in the work of Hebrew and Greek demythologizers. They created a reality focused outside the self, one that could be manipulated the way god-the-potter fingered the world" (p. 47). This happened, for example, when the solar twin, Romulus, actually murders his lunar brother, Remus. Hercules, the quintessential patriarchal solar hero, was born with a lunar twin named Iphicles that few of us remember. In the biblical story of Jacob and Esau, Jacobs steals Esau's birthright and tries to enslave him. Esau, the trickster brother who is close to all animals, especially the water animals, is obviously the lunar twin.

The Hopi Indians have an ancient legend that tells about a red and white brother with solar and lunar traits. "The white brother goes far away to make discoveries that can help both, but his ego becomes so large that he does not return to share his knowledge. As a result, the world loses its harmony (Jacobs, 1998, p. 194). The Kogis of South America also see that light and dark skinned people must work together to keep the Earth in balance. They believe the white race, whom they refer to as Younger Brother, is causing the world to end. Their wise elders, called

Mamas, say Younger Brother must stop desecrating the planet and start *working together* with Older Brother to put the world back in harmony.

Having spent more than 30 years studying solar-lunar mythology and psychology, Howard Teich (2012) believes that Western culture's twin distortions, including the gender labeling of the Sun as masculine and the moon as feminine, represent the loss of an important archetype for a holistic sense of harmony that comes from an equality between solar and lunar forces. This has resulted in repression and oppression that relates to social systems based on a dualistic set of values. When Howard, a good friend and long-time collaborator with Four Arrows, read an early draft of this paper, he expressed concern that readers might see our critical contrast between Indigenous and dominant worldviews as being in itself an overly dualistic proposition. What follows is an effort to rectify this seeming contradiction.

In her 2008 publication, "Thoughts about the Philosophical Underpinnings of Aboriginal Worldviews," Aboriginal scholar and Kombu-merri person Mary Graham writes that there are two major axioms in Aboriginal worldview. One is that the land is the law and the other is that you are not alone in the world. She believes these axioms offer a universal truth and quotes a Kakadu man named Bill Neidjie as saying that Aboriginal law never changes and is valid for all people.

> Aboriginal Law is grounded in the perception of a psychic level of natural behaviour, the behaviour of natural entities. Aboriginal people maintain that humans are not alone. They are connected and made by way of relationships with a wide range of beings, and it is thus of prime importance to maintain and strengthen these relationships.... The land, and how we treat it, is what determines our human-ness. Because land is sacred and must be looked after, the relation between people and land becomes the template for society and social relations. (2008, p. 107)

In other words, she, as we, advocates for the universal application of Indigenous worldview, not, as she continues to say, for "one true way of living in accord with it."

Graham strongly emphasizes that this is not about promoting an ideal system of expression and lifestyle, inferring that cultural manifestations beyond this basic "truth" about living on this planet are and will always be multiple and subject to an eventual balancing or opposites. She writes,

> Aboriginal Law thus cannot be idealogised: it is a locus of identity for human beings, not a focus of identity (p. 109). If one true way is posited, sooner or later individuals or groups are inclined to ideologise it; rigid thinking then follows (or vice versa), and the formation of groups of 'true believers', chosen people, sects, religions, parties, etc., cannot be far behind... Aboriginal law is valid for all people only in the sense that all people are placed on land wherever they happen to be...(Nature is the only constant for human beings.) Ideas are myriad and ever changing. This is why the custodial ethic, based on and expressed through Aboriginal Law, is so essential not only to Aboriginal society but to any society that intends to continue for millennia and wants to regard itself as mature. (pp. 110–111)

Once we accept the foundational prerequisite for healthy life on earth that requires living according to the laws of nature and respect for all living things and their interdependencies, then we can venture without limitation into varying expressions of life, making us artists and creators of individual and collective purpose. From this basic essential respect and holistic understanding of dualities, our structural inequalities are no longer needed and our many mental illnesses can disappear. The unifying source physicists and philosophers keep seeking is nature and our practice of empathy and complementarity with apparent opposites is the unifying behavior that stems from it.

Hegel recognized the need for a unifying factor to resolve the conflicts of dualism, but he uses a Christian God as the factor instead of nature and the wisdom of those who have studied it for hundreds of thousands of years (Lauer, 1982). Using a fully intelligible God that man can logically understand, he sees duality as an illusion because of God's intervention and wisdom. God is the synthesizing agent. For example, he saw "Becoming" (via God) as the complementarity joining the duality of "nothingness" and "being." He borrows from Goethe the idea that every problem that arises in life causes contradictions or disputes, though when the problem is measured in light of a unifying concept, the duality disappears. "God" thus resolves the tension between thesis and antithesis. Maybe Hegel deep down in his own mind saw this differently than most of his interpreters seem to think, but as understood by most, the logical, rational knowledge of "God," the monotheistic power of the universe, seems to be the key for his synthesis. If so, then this becomes one of the ultimate problematic dualities, in light of Christian histories and realities. Four Arrows wrote about such realities in a paper entitled "False Doctrine: The Influence of Christianity on the Failure of Indigenous Political Will" (2014) that speaks of ways that a partnership or pairing between Indigenous spirituality and Christianity is still possible if instead of seeing opposites as a war to sustain one position over the other, Christianity is seen as potential partner to an Indigenous worldview perspective.

The Quechua speaking peoples of the Andean mountains in Peru, another Indigenous culture, offer a clear understanding of the importance of complementary opposites while sustaining the Aboriginal mandate for following the laws of nature. In a research project described in her publication, "The Splendid and the Savage: The Dance of the Opposites in Indigenous Andean Thought," Hillary S. Webb offers a comprehensive analysis of the meaning of three of their words, *yanantin, masintin,* and *chuya* (2012, pp. 69–93). "Yanantin" describes the idea of universal oneness that includes an understanding of a sort of pairing of opposites. "Masintin" is "the active process by which the yanantin pair becomes "paired" and thus moves from a state of antagonism and separateness to one of complementarity and interdependence…" (p. 74). The word "chuya" refers to an entity that may be missing its potential complementary other or is still viewed as being unequal somehow.

According to Webb's research participants, this movement toward complementarity and interdependence is a four-stage process of boundary exploration. The four stages are as follows:

- Tupay (The Meeting)
- Tinkuy (Testing of Boundaries)
- Taqe (The Union)
- Trujiy (The Separation)

Interestingly, the last stage of this pairing process is separation from the attained union in a way that allows it to be a stepping-stone to a more all-encompassing union with the universe.

> …yanantin departs or when you depart from your yanantin. …That separation is only the start of another, much higher level of union…Trujiy represents the capacity to be yourself again once you have experienced that yanantin union. After that, you become one single person again. But in that singleness you are no longer just yourself. You are One—with the yanantin, with God, with the essence. No matter what happens, you are One with all of that (Webb, 2012, p. 152).

Thus, taking these views together, we have but one earth and the systems upon it we call "nature." We can live according to the belief we are part of it intrinsically, physically, and spiritually. We can acknowledge the proven assumptions gleaned after over a million years of surviving and thriving on earth. Or, we can live according to a belief that we are somehow separate from the earth and its life systems, while continuing to ignore, dismiss, or ridicule our Indigenous wisdom. In our view, the evidence is clear for choosing which of these foundational beliefs will best serve future generations. And at the same time, from indigenous knowledge of natural systems we know that diversity and its complementary nature is a crucial dynamic in these systems. Granted that a number of diverse beliefs, values, and actions exist as a result of the dominant worldview and all of them must be studied for their complementarity, but the study can only be successful if we remember that we and the earth are of one mind. The Western worldview has brought new perspectives but at a cost no one can afford to pay. Even with regards to the oneness of yanantin, we learn that the Natives say that not all apparent opposites are suitable for pairing. Harrison, another researcher of this concept, writes, "Quechua speakers persistently distinguish objects which are not well matched or 'equal'" (1989, p. 49).

So what is it that keeps us from living according to the most obvious truths—the laws of nature? How can we be seen as truly intelligent creatures while practicing constant war, oppression of others and a priority of convenience, materialism, and power that causes us to forsake a sacred relation to the water we drink and the air we breathe? We conclude this paper with a largely unconsidered answer that has been realized by our Indigenous cultures since time immemorial that relates to the use of what we today might refer to as "trance based learning."

Trance and Transformative Learning

Although some psychologists and consciousness researchers realize that most learning is formed automatically from immersed experience, most people do not use this knowledge responsibly or toward building good, sustainable lives (instead, the power is used by purveyors to influence the purchase of their products). Unintentional learning has shaped many belief systems from religion to consumerism. Intentional trance learning is another powerful form that has been neglected by modern humans who typically have forgotten the power of trance-state learning. In so doing they have allowed perceived authority figures to take control of it so that many of our beliefs, actions, and inactions are the result of a trance-logic they may not even be aware of that is responsible for their contradictory behaviors. Indigenous Peoples well understood the power of learning while in intentional or spontaneous alternative states of consciousness and had the discipline, focus, and techniques for staying on "the red road."[5] This use of trance phenomenon for learning and acting according to what is real and true may be the missing link for bringing us into integrity with our evolved nature.

In an article about hunter-gatherer studies published in the *American Anthropologist*, Lee (1992) writes,

> We live in an era in which the line between real and non-real has become dangerously blurred. What is real has become a scarce commodity and the pursuit of the "real" sometimes becomes a desperate search....We don't have to search far for evidence of this proposition. The Disney corporation produces and distributes in a single fiscal year, perhaps in a single week, more fantasy material to more people than entire archaic civilizations could produce in a century.

States of the Left, Right, and Center and their bureaucracies also produce prodigious volumes of fantasy. (1992, p. 32)

We would guess that the hegemonic manipulations of culture are even more influential and powerful today than when Lee wrote this. Hegemony, what happens when we believe that the "truths" put forward by those in power must indeed be true even if they benefit only its authors, is so successful in the world because of hypnotic trance logic. Hypnotic learning during alternative states of consciousness and alternate brainwave experience is a part of nature's survival repertoire for a number of animals. Under the dominant worldview, it is placed on the fringes of society, however, as something to be used only by licensed physicians or stage performers. As a result, we lost our own *intentional* hypnotic skills and gave control of the phenomenon to our preachers, peddlers, and politicians—or any other person we allowed to have some authority over us. Such intentional self-hypnotic skills include the ability to "believe in images" via self-induction into appropriate altered states of awareness, as well as giving explicit permission to others such as healers or specialized wisdom keepers to induce trance and implant words. Words were understood as sacred vibrational frequencies. Even Freud, who against the wishes of his friend Jung refused to use hypnosis, said that "Words were originally magic and to this day words have retained much of their ancient magical power" (1917, p. 17). In his text *A Time Before Deception,* Thomas Cooper offers a scholarly study of how words were seen as sacred to American Indians. They understood words as being about describing reality and thought that people who lied had a mental illness in which they could not judge truth from falsity (1998). One might consider this a valid explanation for the behavior we see today.

Indigenous Peoples recognized the importance of trance work long ago for acquiring wisdom and living according to it, but unlike us they never let it slip out of their control. Webb reveals in her study that the Natives told her the best way to learn yanantin was to go into deep trance with mescaline from the juice of a cactus. "It was suggested to me at the beginning of my research that the best way for me to understand and integrate this concept of yanantin was for me to 'download' it—that is, to go into ceremony with the San Pedro cactus" (Webb, p. 78). Plant medicine, however, is but one approach used by Indigenous Peoples throughout time and around the world. A variety of cultural ceremonies, group or individual prayer ceremonies (such as the vapor purification lodge), Vision quests and other forms of isolated meditation, intentional trance-inducing dance rituals (Thomason, 2013), drumming and other forms of music (Amoss, 1978), physical exertion followed by trance induction, fasting, and sensory deprivation (Villoldo & Krippner, 1987) were all widely practiced as ways to embed important knowledge into the psyche and for healing (Walsh, 1996, Thomason, 2013). Often a pre-planned indoctrination into the cultural expectations via stories or a repeating of important cultural rules followed. Sometimes an individual merely put him or herself into the appropriate state of receptivity for a particular set of word instructions. Mike Williams of the University of Reading writes in his text *Prehistoric Belief* (2010) that early humans were likely much more adept at entering trances and used trance-state to solve a number of life-threatening problems.

Unfortunately, such studies are seldom given serious or widespread attention in any study of Indigenous cultures. In fact, Western sciences in general are not supportive of such research. Consider placebo phenomenon for example. For hundreds of years, physicians have witnessed the power of belief to cure, but in the past 50 years when double-blind placebo controls for just about every drug or surgical intervention were required, the outcomes proving the power of hypnosis phenomenon have been all but ignored. Two Harvard scholars, Benson and Kaptchuk, have stood firmly against years of ridicule and dismissal of the facts that show that from 30 to 90% of successful results from the actual drugs or surgery occur with placebo comparisons, even when the patient knows he or she is in the placebo group. Benson's history of this unfortunate process up until 1995 can be found in his text *Timeless Healing: The Power and Biology of Belief* (1996), and his coauthored article in the *Journal of the American Medical Association* back in 1975 entitled "The Placebo Effect: A Neglected Asset." Kaptchuk's journal article of 1998, "Intentional Ignorance" is another good history of this controversy; the other side, which is reflected in a 1994 article in the new *England Journal of Medicine,* that placebo controls themselves are unethical and have little to no efficacy in medical practice (Rothman & Michels, pp. 394–398). For a thorough and up-to-date study of the placebo phenomenon evidence go to Harvard Medical School's website (http://programinplacebostudies.org/publications/) to connect to 85 peer-reviewed publications dated from 1998 to 2014.

Four Arrows has had notable experience in this controversy as well. Prentice-Hall's emergency medicine division, Brady, published his text, *Patient Communication for First Responders: The First Hour of Trauma*, in 1988. Field tested for 12 years, it showed that first responders at the scene of an emergency, especially firefighters, police, and paramedics, were using hypnosis whether they knew it or not, for good or for bad, because patients were in hypnotic states. "All creatures, during times of stress, become hypersuggestible to the communication of perceived authority figures" (Jacobs, 1998, p. 44). Thus, a paramedic or anyone else speaking with authority unintentionally could cause untold harm with an off-beat comment in front of an apparently unconscious person, like "Wow, that knee is messed up. I doubt he'll walk again." Or, with conscious effort based on simple training protocols, could direct a patient to stop bleeding as in a situation where the victim is trapped in a car and direct pressure cannot be applied. After six months on the market and many letters from people around the world giving testimony to the life-saving techniques taught in the book, the book was remaindered because a lawyer or two determined the book should only be used by "licensed medical physicians trained in medical hypnosis." We share this story because one must realize how some things we don't know stay hidden because of the hegemony and because of a dismissal of Indigenous belief systems. But, as Tolstoy reminds us, "Wrong does not cease to be wrong because the majority share in it" (2009, p. 56).

Conclusion

We humans posses essentially the same brain we have had for well over a million years. We are part of nature, whether we have forgotten or disagree. We all have our special skills and reasons for being in the universe. To act with integrity to our place in the mysterious scheme of things, we need to wake up from hegemonic or trauma-based hypnosis and take charge of our own trance states so that we can live as we are meant to live amid the wonder of our natural world. Reclaiming our Indigenous worldview as a baseline for making changes in the world as needed, the process of investigating the two main worldviews considered in this essay can help put our creative decisions, technologies, and learnings into a holistic alignment with the nature into which we are woven. A true reunion with our place in the natural world and a more authentic baseline for remembering how our beliefs are formed will empower us to reclaim our more authentic cultures so that amid our diversity we can maintain those things we share in common for the greater good.

We close with only a cursory list of more specific ways to accomplish this "waking up" process. These suggestions offer immediate opportunities for personal and organization transformation that stem from relearning and honoring the wisdom that guided us for most of human history and allow for careful reflection on what from the two worldviews still works and what doesn't.

1. Start by selecting any important topic requiring you to make a decision.
2. Consider the topic with a sacred awareness that all of nature, including all sentient beings, are relatives and have great significance, including fellow humans and align possibilities accordingly. Give special attention and respect to local place. Keep "the greater good" in mind.
3. Use trance learning with simple and safe self-hypnosis techniques to embed carefully considered (and well-researched) conclusions and to foster right action.
4. Use dialogue with others in the process of understanding various positions and align all goals with a baseline that is likely representative of a more original state.
5. When in conflict with others, do not take things personally nor deviate from truth. Use humor intentionally and remember the goal of conflict resolution is to bring all back into community.
6. Remember the laws of complementarity.
7. Trust the universe with courage and fearlessness.

A useful tool for implementing these guidelines is the CAT-FAWN Connection, detailed in *Primal Awareness* (Jacobs, 1998). CAT= Concentration Activated Transformation and refers to the hypnotic state of awareness. F-A-W-N refers to Fear, Authority, Words, and Nature. Using the Indigenous worldview: Fear is to be seen as a catalyst for practicing virtues (courage, generosity, humility, honesty, fortitude, patience) and moving through it leads to trusting the universe with fearlessness. Authority only comes from honest reflection on lived experience with the awareness that the laws of nature and our interconnectedness are irrefutable. Words are sacred vibrations, whether we speak them to ourselves or to others. Dishonesty and deception are equal to insanity. Finally, nature is all. It is our home, our teacher, our mind. All technologies and financial or creative enterprises must allow for an appropriate balance among natural and vital systems upon which we all depend.

Hypnosis studies reveal that when new objectives or beliefs are deeply imagined while we shift into alternative brain wave activity, we actually change the synapses in our brains to act according to the new image. Although brain hemisphere studies are oversimplified in popular media and are much more complementary than independent in function, the research shows that hypnosis is largely situated in the right hemisphere, the site of holistic, receptive intelligence. Human brain activity may be out of balance with an over-emphasis on left brain functions and an undermining of right hemisphere development early in life and throughout childhood (Narvaez, 2014). Creative activities and free play with others are ways to rebuild the right hemisphere. Dancing, singing, and joking are activities that hunter-gatherers enjoy most of the time. They engage in various communal trance-producing activities and adventures. These are things that we can use to begin to heal ourselves, each following our honest perceptions of right action. For those of you who are in education, we also recommend creating worldview curriculum.[6]

The worldwide crises threatening life systems on Earth call for restoring our positive potential to once again be one with the universe in thought and action. If there is anything we can glean from our Indigenous worldview, it is to focus our energies as best we can on re-knowing our local places in which we dwell and doing our best to find and preserve those who have lived in these places long enough to know the original baseline. We don't have to "go back" per se, but we can go forward with a proven two-million-year-old worldview to help guide us.

Notes

1. This is a secondary source quote and we have put it into plural form rather than the original "man" and "he." We think Laurens van der Post, who offered his recollection of his good friend's original words at age 87 during a 1994 interview, would approve. See http://www.ratical.org/many_worlds/LvdP/quotations.html
2. Four Arrows first introduced this idea in his doctoral dissertation and subsequent book, *Primal Awareness* (1998). In this text, he shows how positive transformation toward and maintenance of appropriate ways to conceive of fear, authority, words, and nature are mediated by intentional or spontaneous hypnosis processes and that Indigenous approaches to understanding these four forces result in very different hypnotic outcomes.
3. Koltko-Rivera's article "The Psychology of Worldviews" is without doubt the most thorough overview of worldview research compacted into an article imaginable. The Society of General Psychology awarded him the Miller Award for an Outstanding Article in 2008. He offers various constructs that different theorists have offered for what makes a worldview, such as the "man-nature" and "relational" dynamics we have emphasized.
4. When referring to groups of people, we use a capital "I" for Indigenous. Here, we refer to living indigenously (small "i") as relating to having lived in one place for long enough to learn the complex physical and spiritual realities of place.
5. *Chanku Luta,* a Lakota/Dakota word for "red road," relates to walking in balance. Ross (1989) contends that American Indians show more right-brain synapses than non-Indian people and therefore are able to use hypnosis and art with more facility as both of these functions require significant right-brain function.
6. An excellent model is Mark Hathaway's "Ecological Worldviews" course at the University of Toronto. His syllabus and bibliography can be found online at http://www.environment.utoronto.ca/Upload/undergradsyllabus/ENV333H.pdf

References

Abram, D. (2010). *Becoming animal: An earthly cosmology.* New York: Pantheon.
Amoss, P. (1978). *Coast Salish spirit dancing.* Seattle: University of Washington Press.
Ani, M. (1994). *Yuguru: An African centered critique of European cultural thought and behavior.* Trenton, NJ: Africa World Press.
Benson, H. (1996). *Timeless healing: The power and biology of belief.* New York: Scribner.
Berry, T. (2006). *The Dream of the Earth.* Berkeley, CA: Counterpoint.
Chesterton, G. K. (1986). *Daylight and nightmare.* New York: Dodd and Mead.
Cobern, W. (2005). *Worldview, science and the understanding of nature.* Retrieved from http://www.wmich.edu/slcsp/SLCSP169/SLCSP169.pdf
Cooper, T. (1998). *A time before deception.* Santa Fe, NM: Clear Light Publisher.
de Witt, A. H. (2013). *Worldviews and the transformation to sustainable societies.* (Doctoral dissertation) dare.ubvu.vu.nl/bitstream/handle/1871/48104/dissertation.pdf
Eisler, R. (2002). *The power of partnership.* Novato, CA: New World Library.
Four Arrows. (2013). *Teaching truly: A curriculum to Indigenize mainstream education.* New York: Peter Lang.
Four Arrows. (2014). "False doctrine." The influence of Christianity on the failure of Indigenous political will. *Critical Education, 5*(13). Retrieved from http://ices.library.ubc.ca/index.php/criticaled/article/view/184496
Four Arrows & Block, W. (2011). *Differing worldviews in higher education: Two scholars argue cooperatively about justice education.* Rotterdam, Netherlands: Sense Publishers.
Four Arrows, aka Jacobs, D. T., & Cajete, G. (2010). *Critical neurophilosophy and Indigenous wisdom.* Rotterdam, Netherlands: Sense Publishers.
Four Arrows, aka Jacobs, D. T. (Ed.). (2006). *Unlearning the language of conquest: Scholars challenge Anti-Indianism in America.* Austin: University of Texas Press.

Freud, S. (1915–17). *The complete introductory lectures on psychoanalysis*. In J. Stachey (Ed. & Trans.), *The standard edition of the complete psychological works of Sigmund Freud* (Vols. 15 & 16). New York: Norton.

Galtung, J. (1990). Cultural violence. *Journal of Peace Research, 27*(3), 291–305.

Graham, M. (1999). Some thoughts about the philosophical underpinnings of Aboriginal worldviews. *Worldviews: Global Religions, Culture, and Ecology, 3*(2), 105–118.

Hallowell, A. I. (1960). *Ojibwa ontology, behavior, and world view*. Retrieved from http://www.newstudiesonshamanism.com/wp-content/uploads/2011/01/Ojibwa-Ontology.pdf

Harrison, R. (1989). *Signs, songs, and memory in the Andes: Translating Quechua language and culture*. Retrieved from http://www.jstor.org/stable/30028006

Jacobs, D. (1988). *Patient communication for first responders: The first hour of trauma*. Englewood Cliffs, NJ: Prentice-Hall.

Jacobs, D. (1997). *Primal awareness: A true story of survival, transformation and awakening with the Raramuri shamans of Mexico*. Rochester, VT: Inner Traditions International.

Jacobs, D. T. (1991). *Patient communication for first responders: The first hour of trauma*. Englewood Cliffs, NJ: Prentice-Hall.

Jung, C. G. (1966). *The practice of psychotherapy: Essays on the psychology of the transference and other subjects* (Collected Works Vol. 16). Princeton, NJ: Princeton University Press.

Kaptchuck, T. J. (1998). Intentional ignorance: A history of blind assessment and placebo controls in medicine. *Bulletin of the history of medicine, 72*(3), 389–433.

Koltko-Rivera, M. (2004). *The psychology of worldviews*. Retrieved from http://www.academia.edu/3089027/The_Psychology_of_Worldviews

Lauer, Q. (1982). *Hegel's concept of God*. Albany: State University of New York Press.

Leavitt, G. C. (1977). The frequency of warfare: An evolutionary perspective. *Sociological Inquiry, 47*, 49–58.

Lee, R. (1999). *Science and constructivism*. Retrieved from https://tspace.library.utoronto.ca/bitstream/1807/17946/1/TSpace0100.pdf

Lippmann, W. (1929/1982). *A preface to morals*. New York: Transactions Publishers.

Momaday, N. S. (1992). *In the presence of the sun: Stories and poems, 1961–1991*. New York: St. Martin's Press.

Narvaez, D. (2012). Moral neuroeducation from early life through the lifespan. *Neuroethics, 5*(2), 145–157. doi:10.1007/s12152-011-9117-5.

Narvaez, D. (2013). The 99 Percent—Development and socialization within an evolutionary context: Growing up to become "A good and useful human being." In D. Fry (Ed.), *War, peace and human nature: The convergence of evolutionary and cultural views* (pp. 643–672). New York: Oxford University Press.

Narvaez, D. (2014). *Neurobiology and the development of human morality: Evolution, culture and wisdom*. New York: W. W. Norton.

Narvaez, D., Gleason, T., Wang, L, Brooks, J., Lefever, J. B., & Cheng, Y. (2013). The evolved development niche: Longitudinal effects of caregiving practices on early childhood psychosocial development. *Early Childhood Research Quarterly, 28*(4), 759–773.

Naugle, D. K. (2002). *Worldview: The history of a concept*. Grand Rapids, MI: William Erdmans Publishing.

Redfield, R. (1953). *The primitive world and its transformations*. Ithaca, NY: Cornell University Press.

Redfield, R. (1956). *Peasant society and culture: An anthropological approach to civilization*. Chicago: University of Chicago Press.

Ross, A. C. (1989). Brain hemispheric functioning and the Native American. *Journal of American Indian Education, 2*(3), 72–76. Retrieved from http://jaie.asu.edu/sp/V21S3bra.htm

Rothman, K. J., & Michels, K. B. (1994). The continuing unethical use of placebo controls. *New England Journal of Medicine, 331*(6), 394–398.

Royal, T. A. C. (2002). *Indigenous worldviews: A comparative study*. Wellington, New Zealand: Te Wananga-o-Raukawa.

Sale, K. (2006). *After Eden: The evolution of human domination*. Durham, NC: Duke University Press

Shepard, P. (1992). A post-historic primitivism. In M. Oelschlaeger (Ed.), *The wilderness condition: Essays on environment and civilization*. Washington, DC: Island Press.

Stokes, P. (2002). *Philosophy: 100 essential thinkers*. New York: Enchanted Lion Books.

Tarnis, R. (2007). *Cosmos and psyche: Intimations for a new worldview*. New York: Plume Publishers.

Teich, H. (2012). *Solar light lunar light: Perspectives in human consciousness*. Skiatook, OK: Fishing-King Press.

Thomason, T. C. (2013). The role of altered states of consciousness in native American healing. *Journal of Rural Community Psychology, 13*(1). Retrieved from https://www.marshall.edu/jrcp/VE13%20N1/jrcp%202013%201%20thomason.pdf

Tolstoy, L. (2009). *A confession*. Franklin Park, IL: World Library Classics.

Turnbull, C. M. (1983). *The human cycle*. New York: Simon & Schuster.

Villoldo, A., & Krippner, S. (1987). *Healing states.* New York: Simon & Schuster.
Vining, J., Merrick, M. S., & Price, E. A. (2008). The distinction between humans and nature: Human perceptions of connectedness to nature and elements of the natural and unnatural. *Research in Human Ecology, 15*(1), 1–11. Retrieved from http://www.humanecologyreview.org/pastissues/her151/viningetal.pdf
Walsh, B. B. (1996). Shamanism and healing. In B. Scotton, A. Chinen, & J. Battista (Eds.), *Transpersonal psychiatry and psychology* (pp. 96–103). New York: Basic Books.
Webb, H. S. (2012). The splendid and the savage: The dance of the opposites in Indigenous Andean thought. *Journal of Transpersonal Psychology, 4*(1), 69–83. http://www.transpersonaljournal.com/pdf/vol4-issue1/Hillary%20Webb.pdf
Wilcox, C. (2004). *Robert Redfield and the development of American anthropology.* Lanham, MD: Lexington Books.
Williams, M. (2010). *Prehistoric belief: Shamans, trance, and the afterlife.* London: The History Press.
Wilshire, B. (2006). On the very idea of 'worldview.' In Four Arrows (Ed.), *Unlearning the language of conquest: Scholars expose anti-Indianism in America.* Austin: University of Texas Press.

SEVEN

Why It Is Possible and Imperative to Teach Capital, Empire, and Revolution— and How

Rich Gibson

Not terribly sophisticated 4th graders can grasp the two-century-old tale *The Spider and the Fly*, written by Mary Howitt in 1829.[1] This is the text:

>"Will you walk into my parlour?" said the Spider to the Fly,
>'Tis the prettiest little parlour that ever you did spy;
>The way into my parlour is up a winding stair,
>And I've a many curious things to shew when you are there."
>
>"Oh no, no," said the little Fly, "to ask me is in vain,
>For who goes up your winding stair
>-can ne'er come down again."
>
>"I'm sure you must be weary, dear, with soaring up so high;
>Will you rest upon my little bed?" said the Spider to the Fly.
>"There are pretty curtains drawn around; the sheets are fine and thin,
>And if you like to rest awhile, I'll snugly tuck you in!"
>
>"Oh no, no," said the little Fly, "for I've often heard it said,
>They never, never wake again, who sleep upon your bed!"
>
>Said the cunning Spider to the Fly, "Dear friend what can I do,
>To prove the warm affection I've always felt for you?
>I have within my pantry, good store of all that's nice;
>I'm sure you're very welcome — will you please to take a slice?"

"Oh no, no," said the little Fly, "kind Sir, that cannot be,
I've heard what's in your pantry, and I do not wish to see!"

"Sweet creature!" said the Spider, "you're witty and you're wise,
How handsome are your gauzy wings, how brilliant are your eyes!
I've a little looking-glass upon my parlour shelf,
If you'll step in one moment, dear, you shall behold yourself."

"I thank you, gentle sir," she said, "for what you're pleased to say,
And bidding you good morning now, I'll call another day."

The Spider turned him round about, and went into his den,
For well he knew the silly Fly would soon come back again:
So he wove a subtle web, in a little corner sly,
And set his table ready, to dine upon the Fly.

Then he came out to his door again, and merrily did sing,
"Come hither, hither, pretty Fly, with the pearl and silver wing;
Your robes are green and purple — there's a crest upon your head;
Your eyes are like the diamond bright, but mine are dull as lead!"

Alas, alas! how very soon this silly little Fly,
Hearing his wily, flattering words, came slowly flitting by;
With buzzing wings she hung aloft, then near and nearer drew,
Thinking only of her brilliant eyes, and green and purple hue —
Thinking only of her crested head — poor foolish thing!

At last,
Up jumped the cunning Spider, and fiercely held her fast.
He dragged her up his winding stair, into his dismal den,
Within his little parlour — but she ne'er came out again!

And now dear little children, who may this story read,
To idle, silly flattering words, I pray you ne'er give heed:
Unto an evil counsellor, close heart and ear and eye,
And take a lesson from this tale, of the Spider and the Fly.

It is unfortunately clear that the crux of the story—spiders *must* eat flies—eludes most of the world's people today.

"...not criticism but revolution is the driving force of history..." Karl Marx (1845)

The core issue of our times is the rise of color-coded inequality and the real promise of perpetual war met by the potential of mass class conscious organized resistance for the clarion call that has driven social movements for centuries: Equality! Revolutionary equality! In the absence of such a social movement, education remains snared by capital and empire, as we shall see, and resistance merely recreates ignorance and despair—Dark Ages' barbarism, in slightly new ways.

This is not a utopian scheme that aims at a far distant tomorrow and refuses to address the necessity to win reforms, or to even defend what is minimally left to poor and working people today. It is, instead, to insist that U.S. unionism as it is—and most of the counterfeit reformist "left"—cannot win even short-term reforms and, moreover, to split the needs of today from the requisite need to transcend capitalism is to lose both.

Or, perhaps more abstractly, to abandon both the theory and practice of revolution is to deny science (quantity into quality and leaps in, for example, evolution), philosophy (dialectics into materialism), history (revolution on revolution to end exploitation, to overcome the master/slave relationship, for freedom), in pedagogy, those transformative "aha" moments when quantities of effort become qualitatively new knowledge, and passion itself—a cornerstone of any movement for change.

To give up even the theory of revolution is to dump the materialist conception of history, replace it with reformist—idealist—fantasies about democracy dominating the capitalist state, to pretend that capitalism can be softened over time, that imperialism will end by ignoring it, or voting it away. It is to deny there is an economic base to today's society, rooted in exploited labor and the unappeasable quest for cheap labor, raw materials, regional control, and markets. It is to pretend the political world is distinct from the economic, and the rich can be voted out of their money and greed (Magdoff, 1978).[2]

For many people, forsaking revolutionary theory is to become what they set out to oppose. They're instruments of their own oppression. To give up on, at least, the theory of revolution is to guarantee the spiders will feed on our great-grandchildren. Using works of Marx and Engels, Chalmers Johnson, Lenin, Lukács, and Luxemburg, I believe it's possible to teach revolution in theory and practice—and survive as an educator (see, for example, Queen, 2014; Ross & Queen, 2013).

In practice, the Rouge Forum is the only education-based organization in North America that has, for 15 years and more, seen class struggle as central to school and society. We are not a revolutionary organization. There may be Rouge Forum members from groups who say they are—and perhaps they are. We have not, however, run from the term "revolution." Indeed we have investigated its aspects with care.

> "And your education! Is not that also social, and determined by the social conditions under which you educate, by the intervention direct or indirect, of society, by means of schools..." (Marx & Engels, 1848)

Given the role of imperialist de-industrialization, school is one of the centripetal organizing points of daily life. There are about 3.9 million school workers organized into the two U.S. unions, the National Education Association and the American Federation of Teachers. If schools are missions for capitalism and empire; the vast majority of school workers—who are not professionals but workers and more so ever year—are their missionaries.

"The parson goes hand in hand with the landlord" (Marx & Engels, 1848). The parallel is clear enough. Most teachers see themselves as witting agents of the capitalist, today corporate, state. Schools are middle class job banks, peopled by school workers full of fear. Even so, as Marty Glaberman (1997) famously said, "as long as work sucks, there will be resistance."

At issue is whether or not resistance makes any sense, or if it flails at phantoms, rushing toward mirages. Teacher work, often wrongly described as professionalism, tracks the same avenues that any job suffers. Teachers, really school workers, are not professionals—until the employer gulls them into buying books, supplies, extending hours, "volunteering" weekend work, etc. Teachers are alienated from the processes and products of their work.

School workers do not control the curriculum. Indeed, many of them could not operate without a pre-packaged set of textbooks. They have, for 20 years and more, been ordered to proctor high-stakes standardized exams: it's Taylorism in the classroom; tests that most of them know measure little more than parental income, race, and home language—and amount to child abuse (Callahan, 1962; Ross, 2010).

The medical, "First do no harm," was nearly never raised by non-professional school workers. Teachers engage the same war of all on all that all workers face: the struggle for jobs—when jobs should be plentiful and class size less than ten. Like any factory worker, "the greatest aid to efficiency is a long line of (people) at the gate" (Foster & McChesney, 2012, p. 115).

In schools, teachers are estranged from students (via grading and tests), from the curriculum (via textbooks and standardized curricula) from parents, and administrators—and each other (via competition for jobs and wages).

Kids, the focus, or "product" of schools, are particularly alienated, distanced from meaningful struggles for what is true, from freedom, from any remote practice of democracy, from equality. For example, as James Loewen (2007) demonstrated in *Lies My Teacher Told Me*, most of the history, particularly historiography, itself, isn't true.

The unjustly structured taxes that make capitalist schooling possible pay the intellectual jailers of those who must attend. Teachers work in segregated schools, by class first, then race, a creation of capitalist inequality in accumulated wealth, income, and geography.

School workers create surplus value in the sense that they prepare the next generation of workers, they manufacture (real or false) hope, and they participate in schools as huge markets. Imagine the costs of iPads, Chromebooks, buses, architects for buildings, test-prep materials, etc. Schools warehouse kids, babysit. It's a tax-funded service for low wage companies. Schooling produces labor power in more ways than one.

Teachers and students are routinely commodified. Test results, revered by real estate agents who churn the market, are one example. Flatly, in every school, every student represents a dollar value. In California, every student is worth about $5,000 a year, carefully pro-rated hour by hour on daily attendance. As with any capitalist relationship, behind compulsory state schooling is violence: truancy laws, threats, fines, and arrests. Alienation, exploitation, and commodification add up to form reification—these processes seen as normal and inevitable. Test scores, again, are a glaring example, but so is the daily life of school: bell schedules, the division of labor in history versus science versus language arts, etc.

Schools, unbeknownst to most in higher education and politicians, are part of society. They are, as we shall see in detail, embedded in capital and empire and face the crises that necessarily take place within those systems: upheavals following periodic stagnation in the economy, and war. To suggest that these factors, then, necessarily lead to revolution, or even mass resistance, would be to mock history. They do not—as the last 20 years of life in schools demonstrates.

On the face of it, these terms could easily be applied to the majority of the United States teaching force, which has done little but acquiesce to their own and their students' oppression: cowardly, racist, nationalist, and superstitious.

Very few teachers would read from American patriot Thomas Paine's "Age of Reason" in a classroom:

> The story of the angel announcing what the church calls the immaculate conception is not so much as mentioned in the books ascribed to Mark and John; and is differently related in Matthew and Luke. The former says the angel appeared to Joseph; the latter says it was to Mary; but either Joseph or Mary was the worst evidence that could have been thought of, for it was others that should have testified for them, and not they for themselves. Were any girl that is now with child to say, and even to swear it, that she was gotten with child by a ghost, and that an angel told her so, would she be believed? Certainly she would not. Why, then, are we to believe the same thing of another girl, whom we never saw, told by nobody knows who, nor when, nor where?" (Paine, 1795/1795)

This could not be read for the following reasons: Too many teachers are mystics themselves. Administrators would hear about it and go wild. Parents would go wilder.

The vast majority of school workers have no conception of the materialist viewpoint in history. They have unsystematic, often inexplicable, worldviews. Nor, though they are daily changing people, do they see themselves as agents of dramatic social change.

There are, certainly, many pressures from above. In California, it is illegal to teach favorably about Karl Marx. Hence, labor history's core is banished from the curriculum. Reason—against superstition—is out, in favor of "tolerance" of all available ontologies except rational ones.

Love, as a matter of sexual pleasure, it largely banned, in favor of teaching fear of sex: AIDS, STDs, pregnancy, etc.

Freedom is out as there is no real freedom practiced in schools. That almost obliterates the key factors of life: Love. Work. Knowledge and the struggle for truth. Freedom.

Trained in mis-education centers, colleges of education, teachers work through a process that too often selects against rebels, even intellectuals, and forges the factors above. Nevertheless, some fight back. They matter.

There are less than 4500 "members" on the closely-held Rouge Forum e-mail list, with no dues, nor a line. But we have held up a beacon for school workers, veterans, parents, students, and others, worldwide, India to Grenada, shining on the reality of class struggle. As important, we have been a community of friends. Clearly, we are not enough, yet. In the absence of a revolutionary movement for equality and justice: savagery.

What Explains Popular Madness?

If you seek barbarized continents, nations, regions, cities, or tribes, look around you: El Salvador, Guatemala, Pakistan, Afghanistan, Iraq, Libya, Mali, Syria, South Sahara, or Detroit inside the heart of darkness itself. Seek the centers of hydrophobic-like barbarism in Washington, DC or Moscow or Beijing—the beast-cooks.

What produced this reality is part of the investigation into why things are as they are—and what to do—as we are responsible for our own histories. Taken from another side: What created the mass hysterical conversion crisis lurching around the world?

Beyond false consciousness, a conversion crisis related to hysteria, is the transference of a mental disorder to physical activity; for example, stress switched to paralysis of a limb. Taken in mass, a hysterical conversion crisis is personified by groups of people who, unable to address the whole of why things are as they are, attack distinct, idiosyncratic symptoms and thus are unable to find a cure. A clear, current indicator of this disorder comes from the Pew Research Foundation (2015):

> The share of countries with a high or very high level of social hostilities involving religion reached a six-year peak in 2012, according to a new study by the Pew Research Center. A third (33%) of the 198 countries and territories included in the study had high religious hostilities in 2012, up from 29% in 2011 and 20% as of mid-2007. Religious hostilities increased in every major region of the world except the Americas. The sharpest increase was in the Middle East and North Africa, which still is feeling the effects of the 2010–11 political uprisings known as the Arab Spring. There also was a significant increase in religious hostilities in the Asia-Pacific region, where China edged into the "high" category for the first time.

That's violent, 6th-century, pathological mysticism running amok. *Rolling Stone* reporter Matt Taibbi (2009) calls it *The Great Derangement: A Terrifying Story of War, Politics, and Religion*.

Wilhelm Reich (1970), in *The Mass Psychology of Fascism*, explored the psychological realm. Reich located what he called an "emotional plague" in the suppression of sexual pleasure, which sweeps across class, churches, parties, families especially, and related social organizations. I will leave it to the reader to interrogate this avenue in greater depth, although my efforts don't show much improvement on his too-often-ignored examinations of the emergence of fascism as a popular movement (Wolfenstein, 2003).

One other, not alternate but additional, element of explanation:

There Is No Left

Nearly all of what is in fact the bogus world "left" has abandoned revolution, except in its most hollow, even reactionary, forms: the Arab Spring; the ultraconservative farces in Egypt and Syria; the Orange revolution (and other Central Intelligence Agency sponsored color-uprisings, the latest in the Ukraine), and earlier—the tragedies that came of Russia and the long revolution in China, and the fictional left in the United States, etc. (see Samuels, 2014).

In the Arab world, and elsewhere, it is reasonably clear that masses of people reject, on one hand, United States imperialism (if not necessarily the draw of U.S. consumerism and culture—not you, Taliban and ISIS), and the obvious failures of Soviet and Chinese "socialism," really capitalism with a purportedly benevolent party at the top (Rogan, 2009).[3] They have turned, alternately to Al-Qaeda, the Taliban, the Islamic State or ISIS (aka Daesh), savagery, or the fascist nationalism of the Ukraine phony rebel and often fascist leadership (see Blum, 2015).

In the United States, the fake socialist left on one hand hides its politics, perhaps believing people must be led to revolution by baby steps: first a union, then a caucus, then a book club, then the party (which keeps revolution a secret, meaning the party is useless, ducking the pedagogy of class consciousness to the people, while the police are fully aware of the party and its "real" politics). There is no proof people learn like this, and a great deal of evidence to the contrary. On the other hand, the sectarian left stands with bullhorns shouting revolution, but refusing to detail the sacrifices and real devastation that any revolution must first create and yet transcend. Environmentalist revolutionaries seem to dismiss the environmental devastation that any revolution would explode and, likely, will be blackmailed by this threat in the future.[4]

Ghost Dancing Against Capitalism and Empire

In the late 1880s and 1890s, despairing Indian tribes, under assault from all angles, took leadership from a "Weather doctor," Wokova, who promised that the Ghost Dance, a circle dance, would restore peace and prosperity for the various tribes. Some enthusiasts apparently believed that the Ghost Dance was a protection against bullets and death (Kehoe, 1989).

Over time, the Ghost Dance spread to the Lakota Sioux at Wounded Knee, South Dakota. The United States sent federal troops to stop them, against the advice of a former Indian agent who complained that other religious services, similar services, were not prohibited nor threatened. Federal troops, on December 15, 1890, opened fire, killing the famous chief, Sitting Bull. Two weeks later, troops killed more than 150 Indians. The Ghost Dance lost its appeal.

The Ghost Dance misread why things were as they were, urged a mystical series of tactics disconnected from any reasonable strategy, and an occult Grand Strategy (popular yet failed for centuries): heaven will wait. They lost, were crushed, by force.

There have been at least five easily recognized Ghost Dances around the world in the last 14 years—and it is more than 100 years later. Indeed, another is occurring as I write, in late February and early March 2015—an "Adjuncts' Day of Action," organized in the main by the Service Employees International Union, a dues collecting machine initially organized by the mob, and embedded with the empire as is the entire AFL-CIO (Scipes, 2005).[5]

Ghost Dances: Taken One at a Time

The first Ghost Dance was, at base, two dances on the same dance floor: the outpouring for war after the superstitious billionaire's terrorist attack of September 11, 2001—and the subsequent idiotic invasion of Afghanistan—a war in response to a crime.

The flip side of that dance included the mass U.S. demonstrations against the war on Iraq—carefully steered by the Communist Party USA and its front, United for Peace and Justice, absent any analysis of capitalism, imperialism, and the rise of the corporate state: fascism.

Today, those who so favored the wars are exhausted by war, perhaps surprised and disheartened that war is hell, and unwilling to fully probe into Syria or the Ukraine, even knowing their over-stretched empire evaporates beneath their feet. The anti-war side now barely exists. It has no notable numbers, and thanks to the CPUSA and UFPJ, few learned anything of import from their opportunist activities.

The CPUSA illustrates the kind of opportunism that sacrifices the needs and goals of real friends and allies for petty advantages about second tier issues. Metaphorically, it is to seek to address separate parts of the organic capitalist machine, hoping this will weaken its development, which in this social situation in particular is an illusion. It's to build on sand. The CPUSA is the leafleting wing of the Democratic Party.[6]

Opportunists may arrive with numbers of people in their base—who know nothing truly important. Those people will be fickle at heart. Lots of people over time becomes few people, most of them vapid. Sectarians, on the other hand, arrive with no people. Sectarians and opportunists produce, at base, very similar results. This marriage of opportunism and sectarianism adds up to a form of liberalism that paves the way for fascism: again, the current corporate state. It's a re-run of the Second International, but dumber.

I believe it became more than reasonable to describe the United States as a fascist empire when two elements combined: (1) the declaration of perpetual war under crusader banners in 2001; and (2) the bank and industrial bailouts of 2008. Wars could have been ended, but now neither can be reversed. The imperfect combination of corporations, government, and militarism is complete.

Liberals seek to moderate capitalism by empowering a government that is not an ally, nor potential ally, but an enemy; the executive committee and armed weapon of the rich. Al Szymanski, more than 35 years ago, described the duties of what is, in fact, monopoly-finance capitalism with a pretense of democratic statehood: a corporate state (bank bailouts, the takeover of the auto industry, endless war—add it up):

- To guarantee the accumulation of capital and profit maximization and make it legitimate.
- Preserve, form, and temper, capitalist class rule.
- Raise money to fund the state.
- Guarantee and regulate the labor force.
- Facilitate commerce.
- Ensure buying power in the economy.
- Directly and indirectly subsidize private corporations.
- State sanction of self-regulation of corporations.
- Advance the overseas interests of corporations. (Szymanski, 1978, p. 198)

Democracy does not command capital. Democracy submits, atomizes voters to individuals huddled in ballot booths asking capital's favorite question: What about Me?

Opportunism denies, or hides from the mass of people, Lenin's thought, following Marx and Engels, that government is an armed force designed to protect the interests of one class against another. The state exists as a demonstration that irreconcilable class antagonisms exist (Lenin, 1917).[7]

Liberal opportunists want capitalism and empire, without their underpinnings in robbed labor and wars. Rather than a bad social system—capitalism in decay—they identify bad people and ratify evil by choosing its lessers time and again, most recently the demagogue, Barack Obama.

There are no significant differences between Republicans and Democrats on the most fundamental issues in the United States: endless war and the militarization of all life; bailouts of Wall Street (finalizing the move to fascism); deportations; greater reliance on deception and force; racist segregation, especially private property; and greater regimentation of schooling. Of course, they're all nationalists.

Sectarianism and opportunism combine to form the fatalistic belief that the world, matter, will surely change in ways we desire. Both finally limit or deny the significance of fully reflective human agency—grasping and changing (upending)—the world at its political and economic roots. We have seen these mis-estimations quickly turn into the opposites of their civic claims far too often.

For the philosophically minded, left Hegelianism, sectarianism, and right Hegelianism, opportunism, change happens along a line of accumulated, predictable, nearly inevitable, ingredients or change happens because we wish it so. Both reality and/or change are constructs of the mind, usually the Mind in charge. Meet the new tyrant, same as the old tyrant.[8]

The resolution of this is a deep probe into the intersections of mind and matter, in the construction of everyday life, in using critical Marxist theory to make the reproductive veils of capital transparent, and to grasp what useful elements of the future are built into the present and to look into the future.

The second Ghost Dance, the massive outpouring for immigrant rights that involved more than a million people marching on Mayday, 2006, perhaps the biggest one day strike in U.S. history, was quickly demolished by flag waving nationalism, religion, Democrats, and unionites and later, Obama (Watanabe & Becerra, 2006).[9]

The third was Occupy Wall Street, a mindless yet heady adventure that claimed no Grand Strategy (distant goals like a world of sharing and freedom: communism), no strategy, meaning the strategy became the dumbest low denominator of whoever shouted loudest in the "people's" mike and no leaders when the leaders were easily spotted by the police, and pretended that it occupied something when it was always swept away with ease. In some instances, OWS was a cultural carnival, with artful puppets in the front. In militarized San Diego, it was always small. On a fall day, a young self-described "graduate student," lay on a sidewalk next to a pricey theater with a sign, "the Constitution Says we Have a Right to Revolution." His little group of comrades, none standing, posed for wealthy theater-goers, on intermission, who photographed them with phones. Told the Constitution did not back revolution and in fact it was written in secret by far too many slavers, he insisted he was right.

Blocks north, a street-marching crowd of about 15 chanted, "We are the 99%!!!" as police cars led them, police motorcycles followed them, and, on adjacent blocks, police armed personal carriers stood ready. In Nebraska, dozens huddled on the cold ground. I met a young woman Occupier's whose legs were broken by the police in Rhode Island. She remained active. In Oakland, California, OWS was militant and politicized. Where is it now?

Occupy Wall Street was destroyed by unionites, Democrats (hand in hand), and some carrots (ballots), and Obama-led, coordinated, police violence.[10]

The fourth Ghost Dance was the anti-tuition fight led by students—segregated by, mainly, class, primarily in California and New York State, but scattered all over the country (note that with minor variations, each Ghost Dance grows smaller). That was again destroyed by unionites, Democrats, and a little state violence.[11] The key error of this Dance was the student leaders' failure to recognize the fact that capitalist education has never been public. Their demand, duplicated before and after their actions, "Defend Public Education," was a call to defend the systematically segregated, stupefying, mis-education of what is now a corporate state. A similar error is made by the demand to "Stop Privatization."

Inherent in "Save Public Schools" is the *nationalist* view that we all share a common goal to educate all kids in a democratic society. That's never been the case. It is, though, a good way to make a war popular. In 1900, in "Reform or Revolution," Rosa Luxemburg warned about this move: the gradual reduction of capitalist exploitation (in our case, in school cost increases) and the extension of social control (the schools of the capitalist state). Following this commonplace unionite logic: "let us return to the halcyon days of truly public education," which never existed.

From the other angle, it again means "Defend the Corporate State," the merger of business, the military, and government (that's how the money moves) in creating schools as illusion mills and human munitions factories—capitalist education.

A second anti-tuition hike error was the failure to merge the leadership from segregated systems like the University of California (the "race horse system" per a former chancellor, Charlie Reed,) and the "work horse system" of the California State Universities, and the "holding pens" of the community colleges. It was easy to see who was doing most of the "leading," and talking, in the coordinating meetings: UC students, who had the least to lose.

And now, the fifth and most recent Ghost Dance as the resistance decays even more, we see the spurious school "test resistance" movement led by the likes of the vacillating reactionary Diane Ravitch, American Federation of Teachers president Randi Weingarten, and National Education Association boss, Lily Eskelsen Garcia. Ravitch is a god-blessing patriot in her own words. Ravitch is now joined by the unionite tops who helped write the No Child Left Behind Act (NCLB), the Race to the Top, and the Common Core, like the $465,000 a year NEA boss Dennis van Roekel and his successor, Lily Eskelsen Garcia. They want the Common Core and tests repaired, as do all those liberal grouplets (FairTest, on the payroll of the National Education Association, and *Rethinking Schools*, come to mind) who refuse to critique the source of the necessity of greater regimentation of the curriculum (always regimented by textbooks), the wellspring being capitalism in crisis and an empire evaporating. Together, they form the three Mother Superiors of the missions for capitalism. They all live very well—off others (see Gibson, 2010).

They (as well as the teacher union rank and file) want less testing (warned for a decade, school workers finally caught on to the logical step of merit pay—the most grotesque opportunism). They also insist they want to "defend public schools," which really means "save my job—I already proved I will conduct child abuse (racist high-stakes exams) to keep it," when (again) capitalist schooling has never been public but always segregated by class and race.

The duplicity of NEA's leadership became glaringly clear when the NEA representative assembly of 2014, 9,000-plus members gathered in Denver, voted by a wide margin to demand the resignation of Obama's Education Secretary, Arne Duncan. Days later, Eskelsen Garcia, new NEA president, met with Duncan, hugged him, and called him "a good man" (Reisnikoff, 2014). Duncan remains on the job. That second-tier demand, "Save Public Schools," worships an apparition. It's the kind of liberalism that aspires to a new master. It also ignores the unpleasant fact that the education agenda is a war agenda: class war and empires' wars.

To carry the personifications of war a bit further: General William H. McRaven, former head of the terrorist Joint Security Operations Command (at base, an huge assassination squad that helped lose the wars in Afghanistan and Iraq) is now the head of the University of Texas system. Janet Napolitano, former immigration boss under the demagogue Obama, the woman who made her name off nationalism and racism, is now the boss of the University of California system. And General Piraeus, failed general who wrote the half-witted "US Counterinsurgency Manual," (done better 2000 years earlier by Sun Tzu in *Art of War*) and disgraced CIA top who turned over top-secret material to his paramour and was fired, prosecuted, and wrist-slapped, is now teaching at City University of New York.

"Wherever We Go, We Have Got the Maxim Gun, and They Have Not"[12]

In the midst of World War I, a general demanded that the schools become "human munition factories" (Hochschild, 2012, p. 112). That capitalist schools serve a capitalist state is key to grasping the war project at hand. Recently the Council of Foreign Relations (led by war-hawk Condoleeza Rice, "We don't want the smoking gun to be a mushroom cloud") issued its Education Task Force Report, demonstrating in clear terms that the education agenda is a war agenda (Blitzer, 2003).

> Human capital will determine power in the current century, and the failure to produce that capital will undermine America's security. Large, undereducated swaths of the population damage the ability of the United States to physically defend itself, protect its secure information, conduct diplomacy, and grow its economy. (Council on Foreign Relations, 2014)

Harry Magdoff spelled out what should be an obvious connection years ago: "Economic theory and analysis which omit imperialism and militarism from their underlying paradigm are far removed from the reality of today's world" (Magdoff, 1978, p. 210).

Imperialist war is a reality that Rouge Forum members pointed to even before 2001. In 1999 we wrote, "If you are teaching middle school children, you are teaching the soldiers in the next oil war." We had no crystal ball, just an understanding of the necessary relationship of imperialism and war. Better than "Defend Public Education" is "Rescue Education from the Ruling Classes."

What will come of this last and smallest Ghost Dance so far? They will lose, just like their predecessors (and the 19th century tragedy that gave rise to the term). Even if they win, they lose. Capitalist schooling can easily appropriate John Dewey or Paulo Freire. Freire's method, ostensibly created to oppose "banking education," is used by banks' training programs.

The people the reformers misled will learn nothing significant about grand strategy, strategy, tactics, nor even the most rudimentary methods of doing criticism. The last dullard to help lead the test resistance crowd, part of which is now claiming the "Patriotic" banner, derisively called the Common Core "socialistic," not National Socialism (Phillips, 2014).

Another Ghost Dance is picking up partners inside the teacher unions, the suburban and whiter NEA and the urban American Federation of Teachers. A self-described "radical," Alex Caputo Peal, recently won election in the second largest local in the United States, Los Angeles.

In Detroit, a long-time teacher, Steve Conn, a member of By Any Means Necessary, a front for the Trotskyist Revolutionary Workers League, finally won the Detroit Federation of Teachers' presidency, after more than five attempts. Conn courageously led the Detroit teachers' wildcat strike of 1999, but was repeatedly cheated out of leadership positions for the remaining years (Gibson, 1999).

In a DFT recount vote, Conn won election by four ballots, 621 to 617 with about one quarter of the members voting. Conn may find himself sandbagged by a dedicated, entirely reactionary, opposition and an apathetic, despairing rank and file, accustomed only to defeat. Conn is probably the most outspoken of the newly elected officers. We shall see how he overcomes the countless obstacles he, and the people of Detroit, face.[13]

In the Chicago Teachers Union, a moderate posing as a radical, Karen Lewis, won election against the past notorious sellout caucus. Lewis led a brief strike, then urged the teachers to return to work under what she posed as a good contract, a victory. Mayor Rahm Emanuel, an Obama foot-soldier, laid off hundreds of teachers subsequently, with a good deal of noise, but no direct action, from the Chicago Teachers Union, an AFT affiliate. Now, Lewis' health forced her to step away from her position, which today is held by Jesse Sharkey, a member of the International Socialists, another Trotskyist sect. Sharkey led CTU's drive to back Chuy Garcia against incumbent Emanuel in a mayoral election. Garcia is a long-time Democratic Party functionary. Less than 35% of Chicagoans voted. Nevertheless, Sharkey and the CTU helped Garcia win enough votes to cause a run-off. Sharkey declared that Garcia would win, "changing Chicago politics forever," a fancy: win or lose. Chuy lost (Felsenthal, 2015).

In Milwaukee, Bob Peterson, a key leader of Rethinking Schools, closely tied to the Democratic Socialists of America, is now the president of his union.

All of these "radicals," have everything in common with the past Ghost Dances:

- No critique of capitalism and imperialism in their organizing or publications;
- No analysis of the capitalist state, now a fascist corporate state, in favor of "our democracy";
- A second tier analysis of the roles of racism and sexism—the former a creation of the development of capitalism and the latter a centuries-old remnant, still powerful within capital;
- No open declaration of class war or opposition to imperialist war from their official union positions (and in DSA, none at all);
- "addressing only the distinct, separate parts of a lifeless machine," artificially isolated "facts" that are truly part of a totalizing process (Luxemburg, 1900);
- All these struggles are designed to remain within parameters set by capital and empire, so any victory, temporary as it may be, is theirs;
- Hence, support for the system of capital and its decaying U.S. empire—convincing people fundamental change is impossible.[14]

While some may openly be members of socialist sects, and others may be not so openly aligned, they all behave as nationalist liberals. Bob Peterson is probably not the most radical of this group of opportunists, but his reach, via Rethinking Schools, is wide. Indeed, he publishes in what many call the "voice of U.S. intelligence," the *Washington Post*. For that reason, and the fact that the others' public positions so closely parallel his, I will use his *Washington Post* piece as an example (Peterson, 2015).

In his piece, Peterson argues that teacher unions are under attack. While he focuses on the Republican assault that eliminated what I would call forced dues collection, and what Peterson calls "collective bargaining" that originated with a (popular) governor and legislature, he does note that Democrats have joined the fray as well. Peterson believes a "new" (he knows his history better) kind of "social justice unionism" can revitalize the teacher unions and communities as well. His description of social justice unionism:

> Three components of social justice unionism are like the legs of a stool. Unions need all three to be balanced and strong: We organize around bread and butter issues. We organize around teaching and learning issues to reclaim our profession and our classrooms. We organize for social justice in our community and in our curriculum. (Peterson, 2015, para. 15)

Peterson proposes that tactical work through coalitions with parents and related community groups, a la Chicago, is key to their efforts. Among his coalition partners are the usual suspects: NAACP, ACLU, Parents For Public (sic) Schools, and others.

Peterson wants to enhance teacher "Professionalism." To beat this dead horse to death, again: Teaching was never a profession; school workers don't set their hours, wages, methods of work, the curriculum, and now not the tests. It's a working class job—professionalism is an elitist dodge that allows, for example, principals to demand teachers buy supplies, work hundreds of unpaid hours, etc. and see themselves as educated superiors to blue collar workers—the allies they need most.

In this, Peterson managed to get his "union" to train teachers on the districts' "student learning outcomes" a move well within the management box. He's proud of the union's burgeoning electoral efforts, despite the fact that this was the key union that sought to recall Governor Scott Walker, and lost, positioning Walker as a 2016 presidential candidate. Rather than a state-wide strike, actions similar to what gave birth to the distorted baby, collective bargaining, unionites in Wisconsin empowered their enemies.

Peterson wants to fight "privatization," a second or third level issue, and on those grounds, he fears what amounts to fighting back too hard, speaking out of turn, "…speaking out can play into the hands of the privatizers as they seek to expand privately run charters…" (Peterson, 2015, para. 56). The only mention of a strike is historical, about Chicago—not something that would be openly planned in Milwaukee—when it was only strikes, most of them illegal, which won the earliest rights to collective bargaining.[15] Not surprisingly, Peterson never gets to exactly what his hobby horse of "social justice" is. And it is unsurprising that the *Washington Post* so easily carried his work.

It is impossible for any knowledgeable radical, set aside a revolutionary, to read this series of what are in fact but tactics, never really reaching into the respectability of a simple strike strategy, and not think, perhaps stridently, "petty bourgeoisie opportunism with a middle class core." In this sense, per Marx, he's both a reactionary and a utopian.

While many honest and relatively innocent people involved themselves in these Ghost Dances, it remains that each has been led by people in leftist groups who deliberately reject the notion of simply telling people about the easily seen realities of class war and failing empires.

The ruling classes see it and worry about the relationship of inequality and uprisings. See their writing at about the crises of inequality and the potential of class-consciousness in, for example, the Council on Foreign Relations (2014). Even the French worry about inequality on behalf of Americans: Thomas Piketty's *Capital in the 21st Century*, which unfortunately ends with a request for the rich to give up their riches.

At base, part of the imitation left lies to people in order to trick them into revolution: to appropriate one favorite Trotskyist term, "putting people in motion," which will somehow make them smart. The lies come from two poles—hiding the reality of capitalism's failures and at the other end, the fact that any kind of social change will cause a great deal of suffering and destruction. Things will not get better fast after a revolution. Indeed, for some time they will get worse.

Perhaps this "left" wants to imitate the Bolsheviks who famously gave the bourgeoisie the rope to hang themselves with; then moved to power when the bourgeoisie couldn't rule. But then came the Bolshevik failure in quickly restoring capitalism with a purportedly benevolent party at the top, Bolshevism: tricked by the bourgeoisie within its own midst.[16]

The phony U.S. left did all it could to prevent the rise of a mass, class conscious movement. Hence, the importance of ideas and the ideological battle. On one hand, what defeats men with guns? On the other hand, what easily understood singular belief holds together a movement that must suffer to win a better world? Ideas. That is likely to be the only worthwhile lesson of the Arab Spring. That is why the ideological battle is important. The core idea? Equality—true in science and society.

Settling Scores

What does the fake left dodge? The reality of the domination of capitalism and imperialism, as we have seen. Per Rosa Luxemburg:

> ...capital in its struggle against societies with a natural economy pursues the following ends: (1) To gain immediate possession of important sources of productive forces such as land, game in primeval forests, minerals, precious stones and ores, products of exotic flora such as rubber, etc. (2) To 'liberate' labour power and to coerce it into service. (3) To introduce a commodity economy. (4) To separate trade and agriculture. (Luxemburg, Chapter 27, 1913)

Everywhere in the world now, children of the poor kill other children of the poor on behalf of the rich in their homelands. Militarism invades every aspect of life in the United States Empire come to ensnarl everything, as William Appleman Williams put it: "Empire as a Way of Life." He also warned it will inevitably lead to nuclear death (Berger, 1995, p. 375).

The U.S. military budget, if we take it at face value (and we won't) at about $640 million in 2014 takes up about 55% of the total budget while education gets about 6%. It is more than the combined military spending of China, Russia, Saudi Arabia (yes, third), France, United Kingdom, Germany, Japan, France, and India (Peterson Foundation, 2014). The real military, "defense," budget is now well over the one trillion dollars that Chalmers Johnson (2008) described as far back as 2008. Much of that budget is secret—black?

The 2014 "Quadrennial Defense Review," issued by the Department of Defense, describes three pillars of empire:

1. Protect the homeland, to deter and defeat attacks on the United States and to support civil authorities in mitigating the effects of potential attacks and natural disasters.
2. Build security globally, in order to preserve regional stability, deter adversaries, support allies and partners, and cooperate with others to address common security challenges.

3. Project power and win decisively, to defeat aggression, disrupt and destroy terrorist networks, and provide humanitarian assistance and disaster relief.

These pillars are mutually reinforcing and interdependent, and all of the military Services play important roles in each. Our nuclear deterrent is the ultimate protection against a nuclear attack on the United States, and through extended deterrence..." (Department of Defense, 2014, p. v)

Empire is temptation. War means work: jobs.

College and university campuses are littered with military recruiters, intelligence agencies, high-tech operations that build, for example, drones. High schools and community colleges in poor and working class areas are awash with militarist hustlers in uniform distributing materials and in the classroom teaching—patriotic veterans. Now, the military poses its mission as "a job, not an adventure," as it moves to recruit women for combat because American men are too uneducated, too addicted, too convicted, and too unfit to fill the numbers needed for cannon fodder.

The deadening "Thank you for your service" is routinely offered to strangers in uniform. And, to beat an already dead horse, "American Sniper" rules the culture along with baseball played in camouflage, football games with flyovers. I frequently meet educated Americans, like my Kaiser doctor, who are surprised Guantanamo is still open and reject the claims made in the brilliant and tragically funny Guantanamo Diary (Slahi, 2015). Paraphrasing Chalmers Johnson (2000): "History is so eradicated that Americans cannot connect cause and effect."

Today, monopolized finance capital dominates industrial capital in the United States It has for 100 years. Now, however, that domination is full blown and especially poisonous. Evidence: finance capital won $12.9 trillion in the 2008–2009 bailouts while industrial capital only stole about $700 billion. We'll repeat this below, for emphasis.[17]

One implication of this overwhelming rule of finance capital was witnessed by the billionairess Lady Astor who said (paraphrasing), "We the wealthy once looked ahead 50, even 100 years. We built industry, commerce, productive fields. We worried about the poor. Today, the newly rich just run higgidly piggidly after the nearest dollar." Or, "after me, the deluge" (Brooke Astor, 2007).

The recent, "Flashboys, A Wall Street Revolt," demonstrates not only the domination of finance capital, but also shows the rush for the nearest penny, in nano-seconds, the class nature and corruption of the rigged stock exchange, and the players' utter lack of interest in the long term, a psychological issue addressed soon on these pages (Lewis, 2014).

From time to time, greed vastly outweighs ruling class patriotism, though they know well they hide behind the national military—everywhere. Take for example, Jamie Dimon of what was JP Morgan and is now JP Morgan Chase (big fish eat little fish). In the fall of 2008, when the U.S.' bankers faced a watershed crisis, the collapse of the U.S. banking system and, most likely, the world economic system; to be predictably followed by mass riots and social unrest, Hank Paulson, then head of the Treasury, approached Dimon for assistance in a bailout. Dimon: "Hank, I would do anything for the United States, but not at the expense of J.P. Morgan" (Sorkin, 2009). Dimon and his cohort, white men meeting on a weekend, in secret, did win the bailout battle. There were quid pro quos. They promised to allow for more regulation of the banks, to carefully supervise loans but to offer them to the deserving, and to stop the rampant greed made too obvious in the multi-million dollar bonuses they received in the past. At this writing, the bankers have defeated the regulations, they are not offering loans to many solvent people but the student debt crisis is rising—more than one trillion dollars. And, in 2013, Dimon got a 70% raise to $20 million (Moore, 2013).

With monopoly finance capital ruling the corporate state, short term views, the absence of grand strategy, combine to devastate the nation's cities, its infrastructure, international imperial politics, and, horrifically, the world climate itself (Gibson, 2013).

> In its pure form, fascism is the sum total of all irrational reactions of the average human character. To the narrow-minded sociologist who lacks the courage to recognize the enormous role played by the irrational in human history, the fascist race theory appears as nothing but an imperialistic interest or even a mere "prejudice." The violence and the ubiquity of these "race prejudices" show their origin from the irrational part of the human character. The race theory is not a creation of fascism. No: fascism is a creation of race hatred and its politically organized expression. Correspondingly, there is a German, Italian, Spanish, Anglo-Saxon, Jewish and Arabian fascism. (Reich, 1933)

Another element of fascism is secrecy, on the one hand, and mass surveillance on the other. Liberal author and former *New York Times* reporter James Risen describes this pervasive reality in the United States in "Pay Any Price; Greed, Power, and Endless War." In regard to secrecy and surveillance, Risen notes *The New York Times'* suppression of his own work on the National Security Agency's constant intrusions into the e-mail and web traffic of both Americans and foreigners—the latter illegal on the face of it, but constant never the less—a fact later revealed by Edward Snowden. Risen (2015) concludes: "In 2009, I realized…that the war on terror had become a bi-partisan enterprise. America was now locked into an endless war and its perverse and unintended (sic) consequences were spreading" (p. 273).

Fascism is now a popular mass movement in the United States and much of the world, taking on somewhat different forms, but in essence largely the same. Witlessly supported, passively or actively backed; that is what is. The United States is a consumerist, not industrialist, society, the result of imperialist out-sourcing and finance capital in stagnation, fashioning gargantuan debt. Between two thirds and three fourths of the economy is rooted in consumption. This is not a post-Fordist argument. Fordism (an extreme division of labor, aggregative industrial production, standardization of parts and methods of production, interchangeability; Taylorism, a mass of overseers of all forms of work and life, etc.) exists worldwide; many aspects appearing in U.S. schools.

Industrial production shifted; did not disappear. Hence, the post-modernist turn, really the whining of the vanishing middle class intelligentsia, is not mine. Culture nests in an economic base, a whole that cannot be ignored. The mass psychological impact of this material reality, hinted above, is this: industrial society is easily seen as a class war, not as easily recognized as a form of exploitation as slavery, but in the late 18th century, class war was widely admitted. The obvious, conscious solidarity of factory work: everyone must join together to create a product and, to control the processes and products of that creation, even to a degree, it's necessary to act in solidarity—an injury to one preceding an injury to all or, in the case of a strike—"don't scab!" (Wierson, 2013).

Consumerist mass psychology, however, is different. It's truly a war of all on all. "I wish to offer you as little as possible for your product," and vice versa. It may be the high point of human alienation. A consumerist society, which must involve the individualistic thrust to the front, is an even more narcissistic society than what Drs. Jean Twenge and Keith Campbell (2010) noted in "The Narcissism Epidemic," and was played out in the "Too Big to Fail," Wall Street inverted laissez faire greed-festival before and after the collapse of 2008.

While class consciousness, or its absence, is not solely located in an economic base, in this case a consumer society, that undergirding reality has to be a consideration to explain this "Great Derangement." Consumerism is, assuredly, contradicted by booming inequality and a huge underclass. The poor can only buy so much, especially with a color-coded two million of them in prison. The ruling class, married to the governing class, exhibits a top-down ad hoc, make-shift, set of moment to moment tactics with plenty of pyrotechnics and little grand strategy, and the remainder of the people experience a "what about me at this moment"; a mass population especially susceptible to spectacles, despair, and manufactured panics. Mix in the formidable displays of police violence against protestors from Oakland, California, to Ferguson, Missouri—ruthless ferocity to be seen by all, Tweeted, YouTubed, Facebooked, and televised, probably to not too much consternation of the authorities.

In school, however, an overblown culture of fear exists. In 2009, Susan Harman, a former school principal, and Robert Apter, Marxist scholar and retired union organizer, and I visited nearly every county in California, meeting with hundreds of school workers, parents, school board members, and community personnel. Our overarching conclusion is that the primary affect of schooling is fear, the result of increasing authoritarianism in most aspects of school life. Nevertheless, Apter and I came to believe that much of that fear is, in fact, an overestimation of the power of school bureaucrats and a lack of courage to act.

Fear, in schools and out, has a material footing in the economy. Massive debt, calculating competition for low-wage jobs, widely televised police violence against non-violent innocents, all add up, but in most instances the worst-case scenario in schools is dismissal. Who, of any weighty consequence, has never been fired and/or jailed?

All of this begins to sum up to be a significant part of why people of the United States are so easily led into, and out of, Ghost Dances.

The Rise of Corporate States, Fascism, in Varying Forms Worldwide

R. Palme Dutt (1935/1974) in *Fascism and Social Revolution* argued fascism is an inevitable result of capitalism and its decay if the social revolution is delayed.

> Fascism is the logical result of the fact that the form of private ownership of the means of production can progress no further and must create violent crises, stagnation, and decay. Only the social organization of production can sanely organize production, and this can only come through social revolution. (p. 264)

The world available for capitalist exploitation now contracts. Fascism is a further stage of capital in crisis. A massive world army of unemployed people grows, and as this world crisis grows, so does the need of bosses to lower the costs of production. There are but two alternatives, social revolution or destruction. The class struggle now intensifies…

Here we will need, for brevity's sake, to use a footnote for the more critical reader to enter into an expansion of precisely what fascism is, where it originates, who it serves, its backers, and hence, how to fight it and why (Gibson, 2001; Pilger, 2015).

The Quisling role of the "labor movement," as partners of the unified parties of capital, that is, the war parties. No significant labor boss in the United States will state that employers and workers have contradictory interests. More, they are all steeped in nationalism and the practices of empire. This became glaringly clear in the National Education Association's Representative Assembly of 2010, when about 10,000 mostly rank and file practicing school workers voted "not to discuss" the wars as it might disturb the feelings of the attendees. This wasn't an orchestrated parliamentary trick; it was the raised hands of more than 90% of the room. In 2011, the NEA voted to endorse Obama, despite his Race to the Top attacks on school workers and the wars that were destroying so many recent graduates (Gibson, 2013).

That school workers are among the last in the United States to have fairly decent wages, health benefits, some forms of tenure like "just cause," and pensions, is indicative of the empire's bribe. It creates what Marx and Engels called the "labor aristocracy." Engels wrote, "Participation in the world market was and is the economic basis of the English working class' nullity" (Hunt, 2011, p. 320). He wasn't just pointing to labor "leaders." Lenin (1916) addresses the empire's payoff to its junior partners:

> The receipt of high monopoly profits by the capitalists in one of the numerous branches of industry, in one of the numerous countries, etc., makes it economically possible for them to bribe certain sections of the workers, and for a time a fairly considerable minority of them, and win them to the side of the bourgeoisie of a given industry or given nation against all the others. The intensification of antagonisms between imperialist nations for the division of the world increases this urge. And so there is created that bond between imperialism and opportunism, which revealed itself first and most clearly in Great Britain, owing to the fact that certain features of imperialist development were observable there much earlier than in other countries. Some writers, L. Martov, for example, are prone to wave aside the connection between imperialism and opportunism in the working-class movement…(Chapter 10)

What's new? The powerful remnants of mysticism: 42% of Americans are creationists, others believe God created evolution (Newport, 2014). The pretend-left is as afraid to say, "People make gods, gods don't make people. Believe that and you will believe anything. You have fairies dancing in your head," as the United States is unwilling to say the same thing to the Taliban, Muslim Brotherhood, Al Qaeda, IS, Opus Dei, and Israel. "No gods, no masters" is the only possible response to religious barbarism. Otherwise, it is "My God can beat up your god," and endless religious wars: an element of today's educated barbarians at much of the top of the United States and the Middle East, and the world.

Nationalism, the curse of the last 2 ½ centuries. A geographical accident of births unites the slaves with the masters, often in the name of freedom. "You're not a slave! You're free! Your problem is the slaves of the Master over there! Kill them!"

The necessity of revolution and the suffering that any revolution will make, victorious or not, for some time. The failure to take on the "whole" of society, described in brief above, means movements typically lack grand strategy (an equitable just society of free people living in harmony), strategy (revolution taking place in different forms in different times in different areas), and tactics (strikes, demonstrations, propaganda, etc.) (see, for example Perlman, 1984). This leaves the initiative solely in the hand of capital, as the "left" chases its symptoms and false flag creations. This means movements flail at shifting effects of capitalism, effects frequently manipulated by elites (Occupy Wall Street, union elections, educational testing opt-outs, etc).

As they leap from second tier mission to second tier mission, they also adopt utopian solutions (save "our" schools and let them return to the pristine days of the past) with no inkling of how to get from the compartmentalized and partial here to there.

What Is a Revolution? It's Reasonable to Teach It

There are two words in Chinese that describe "revolution." One is *fanshen* (see William Hinton's brilliant book on the Chinese revolution by that title). Fanshen means to dig into and turn over the soil. What is on top is new, but what is below is still there. The other word means "to withdraw the mandate from heaven." That's a legitimacy crisis: when the people realize the emperor is a mere mortal, no better than others, has no honor from God, and is indeed, worse, because the ruler has mis-served the people by theft, nepotism, etc.

> The bourgeoisie itself, therefore, supplies the proletariat with its own elements of political and general education, in other words it furnishes the proletariat with weapons for fighting the bourgeoisie. (Marx & Engels, 1848, Chapter 1)

Chalmers Johnson was a CIA asset whose work on revolution is a benchmark for all similar modern studies. Of course, at the time of the writing, Johnson was seeking to oppose revolutions, but he wrote a cookbook. Revolutionary violence must attack the central seat of power. Decentralized violence often leads to reform. Societies are rooted in coercion, forms of violence applied inequitably in inequitable societies. When hope vanishes, and people are just scavenging for food, revolution may be at hand. I paraphrase from Johnson: "The most important value system in a society is to legitimize the use of force."

Johnson's sources of change:

1. External: world wide communications system, foreign travelers returning, international communist parties, external warfare, etc.
2. Internal: changes of values brought about by intellectual activity, scientific discovery, acceptance of innovations that are not incorporated into "normal" society.
3. Ideology, an alternative value system, plus much more, is key to revolution. In this sense, ideology would mean a program of values, a coherent or at least understandable method of analysis and plans of action: Grand Strategy, strategy, and tactics.

Such an ideology will "supply intellectually and emotionally satisfying explanations of what is wrong with the social system," why one who personifies the prevention of change promises some methods of suggesting that success of change is possible and offers some view of a better way to live. Revolutionary ideologies, thus, offer a method of thinking; apply it to criticism of things as they are (the existing social order) to produce a culture that shows how things can change, reveals long term goals, and, during revolutions, these ideologies often shift in order to explain deficiencies within them as social practice tests them.

Revolutionary ideologies are, typically, imminent. That is, they do not argue for postponing change but seek to hasten it. High degrees of generality, or correctness in terms of explanation and practice, mean that revolutionary ideologies can spread between and among dissident groups; solidarity grows. Related causes include power deflation (dependence on more and more force); loss of authority, use of force seen as illegitimate (lost foreign wars); and accelerators (events that make armies mutiny, revolutionary leaders decide to move, etc.).

In order to retain power, elites must do two things: recognize disequilibrium and move, convincingly, to act on it. One common method to retain power is to coopt opposition leadership. This ends the summary of Chalmers Johnson on revolutionary change.

Revolution is an academic field that gets far too little attention. And, in practice, everything is in place for a dramatic, revolutionary upheaval. But there is no left.

Class Consciousness to Connect Reason to Power

What, after all, is class consciousness?

Per Ron Eyerman (1981), class consciousness is the awareness that one is

> Part of a social group that, through common work activity at the same time reproduces a social system and others in it who do not have the same interests regarding that system, and who do not participate in it in the same manner…it is an orientation toward political action…an awareness of others, of those who are similar and those who are different with regard to their long-term interests, and an awareness of the social structure that makes their differences real. (p. 283)

Class consciousness implies anti-racism, anti-capitalism, as well as a vision of a better future against which today's actions can be examined. This is not to simply reduce every question of race, sex, religion, or ethnicity immediately to greed, profits, but it is to say that the war for surplus value has, at the end of the day, decisive influence in setting up all the social relations of capital.

Capital's schools, racism, nationalism, sexism, and religion all disguise social problems, problems of class, as problems of individual people, competing races/crafts/industries/nations, or fate. That is, capital's schools and U.S. forms of unionism are designed, above all, to create a veneer of limited knowledge, but to wipe out class consciousness. To date, this is succeeding.

Following Eyerman, class consciousness has been seen as:

1. a logical and necessary result of the advance of productive forces, that is, when the world is industrialized, people will become class conscious;
2. an awareness of the whole picture of capital, through the daily bitter experiences that capital must offer the working class, and the intervention of an advanced party;
3. an offering to working people from organized intellectuals and dedicated activists, especially as crises arise;
4. workers' spontaneous response to their collective, persistent, problems, as work is always alienating; and

5. class consciousness has been seen as the natural product of intellectuals produced by the working class itself, organic intellectuals, whose ideas can be more easily grasped and accepted. None of these formulas has worked well so far, or yet.

Class consciousness, then, is a pedagogical and practical problem that has not been resolved. Its absence plagues the working classes of the world as crises of capitalist inequality, imperialist war, racism, rising irrationalism, international bankruptcies, militarism, etc. make the current situation especially menacing and urgent.

The crux of the pedagogical issue goes beyond transcending racist alienation and defeating exploitation. At the heart of the question is the view that people can overcome the master/slave relationship, consciously, yet not recreate it at a new level; to forge a new society, a caring community, from the wreckage of the old, to forge reason from unreason.

Justice does demand organization. Organization requires discipline. That, too, is a problem, a contradictory relationship of taking direction, at bottom obeying orders from those with the broadest view, to paying careful attention to those with specific knowledge of particular circumstances.

In practice, this has meant that those in relatively secret sections of revolutionary organizations, which must exist, have to operate with limited knowledge of all sorts: who is who, what the next steps will be—and they frequently cannot question directions. They must grasp the "whole," without knowing many of its revolutionary parts.

Lukács, in *History and Class Consciousness*, locates "imputed consciousness," among the oppressed as taking corporeal form, bodily form, inside a Marxist party; in his case, the temporarily successful Bolsheviks. That consciousness is then transferred, through various forms of educational efforts or propaganda, to the exploited.

Perhaps this became, primarily, a one way, top-down message. It surely did within the CPUSA where many old members remember the main message as: "Do what you're told." Class consciousness must be dialectically pressed on organizers, and from organizers back and forth to masses of people. Organization must be moral, ethical, to win the trust of the masses, and to set an egalitarian standard—which recognizes the vital role of leadership—against which opportunism can be judged.

But the crux of education, of organization, and of pedagogy itself, is the fact that we can understand and transform the world. We make our own histories, are subjects who can create change, or an unacceptable, soon-to-be-disastrous, false continuity (Lukács, 1971).

The path to a loving society, a community where people can live creatively, consciously, collectively, and not merely democratically, free of the rule of private property, exploitation, and empire, is probably only possible through great suffering. We should not despair in that, because that is the home of hope.

People who have suffered and struggled define themselves in that process and achieve a standing that is unavailable to others.

People who have suffered can transcend fear, the host of hate, because they will have had to truly move in understanding from what appears to be, to what is, to what can be. The process of their suffering gives them a better understanding of what is essentially a master/slave relationship than the masters can ever attain, and their daily lives serve as proof to the masters' lies. In doing that they may be able to fashion a society that lives by the idea, which will require a massive international change of mind (and a calling off of the massive scientific industrialized slaughter), an idea whose time has come: from each according to their commitment, to each according to their need. This stands in clear opposition to the zenith of capitalism today, summed up by Conrad in *Heart of Darkness* as the ultimate declaration of imperialism: "Exterminate all the brutes."

Yes, of course today there is a gap between the present state of unconsciousness (or madness), class consciousness, and a revolution (which is no more inevitable than the temporary victory of fascism). Obviously the balance of forces, everywhere, is not good. In the United States the usually vacillating petty bourgeoisie, in schools and out, are not just tilting to the ruling class, they toady for it. Still, if there is never to be a revolution, there will be nothing but repeatedly "perishing in the death throes of capitalism" (Lukács, 1971, p. 263).

The specter of World War III is real to former USSR top, Gorbachev, and me (Defotis, 2015). Between here and there is a fight. It would be unwise to offer a prescription that could be applied to every community, detailing the old "what is to be done," question. But direct action (control of workplaces and communities at key choke points), relentless agitation for class consciousness, and, importantly, close personal ties across all the barriers that capital creates seem key.

It is fair to ask: What has the Rouge Forum done? We led the initial test resistance with boycotts in the early 1990s, direct action in the "professional organizations" and unions—always pointing to the war agenda that drives capitalist schooling. We were involved at all levels in the Detroit teachers' wildcat strike (Gibson, 1999). We help fight the NCLB, Race to the Top, and Common Core, placing them in their social context. We engage the battle for ideas. We hope these ideas will defeat men with guns who fight on behalf of a tiny minority of the world's people.

Capital has united the world via systems of production, exchange, communications, and exploration and divided the world by class, race, nation, mysticism, and sexism. It is a social system that has far outlived its usefulness. Indeed, everything Chalmers Johnson (2000; 2008) described as the backdrop for the possibility of revolutionary change is well in place. Capital has nothing left to offer masses of people. Even before the NASDAQ collapse, people with three SUVs began to notice that such good luck was just not fulfilling.

Capital has inverted science; consider the huge scientific advances in weaponry and gas-masking, while 25% of the kids in parts of New York City are cursed with environmental asthma.

Capital is attacking all that is beautiful, from rationality to aesthetics—the drooling fundamentalist snake-handling top office-holders who cloak the breasts on statues. But overcoming the processes of capital is going to require a massive change of mind, an urgent change if we are going to go beyond industrialized slaughter.

Changing minds is the daily life of every school worker. School workers are situated at the centripetal organizing point of North America's de-industrialized life. They do not have to operate the school-to-war pipeline. Indeed, if they begin to recognize the contradiction between why they think they are in capitalist schools, and why elites want them there, perhaps those educators can rescue education from the ruling classes—then help to expose the false mandate from heaven that offers dishonest and incompetent leaders legitimacy they do not deserve.

War and more war is inevitable within the systems of capital and empire; as inevitable as the betrayal of the promises of nationalist liberals in socialist garb. If history is any kind of guide, the lessons of the Second International should be enough.[18]

What we do counts, more than ever. There is no guarantee we will win. But we must. That will not happen by simple reasoning. The Masters will not adopt the ethics of the slaves. We will win by resisting, with a plan to overcome, and by learning from our resistance—outfoxing the destruction of reason and wisdom.

The core issue of our times is the rise of color-coded inequality and the real promise of perpetual war met by the potential of mass class-conscious resistance for the clarion call that has driven social movements for centuries:

A single-minded aim: Equality! Revolutionary equality! We will not be fed willingly, witlessly, to the spiders.

Notes

1. I urge the reader to get the 2012 Deluxe Edition of *The Spider and the Fly*, brilliantly illustrated, published by Simon and Schuster. Read it to adults. There are many online editions.
2. Magdoff (1978) is a fine beginner's text on empire with short essays that can be read by high school students. He notes there have been three full years of war for every year of peace for the United States since the Revolution (p. 199).
3. Rogan, unfortunately, completely misread the Arab Spring, predicting it would begin to offer proof that the Arab people can build democracy. It has done anything but. Nevertheless, his analysis of the past, up to say 2009, the date of the publication of the hardback edition, is unsurpassed.
4. At this writing, it is not possible to determine what will come of the anti-racist demonstrations that took place since a series of police and white civilian murders after the killing of Trayvon Martin, Michael Brown, and other black youth. However, without left leadership, the protests will remain, at best, protests and little else.
5. A classic in labor studies, which describes the bourgeoisie nature of labor boss, is Mills (1948).
6. For a detailed examination of the bizarre trajectory any loyal rank and file Communist Party USA member would have followed see Gibson (2006).
7. See also Reich (1970) arguing that liberalism leads to fascism, p. 73.
8. Hegel expert of Western Michigan University Rudolph Siebert, simplified the left/right Hegel dichotomy as, in the Second World War, Stalin represented the Left Hegelians, and Hitler the Right—mechanical materialism versus mysticism. The reader seeking a shortcut, or guide, to Hegel—always wise—may look here first: http://www.philosophybasics.com/movements_hegelianism.html. A much longer examination of the left/right issue is here: http://www-rohan.sdsu.edu/~rgibson/freirall.htm
9. I use the term "unionite," deliberately, distinct from "unionist," as an insult as today's unions are not what most people think of as unions, but dues collection machines working on behalf of capital and empire. For an extension, see Gibson (2013).
10. See the attack on an Iraq veteran in Oakland: http://www.youtube.com/watch?v=61lQUaLknPc
11. For a visual display of the police violence, witness the casual work of Lt. John Pike at University of California, Davis: https://www.youtube.com/watch?v=6AdDLhPwpp4
12. British imperial chant.
13. The DFT Election Committee reported March 5 that the official recount of the January presidential election resulted in Steve Conn garnering 621 votes. Edna Reaves received 617 votes. Retrieved from the DFT web site, March 15, 2015. http://dft231.mi.aft.org/
14. Chalmers Johnson alternately described the United States as a fascist state and a state where fascism was emerging in his books, articles, and videos. Here is but one: http://www.truthdig.com/arts_culture/item/20080515_chalmers_johnson_on_our_managed_democracy. Johnson's Nemesis Trilogy, which began with *Blowback*, then *Sorrows of Empire*, and concludes with *Nemesis*, remains the best on the issue of the decaying U.S. empire, despite the fact he was a lifelong anti-Marxist and for a good part of his life, a CIA asset. Johnson's death in 2010 was a terrible loss for those who do serious analytical work. His resources, methodology, and conclusions were brilliant, and nicely referenced.
15. Probably the easiest way into this history is the film *With Babies and Banners, The Great Flint Strike at General Motors*. It is about 50 minutes long, perfect for most classrooms, and demonstrates the efforts of real radicals, surely not revolutionaries, in the Communist Party USA of the 1930s. It is online at https://www.youtube.com/watch?v=pa75V-tdBko (disclosure, many of the people involved in making the film were friends).
16. Lenin picked up this strategy from Marx and every revolution since pursued this path: China to Cuba to Grenada. It hasn't worked and is one of several Achilles' heels of socialism as we have known it. See Marx's "Address of the Central Council to the Communist League," in Bender, Frederic (1967) *Karl Marx, Essential Writings*, Chapter 26, p. 264.
17. Lenin's "Imperialism, the Highest Stage of Capitalism" begins with the role, in the early 1900s, of monopoly-finance capital. What is often missed by radicals is Lenin's examination of the relationship of empire and bourgeoisie leftists, bought off by imperial bribes. And John Bellamy Foster (2014) follows that path and brings it up to date in *The Theory of Monopoly Capitalism*.
18. For a detailed description of the opportunism, which I have used interchangeably with liberal nationalism, see Lenin, V. I. (1915).

References

Berger, H., (Ed.). (1995). *A William Appleman Williams reader*. New York: Elephant Books.

Blitzer, W. (2003, January 10). Search for the smoking gun. CNN. Retrieved from http://www.cnn.com/2003/US/01/10/wbr.smoking.gun

Blum, W. (2015, January 25). The U.S. and Ukraine: Dumb and dumber. *Foreign Policy Journal*. Retrieved from http://www.foreignpolicyjournal.com/2015/01/24/the-us-and-ukraine-dumb-and-dumber/

Brooke Astor, First Lady of Philanthropy, Dies. (August 13, 2007). *The New York Times*. Retrieved from http://www.nytimes.com/2007/08/13/obituaries/13cnd-astor.html?pagewanted=all&_r=0

Callahan, R. (1962). *Education and the cult of efficiency*. Chicago: University of Chicago Press.

Council on Foreign Relations. (2014). *The income inequality debate*. Retrieved from http://www.cfr.org/united-states/income-inequality-debate/p29052

Council on Foreign Relations Task Force. (2014). *U.S. education reform and national security*. Retrieved from http://www.cfr.org/united-states/us-education-reform-national-security/p27618

Defotis, D. (2015). *Gorbechev: Russia, Ukraine, and Europe risk nuclear war*. Retrieved from http://blogs.barrons.com/emergingmarketsdaily/2015/01/09/gorbachev-russia-ukraine-europe-risk-nuclear-war/

Department of Defense. (2014). *Quadrennial defense review: Executive summary*. Retrieved from http://www.defense.gov/pubs/2014_Quadrennial_Defense_Review.pdf

Dutt, R. P. (1974). *Fascism and social revolution*. San Francisco, CA: Proletarian Publishers. (Original work published 1935).

Eyerman, R. (1981). *False consciousness and ideology in Marxist theory*. Stockholm: Almqvist & Wiksell.

Felsenthal, C. (2015, February 25). Sharkey believes Chicago politics are changed. *Chicago Magazine*. Retrieved from http://www.chicagomag.com/Chicago-Magazine/Felsenthal-Files/February-2015/Jesse-Sharkey-Election/

Foster, J. B. (2014). *The theory of monopoly capitalism*. New York: Monthly Review Press.

Foster, J. B., & McChesney, R. (2012). *The endless crisis*. New York: Monthly Review Press.

Gibson, R. (1999). The Detroit teachers' wildcat strike. *Cultural Logic, 2*(2). Retrieved from http://clogic.eserver.org/2-2/gibson.html

Gibson, R. (2001). What is fascism? Retrieved from http://www.thirdworldtraveler.com/Fascism/What_Is_Fascism_Gibson.html

Gibson, R. (2006). The torment and demise of the United Auto Workers union as performed by the auto bosses, the labor leaders, counterfeit radicals, fictional revolutionaries, and all those who know they are not innocent either. *Cultural Logic, 9*. Retrieved from http://clogic.eserver.org/2006/gibson.html

Gibson, R. (2010, July). *The NEA Representative Assembly 2010: A longer view*. Retrieved from http://richgibson.com/NEA-RA2010LongerView.html

Gibson, R. (2013, October 23). The counterfeit unionism of empire. *CounterPunch*. Retrieved from http://www.counterpunch.org/2013/10/23/counterfeit-unionism-in-the-empire/

Gibson, R. (2013, March 28). Barbarism rising, Detroit and the international war of the rich on the poor. *Counterpunch*. Retrieved from http://www.counterpunch.org/2013/03/28/detroit-and-the-international-war-of-the-rich-on-the-poor/

Glaberman, M. (1997). Workers have to deal with their own reality and that transforms them. Retrieved from https://www.marxists.org/archive/glaberman/1997/xx/workersreality.htm

Hinton, W. (1966). *Fanshen: A documentary of revolution in a Chinese village*. New York: Monthly Review Press.

Hochschild, A. (2012). *To end all wars*. New York: Mariner Books.

Hunt, T. (2011). *Marx's general*. New York: Metropolitan Books.

Johnson, C. (2000). *Blowback*. New York: Holt.

Johnson, C. (2008). How to sink America. *TomDispatch*. Retrieved from http://www.tomdispatch.com/post/174884

Kehoe, A. B. (1989). *The ghost dance: Ethnohistory and revitalization*. New York: Holt, Reinhart, & Winston.

Lenin, V. I. (1915). *The collapse of the Second International*. Retrieved from http://www.marx2mao.com/Lenin/CSI15.html

Lenin, V. I. (1916). *Imperialism, the highest stage of capitalism*. Retrieved from https://www.marxists.org/archive/lenin/works/1916/imp-hsc/

Lenin, V. I. (1917). *State and revolution*. Retrieved from https://www.marxists.org/archive/lenin/works/1917/staterev

Lewis, M. (2014). *Flashboys: A Wall Street revolt*. New York: Norton.

Loewen, J. (2007). *Lies my teacher told me* (Revised Ed.) New York: Touchstone.

Lukács, G. (1971). *History and class consciousness*. Cambridge, MA: MIT Press.

Luxemburg, R. (1900). *Reform or revolution*. Retrieved from https://www.marxists.org/archive/luxemburg/1900/reform-revolution/ch05.htm

Luxemburg, R. (1913). *The accumulation of capital* (Chapter 27, The Struggle Against Natural Economy). Retrieved from https://www.marxists.org/archive/luxemburg/1913/accumulation-capital/ch27.htm

Magdoff, H. (1978). *Imperialism: From the colonial age to the present*. New York: Monthly Review Press.

Marx, K. (1845). *The German ideology*. Retrieved from online at https://www.marxists.org/archive/marx/works/1845/german-ideology/ch01b.htm

Marx, K. (1967). Address of the Central Council to the Communist League. In F. Bender, (Ed.) *Karl Marx: Essential Writings*. New York: Harper Torchbooks, (Original work published in 1850).

Marx, K., & Engels, F. (1848). *Communist manifesto*. Retrieved from https://www.marxists.org/archive/marx/works/1848/communist-manifesto/ch02.htm

Mills, C. W. (1948). *New men of power*. Urbana: University of Illinois Press.

Moore, M. (2013). JP Morgan gives Dimon 70% raise to $20 million. *Bloomberg* News. Retrieved from http://www.bloomberg.com/news/articles/2014-01-24/jpmorgan-increases-dimon-s-total-pay-to-20-million-for-2013

Newport, F. (2014). 42% of Americans are Creationists. Gallup Poll. Retrieved from http://www.gallup.com/poll/170822/believe-creationist-view-human-origins.aspx

Paine, T. (1794/95). *Age of reason*. Retrieved from http://www.ushistory.org/paine/reason/singlehtml.htm

Perlman, F. (1984). *The continuing appeal of nationalism*. Retrieved from https://libcom.org/library/continuing-appeal-nationalism-fredy-perlman

Peterson, B. (2015, February 13). Social justice unionism. *Washington Post*. Retrieved from http://www.washingtonpost.com/blogs/answer-sheet/wp/2015/02/13/how-teachers-unions-must-change-by-a-union-leader/

Peterson Foundation. (2014). *U.S. defense spending*. Retrieved from http://pgpf.org/Chart-Archive/0053_defense-comparison

Pew Research Foundation. (2015). *Religious hostilities hit six year high*. Retrieved from http://www.pewforum.org/2014/01/14/religious-hostilities-reach-six-year-high/

Phillips, E. (2014, April 9). We need to talk about the test. *The New York Times*. Retrieved from http://www.nytimes.com/2014/04/10/opinion/the-problem-with-the-common-core.html

Pilger, J. (2015, February 27). *Why the rise of fascism is again an issue*. Retrieved from https://zcomm.org/znetarticle/why-the-rise-of-fascism-is-again-the-issue/

Queen, G. (2014). Class struggle in the classroom. In E. W. Ross (Ed.), *The social studies curriculum: Purposes, problems, and possibilities* (pp. 313–334). Albany: State University of New York Press.

Reich, W. (1970). *The mass psychology of fascism*. New York: Touchstone.

Reisnikoff, N. (2014). *NEA leader inherits tensions*. MSNBC. Retrieved from http://www.msnbc.com/msnbc/incoming-nea-head-inherits-tension-arne-duncan

Risen, J. (2015). *Pay any price, greed, power, and endless war*. New York: Houghton Mifflin.

Rogan, E. (2009). *The Arabs: A history*. New York: Basic Books.

Ross, E. W. (2010). Clockwork: Taylorism and its continuing influence on work and schooling. In E. Heilman (Ed.), *Social studies and diversity teacher education: What we do and why we do it* (pp. 33–37). New York: Routledge.

Ross, E. W., & Queen, G. (2013). "Shut up. He might hear you!" Teaching Marx in social studies education. In C. S. Malott & M. Cole (Eds.), *Teaching Marx across the curriculum: The socialist challenge* (pp. 203–228). Charlotte, NC: Information Age Publishing.

Samuels, D. (2014). How Osama Bin Laden outsmarted the U.S. and got what he wanted. *Tablet*. Retrieved from http://tabletmag.com/jewish-news-and-politics/160156/how-bin-laden-won

Scipes, K. (2005, July 19). Free labor from the empire. *MRZine*. Retrieved from http://mrzine.monthlyreview.org/2005/scipes190705.html

Slahi, M. (2015). *Guantanamo diary*. New York: Little Brown.

Sorkin, A. (2009). *Too big to fail*. New York: Viking Press.

Szymanski, A. (1978). *The capitalist state and the politics of class*. Cambridge, MA: Winthrop.

Taibbi, M. (2009). *The great derangement: A terrifying story of war, politics, and religion*. New York: Spiegel and Grau.

Twenge, J., & Campbell, K. (2010). *The narcissism epidemic: Living in the age of entitlement*. New York: Atria.

Watanabe, T., & Becerra, H. (2006, March 26). 500,000 March in Los Angeles. *Los Angeles Times*. Retrieved from http://articles.latimes.com/2006/mar/26/local/me-immig26

Wierson, M. (2013). Is the U.S. consumerist society flawed by design? *Market Realist*. Retrieved from http://marketrealist.com/2013/09/u-s-consumerism-economy-flawed-design/

Wolfenstein, E. (2003). *Psychoanalytic-Marxism: Groundwork*. New York: Guilford Books.

EIGHT

Class Struggle and Education: Neoliberalism, (Neo)conservatism, and the Capitalist Assault on Public Education

Dave Hill

Neoliberalism and (Neo)conservatism

Neoliberalism—marked, *inter alia,* by the marketization, commodification, degradation, managerialization, and privatization/pre-privatisation of public services (Giroux, 2004; Harvey, 2005; Hill, 2013a, b; Hill and Kumar, 2009; Hill and Rosskam, 2009)—does not come unaccompanied. It usually has a twin—neoconservatism—albeit, a twin with which it has an often fractured relationship (Gamble, 1988). As Saad-Filho puts it,

> In essence, neoliberalism is based on the systematic use of state power, under the ideological guise of 'non-intervention', to impose a hegemonic project of recomposition of the rule of capital at five levels: domestic resource allocation, international economic integration, the reproduction of the state, ideology, and the reproduction of the working class. (Saad-Filho, 2011)

The strength of the neoliberal alliance with (neo)conservatism, with conservative forces, is particularly strong in Turkey, where the Erdogan government is very nakedly pushing forward with Islamicization of society and the education system, and with brute use of the repressive apparatuses of the state—as seen in the summer 2013 national police brutality against the Gezi Park resistance movement. Thus, in Turkey, neoliberalism is accompanied by traditionalist, Islamic conservativism in and through the ideological state apparatuses of the media, the mosque, and the education system, accompanied by the naked use of the repressive state apparatuses—such as the bullets, tear gas, and chemically treated water cannon used across Turkey through summer 2013.

Today we have been experiencing both neoliberalization and neoconservatization in England, in Europe generally, in Turkey, and globally. There are, of course, resistances within neoliberalized states, and also isolated states resisting neoliberalism, such as the governments and states of Cuba and Venezuela. Britain, in contrast, with the United States, is and has been one of the centers of this neoliberal/neoconservative transformation of economy, society, and of education.

It is important to make clear that neoliberalism is simply the latest stage of capitalism. It is current capitalism. This article is written as a critique of neoliberal capitalism and its (neo)conservative allies. But, importantly, this critique is, *in essence*, a critique of capitalism itself, of capitalist economic relations, of capitalist social relations, of the capital-labor relation. Removing neoliberalism and (neo)conservatism, for example through social democratic reforms may lead to a more compassionate society with some valuable welfare, workers' rights reforms and even a slight equalization of income and wealth and power in society. But such reforms, while, to repeat, hugely valuable, will not remove class exploitation by the capitalist class of the labor power of the working class.

One purpose of this article is to show, to warn of what a neoliberal/neoconservative future might look like as it develops. National capitalism in Turkey is already adopting and adapting the neoliberal Anglo-Saxon model of profiteering and privatization, of diktat and control, of increasing immiseration and degradation of public services, public service workers, and those in society dependent on public services (Hill, 2012a, 2013b).

Neoliberalism and (Neo)conservatism and the Nature and Power of the Resistance

The paths of neoliberalization and (neo)-conservatism are similar in many countries. But each country has its own history, has its own particular context; each country has its own balance of class forces, its own level of organization of the working class, and levels of confidence within the working class and within the capitalist class. In countries where resistance to neoliberalism is very strong, as in Greece, then the government has so far found it actually very difficult to engage in large-scale privatization. When the Greek government tries to privatize public-sector activity, the ports, the buses, the trains, the museums, and so on, these efforts are met with general strike. In Greece, working-class consciousness and class organization, in a situation of naked class war from above, are highly developed.

But in some countries, where trade-union resistance and working-class organizations' resistance are historically very weak, for example, Ireland and the United States, then neoliberalism and the capitalist class have an easier path. There has been little resistance even to extreme measures taken by, for example, recently in Wisconsin, the state government's passing a law that made it illegal to negotiate with trade unions. In other words, it has said there would be no more collective bargaining with trade unions. There were major demonstrations, and trade union protests—but the law passed, even if it did electrify the left and the trade union movement in the United States.

To leftists in Britain this was incredible, in the sense of it being hard to believe. Although there has been as succession of neoliberal and neoconservative governments in Britain both Conservative and New Labor, the trade unions still have great strength. The Trade Unions

Congress (TUC) in Britain has around six million members. On October 20, 2012, 150,000 of us went on the march in London against austerity. That followed on from the student and worker marches against education cuts of 2010 and 2011.

When the organized working class wakes up, then we can take very strong action. But some trade-union leaders sometimes live comfortable lives; sometimes they have good relations with the government and are incorporated into the (capitalist) state apparatuses. Not all the trade-union leaders are radical. However, some union leaderships are Marxist. In Britain the Communist Party of Britain has some power in unions at the top level; so does the Trotskyist group called the Socialist Party, the Committee for a Workers International, and so does the Socialist Workers Party. And of course, socialists and Marxists are very active within the membership of trade unions, pushing the leaderships into more radical action. The power of the organized working class, if spurred into action, can have very considerable impact. We hope in Britain to have a general strike against "Austerity Capitalism." We (Marxists, activists) are working toward that. This would be only the second general strike in British history, the first since 1926.

Levels of resistance vary much in different countries. In Portugal, for example, recently there were one million on strike, one million in demonstrations. That is in a small country of eight million people. In Ireland, there are very small demonstrations. The most noteworthy action in Ireland against austerity and neoliberalism was one worker driving his big digger truck into the gates of parliament.

Levels and types of resistance against neoliberalism and austerity capitalism in the United States, England and Wales (Canaan et al., 2013), Greece, Ireland, and Turkey (Inal & Ozturk, 2013) are described and analyzed in great detail from a Marxist perspective in the chapters on resistance in *Immiseration Capitalism and Education: Austerity, Resistance and Revolt* (Hill, 2013b).

The Neoliberal/Neoconservative Education Revolution in Britain

Education and other public services in Britain have been subject to neoliberalization since the Margaret Thatcher (Conservative Party) governments of 1979–90, in particular with the Education Reform Act of 1988. This established classic neoliberal policies of prompting the marketization of schooling (through so-called "parental choice" and through "league tables" of schools, whereby the exam results and academic test results of each school are published in league table format). It also (together with the 1986 Education Act and subsequent legislation) changed the composition of school-governing bodies, adding "business" governors, and reducing the numbers and influence of governors appointed by locally democratically elected councils. And under the "Local Management of Schools" (LMS) section of the 1988 act, local authority/school district influence was further weakened when most budgetary control was handed to school head teachers/principals and governing bodies (Ball, 1990; Hill, 1997, 2001).

Since Margaret Thatcher's governments of 1979–1990, successive Conservative (1990–1997 under John Major), New Labor (1997–2010 under Tony Blair and Gordon Brown) and Conservative–Liberal Democrat Coalition (2010–present under David Cameron) governments have intensified the neoliberalization of schools and of universities dramatically, alongside cuts in funding.

One notable recent cut in public expenditure was (from September 2011) that of EMAs, "education maintenance allowances," paid to young people aged 16–19 from poor families, of (usually) £30 a week, to encourage them to stay on at school. I benefited from a similar scheme in the 1960s; one of my grandsons received an EMA, 2006–2009. For university students the free university education that, I, for example, received has been replaced by the imposition of annual university tuition fees of (usually, currently) £9,000 per annum (see Hill, 2010a). (The New Labor government of Tony Blair, abandoned free university education and introduced university tuition fees in 1998.)

Ideologically these neoliberal developments such as marketization and the introduction of "New Public Managerialism" (management methods drawn from private enterprise) can be interpreted as "the businessification" of education (Rikowski, 2002, 2003, 2007), the softening up, the preparation for the wholesale privatization of schools, vocational colleges (called, in Britain, further education colleges), and universities.

Currently (2013) there is only one private university in Britain, but degree-awarding powers have been granted to a number of other organizations, and the current Conservative–Liberal Democrat Coalition government in Britain is planning more private universities. It is, indeed, likely that in the fairly near future, some currently public/state universities in Britain will become private, bought and sold on international stock markets by transnational corporations and hedge funds. Ball (2012) is very clear on such developments, regarding schools, colleges, and universities, detailing such developments in Britain and globally. This development was warned about/foreseen by Rikowski (2003) and Hirtt (2004). Hirtt warned, in 2004, about state education provision and state health provision being "the last great El Dorados" for capitalist privatization and profit from public-sector-provided services.

Marketization/Competition/Choice: "Parental Choice," League Tables, and High-Stakes Testing

Let me now go into more detail about some of the main aspects of neoliberalism, marketization, and privatization/ pre-privatization in schools and universities in Britain (or, to be more precise, England. Wales, Scotland, and Northern Ireland have a degree of autonomy/self-government regarding education policy and provision).

With schools there is now a system of market competition between individual schools. Under the 1944 Education Act, which the Thatcher 1988 Education Act replaced, local authorities/school districts (which were directly elected) had allocated children/students to schools, sometimes taking into account a degree of parental choice, but sometimes attempting to ensure that within a largely "comprehensive"/all-ability intake of students, there was a mix of students of all "bands" of ability/attainment (Hill, 1997, 2001), what in the United States is termed all "tracks" of students.

The conservative governments in Britain, those of Thatcher (1979–1990) and of John Major (1990–1997), introduced and extended what they termed "school choice," or, more specifically, "parental choice." However, in such systems it is not the parents who choose; it is the (more prestigious, "high attaining") schools that choose the children/students, the "preferred" children/students being those with high test scores and "acceptable" (high status, "middle class") cultural capital (Gewirtz et al., 1995; Gillborn & Youdell, 2002; Weekes-Bernard, 2007; Sellgren, 2013).

This has led to considerably increased hierarchy and elitism within the state education system, elitism that is social class based, and also based on ethnicity (Weekes-Bernard, 2007).

This leads to much increased hierarchy and elitism within the state education system, elitism that is "raced" social-class based. The Academies Commission Report of January 2013, *Unleashing Greatness* (Academies Commission, 2013) says it has received numerous submissions suggesting that academies are finding methods to select "covertly," that some academies may "covertly" select pupils by using extra information on families or holding social events with prospective parents (Sellgren, 2013). The report says it has received evidence that some popular schools, including academies, attempt to select and exclude pupils, despite the fact that the government admissions code says that schools cannot interview children or parents, or give priority to children whose parents offer financial or practical support (Sellgren, 2013).

That is one aspect of the neoliberalization in schooling, a class-based increased hierarchicalization of schools. And this choice is facilitated by the creation of the league tables of schools and of universities, league tables of schools (and universities) sorted by exam results, by "high-stakes testing." (It needs noting that this discussion is about state schools, that is, publicly funded schools. In the UK, 93% of school pupils/ students attend state schools, with 7% attending private schools.)

Neoliberalism requires that in a market, it is necessary to be able to test the efficiency and value of the products. In England there is now a very rigid system of testing children at different ages, even when they first enter the schools. That could be either at age four or five. As result of the assessment results of the children, there becomes a league table in every municipality; in every part of the country, in every area, there are league tables of schools. It is "middle-class" parents who have the means, the cars, the ability to pay transport costs, to take their children to the schools that have higher results, which may be some distance away.

As a result of "parental choice" and published/public league tables, there has been a notable increase in differentiation between the high-achieving schools and low-achieving schools. In Britain 13% of children have "free school meals" (FSM); the poorest 13% have free dinners at school. I did when I was a boy. If we look at two maps in England, the map showing who receives free school dinners, and the map of exam results, the maps are virtually identical. The map showing assessments at tests and exams, the map of high and low attainment on school tests, mirrors the map of the existing income inequality.

Privatization/Pre-Privatization of Schooling: Academy Schools (State-Funded Schools Managed and Controlled by Corporations)

In Britain, the government is engaging with schools on a program of pre-privatization, setting up a so-called "academy system" where numerous state schools remain state funded, and within the state system, but are re-designated as "academies." Thus, in the school sector, state-funded schools are actually being handed over to private companies, to chains of schools, to a variety of religious organizations, to become "academies" (formerly known as City Academy Schools) (Beckett, 2007; see also Benn, 2011; and Anti-Academies Alliance, n.d.). These schools (currently more than half of all state secondary high schools, and increasing numbers of primary/elementary schools) are taken away from democratically elected local authority/school district control and residual funding, to become quasi-independent schools, actually receiving their funding directly from central government. At the stroke of a ministerial pen they could easily, at some stage, become fully independent, fully private schools, offered for sale on the market.

An academy school is where government gives to any religious group, Muslim, Jewish, Christian, or to any rich businessmen or businesswomen, for example, and can say, "Look, have this school, you can call it and name it with your name, after your wife or your business/company. You can name it, and then you can have control over the school! You can appoint a majority of the governors, the people who run the schools, people who oversee the head teacher. You can ultimately change the contracts of the teachers. You can change the skill mix of staff, that is, the numbers of fully qualified teachers, and the numbers of less-well-qualified (and much-lower-paid) 'teaching assistants.' You can have fewer teachers and more teaching assistants. You can change the length of the school day and you can change the curriculum." If you want much more religion, for example, fundamentalist religion, more fundamentalist Christian religion, then the government says that is fine.

This, academy schooling, is an aspect of pre-privatization. At the moment all these academies are "not-for-profit" organizations. At the minute, in England, those who control schools cannot make a profit from actually running schools. But the new "owners" can pay themselves inflated salaries and award contracts for services such as cleaning services to their friends and business associates. (See Hill et al., 2013 for detail on this). We can also look at the United States, where there are charter schools, and we can see that some of them are "for profit," with multinational and national capital companies/corporations making profits from running state schools!

Neoconservatism

Neoconservatism here refers first to "order and control" and second to "traditional morality." The systematic use of state power referred to by Saad-Filho at the beginning of this article is the use by governments of the repressive state apparatuses such as law, the police, the judiciary, the security services, the armed forces, and the surveilling and intimidatory forms of management control within institutions and places of work. As Althusser (1971) noted, the repressive state apparatuses have ideological functions and impacts—and these currently reinforce the individualistic, competitive, commonsense pro-capitalist ideology (Gramsci, 1971) and serve to naturalize capital, rendering capitalist economic relations and capitalist social relations, and making the Capital-Labor relation seem only natural.

Concerning the "traditional morality" aspect of neoconservatism, this varies in space and time, from country to country and at different periods. It generally, but not always, includes a veneration of the family and heterosexual relationships. This varies, so for example, the current British prime minister is socially liberal, in contrast to his "Victorian morality" enthusiast predecessor, Margaret Thatcher, and in contrast to Erdogan, the current, conservatizing prime minister of Turkey.

However, a second aspect of conservatism and neoconservatism is that, universally, it involves and seeks to enforce an acceptance of elitism and hierarchy—and of one's place in that hierarchy. That hierarchy is "raced" and gendered, a racial hierarchy, and a gender hierarchy as well as a social class hierarchy (Hill, 2013a).

Neoconservatism in England

Neoliberalism is often but not always accompanied by neoconservatism. Because the capitalist class, and the governments they control, have to make sure that this freedom in the market is controlled, in Britain the Thatcher government in the 1988 Education Reform Act instituted a national curriculum. Prior to 1988, schools and local education authorities (LEAs)/school districts had considerable autonomy over curriculum design and also teaching methods/pedagogies. However, the national curriculum for state schools—and the accompanying assessments—are quite rigid, and it is a conservative curriculum. Margaret Thatcher herself looked at some of the curriculum proposals and said "No, that is too liberal." She herself changed the curriculum (Hill, 1997). That is an element of state control, control of the free market: an example of where neoliberalism, "free choice," is accompanied by state supervision/control, and a rigid control of the curriculum for state schools. Not, interestingly, for private schools. They decide their own curriculum. (In Britain, the 7% of children who go to private schools are overwhelmingly middle class and upper class. Almost 100% of the ruling capitalist class send their children to elite private schools.)

For teachers and schools, the (privatized) school-inspection system, the Office for Standards in Schools, Ofsted, has changed from its (pre-1988) role of "light touch"/supportive school inspection to its current, feared, draconian role with regularly used powers to close what it regards as "failing" schools and/or force them to become Academies—often against the wishes of parents, teachers, and governors (Anti-Academies Alliance, n.d.; Benn, 2011; Local Schools Network, n.d.).

And for radical and critical educators in general, those of us trying to engage in "deep critique" (Rikowski, 2008) of capitalism, of capitalist economic, social, and political relations, and how these operate within schools and universities, there is often marginalization, non-promotion, dismissal, pressure to conform to, to comply with pro-capitalist norms in ideology. And there is the pressure of performativity, of the endless form-filling and surveillance and control of teachers.

Neoconservatism in Turkey

The Islamicization of Turkey's social and education systems may be described, in relation to jihadi Islamicization in Pakistan, Afghanistan, Somalia, Mali, Egypt, for example, as "soft İslamicization." There are no beheadings, amputation of limbs, widespread killings of religious minorities.

But for those choking on tear gas in Istiklal Street and Gezi in Ankara, or in Kezilaye in Ankara (as I was, accompanied by brave comrades from leftist movements in Turkey) or for those tragically killed and blinded by Turkish police in recent demonstrations, there is nothing soft about the state repression of dissent by the Turkish government. In Turkey, neoliberalism is accompanied by a conservatization of society and education, backed up by police batons. It may not be of the same nakedness and institutionalized brutality as during the Turkish military dictatorship. But what is happening now is perhaps even more dangerous. In schools for example, the new curriculum, introduced by the AKP government, including, for the first time since the Kemalist revolution nearly a century ago, the study in schools of two hours a week on the Koran, and two hours a week on the life of Muhammed is, for leftists and secularists (and liberals) very worrying. İt is very convenient for capitalism if major sections of the population start to become more religious, more subservient to the afterlife, more subservient to conservative morality as opposed to Marxist collectivist morality.

I am also very well aware that leftists in schools and universities in Turkey feel pressures—not so much in the largest, most prestigious universities, but in small universities. Numerous comrades have told me of the increasing official pressures against them because of their Marxist/Communist beliefs. In the small universities, I have comrades who are saying it is much more difficult for them to teach critical pedagogy, for them to teach Marxist analysis of society. This is a dangerous, repressive development. Fevziye Sayilan and Nuray Turkmen describe and analyze in detail this neoliberalism and neoconservatism in Turkish society and education (Sayilan & Turkmen, 2013).

> In the last decade, Islamic conservatism has left its mark….Public education has evolved dramatically under siege by both religion and market. While on the one hand the subsidy for public education has been gradually reduced, private schools and universities are encouraged and as a result, education and schools have accorded with the class and status structure of capitalism more clearly than the previous period. On the other hand, the content/curriculum and structure of education have been Islamized. Today the integration of Turkish capitalism with global capitalism has been largely completed. The economy has been restructured to provide the terms of the expansion of capital accumulation. Over a period of more than thirty years, schools and universities have been the most affected areas by all of these changes….In this process, the basis of relatively democratic society, which was formed on the basis of the relationship between the state, market and society, has also dissolved. Accordingly, the modernist ideology (scientific, secular and co-educational) that created a historically dominant philosophy of education in Turkey is also undergoing a major change.

Fevziye Sayilan and Nuray Turkmen continue,

> As in the rest of the world, marketization of education was realized in both hidden and open ways (see Ball & Youdell, 2007). Privatization and commercialization policies in education have openly focused on reducing state subsidies for the financing of public schools, using the subsidies, instead, in favour of private schools, and charging families for education at every level under the name of 'contribution' (Ercan, 1998; Gök, 2004; Sayilan, 2006; İnal, 2012). The education share of national income continued to decrease (Ercan, 1998; Kurul, 2012).

Sayilan and Turkmen further continue,

> The other face of educational inequality is the growing inequalities between schools. Insofar as much as the financing of schools and education is left to the families, the inequality between the elite state schools and ordinary state schools with regard to the quality of education and the learning environment has also increased. Furthermore, private schools, because of their having infrastructure, proper learning environment and social facilities, cause the increase of inequality between private schools and ordinary state schools. As a result of these policies, the schools became ever more openly characterized by their social class characteristics. So neoliberalism consolidates the reproduction of capitalist social relationships through education and schools.

It is of course what the U.S. government and transnational/national capitalist classes want. The U.S. and multinational capital are very happy now to work with pro-business, pro-neoliberal—what they regard as "moderate İslamic"—states. The United States has clearly seen Turkey as a possible future model for Egypt, and Libya. It is notable in Egypt, where the strong trade unions and workers' organizations have a long history, that one of the first acts of the so-called "democratic" new Egypt was to attack trade union rights and trade unionists, a policy continued by the new post-Morsi military dictatorship. For the United States for capitalism, nothing must get in the way of the reproduction of capitalist social relationships and capitalist economic relationships.

Schools and Universities as Ideological State Apparatuses: Stimulating Individualistic Competitive Entrepreneurship in Schools and Universities

In many countries there is now in schools and universities an emphasis on designing, applying, and updating education and school teaching programs that seek to develop and stimulate students to develop very specific values/value systems. In some U.S. states these values are Christian fundamentalist, socially illiberal, and economically individualistic. In Turkey, religion plays a similar role. While the values are Islamic and specifically Turkish and Islamic conservative, the same partnership thrives—the partnership between social illiberalism and conformity with economic individualism. In Britain, the hold of religion is very weak; it is a far more secular society than the United States or Turkey. The specific value system being advanced by governments is for students to become individualistic, entrepreneurial, and competitive. For example, some British universities now have institutional targets such as "at least 7% of students will go on to set up their own business."

This is very good demonstration of what Louis Althusser (1971) wrote about education being one of the major ideological state apparatuses. The major ideological state apparatuses are the capitalist-controlled mass media and the (again, capitalist-controlled through governments of political parties bankrolled by capital) state education systems. In every capitalist country, and in England, capitalists have an ideological agenda. Children are told to be competitive, individualistic; children are told to set up businesses, to value moneymaking, and "the spirit of enterprise." This is against leftist notions of collectivity, solidarity, public service, and public good.

Effects of Neoliberalism and Conservatism on Teachers in Schools: Managerialism, Surveillance, and Control

Neoliberalism is enforced through increased forms of surveillance and control in society, such as, for example, by the importation into public services, such as education of "new public managerialism"—more brutalistic, finance-driven, authoritarian forms of management (Beckmann & Cooper, 2004; Beckmann, Cooper & Hill, 2009; Deem, 1998). Public services, such as schools and universities, are increasingly run in accordance with the principles of "new public managerialism based on a corporate managerialist model imported from the world of business. As well as the needs of Capital dictating the principal aims of education, the world of business also supplies the model for how it is to be provided and managed." (Beckmann & Cooper, 2004).

Stevenson (2007) is one of many analysts (see also Lewis, Hill, & Fawcett, 2009) who note that:

A key feature of current school-sector reform in England is the restructuring of teachers' work and the increased use of support staff to undertake a range of activities previously undertaken by teachers. Supporters speak of a new teacher professionalism focused on the "core task" of teaching. Critics fear deprofessionalization through a process of deskilling, work intensification, and labor substitution.

Stevenson continues, describing a:

…relentless drive to raise productivity, teachers have often found themselves the victims of unwelcome change in which they have had their professional judgment curtailed, witnessed the increasing managerialization of the educational process, and been subjected to ever more forensic scrutiny of their work by external agencies (Ball, 2003)….These developments have inevitably affected the work pressures on teachers and resulted in an intensification of the labor process of teaching. (Smyth, Dow, Hattam, Reid, & Shacklock, 2000).

In the section below I use some primary research about "teachers' work" carried out between September 2012 and January 2013 by James Lloyd Hill, who has worked in four different secondary (high) schools in England (Hill, J., 2013).

James quotes a colleague who:

…summarized her view of being a teacher as 'you're not a teacher anymore, you're someone who works in a school'—she's been teaching 6 months, and was backed up by another colleague in the room with 12 years teaching experience behind her. The same teacher also said 'I didn't get into teaching to deliver lessons which are already pre-planned for me which I have to follow, or teach subjects which I never trained for and to only deliver other peoples' resources, I wanted to inspire them to learn History' (her subject).

James's view is that:

It seems to me the ability (time/insight) to inspire is taken up with filling in tracking data, data in-putting, filling in spreadsheets when homework has been set, making sure your room is not untidy for fear of senior management noticing and 'having a word'. The extra work that teachers now have to do has very little to do with the delivery of lessons, but ticking the boxes which senior management feel they should have ticked, in case Ofsted come calling. There is a lot of talk among heads of department about 'how can we show this?' and 'where's our evidence for that?', and as a result, we don't hear as much of 'I think I'm going to try this with that group of students'.

This view exemplifies research carried out by MacBeath in 1995 (p. 12), not long after the National Curriculum and its testing and surveillance regime came into operation. MacBeath quotes a student teacher as saying "I used to feel that this school cared about how well I was doing. Now I just think it cares about how well **it's** doing."

James continues,

I'm not suggesting that as teachers we are not accountable for students' attainment in our lessons, but there is a limit on our ability to be accountable, and certainly a limit on how that accountability is tracked; lesson plans, intervention documentation by teachers—what have you done about student x, y and z? Why are they still failing?! Documentation on each student, and each aspect of a student accounted for on your lesson plan (such as average reading age; SEN status; Gifted and Talented status; preferred learning style (VAK), learning goal; current grade.

James talks not just of the intensification of accountability, but of a managerial culture of control and fear:

> The voices of the Unions are quieter than they once were in schools, there are still those brave enough to speak out on behalf of those who must not be named to senior management, even though they do ask 'and who thinks that?' but more recently it has had to be a case of safety in large numbers. We had a Joint Union meeting of the NUT (National Union of Teachers) and NASUWT (National Association of Schoolmasters/Union of Women Teachers) where we agreed on 'work to rule' principles the unions had set out, but the added pressures being placed on staff meant that we signed a petition. One member of staff set it up, and had to guarantee at least 60 signatures before he would show it to the head. Staff feel they can be got rid of so easily now. Having spoken to a Union leader in the school, she said staff are just too afraid to speak out now, because they know that if senior management want rid of you, they can do it now.
>
> Senior management can observe you with their performance management duties (in some schools this may be once a year, in this, once every term). There are the 'learning walks' where they can 'pop into' your lesson (for however long they choose—this may have a different label, but it has the same effect on their view of your teaching, and your anxiety levels). There are also 'book looks', which have always been done, but now they must be standardized (making sure there are comments on how students can improve, and asking a 'Learning Development Question', which the students must answer. This is to tick another box in case Ofsted arrive). And the over-riding view of the reasons for many of these quality initiatives is that if Management want you out, they will force you out with the amount of pressure they will place on you from the observations, or you will slip up in an observation, which can then be used against you.
>
> I was observed on a learning walk by a member of senior management, she came in as the class was doing an activity, there was music on in the background, I was sat at my desk looking over a student's book. The member of staff left after a few minutes. At the end of the day I received an email from my head of department, who had received an email from the senior management observer. It was a complaint that I hadn't got up and gone over to greet her at the door. She didn't see the reason why I was playing that music and so therefore thought it questionable. The fact I was sat at my desk also gave her cause for concern, especially as another member of staff had also seen me sat at my desk once when they had walked past my classroom and looked inside through the window in the door.
>
> This type of micro management is something you may expect from working in a cubicle in an office. How teachers relate to students, how they engage them, is being written out in a memo, so Ofsted can tick it off.

MacBeath (1995) is among many who note that:

> ...inspections carry high stakes for schools and teachers and where the press for accountability overshadows the improvement motive. It also assumes that inspectors are able not only to 'see' schools as they are but are able to tell the story in ways that depict the complexity, vitality and dynamic of a school's character. Snapshots are by nature limited by both frame and focus.

James continues,

> You hear they're (Ofsted) in the area, you panic. They call, you plan like you've never planned before (because it's impossible to do that amount of planning for 9 different teaching groups who you see at least 2/3 times a week, with the amount of detail the school thinks Ofsted

require). They observe your lesson: the students are amazing, because there's a new person in the room who looks important. Your nerves are hanging by a thread because you don't know if you've demonstrated 3 levels of progress in the 15 minutes the inspector has been in your room (possibly not, because they came in right in the middle of the activity). By the end of the lesson, the students may have learnt something, but if it hasn't been measured by the inspector, you're not a 'good' teacher. So you'll be observed again, and again, and again.

Resistance, Critical Education, and Critical Educators

Critical Education and Critical Educators

In schools, colleges, and universities, many radical and Marxist critical educators try to affect four aspects of learning and teaching, asking questions about (at least) four aspects (see Hill, 2012b, 2012c). Some critical educators question the teacher-centered *pedagogy*, the pattern of teaching and learning relationships and interaction, and try to use democratic participative pedagogy that breaks down patterns of domination and submission and listens to children's, students', and local communities' voices—but not uncritically. This is no uncritical, postmodernist, or liberal, uncritical acceptance of polyvocality. Critical Marxist educators engage in critique that frames educational experiences within the conditions of capitalism and its current neoliberal form. Critical Marxist educators also attempt to utilize different types of pedagogy in teaching, to engage in non-hierarchical, democratic, participative teaching and research, while by virtue of their role in actually teaching, may maintain an authoritative stance where appropriate. Such approaches are rooted in social constructivist Vygotskyan understandings of learning, and are also aimed both at producing co-learning, by teachers as well as students, and at overtly welcoming and valuing more cultures than are commonly valued in a transmission mode of teaching. Of course critiques of over-dominant teacher-centered pedagogy are not restricted to Marxist educators. They are also made by liberal-progressive, child/student-centered educators and by some conservative educators, concerned about teaching effectiveness and preparation for the workplace.

But critical education is about far more than pedagogy (Hill, 2014). Indeed, it takes place outside schools and universities, as well as inside (Hill, 2012a, 2013a,), as the rise of alternatives to the English university indicates. (Canaan et al., 2013; Hill, 2013b). There is educational resistance outside the state-controlled education structures, in connection with the teach-ins at Tent Cities, a Free University movement, and through oppositional media and cultural workers, as well as within trade union and student groups.

A second question Marxists can and should ask is about the *curriculum*—who selected the content and how rigid is it? Even where the curriculum is very tightly controlled, even where it is very rigidly prescribed, there are, as Gramsci taught us, always spaces, little spaces for us to infiltrate, to use, to colonize. For example this can be seen in the teaching schools, prisons, youth clubs, universities and vocational colleges, and in "tent cities," teach-ins and teach-outs, and in emergent alternatives.

Marxist educators, indeed critical educators in general, can, with students, look at the curriculum and ask: Who do you think wrote this? Who do you think decided on including this in the curriculum? What do you/we think should be in the curriculum that is currently absent? Why do you think it is absent? Who do you think benefits and who loses from this curriculum?

What is the ideology behind this book/task/lesson/curriculum piece? These questions can be asked with 10-year olds, 16-year olds, 40- or 70-year olds.

However limited the spaces within a school, university, or educational site, within a curriculum, are, we can always find some possibility to question and to encourage the children/students to do this as well, so that they are, in effect, developing an awareness of what can be called "ideology critique" (Kelsh & Hill, 2006). And then we can suggest, and seek from students, an alternative, perhaps even if only for five minutes in a lesson/session. We can question existing versions of history. We can ask, Is there a different version or view of the past, the present, or the future? So, looking at the work of Marxist, Communist teachers and critical educators, we can affect the content of curriculum. If that is, at any particular time/space, almost impossible, we can seek to develop ideology critique, an understanding of the capital-labor relation, of capitalism and its relationship to education systems, of ideological and repressive state apparatuses, and of how schools and universities are shaped and controlled into producing politically and ideologically quiescent and hierarchically organized and rewarded labor power. Where Marxist educators, and revolutionary critical educators (McLaren, 2005; McLaren & Jaramillo, 2010) differ from more social democratic and liberal critical educators is in the emphasis placed on resistance and socialist transformation (Kelsh & Hill, 2006; Skordoulis & Hill, 2012; Hill, 2014).

A third question in education that critical/Marxist educators can and should ask is about *organization of the students.* How should children of different social class, gender, and ethnic backgrounds and different sexual orientations be organized within classrooms, within institutions such as schools and universities, and within national education systems? Are some groups, such as girls, such as ethnic minorities, such as the poorer sections of the working class, in fact systematically labeled, segregated, divided, demeaned? In some countries virtually all children go to the same *type* of school. But children tend to go to schools where their own class predominates. There is also a question of how the education system inculcates a differentiated sense of class awareness in working, middle, and ruling class students. And it tries to keep the working class as a working class that is obedient, subservient, individualistic, interested in only themselves not in collectivity, not in community. Marxist educators clearly prefer and work for what in Britain is called "comprehensive" schools, and in India, for example, is called "the common school." But then, even where this happens (as in Finland, where there are only a handful of private schools, where students up to the age of 16 are taught in common/ comprehensive schools in "mixed ability" classes) there are internal informal mechanisms, the hidden curriculum of differential ("raced," gendered, and "sexually oriented" expectations and responses to different cultural capitals) (Reay, 2006; Hill, 2009).

A fourth question Marxist educators ask is about *ownership and control of schools* (and, indeed, universities). Who should own, control, and govern schools, further education (vocational) colleges, and universities? Of course we cannot change the law at a stroke, but we can lead a movement that at some stage—in 2 years' time, 10 years' time, 20 years' time—the ownership and governance of schools can be changed, made democratic, and secular and can attempt to be egalitarian. Instead of, as in some countries, schools, colleges, and universities being run by a religious state, by transnational corporations (Ball, 2012), or by religious organizations themselves, by "for-profit" private companies, by companies that are in theory and public discourse not-for-profit (but that reward handsomely their executives and their friends), or schools that are run and governed by rich businessmen or women. Marxist educators (and others, of course) believe that schools, colleges, and universities should be run democratically, with education workers and students, as well as elected representatives of local communities, having powers in and over those education institutions, within a secular, democratic national framework. Explicit in this is the assertion that education is a public good and a public right that should not be distorted and corrupted by private ownership—there should be no private schools, colleges, or universities. (For an attempt to address these various aspects of education, in developing a socialist policy for education, see Hill, 2010c.)

Of course the number of critical, radical, Marxist, counter-hegemonic school teachers and university teachers is limited, and it takes courage to be one in the face of the repressive aspects (non-promotion, dismissals, harassment by management) of and within the education state apparatuses.

Educate, Agitate, Organize

We Marxists and critical educators in general seek to serve and advance the interests of the working class. We, as teachers, as educators, are working class too; we sell our labor power to capitalists and to the apparatuses of the capitalist state, such as schools and universities. We have to consistently and courageously challenge the dominant ideology, the hegemony of the ruling class, the bourgeoisie, the capitalist class. We are in a battle for dominance of our ideas; there are "culture wars" between different ways of looking at/interpreting the world. We have to contest the currently hegemonic control of ideas by the capitalist state, schools, media, and their allies in the religions. If we sit and do nothing, if their ideas are not contested, then capitalism will continue to rule, to demean, to divide, to impoverish us, and the planet.

At certain times in history, and in certain locations, the disjunction—the gap, the difference—between the material conditions of workers' existence on the one hand, our daily lived experience, and, on the other hand, what the newspapers and the media and the imam and the priest and the rabbi say/preach, that gap becomes so stark, so obvious, that workers' subjective consciousness changes. At this moment—now—in some countries in the world, the gap between the "official" ideology that "we are all in together" and that "there is no alternative" (to austerity), or in schools and universities faced by commodification and managerialism and (pre)-privatization—that gap becomes so large that the ruling party, and the ruling capitalist class, and capitalism itself, loses legitimacy. And so, as in Greece now, and in Portugal, in Spain, in Turkey and Brazil, and in other countries such as Britain, we Marxists are necessary. We are necessary in leading and developing changes in consciousness, a change in class consciousness, and in playing a leading role in organizing for the replacement of capitalism.

Program

In 1938, in "*The Transitional Program,*" Trotsky addressed the types of programs moving the discussion beyond the *minimum program* (minimum acceptable reforms, such as those to protect and improve existing rights and entitlements, such as rights at work, social and political rights) and the *maximum program* (socialist revolution, with the type of society ultimately envisaged by Marx, a socialist non-capitalist/post-capitalist society) that were advanced by late -19th- and early -20th- century social democrats and by communists of the Third International and articulated a new type of program: **the** *transitional program*. Trotsky, with a distinct resonance to today's struggles, wrote:

The strategic task of the next period—prerevolutionary period of agitation, propaganda and organization—consists in overcoming the contradiction between the maturity of the objective revolutionary conditions and the immaturity of the proletariat and its vanguard (the confusion and disappointment of the older generation, the inexperience of the younger generation). It is necessary to help the masses in the process of the daily struggle to find the bridge between present demand and the socialist program of the revolution. This bridge should include a system of transitional demands, stemming from today's conditions and from today's consciousness of wide layers of the working class and unalterably leading to one final conclusion: the conquest of power by the proletariat.

Classical Social Democracy, functioning in an epoch of progressive capitalism, divided its program into two parts independent of each other: the minimum program which limited itself to reforms within the framework of bourgeois society, and the maximum program which promised substitution of socialism for capitalism in the indefinite future. Between the minimum and the maximum program no bridge existed. And indeed Social Democracy has no need of such a bridge, since the word socialism is used only for holiday speechifying. The Comintern has set out to follow the path of Social Democracy in an epoch of decaying capitalism: when, in general, there can be no discussion of systematic social reforms and the raising of the masses' living standards; when every serious demand of the proletariat and even every serious demand of the petty bourgeoisie inevitably reaches beyond the limits of capitalist property relations and of the bourgeois state.

Trotsky continued,

> Under the menace of its own disintegration, the proletariat cannot permit the transformation of an increasing section of the workers into chronically unemployed paupers, living off the slops of a crumbling society. The right to employment is the only serious right left to the worker in a society based upon exploitation. This right today is left to the worker in a society based upon exploitation. This right today is being shorn from him at every step. Against unemployment, "structural" as well as "conjunctural," the time is ripe to advance along with the slogan of public works, the slogan of a sliding scale of working hours. Trade unions and other mass organizations should bind the workers and the unemployed together in the solidarity of mutual responsibility. On this basis all the work on hand would then be divided among all existing workers in accordance with how the extent of the working week is defined. The average wage of every worker remains the same as it was under the old working week. Wages, under a strictly guaranteed minimum, would follow the movement of prices. It is impossible to accept any other program for the present catastrophic period.
>
> [...] The question is not one of a "normal" collision between opposing material interests. The question is one of guarding the proletariat from decay, demoralization and ruin. The question is one of life or death of the only creative and progressive class, and by that token of the future of mankind. If capitalism is incapable of satisfying the demands inevitably arising from the calamities generated by itself, then let it perish. "Realizability" or "unrealizability" is in the given instance a question of the relationship of forces, which can be decided only by the struggle. By means of this struggle, no matter what immediate practical successes may be, the workers will best come to understand the necessity of liquidating capitalist slavery. (Trotsky, 1938)

The "decay, demoralisation and ruin" Trotsky speaks of are, for many millions of workers' families—including what in the United States and elsewhere are called "middle class" workers—an everyday reality in this current era of capitalism, neoliberal capitalism, or "immiseration capitalism." The precise organisation and characteristics of the resistance to the depredations is a matter for strategic and tactical considerations, relating to the current balance (strength, organizations, (dis)unity) of class forces in specific local and national contexts. What is clear, though, is that the problematic regarding capitalism, for Marxist activists and educators, is not just to reform it, welcome though such reforms, such as "minimum program," are, and active in campaigning for and to protect such reforms we must be. But, regarding capitalism, our task is to replace it with democratic Marxism.

Acknowledgments

This to thank James Lloyd Hill for carrying out a series of semistructured interviews and personal ethnography in relation to the intensification and managerialization of teachers' work.

References

Academies Commission. (2013). *Unleashing greatness: Getting the best from an academicised system*. London: RSA and Pearson. Retrieved from http://www.thersa.org/__data/assets/pdf_file/0020/1008038/Unleashing-greatness.pdf
Althusser, L. (1971). Ideology and state apparatus. In L. Althusser, *Lenin and philosophy and other essays*. London: New Left Books.
Anti-Academies Alliance. Retrieved from http://www.antiacademies.org.uk/
Ball, S. (1990). *Politics and policy-making in education: Explorations in policy sociology*. London and New York: Routledge.
Ball, S. (2003). The teacher's soul and the terrors of performativity. *Journal of Education Policy 18*(2), 215–228.
Ball, S. (2012). *Global Education Inc.: New policy networks and the neoliberal imaginary*. London: Routledge.
Ball, S. J, & Youdell, D. (2007, July). Hidden privatisation in public education. Preliminary report. *Education International* 5th World Congress.
Beckett, F. (2007). *The great city academy fraud*. London: Continuum.
Beckmann, A., & Cooper, C. (2004). 'Globalization', the new managerialism and education: Rethinking the purpose of education. *Journal for Critical Education Policy Studies*, *2*(1). Retrieved from http://www.jceps.com/index.php?pageID =article&articleID=31
Beckmann, A., Cooper, C., & Hill, D. (2009). Neoliberalization and managerialization of 'education' in England and Wales – a case for reconstructing education. *Journal for Critical Education Policy Studies*, *7*(2). Retrieved from http://www.jceps.com/index.php?pageID=article&articleID=170
Benn, M. (2011). *School wars: The battle for Britain's education*. London: Verso.
Canaan, J., Hill, D., & Maisuria, A. (2013). Resistance in England. In D. Hill (Ed.) *Immiseration capitalism and education: Austerity, resistance and revolt*. Brighton, UK: Institute for Education Policy Studies.
Deem, R. (1998). 'New Managerialism' and higher education: The management of performances and cultures in universities in the United Kingdom. *International Studies in Sociology of Education, 8*(1). Retrieved from http://www-e.unimagdeburg.de/evans/Journal%20Library/New%20Education%20Market/Deem%20New%20Managerialism%20in%20HE.pdf
Ercan, F. (1998). 1980'lerde Eğitim Sisteminin Yeniden Yapılanması: Küreselleşme ve Neo Liberal Eğitim Politikaları, (Restructuring of the education system in the 1980s: Globalisation and neo-liberal education policies). *75 Yılda Eğitim. (23–38)* Türkiye İş Bankası yayını. İstanbul.
Gamble, A. (1988). *The free society and the strong state*. Basingstoke, UK: MacMillan.
Gewirtz, S., Ball, S., & Bowe, R. (1995). *Markets, choice and equity in education*. Milton Keynes, UK: Open University Press.
Gillborn, D., & Youdell, D. (2002). *Rationing education: Policy, practice, reform and equity*. Milton Keynes, UK: Open University Press.
Giroux, H. (2004). *The terror of neoliberalism: Authoritarianism and the eclipse of democracy*. Boulder, CO: Paradigm.
Gök, F. (2004). Eğitimin Özelleştirilmesi, (Privatization of Education). *Neoliberalizmin Tahribatı: 2000'li Yıllarda Türkiye*. (94–110) 2. Cilt. Metis Yayınları. İstanbul.
Harvey, D. (2005). *A brief history of neoliberalism*. Oxford, UK: Oxford University Press.

Hill, D. (1997). Equality in primary schooling: The policy context of the reforms. In M. Cole, D. Hill, & S. Shan (Eds.), *Promoting equality in primary schools* (pp. 15–47). London: Cassell. Retrieved from http://www.ieps.org.uk/papersdh.php

Hill, D. (2001). Equality, ideology and education policy. In D. Hill and M. Cole (Eds.), *Schooling and equality: Fact, concept and policy* (pp. 7–34). London: Kogan Page. Retrieved from http://www.ieps.org.uk/papersdh.php

Hill, D. (2009). Theorising politics and the curriculum: Understanding and addressing inequalities through critical pedagogy and critical policy analysis. In D. Hill & L. Helavaara Robertson (Eds.), *Equality in the primary school: Promoting good practice across the curriculum*. London: Continuum. Retrieved from http://www.ieps.org.uk/PDFs/Ch20HillandRobertson2009.pdf

Hill, D. (2010a). Students are revolting—and quite right too. *Radical Notes*. Retrieved from http://radicalnotes.com/journal/2010/12/03/students-are-revolting-education-cuts-and-resistance/

Hill, D. (2010b). A socialist manifesto for education. *Socialist Resistance Online*. Retrieved from http://socialistresistance.org/?p=905

Hill, D. (2010c). A socialist manifesto for education. *Socialist Resistance Online*. Retrieved from http://socialistresistance.org/?p=905

Hill, D. (2012a). Immiseration capitalism, activism and education: Resistance, revolt and revenge. *Journal for Critical Education Policy Studies*, 10(2). Retrieved from http://www.jceps.com/index.php?pageID=article&articleID=259

Hill, D. (2012b). Fighting neo-liberalism with education and activism. *Philosophers for Change*. Retrieved from http://philosophers.posterous.com/fighting-neo-liberalism-with-education-and-ac

Hill, D. (2012c). The role of Marxist educators against and within neoliberal capitalism. *Socialist Resistance. 26 Feb*. Retrieved from http://socialistresistance.org/3184/the-role-of-marxist-educators-against-and-within-neoliberal-capitalism

Hill, D. (2013a). *Marxist essays on education: Class and 'race', neoliberalism and capitalism*. Brighton, UK: The Institute for Education Policy Studies.

Hill, D., et al. (2013b). *Immiseration capitalism and education: Austerity, resistance and revolt*. Brighton, UK: Institute for Education Policy Studies.

Hill, D. (Ed.). (2014, forthcoming). *Critical education, critical pedagogies, Marxist education*.

Hill, D., & Kumar, R. (Eds.). (2009). *Global neoliberalism and education and its consequences*. New York: Routledge.

Hill, D., Lewis, C., Yarker, P., & Maisuria, A. (2013). Capitalism and education in Britain. In D. Hill (Ed.), *Immiseration capitalism and education: Austerity, resistance and revolt*. Brighton, UK: Institute for Education Policy Studies.

Hill, D., & Rosskam, E. (Eds.). (2009). *The developing world and state education: Neoliberal depredation and egalitarian alternatives*. New York: Routledge.

Hill, J. L. (2013). *Interview and personal ethnography research data gathered on secondary school teachers' perspectives on and reactions to the intensification and managerialisation of teachers' work*. Unpublished.

Hirtt, N. (2004). Three axes of merchandisation. *European Educational Research Journal*, 3(2), 442–453. Retrieved from http://www.wwwords.co.uk/eerj/

İnal, K. (2012). The educational politics of the AKP: The collapse of public education in Turkey. In K. İnal and G. Akkaymak (Eds.), *Neoliberal transformation of education in Turkey* (pp. 17–32). New York: Palgrave Macmillan.

İnal K., & Ozturk, H. T. (2013). Resistance in Turkey. In D. Hill (Ed.), *Immiseration capitalism and education: Austerity, resistance and revolt*. Brighton, UK: Institute for Education Policy Studies.

Kelsh, D., & Hill, D. (2006). The culturalization of class and the occluding of class consciousness: The knowledge industry in/of education. *Journal for Critical Education Policy Studies*, 4(1). Retrieved from http://www.jceps.com/index.php?pageID=article&articleID=59

Kurul, N. (2012). Turkey under AKP rule: Neoliberal interventions into the public budget and educational finance. In K. İnal & G. Akkaymak (Eds.), *Neoliberal transformation of education in Turkey* (pp. 83–94). New York: Palgrave Macmillan.

Lewis, C., Hill, D., & Fawcett, B. (2009). England and Wales: Neoliberalised education and its impacts. In D. Hill (Ed.), *The rich world and the impoverishment of education: Diminishing democracy, equity and workers' rights* (pp. 106–135). New York: Routledge.

Local Schools Network. Retrieved from http://www.localschoolsnetwork.org.uk/campaigns/transparency-academies-freeschools/page/3/

MacBeath, J. (1995). *Self-evaluation and inspection: A consultation response for the National Union of Teachers*. London: National Union of Teachers. Retrieved from http://www.teachers.org.uk/.../Future_of Inspection-MacBeath_response.d

McLaren, P. (2005). *Capitalists and conquerors: A critical pedagogy against empire.* Lanham, MD: Rowman & Littlefield.

McLaren, P., & Jaramillo, N. (2010). Not neo-Marxist, not post-Marxist, not Marxian, not autonomist Marxism: Reflections on a revolutionary (Marxist) critical pedagogy. *Cultural Studies—Critical Methodologies, 20*(10), 1–12.

Reay, D. (2006). The zombie stalking English schools: Social class and educational inequality. *British Journal of Education Studies, 54*(3), 288–307.

Rikowski, G. (2002). *Globalisation and Education,* A paper prepared for the House of Lords Select Committee on Economic Affairs, Inquiry into the Global Economy. Retrieved from http://www.leeds.ac.uk/educol/documents/00001941.htm

Rikowski, G. (2003). *The profit virus: The business takeover of schools. The flow of ideas.* Retrieved from http://www.flowideas.co.uk/?page=articles&sub=The Profit Virus – The Business Takeover of Schools.

Rikowski, G. (2007). The confederation of British industry and the business takeover of schools. *The Flow of Ideas,* 3rd June. Retrieved from http://www.flowideas.co.uk/?page=articles&sub=The%20CBI%20and%20the%20Business%20Takeover%20of%20Schools

Rikowski, G. (2008). The compression of critical space in education today. *The Flow of Ideas.* Retrieved from http://www.flowideas.co.uk/?page=articles&sub=Critical Space in Education.

Saad-Filho, A. (2011). Crisis in neoliberalism or crisis of neoliberalism? *Socialist Register, 47.*

Sayilan, F. (2006). "Küresel Aktörler (DB ve GATS) ve Eğitimde Neoliberal Dönüşüm," (Global Actors and the Neoliberal Transformation in Education). *TMMOB Jeoloji Mühendisleri Odası. Aylık Bülten Eğitim Dosyası.* Kasım-Aralık, 44–51.

Sayilan, F., & Turkmen, N. (2013). Austerity capitalism and education in Turkey. In D. Hill (Ed.), *Immiseration capitalism and education: Austerity, resistance and revolt.* Brighton, UK: Institute for Education Policy Studies.

Sellgren, K. (2013, January 10). Academies could 'fuel social segregation.' *BBC.* Retrieved from http://www.bbc.co.uk/news/education-20960500

Skordoulis, C., & Hill, D. (Eds.). (2012). Introduction. In *Proceedings of the First International Conference on Critical Education,* 2011. Athens: University of Athens.

Smyth, J., Dow, A., Hattam, R., Reid, A., & Shacklock, G. (2000). *Teachers' work in a globalizing economy.* London: Falmer Press.

Stevenson, H. A. (2007). Restructuring teachers' work and trade union responses in England: Bargaining for change. *American Education Research Journal, 44*(2), 224–251. Retrieved from http://aer.sagepub.com/content/44/2/224.full

Trotsky, L. (1938). The death agony of capitalism and the tasks of the fourth international: The transitional program. Retrieved from http://www.marxists.org/archive/trotsky/1938/tp/tp-text.htm – m

Weekes-Bernard, D. (2007). *School choice and ethnic segregation: Educational decision making among Black and ethnic minority parents.* London: Runnymede Trust. Retrieved from http://www.runnymedetrust.org/uploads/publications/pdfs/School%20ChoiceFINAL.pdf

PART III

Social Justice Education in the Classroom

NINE

Social Justice in the Classroom? It Would Be a Good Idea

Doug Selwyn

Both class and race survive education, and neither should. What is education then? If it doesn't help a human being to recognize that humanity is humanity, what is it for? So you can make a bigger salary than other people?

—Beah Richards

More money is put into prisons than into schools. That, in itself, is the description of a nation bent on suicide. I mean, what is more precious to us than our own children? We are going to build a lot more prisons if we do not deal with the schools and their inequalities.

—Jonathan Kozol

The single largest variable that predicts SAT scores is family income. If you want higher SAT scores, you need to get your kids born into wealthier families. You know, it's great to tell kids to pull themselves up by their own boot straps, but you better put boots on them first.

—Paul Houston

Many of us begin our work for social justice in our classrooms by closing the classroom door. We know the difficult lives of some of our students: living in trailers with no heat in the middle of an Adirondack winter, eating two meals (provided by the school) a day on school days, and hoping for even one meal on weekends or during vacations; using the emergency room as their only health care; experiencing incredible stress living in families that are just getting by, or not quite getting by; caring for younger brothers or sisters while parents work an evening job, a second or third job to make ends meet; moving once, twice, or more during the school year; sleeping in cars, or living with other families in small, cramped apartments; living in neighborhoods filled with unemployment, no hope, and the consequences of those dead ends; dealing with racism, institutional and individual, that is still so obviously with us…

We do what we can, and more than we can to make the experiences of our children as positive and useful as possible, no matter what lives they live when they are not with us. We support our students to gain academic skills that we hope will help them to open doors to more education, a good work life, and that will help them to become active, responsible, and caring members of their communities. We sit with them to problem solve emotional and social problems, to balance the complexities of their lives, in school and out, and to chart out their most productive paths forward. We have done so within our classrooms or in concert with others in the building of community, focusing on what logic and experience has told us is within our power to affect change. And to do that many of us have chosen to shut our doors to the bureaucratic stone walls surrounding our classrooms, to the political "pas de duh" between (self-proclaimed) billionaire education experts and candidates running for one more office, and we shut our doors against the relentless hunt by publishing companies for profits.

The problem is that, even with our often heroic efforts to do what we can within our classrooms, things continue to get worse, and we continue to lose what little control we have now inside that closed door. As testing and the demand for accountability ramps up, as states and the feds overreach their constitutional mandates in order to take over control of the schools, perhaps on the way to dismantling them, and as more public school decision making is made by private for-profit publishing companies such as Pearson, we find ourselves clinging to a tinier and tinier piece of the education shoreline, as the waters rise around us.

It becomes more and more clear that schools do not exist in isolation, and that attempts to improve public education cannot be done by simply focusing within education. If we are to work for social justice, we are going to have to reach out to our colleagues in the school, in the district, across the state, and across the country, but also others in the communities in which we work. It is no longer enough to make things a little better in our classrooms, as the gap between rich and poor continues to widen, and the overall health and well-being of our communities is worsening. I will make the case in this chapter that the only possible response to what is happening in our communities, including our schools, is to join together to stand up for the democracy we are rapidly losing, and to recognize that the health and well-being of our children, our communities, and of our democracy are inextricably interconnected; we cannot focus on one of them without focusing on the underlying issues that govern all of them. Our work for social justice in the schools must include working for social justice within the larger society in which the schools exist.

Social Justice, the Concept

The term "social justice" is used in our school of education to describe the work we do, the direction we are working toward as we help to prepare the next generation of teachers, but I'm not sure we agree on what the term actually means, or that we all recognize the layers of meaning and the assumptions it contains. For example, consider these questions: Can there be social justice in any school or any classroom in an increasingly unequal society? Is it possible to recognize inequality outside of school and still assume that we can bring social justice by educating all children such that they are operating on a level playing field within the walls of the school? Are we serving our students and working toward social justice if we are teaching our students so that they pass the standardized tests that allow them to move on and graduate if we also know those standardized tests are actually destroying public education, and compromising those students as people who can think critically and ethically? Who benefits from public schools, and at what cost? Are schools serving as gatekeepers that help to maintain the status quo?

It may be a fool's game to attempt to land on one definition for social justice since it is a term/phrase used by many people in many different ways, but sampling a number of definitions leads to some common features. Most seem to include several of the facets identified by the Center for Nonviolence and Social Justice in their definition, in which they state that social justice:

> "…embodies the vision of a society that is equitable and in which all members are physically and are psychologically safe. Social justice also demands that all people have a right to basic human dignity and to have their basic economic needs met. Our commitment to social justice recognizes that health is affected by a host of social factors. It is not possible to address trauma and violence without also wrestling with poverty, racism, sexism, classism, homophobia and all other forms of stigma. Because of this, we cannot ignore deep seated inequalities as we seek answers to problems like violence and trauma…" (Center for Nonviolence and Social Justice, 2014).

When we talk about social justice in the classroom we have to begin with the recognition that our children are not living in an equitable society, and that children cannot come to school equally ready to learn, given the inequities of the system. When politicians, venture capitalists, and the Secretary of Education advocate the use of standardized tests and a Common Core curriculum so the children in rural Louisiana, or Mississippi, or upper upstate New York have the same educational experience and opportunity as those children living in Westchester, New York, or Grosse Point, Michigan, we know that politics and economics are the lenses through which they are looking; there is nothing standardized or common about the ways in which our children are living. In fact, as education researcher Jerry Bracey said many years ago, there is no such thing as a standardized child, which brings the lie to any notion of a standardized test. The fight over standardized testing, over the Common Core curriculum, and over the value of teachers takes place between those who actually know teaching and learning, and those who make the unsupported (and unsupportable) claim that all is equal (or can be made equal) within the schoolhouse, that good teachers can miraculously make up for the extreme inequalities of our society, and that we can legitimately compare the experiences of children across the country as a meaningful exercise. It is a lie and one that is used to batter and defame teachers and public education.

Where We Are

We are, as a society, experiencing a health crisis, and our children are suffering increasing challenges that show up in statistics in many different areas. The United States is perhaps the richest nation in the history of the world, and yet 22% of children, approximately 16 million children, lived in poverty in 2010. Between one fourth and one fifth of children in the United States go to bed hungry. In statistics compiled by the Southern Education Foundation, in 40 of the 50 states, low-income students comprised no less than 40% of all public schoolchildren. In 21 states, children eligible for free or reduced-price lunches were a majority of the students in

2013, and more than half of all public school students are currently living in poverty (Southern Education Foundation, 2014).

In a piece written nearly 15 years ago, I likened the experience of children in public school to European American "settlers" getting ready to head west from Independence, Missouri in 1840. Here's what I wrote back then:

> Picture the K-12 educational experience as a journey akin to traveling the Oregon Trail in 1840. Students enter kindergarten in Independence, Missouri, and the plan is for them to exit in the Oregon Territory (at twelfth grade). The only thing that matters on this journey is whether they arrive at appointed checkpoints at the appointed times. Our directive (teacher as wagon master) is to make sure the wagons reach Colorado (for example) on a certain Tuesday in May.
>
> There are many factors that are not considered as the wagons head west towards that checkpoint in Colorado. Some students are rolling along in well-oiled wagons pulled by teams of healthy oxen, while others are pulling the wagons themselves. Some are riding in wagons with only three rusted wheels, and some are walking. Some have twenty people in their wagons, including cousins, neighbors, grandchildren, or friends. When those sitting at the checkpoints fill out their reports, they do not mention that some travelers started in Independence, Missouri, some in Philadelphia, Pennsylvania, some in chains on plantations in the south, and others from across the Atlantic or the Pacific. The reports note simply who came through the checkpoint, and when they arrived.
>
> We educators are given conflicting sets of directions. We are cajoled and inspired by experts in the various disciplines to help our students to fully experience and understand the road they are traveling. We must begin with the first step of the journey, they say, wherever it is, and move at a pace appropriate to the conditions. We are encouraged to work with our students in various configurations, considering the ways that they learn, the experiences they have had, and the demands of the discipline; our work is to integrate the students and the curriculum. It is heady work and takes time. And we have to arrive in Colorado by 4:00 on Tuesday. No excuses. (Selwyn, 2000)

Sadly, the situation today is worse than it was in 2000, when the article was written, preceding No Child Left Behind, Race to the Top, Common Core, and the hysterical demands for increased accountability. The gap between the rich and poor in this country, the growing inequality between the rich and poor is approaching the greatest it's ever been, which guarantees that there can be no real justice for our children, inside or outside of schools no matter what heroics occur in classrooms.

Poverty and Rising Inequality Lowers All Boats

Researchers Richard Wilkinson and Kate Pickett, in their book *The Spirit Level*, present compelling evidence that increasing levels of poverty and inequality are having a significant impact on the health and well-being of all in our society, most specifically on our children. Wilkinson and Pickett have identified the destructive impact that rising inequality within societies has on the health of all, though they are clear that the most significant impact is on those who have the least. Their data focus on a wide range of categories, from infant mortality and health, through physical health and life expectancy, mental health and drug use, educational performance, teen pregnancy, violence, and imprisonment. Their thesis is clear; societies that are more equal experience better health across the board. Overall health is worse the more unequal the society, state, or nation. The data are consistent across virtually all health categories, and are consistent across countries and states. As our society has become more unequal, our health has worsened. One of the most significant factors in the state of health of an individual or a community is the stress in which the people live. Chronic stress is often debilitating, and it can be fatal. Wilkinson and Pickett are clear that there is much greater stress in unequal communities, and the consequences are, among other things, compromised health.

Stress

One of the most significant contributors to the overall health of individuals and communities is stress. Clinicians from the Mayo Clinic recognize the significant difference between our reaction to an immediate perceived threat and chronic stress.

> When you encounter a perceived threat — a large dog barks at you during your morning walk, for instance — your hypothalamus, a tiny region at the base of your brain, sets off an alarm system in your body. Through a combination of nerve and hormonal signals, this system prompts your adrenal glands, located atop your kidneys, to release a surge of hormones, including adrenaline and cortisol.
>
> Adrenaline increases your heart rate, elevates your blood pressure and boosts energy supplies. Cortisol, the primary stress hormone, increases sugars (glucose) in the bloodstream, enhances your brain's use of glucose and increases the availability of substances that repair tissues.
>
> Cortisol also curbs functions that would be nonessential or detrimental in a fight-or-flight situation. It alters immune system responses and suppresses the digestive system, the reproductive system and growth processes. This complex natural alarm system also communicates with regions of your brain that control mood, motivation and fear….The body's stress-response system is usually self-limiting. Once a perceived threat has passed, hormone levels return to normal. As adrenaline and cortisol levels drop, your heart rate and blood pressure return to baseline levels, and other systems resume their regular activities.
>
> With chronic stress, a person constantly feels under attack, and the fight or flight reaction stays turned on. The long-term activation of the stress-response system — and the subsequent overexposure to cortisol and other stress hormones — can disrupt almost all your body's processes. This puts you at increased risk of numerous health problems, including anxiety, depression, digestive problems, heart disease, sleep problems, weight gain, and memory and concentration impairment. (Mayo Clinic, 2015)

University of Washington physician Stephen Bezrushka says that chronic stress (that never turns off) turns out to be responsible for half of the diseases of modern society, from diabetes, to high blood pressure to heart attacks. Stress debilitates, and it can be a killer, and as our society becomes more unequal, more of our families are living with chronic stress (Bezrushka, 2005).

Poverty and Stress

There are some segments of our population that are more likely to be living under chronic stress, brought on by factors ranging from the struggle to meet their basic physical needs on a regular basis (food, clothing, shelter, sleep), their emotional needs, their economic needs, or the stress of living within environments filled with danger, unemployment, hopelessness, drugs, and toxic waste, and the toxicity of racism....A study carried out to assess the impact of the financial crisis of 2008 on children began by looking at the impact of previous financial crises. They found that:

> There is sufficient accumulated evidence from previous crises showing that exposure to situations of deprivation and increasing social inequalities are damaging to children's health in the short and long term....This is likely to impact on the most vulnerable groups in both industrialized and developing countries. The poorest populations from urban areas are the most vulnerable to food insecurity and malnutrition. In developed countries, children living in families without resources or without social protection mechanisms due to austerity measures are at greater nutritional risk, including both obesity and under nutrition. The results of the present review highlight the potential nutritional risk for the most vulnerable populations (Rajmil et al., 2008).

Poverty has recently been found to actually bring changes to the brain itself. Carolyn Gregoire reports that a major new study of the effects of family income and parental education on child and adolescent brain development has found significant differences in the brain size of children living in different income brackets. Gregoire says that:

> The researchers studied nearly 1,100 individuals between the ages of 3 and 20, collecting data on their socioeconomic situation and conducting MRI brain scans and cognitive tests measuring executive functions like self-control and anticipation of consequences....The results revealed a strong positive association between family income and brain surface area, largely in those brain areas that are linked to skills instrumental in learning and academic success.

Gregoire reports that the researchers found that the brain of a child living in poverty is about 6% smaller in surface area than the brain of a child living in a high-income family, and that the most dramatic differences were found in children living in poverty. Gregoire says that the differences in brain size are most likely due to better nutrition, health care, schools, play areas, air quality, and other environmental factors (Gregoire, 2015).

Further research is also now showing that poverty not only changes the brain, but it also changes the way we think. In a story reported on NPR, scientists found that the stress of dealing with the consequences of poverty is often so intense that it can overwhelm a person and preclude thinking about anything else. Correspondent Laura Starecheski quotes Princeton psychologist Eldar Shafir, who calls this problem bandwidth poverty. He says, "When you're bandwidth poor, you're thinking about how to pay for food and make rent today — and it's almost impossible to think about the future." Dr. Shafir says that the poor are often judged for being myopic—for not saving money for the future, or not making better decisions. But what looks like short-sightedness from the outside is actually bandwidth poverty, trapping people...in the moment to such a degree that they literally can't think about the future (Starecheski, 2014).

Race, Poverty, and Stress

The American Psychological Association has linked chronic stress to the experiences of those who have experienced discrimination due to race, sexual orientation, economic hardship, and environmental degradation. Here are a few highlights of what they found:

- Perceived discrimination…has been found to be a key factor in chronic stress-related health disparities among ethnic/racial and other minority groups.
- African Americans, Native Hawaiians, and Latin Americans have been impacted greatly by hypertension and diabetes due to chronic stress resulting from discrimination.
- Stress due to experiences of racism can contribute to adverse birth outcomes, when combined with the effects of general and maternal stress.
- Perceived discrimination/racism has been shown to play a role in unhealthy behaviors such as cigarette smoking, alcohol/substance use, improper nutrition, and refusal to seek medical services.
- Perceived discrimination has been shown to contribute to mental health disorders among racial/ethnic groups such as Asian Americans and African Americans.
- Socioeconomic status and environmental stress has been found to contribute to many health disparities among ethnic/racial groups.
- Acculturation stress is the stress that accompanies efforts to adapt to the orientation and values of dominant culture. It can have an influence on physical and mental health disparities such as hypertension and depression.
- Acculturation stress was found to be significantly associated with substance dependence and anxiety disorders.
- Empirical studies on immigrant adolescents and the children of immigrants found that acculturative stress increased depressive symptoms.
- Regardless of age at immigration, foreign-born women experience more depressive symptoms than native-born women during early adulthood.
- Daily stress, associated with lower social position and poor family functioning, can lead to adverse health outcomes (American Psychological Association, 2015).

There is substantial evidence to show that the most significant period of a person's life is the time from pregnancy through the first two or three years. What happens during that time period really sets the stage for the rest of that person's life. Writing for the Urban Child Institute, Barbara Holden Nixon says that stress has a lasting effect on a child's development. She reports that

> "…the brain is the primary stress organ. It is responsible for activating, monitoring and shutting down the body's reactions to stress. Infants' developing brains are particularly vulnerable; babies are affected by stress even in the protective environment of the womb. Since maternal cortisol levels affect the developing fetus, a mother's level of stress is directly related to the well-being of her baby….Toxic stress increases the risk of preterm delivery, low birth weight and other complications. It is also associated with impaired mental, behavioral and motor development in infancy."

She defines toxic stress as "persistent, unhealthy amounts of stress caused by chronically stressful conditions without the protective benefits of healthy caregiving. These stresses can eventually cause permanent damage…" (Nixon, 2012).

Dr. Bezrushka, from the University of Washington, in talking about the impact of the early years on adult health, says:

> "The lower down you are in society's pecking order, the lower your income, status, wealth, job rank, education level, skin color, accent, the more cortisol you produce….The science is clear:

we are not all born equal. Those from more disadvantaged early life situations are already slated to be less healthy at birth and to become sick later. This is evident from their having low birth weights and being born prematurely which are both highly correlated with adult disease. All this happens before birth (Bezrushka, 2005).

Schools, Poverty, and Stress

We can't ignore the increased stress and anxiety experienced by the children we teach who grow up in poverty, and who experience the inequalities mentioned in the previous sections of this chapter. This stress has an impact on their health, on their ability to concentrate and learn, and on their sense of whether education will make any difference in their futures, in their sense of hope and possibility. Teachers can have a significant impact on what happens in children's lives, but they are only a small part of the picture.

David Berliner, professor emeritus at Arizona State University, has spent much of his career devoted to the issue of poverty and its impact on education. He has found that what happens in schools cannot be divorced from the larger lives that children lead. Berliner identified the most significant factors that influence student performance in school, and found that many of them are located outside of school. He notes that while schools can make some difference, they cannot fully mitigate what happens outside of school. The out of school factors that he identifies are: low birth weight and non-genetic prenatal influences on children; inadequate medical, dental, and vision care, often a result of inadequate or no insurance; food insecurity; environmental pollutants; family relations and family stress; and neighborhood characteristics. What ties most of these factors together is poverty. And what also ties these factors together is that they all relate to student health, whether students are coming to school ready and able to learn, or whether their health has been irreparably compromised by factors out of the control of schools or teachers (Berliner, 2009).

Public Schools Are Not All Created Equal

Public schools are dealing with nearly the full range of students living in the United States, from the wealthy to the poorest of the poor. They receive a certain amount of money from the state to educate each student, and additional local moneys, raised through property taxes, parent teacher organization fundraisers, grants, and other sources. There is quite a wide gap in the money raised and available in different communities such that some schools have more than twice the money per student to spend on students in a neighboring community. This also leads to a significant difference in the education experienced by the students in different schools.

In 1980, Jean Anyon wrote that it was a mistake to talk about public schools as if they were in any way comparable to each other. She found that there was not one public school system, but several systems serving different members of our society differently, with a different sense of mission in each.

Anyon found that the schools located in the poorest communities were training their students to follow instructions, to do as they were told, to read just enough to follow directions. Students leaving these schools might be educated to work in convenience stores, stockrooms, gas stations, or other menial positions. She found that the children of middle class families were trained for jobs that ranged from skilled, well-paid workers such as printers, carpenters, plumbers, and construction workers to middle level white-collar jobs, such as women in office jobs, technicians, supervisors in industry, and city workers such as such as firemen, policemen, and teachers.

The children of those in the top economic class, which she labeled the capitalist class, were being trained to be owners, decision makers, and "the deciders." Children in those schools were not spending their days filling out mind numbing worksheets and prepping year round for standardized tests. These differences in schooling are even truer today than they were 35 years ago, when Anyon was writing. Today's leaders make sure to have their children attend schools that will groom them for leadership (Anyon, 1980).

Chicago mayor Rahm Emanuel, for example, has chosen to send his children to the University of Chicago Lab School, a private school that does not have students take high-stakes tests. The Lab School has seven full-time art teachers to serve a student population of 1,700. By contrast, only 25% of Chicago's "neighborhood elementary schools" have both a full-time art and music instructor. The Lab School has three different libraries, while 160 Chicago public elementary schools do not have a library.

Writer Mike Elk quotes the director of the Lab School, David Magill, as saying on the school's website in February 2009 that:

> "Physical education, world languages, libraries and the arts are not frills. They are an essential piece of a well-rounded education." Magill also is quoted as saying, "Measuring outcomes through standardized testing and referring to those results as the evidence of learning and the bottom line is, in my opinion, misguided and, unfortunately, continues to be advocated under a new name and supported by the current [Obama] administration. (Elk, 2012)

The irony of Emanuel sending his children to a school that does not administer standardized tests while sentencing all of Chicago's public school children to a system centered on high-stakes standardized tests is not lost on former Chicago Teacher's Union President Karen Lewis.

> The new mayor seems to recognize how school funding impacts school quality. We understand why he would choose a school with small class sizes, a broad rich curriculum that offers world languages, the arts and physical education, a focus on critical thinking not test-taking, a teacher and an assistant in every elementary classroom, and paid, high-quality professional development for their teachers.... It's wonderful that he has that option available to him. (University of Chicago Lab Schools, 2011)

Schools and Social Justice

Public schools have been labeled as institutions that level the proverbial playing field, that help address the inequalities that mark this society, beginning with Horace Mann in the middle 1800s. At that time, Mann, often referred to as the father of public education, said, "Education then, beyond all other devices of human origin, is the great equalizer of the conditions of men, the balance-wheel of the social machinery" (Mann, 1849). He also noted that the role schools played as an investment in the health of society was crucial. "Jails and prisons are the complement of schools; so many less as you have of the latter, so many more must you have of the former." Looking on the current statistics related to prisons in the United States, where more are imprisoned than anywhere else in the world, it serves as a stimulus for asking about the role that schools are playing now. If so many are in prison, was Mann wrong, or has the role of schools changed?

One of the prevailing myths of the United States is the myth of Horatio Alger, the self-made man who pulls himself up by his bootstraps. The myth is that anyone can grow up to be president, or at least very successful. In *The Spirit Level*, Wilkinson and Pickett show that the Horatio Alger myth is just that: there is less movement from poverty to wealth in the United States than in virtually any other society. Those who grow up in unequal societies have a more difficult time climbing out of their low status than is true for those living in more equal societies. Schools have been sold to us as the avenue out of poverty, but Wilkinson and Pickett make clear that there is very little traffic along that road. What this also means is that the cycle of poverty, chronic stress, diminished health, and a life compromised by prison or an early death is passed on from generation to generation.

What Does This Mean?

If we are finding that more and more of our children are suffering from the consequences of food insecurity, a lack of health care, neighborhoods containing toxic chemicals (disproportionately positioned in communities of color and other underrepresented populations), and living in families overwhelmed by stress, why is it we are choosing to worry about their test scores, rather than their health? Why are we deciding as a society, to ignore the factors undercutting the health and potential of our young people and demanding that our educational system focus its considerable energy and resources on raising scores on standardized tests as a means to the end of bringing our children closer to equality across the board? Will that focus on test scores offer the prospect of greater equality to the full range of students with whom we work? Is it enough to worry about how we can help them to raise their test scores, or is it more important to help to make changes so that more of our children are healthy? I would clearly argue for the later, and want to turn more directly to that topic.

Health, Well-Being, and Social Justice

So what would it look like if we steered our decision making by the twin stars of social justice and the health/well-being of our children? It would have to be an effort that reached beyond any one classroom or teacher, no matter how skilled or committed. It would take a community, the proverbial village focused on "the vision of a society that is equitable and in which all members are physically and are psychologically safe. Social justice also demands that all people have a right to basic human dignity and to have their basic economic needs met. Our commitment to social justice recognizes that health is affected by a host of social factors." This suggests that a community focus on health and well-being would be a good place to start our efforts at bringing social justice to our classrooms and neighborhoods.

I interviewed a number of teachers, parents, social workers, doctors, and students to get their help and perspectives on what we might mean by the term health, especially as it pertained to school aged children. Health was a complex concept for my informants, comprised of physical, social, psychological, and, for some, spiritual health. They began with physical health, which by consensus they defined as more than the absence of disease. They spoke to characteristics including energy, a curiosity to explore, to question, to know about the world. They said healthy children were resilient, able to deal with frustration, and able to deal with others. Finally, healthy children were willing and able to learn because they were willing to risk, to try new things, and willing to learn from their efforts.

They talked about children who felt safe and secure in the world, who were comfortable with themselves, and who were not afraid to make mistakes and to learn from them. Children who were able to be with others and with themselves, who had hope for their future, and a confidence that they would find their place in the world.

When I asked about those factors that contributed to, or undermined health, there were again several areas of agreement. Crucial elements include the consistent involvement and support of family, or at least one adult who absolutely loves and stands with them. Healthy children need adequate food, sleep, shelter, opportunities to learn and grow, and adults who model how to take advantage of those opportunities. Children are most likely to be healthy if we communicate to them a feeling of belonging, of value, of belief in the possibility that there is a valued place in the world for them. This focus on the health and well-being of children also means that, in classrooms, we offer them every chance to succeed, to learn through their strengths and interests even as they are supported to develop their weaker areas of learning.

Many of the steps we need to take to bring a more just, healthy, and supportive community is beyond the reach of any one school or even school district. We have to take steps to support all members of the community, to narrow the gap between the rich and poor, with particular focus on those who are living in poverty. We can't expect our children to come to school ready to learn if they do not have enough to eat, do not have secure and consistent housing, and lack sufficient health care. We can't expect them to be ready to learn if they are living in chronic stress caused by dynamics within the family (often the consequence of living in poverty), or within the community, often the consequence of poverty and a sense of hopelessness. If we truly want to work toward social justice we need to focus on the larger societal issues in which we all live. There are, however, several steps schools can take to reduce the debilitating stress experienced by their students. Some of these steps can happen within the classroom, some within the school and/or district, and some can be the consequence of schools working with their communities. I will explore the steps we can take in classrooms and schools briefly, as they are relatively clear, and have been taken in some locations already, and then will take more time to explore some actions that schools can take with their communities.

Within Classrooms

Teachers do extraordinary things to reduce the stress and anxieties of their students, and to create safe, secure, and supportive learning environments. They create classroom communities that emphasize sharing, mutual support, an environment that welcomes and values all students. They establish firm and clear expectations that students will act with respect and appreciation for all in the room; put downs and discriminatory acts and statements are not allowed, and all are expected to work with each other.

Further, teachers take the time to get to know their students, their ways of knowing and learning, their interests, their home situations, and to find ways to offer as much support as they can. This can range from making sure there is a time and place for students to do homework if that is not possible at home, to finding ways to provide school supplies, winter clothing, nutritious food, connections to community resources, books, and anything else students need. Teachers also make contact with families to figure out how they (teachers and families) can work together to provide a good educational experience for the child. This often involves ways of supporting the adults in families who have their own needs and challenges. Supporting the adults is often a necessary step toward making sure the student has all the support that is possible.

Within classrooms, teachers also offer students an engaging and relevant curriculum that helps them make connection between what is happening in their own lives and communities and what is happening in schools. Teachers offer students an opportunity to learn through their strengths and interests even as they are also supporting students to develop their skills and confidence in learning through areas that are not so strong. Repeatedly forcing children to run into their own particular brick walls as learners does service to no one, as it serves no one to raise your voice in hopes of communicating more effectively with someone who does not speak your language. Teachers offer their students a safe place to risk, to try new things, to explore new territory, to learn to deal with change, with frustration, and with the process of learning. We all learn in fits and starts; picture the way a young child learns to walk or talk. There are many missteps and mistakes along the way, but through supportive trial and error, through nurturing feedback, through observation and modeling, the child learns to walk and talk. This is how we all learn, and to pretend it is a straight line forward, that happens on a pre-set schedule, is to misunderstand and/or misrepresent reality. Good teachers know this and create learning environments that support all learners where they are, and offer them the tools and room to grow starting from where they are. These steps bring social justice into the classroom.

Within Schools

Schools provide resources to support what goes on in any classroom. Specialists include special educators, librarians, nurses, occupational and physical therapists, psychologists, nurses, translators, family support workers, food service personnel, and others, all of whom contribute to the well-being of students in the building. In ideal situations the relevant personnel get to know the students and families within their buildings and coordinate to get students what they need. Administrators can play a strong role in this, as they organize the resources in their buildings to maximize the focus on meeting student and family needs.

Schools operating within more stressed communities often need to play larger roles in meeting the needs of students and families, and that is complicated by the fact that schools operating in those communities often have fewer resources themselves, as there is less money available through local taxes. Still, there are steps that the school can take, and there are steps that the school district can take, from allocating resources to the ways in which they administer and support schools to make a difference.

Schools and Community

There are significant questions that communities, states, and the federal government need to consider regarding education. What does it mean to be educated in 2015, and what should it mean as we continue on in the 21st century? What should students know and be able to do to best prepare them for their future lives? Do schools in their present form make sense going forward, or are there other designs, other structures that might better serve the needs of learners? Who should be the decision makers with regard to education, and what is the balance of power and involvement among the various stakeholders and constituents, including the local school boards, administrators, teachers, students, parents/families, and the state and federal authorities. How will those charged with administering education interact with other agencies and departments at the local and state level to coordinate services and resources to best serve the children? These questions are complex and will not be resolved quickly, but it is important that conversations about them are started, with parents, teachers, administrators, community members from all involved groups, and, when appropriate, the students.

There are other actions the schools and communities can take together without waiting for resolution of those larger issues. Schools working with the communities in which they are located can make a difference in supporting the health and well-being of the students, teachers, and families in those communities, with particular attention on actions aimed at reducing the chronic stress experienced by many in the poorest communities. Chronic stress, as we have seen, is often debilitating, dispiriting, and destructive, and leaves students feeling hopeless and powerless.

Schools and communities can do much together, from findings ways to use the schools to support the larger population of the community by concentrating needed resources and services as multi-service centers so that parents and families can find many supporting services on the same physical site that the school is located so that they do not have to run all over town for the things they need. Childcare can be offered at schools so that parents and family members could volunteer at the school, or be free to find their own work or schooling. Families can become more involved in the life of the classroom, and classrooms can use more of the community as an extension of their own classrooms. The place in which the school resides can become a focus of study so that all children learn more about the place they share, and can appreciate the many facets of where they live, moving past judging toward an understanding of why things are the way they are. They can also identify and work together to make changes in their shared environment, appreciating the value of community and experiencing a sense of efficacy. Elders can share their stories and help students know the history of the town through their eyes, and the students can offer the elders their attention and eagerness to hear and learn. There are ways in which all can work together to clean up and maintain the common spaces in the community, can plan and create new spaces that will better serve those in town, can work in community gardens producing food for those in need.

High-Stakes Testing, Stress, and Community Action

But little or none of this work will be done, or even considered until there is clarity and resolution to the intertwined issues of high-stakes testing, the Common Core, school funding, and decision making is addressed and resolved. In the past two decades, schools have been turning into test prep factories and all available resources have been mobilized to insure that as many students as possible pass the yearly English Language Arts (ELA) and math tests given toward the end of every school year. That is now the sole measure of whether a student has been successful, and the rubric by which schools and teachers are judged as effective, or not, and the results of these tests are the basis for making high-stakes decisions about children, about programs, about schools, and about budgets. Schools are not like they were when many of us went to school; they are not even what they were 10 years ago, and those changes have not been for the better. Classrooms, hallways, and homes are now filled with stress, frustration, anger, and fear, brought on by these changes, and those who are feeling the changes most are the children most in need of the love, support, and welcome of the school community.

Standardized Testing and Stress

The current educational reform movement has high-stakes testing at its center; all decisions are made based on the scores that students receive on two standardized tests taken at the end of each school year, from third through eighth grades. All decisions about teachers, administrators, schools, school budgets, and even who gets to make decisions are tied to those test results; nothing else matters, which brings incredible stress to the entire community, considering the enormous consequences involved. The tests are controversial to many; they are seen as developmentally inappropriate, riddled with errors, incredibly expensive, and inappropriate for use in making high-stakes decisions. Children spend their entire year being prepared to take these standardized tests, and spend six days or more actually taking the tests. Some have gone so far as to label this as child abuse.

This statement from The National Center for Fair and Open Testing (Fairtest) makes clear many of the concerns about using standardized tests in a high-stakes manner:

> Testing experts and the test-makers themselves have consistently warned against using standardized tests for high-stakes decisions such as graduation or retention, or to hire, fire, or reward teachers (AERA, 2000). The tests provide only a snapshot of a limited range of knowledge and skills, so they can provide only limited information to teachers. Because the tests are not designed to determine teacher effectiveness, no accurate conclusions can be drawn about an individual teacher from her students' test scores. Research indicates that a teacher's impact on student learning cannot be reliably isolated from the myriad other factors that impact student learning (FairTest, 2013).

Students and Stress

Daniel Edelstein quotes Scott Paris, a professor of psychology at the University of Michigan, who speaks on the impact of the increased emphasis on high-stakes testing. "This tendency has forced teachers at all grade levels to orient students to performance goals and comparative standards of excellence instead of internal mastery goals." The emphasis on external goals, Paris suggests, has created an unhealthy classroom scenario in which "standardized tests provoke considerable anxiety among students that seems to increase with their age and experience." Edelstein also quotes Nicky Hayes, editor of *Foundations of Psychology*, saying that common responses to "exam stress" include disturbed sleep patterns, tiredness, worry, irregular eating habits, increased infections, and inability to concentrate. Students are actually learning less due to the chronic stress they are experiencing under the high-stakes testing regime. Researchers studying cognitive impairment report decreased memory capacity in stressed individuals. Studies employing Magnetic Resonance Imaging (MRI) technology also indicate that chronically stressful conditions correspond with selective atrophy in the human brain (Edelstein, 2000).

Rebecca Klein reports on a survey done by the NY State Parent Teacher Association that shows students are more stressed than they have ever been. The survey shows that 78% of students who have special needs or who have received special services for various reasons are more stressed than they have been in recent years, and 75% of all children are more stressed than they have been (Klein, 2014).

This level of stress is most intensely felt by those who struggle with academics or with the school culture to begin with, and those who come to school already stressed due to out-of-school factors mentioned earlier in the chapter, and this extra level of stress is compromising their health, their ability to learn, and their sense of well-being. And so are their teachers.

Steven C. Ward (2015), professor at Western Connecticut State University, wrote that "The 2012 MetLife Survey of Teachers found that teacher job satisfaction declined from 62% of teachers feeling 'very satisfied' in 2008 to 39% by 2012. This was the lowest in the 25-year history of the survey. The survey also showed how stressed teachers in America were. It found that over 'half (51%) of teachers report feeling under great stress several days a week,' an increase of 70% from teachers reporting stress in 1985. "Ward goes on to say that general estimates are that nearly 50% of all teachers leave the profession within five years.

It is also clear that the high-stakes approach and the hyper focus on accountability is having a dramatic impact on those who are choosing to come into education; applications to teacher education programs are down across the country. As these young people choose other professions, and as our current teachers retire, who will teach the next generations of public school students? It is a question.

How Did We Get Here? A Brief Overview

The federal government was not really involved at all in education until the Supreme Court intervened in 1954 in the Brown v. Board decision desegregating schools (at least legally). The Elementary and Secondary Act of 1965 (ESEA) was part of the Civil Rights movement, and required schools to educate all students, attempting to stop the marginalizing of certain populations (particularly African American students). One of the requirements of the ESEA is that Congress must reauthorize the legislation every five years. The last time Congress did so was 2002; at that time there were significant changes made and the act came to be known as No Child Left Behind (NCLB). That law is still in place; Congress failed to reauthorize it in 2007, scared by its ineffectiveness, its price tag, and its unpopularity. No Child Left Behind brought dramatic change to education, in the form of an increased role for the federal government, mandatory high-stakes testing on a yearly basis, and a system of compliance backed up by an escalating series of punishments.

NCLB

No Child Left Behind was passed by Congress in 2002, just a few months after the 9–11 attacks on the World Trade Center. There was little debate at that time; many supporters hoped that it would bring more equity to the schooling that children were receiving as it required all students to be tested, grades three through eight, and made it law that no segment of the population could be ignored or underserved. NCLB brought yearly, high-stakes testing to public education and the demand that all students be at grade level by 2014, a demand that was clearly impossible to meet, especially because Congress never matched its demands with adequate funding. NCLB introduced an increasingly heavy hand of the federal government to public education, through the leverage of federal funding, and redefined successful education as scores on tests. It became clear that the overwhelming majority of schools and districts would fail to meet those 2014 targets, and politicians quietly walked away from NCLB, failing to reauthorize it in 2007, as was required by law; the 2002 version of the law is still in place, though it carries much less weight due to the arrival of Race to the Top.

Race to the Top was introduced in 2009, inserted into the vacuum created by the failure and semi-abandonment of NCLB. President Obama came into office with harsh words for the heightened emphasis on testing that NCLB brought to education, and vowed to change things. States were reeling from the financial crash of 2008 and many state treasuries were sitting on empty, desperate for money from wherever they could find it. The president and his secretary of education moved into this financial and educational vacuum with Race to the Top, a four billion dollar grant program that states could apply for through a lengthy, expensive, and complicated process.

In order to qualify as a Race to the Top winner, states had to agree to several requirements including: creating a data collection system that would track all students in hundreds of categories; making a link between teacher evaluations and student test scores; agreeing to adopt the Common Core state standards and the tests that would come with it; agreeing to commit to starting hundreds of charter schools within the state; changing the way that student teachers were evaluated, putting more emphasis on outside evaluators, and on testing; and agreeing to close down the lowest performing schools, or bringing in private, for-profit managers for those struggling schools.

There were several states that "won" Race to the Top grants, and as a consequence schools and districts had to almost entirely revamp their educational systems, including their basic curriculum, the ways in which teachers were evaluated, the kinds of data they collected, and how that data was managed, even as they were continuing to serve the millions of children in their schools. The irony is that it costs most districts more money to meet the requirements of Race to the Top than they receive from the grant, so schools and districts are losing money to deliver a poorer quality education to their students. What a deal! Schools found that there was even more pressure on students, teachers, and administrators to meet the high-stakes demands of the Common Core curriculum and the high-stakes tests given at the end of the year, in ELA and math, and the overwhelming stress experienced by all has led to serious consequences.

High-stakes tests and all that is connected with them has brought increasing and unavoidable stress, undermined any attempts at bringing more equity to schools and communities, and drained districts and schools of their resources, both economic and human. The obsession with testing has been so far out of control such that schools are punishing the children of families who are refusing the tests. Some follow a policy known as "sit and stare"; children not taking the test are forced to simply sit and stare while their classmates test around them. Today, as I write this, is the first day of the ELA tests in New York State and the pressures around the state are at fever pitch. Superintendents were told at a recent meeting that their jobs were in jeopardy if they were not doing everything they could to make sure that all students took the tests, and if they were not doing everything in their power to resist those who would refuse the tests. In one school, the principal brought food for those who were taking the test and pointedly refused food to those children not taking the tests; what message are we sending to our eight year old children? Some principals and state officers have resorted to threatening and lying to the public they were hired to serve, saying that their schools would be closed down if too many students refused the tests, and that the schools would lose funding. Families were told that their students would be placed into special services if there was no testing data, and in fact one of my university students has a daughter who is now receiving both special services (for students with academic needs) while she is in a program for gifted and talented learners. The town of Rochester, New York has pushed to identify teachers who are encouraging families to opt out—McCarthyism in our own time. The public has become the enemy in a fight to control what happens to our children. The pressures and punishments of high-stakes tests have transformed many who once came into classrooms full of a love of learning and a love of children into administrators seemingly willing to do anything in service to state directives to test, test, test…and to punish or be punished.

When we think about working toward social justice in our classrooms, in our schools, we have to begin with what will protect and maintain the health and well-being of our students, and to bring more equity to all of the children. Currently there is nothing more damaging to the health and well-being of our students and to public education than this obsession with high-stakes testing, and so the most productive action open to those fighting to save public education is to challenge those tests. And the most effective way to do that is to refuse the tests, to deprive states and the feds of the testing data they are using to attack teachers and public education.

Refusing the Tests: An Act of Civil Disobedience

The heart of the high-stakes testing movement is data. Data are collected or gathered on students from the moment they walk through their first public school door, and those data are kept until after the student graduates or leaves school. Once upon a time the data were kept within the school district "walls," so to speak, and were not shared with anyone outside of the district. There were and are protections in place that keep the health and family data from being shared with any third party outside of the district and limits how those data can be shared even within the district. The education reform proponents have worked to change the laws such that data, and now even personal family health and income records, student disciplinary records, and other data, once off limits, can now be shared with third parties, including for-profit corporations and companies that use that data to create educational products they sell to districts at great profit.

Why Refusals?

The refusal movement is a cooperative effort between parents and educators to deny the state the data they are using as a weapon to attack teachers and public education. Parents are properly taking the lead in this effort, for several reasons. First, it is their (our) children who are at the center of this struggle. We care deeply about them, which includes how they are educated, how they are assessed, and how they are treated. Second, parents and families can't be fired. Many educators, including teachers and administrators, have been silenced by threats of disciplinary actions, including dismissal for speaking out against the tests. Third, there are parents who have more time and energy to devote to this effort, where educators are overwhelmed by the demands of their jobs. Fourth, we will still be here, as parents, long after the so-called education reformers have moved on….

The test refusal movement is based on several very simple ideas. The first is that the data that is being collected from the tests is neither valid nor reliable. No reliable assessment expert would advocate making high-stakes decisions based on an individual test, and there are so many factors that influence a child's performance on any test on a particular day that they are anything but reliable. The tests provide no useful data to guide teaching and learning, swallow up large chunks of the school year such that children are learning less and testing more, and are being turned off as learners.

Second, the tests are created, administered, and scored by private, for-profit companies that are making enormous profits through this process. No one is allowed to see the tests or question the scoring and scaling of those tests, the cut scores are established after the tests are completed, and the overall cost of the operation is hidden. The states contract with the publishing companies (Pearson in New York) to create the tests; print and distribute the tests; score the tests; provide professional development, tutoring, and other instructional materials; and so on. They also produce textbooks closely aligned with the actual tests (sometimes actual passages from a Pearson text show up on a Pearson created test), and so districts buy those materials in hopes of better scores.

Third, they see that as the role of the testing increases, the amount of local control decreases. They hear from their children's teachers that they have been ordered to devote most of their year to test preparation in ELA and math, at the expense of social studies, science, the arts, music, recess, physical education, hands-on learning experiences, field trips, and the actual interests and questions the children bring to class. School is much less fun, much more pressured, and their children are not nearly as happy as they once were. Neither are their teachers, nor their administrators. In fact, principals and superintendents report that they have been threatened by the state department of education and by the feds; they must actively advocate for children to take the tests, and work to minimize resistance to the tests or they, the superintendents and principals, risk being disciplined or even fired.

Fourth, it has become more and more clear that, instead of closing the gap between those districts with resources and those without, the emphasis on testing has actually widened the gap, in both test scores and in terms of the actual experience of students in those districts. As mentioned earlier, students from middle and upper middle class homes and districts score higher on these tests (on average), and so schools in these settings do not have to worry so much about their overall test scores. This gives them the room to explore issues in depth, to offer many of those programs that poorer scoring schools and districts no longer offer. They also tend to retain their teachers longer, and that continuity allows for more in-depth instruction.

The fifth reason is that we all know that some students test more effectively than others, and that children from certain demographic groups (second language learners, students with special needs, students who are emotionally fragile, students who learn and communicate most effectively through other means, students who are living in poverty, or who have experienced trauma, or who are living with chronic stress, whatever the reason) will never score as highly as those who come from relative stability and privilege. Families whose children are being judged by this one measure, and teachers who saw their students, who might shine and excel in ways not measured on paper and pencil tests, recognized the injustice being carried out.

So what does it mean to refuse? Parents/families write letters to the school declaring that they are refusing to have their child take the state mandated tests (note, this does not include the regents exams in New York State): not the math, not the ELA, and not the field tests that some schools agree to give. In New York they can request that their child be scored a category 999, which means their scores do not count at all against the child, against the teacher, or against the school. The child does not write on the test booklet at all. More details about this process, the reasons for it, and the current state of things can be found at several websites, including www.nysape.org, www.fairtest.org, www.unitedoptout.org, and www.classsizematters.org.

The ELA testing is finished for 2014; with 63% of the districts across New York State reporting, more than 177,000 test refusals have been reported, and the final results are expected to be greater than 200,000. More refusals are expected in the future.

Why Parent-Led Refusals Are the Best Next Step
Let's make no mistake. Refusing the tests is only a small step to take within the larger picture of bringing social justice to our classrooms. We do need to have larger, deeper conversations about what our society should be like, about what education should look like. We need to come together to decide how we can best educate our children for their futures, and ours, how we can make sure that the focus of education is on serving individual students and the common good, and how we can organize and educate so that all students are well served, bringing more and more social justice to our commons. These are large, complex questions to take on, there are many different views on what our best directions and next steps might be, and there are powerful forces that will resist any attempt to make changes in a system that serves them at the expense of the rest of us. These questions will not be resolved soon, and the even larger questions of capitalism and the larger society in which schools and communities sit will take even longer. Our children cannot wait for these questions to be resolved before we act.

Refusing the tests costs virtually nothing; we simply do not allow our children to take the tests. We approach administrators, school boards, parent groups, politicians, the news media, and other relevant audiences to make clear that high-stakes testing is bringing great harm to our children and to public education. It is a public health issue; high stakes testing is raising the stress levels on children, educators, and families, and there is disproportionate stress felt by those in the communities already living with chronic stress. We make clear that this is a pro-schools, pro–public education, and pro-child act of civil disobedience addressed to those at the top who are ignoring the voices of families and educators who have been trying more sanctioned means of communicating with them.

Parents know their children, and know in increasing numbers that the direction education is going is raising stress levels and lowering the quality of the educational experience their children are having. Refusing the tests is an act of civil disobedience that challenges that which is causing harm. The high-stakes testing is increasing the gap between haves and have-nots, driving out those aspects of the school experience that bring most comfort, joy, and value to the students, and serves as a means by which communities lose local control over their schools.

This movement, which is growing exponentially, has also served to activate and organize parents and educators across the country. This is only the first act of a very long set of next steps as we work to reclaim and refocus public education so that it serves the needs of the students, the community, and our democracy. We are talking with each other, and today's technology allows for instant communication across the state and nation. We are many and these are our children, our teachers, our schools, and our communities. We have the most at stake, and we are not going anywhere. They are few; they have money, power, and a willingness to do what they have to do to get more money and more power, but they really don't care about either education or us; if something shinier comes along they will chase that. So, there is great potential benefit to be gained by refusing the tests, as a first step toward reclaiming our schools and our democracy. It is a step toward justice, toward bringing our schools closer to the ideal of serving the students, and working for the public good.

References

American Psychological Association. (2015). *The role of chronic stressors in health disparities among racial/ethnic groups*. Retrieved from http://www.apa.org/topics/health-disparities/fact-sheet-stress.aspx

Anyon, J. (1980). Social class and the hidden curriculum of work. *Journal of Education 162*(1), 67–92.

Berliner, David C. (2009). *Poverty and potential: Out-of-school factors and school success*. Boulder, CO: Education and the Public Interest Center & Education Policy Research Unit. Retrieved from http://epicpolicy.org/publication/poverty-and-potential

Bezrushka, S. (2005, April 19). From womb to tomb: The influence of early childhood on adult health. *Alternative Radio*. Retrieved from http://www.unnaturalcauses.org/assets/uploads/file/BEZS2-Womb.pdf

Center for Nonviolence and Social Justice. (2014). *What is social justice?* Retrieved from http://www.nonviolenceandsocialjustice.org/FAQs/What-is-Social-Justice/43/

Edelstein, D. (2000, July 12). Test + stress = Problems for students. *Brain Connection*. Retrieved from http://brainconnection.brainhq.com/2000/07/12/tests-stress-problems-for-students

Elk, M. (2012, September 11). Director of private school where Rahm sends his kids opposes testing for teacher evaluations. *In These Times*. Retrieved from http://inthesetimes.com/working/entry/13824/director_of_private_school_where_rahm_sends_his_kids_disagrees_on_standardi

FairTest. (2012). *Massachusetts statement against high stakes testing*. Retrieved from http://www.fairtest.org/massazchusetts-statement-against-highstakes-standar

Gregoire, C. (2015, March 30). Study reveals sad link between poverty and children's brain development. *Huffington Post*. Retrieved from http://www.huffingtonpost.com/2015/03/30/brain-development-poverty_n_6968758.html

Klein, R. (2012). New York students are incredibly stressed out about standardized testing, survey says. *Huffington Post*. Retrieved from http://www.huffingtonpost.com/2014/02/07/new-york-common-core-stress_n_4747863.html

Mayo Clinic. (2015). *Chronic stress your health at risk*. Retrieved from http://www.mayoclinic.org/healthy-lifestyle/stress-management/in-depth/stress/art-20046037

National Center for Education Statistics. (2015, May). *Children living in poverty*. Retrieved from https://nces.ed.gov/programs/coe/indicator_cce.asp

Nixon, B. H. (2012). *Stress has lasting effect on child's development*. The Urban Child Institute. Retrieved from http://www.urbanchildinstitute.org/articles/editorials/stress-has-lasting-effect-on-childs-development

Rajmil, L., et al. (2008). *Impact of the 2008 economic and financial crisis on child health: A systematic review* on Behalf of the International Network for Research in Inequalities in Child Health (INRICH). Retrieved from http://www.ncbi.nlm.nih.gov/pmc/articles/PMC4078594/

Southern Education Foundation. (2014). *New majority update: Low income students in the south and nation*. Retrieved from http://www.southerneducation.org/News-and-Events/posts/April-2014/Juvenile-Justice-Education-Programs-in-the-United-aspx.aspx

Starecheski, L. (2014, July 14). *This is your stressed-out brain on scarcity*. National Public Radio. Retrieved from http://www.npr.org/blogs/health/2014/07/14/330434597/this-is-your-stressed-out-brain-on-scarcity

University of Chicago Lab Schools: Rahm Emanuel's children will attend next year. (2011). Retrieved from http://www.huffingtonpost.com/2011/07/21/university-of-chicago-lab_n_906166.html

Ward, S. (2015). American teachers, more demoralized than ever, are quitting in droves. *Quartz*. Retrieved from http://qz.com/378581/american-teachers-more-demoralized-than-ever-are-quitting-in-droves/

TEN

Poverty, Politics, and Reading Education in the United States

Patrick Shannon

"We are behind" is the popular trope driving American school reform for the last three decades. From A Nation at Risk (1983) through America 2000 to No Child Left Behind (2002), Race to the Top (2009), and Common Core (State) Standards (2014), politicians, philanthropists, and pundits have pointed toward international reading tests scores to justify curriculum overhaul, more rigorous graduation standards, standardization of beginning reading instruction, tying teacher evaluations to student test scores, and national standards with national testing. We're told that American aggregate reading scores hover below those of students from other developed countries and just above those from developing countries. That relative position bodes ill for America, they say, because "whichever country out-educates the other is going to out-compete us in the future. That's what's at stake – nothing less than our primacy in the world" (Obama, 2010).

But the trope is only half correct. Some Americans—just over half (Rich, 2015)—could be considered behind or below on international reading test score comparisons. Analyses of international test scores reveal a two-tiered school system in America (Berliner, 2009). In schools serving predominately middle and upper middle class communities, American students score higher than all other nations. But schools servicing poor and low-income communities produce reading test scores among the lowest nations internationally. Despite a century of reading research and billions of dollars invested in reading education, students from low-income families—cofounded by race (Vigor, 2011), immigrant status (Swartz & Stiefel, 2011), and segregated location (Burdkick-Will et al., 2011)—continue to "struggle" with school reading. Although some schools have made modest improvements (Rowan, 2011), the overall income achievement gap has increased by 40% since the Reagan Administration (Reardon, 2011). That's correct; all the school reforms have actually weakened teachers' abilities to help poor and low-income students—now the majority in public schools—to learn to read well. Poverty has everything to do with American public schooling in general and reading education in particular: how it is theorized, how it is organized, and how it runs. Competing representations of poverty underlie school assumptions about intelligence, character, textbook content, lesson formats, room arrangements, standards, testing, and even business/school partnerships.

According to the *New York Times*, "no one seriously disputes the fact that students from disadvantaged households perform less well in school" (Ladd & Fiske, 2011, A 23). If that were true, then what prevents us from doing whatever it takes in order to overcome the systemic disadvantages, leveling the tiers of reading education? The Harvard and Stanford Collaboration for Poverty Research (CRP) provide an explanation.

> Among those who regard poverty as a major social problem, the conventional view is that we should respond by declaring a new "war on poverty," then introduce initiatives that would lower the poverty rate, and thereby reduce the poverty rate in the U.S. However sensible such an approach may seem, there are real political hurdles that in the U.S. context make it difficult to take on poverty in any concerted way, and one might therefore focus additionally on measures that reduce the negative effects of poverty among those experiencing it. (CPR, 2010)

In what follows, I explore the facts of being economically disadvantaged in America, its effects on students' abilities to learn to read, and the politics of reading education that keep teachers nipping at symptoms without tackling the root causes of disadvantage. By reading poverty, reading educators can craft a response to the rhetoric that positions teachers as solely responsible for America's future (Shannon, 2014).

Poverty Is Real and Growing

Carnoy and Rothstein's (2013) analysis of international reading scores show that both rich and poor Americans score higher than their counterparts abroad. Relatively affluent American students score higher than other nations' affluent students and poorer Americans outperform the poorer students of other countries as well. What weighs the aggregate American reading test scores down to the middle of the pack is the higher percentage of impoverished students in American public schools when compared to any other country in the Organization for Economic Co-operation and Development (OECD) comparisons. According to the National Center for Educational Statistics (Southern Education Foundation, 2015), 51% of American students are now eligible for the National School Lunch Program. (In 1989, less than 32% of American students were eligible for a free or reduced school lunch.) By comparison, child poverty rates in most European Union countries are below 10%. That's a five-to-one ratio for a topic on which it is legitimate to say that America is behind other countries!

It could be argued, however, that this comparison is poorly made because eligibility for a reduced-price lunch runs up to 185% of the U.S. poverty line. The poverty line is the cutoff for free lunch (Federal Register 2014). Nationally, 44% of American students are eligible for free lunch (50% in the South; 44% in the West, 38% in the Midwest, and 36% in the Northeast). It's 58% in the District of Columbia (Southern Education Foundation, 2015). Considering free lunch eligibility alone, American children still suffer at a 4-to-1 ratio when compared to the EU and 6-to-1 where the U.S. Congress rules.

Nevertheless, additional support for the 5-to-1 ratio could be found in the antiquated and inadequate definition of poverty in the United States. Since 1963, the official U.S. definition of poverty has been based on a simple formula in which food was estimate to account for one third of a reasonable household budget. Currently, food occupies only a seventh of the average family budget. In 1963, the poverty line was set at $3000 ($2.736 for daily meals X 365 X 3). Today, a family of two becomes eligible for free lunch at school when its income is below $15,730–that's $14.365 to feed both daily—and for reduced lunch with an income below $29,100 ($26.434 for daily meals). After meals are subtracted from the annual household budget, a poor family has $10,499 (or less) remaining to account for housing, clothing, health care, transportation, childcare, utilities, and entertainment.

A second argument in favor of the 5-to-1 ratio is found in the porous boundary between poverty and low-income status. According to the Dynamics of Economic Well Being report (U.S. Census, 2011), poverty is a temporary condition for many Americans. Families exit poverty as well as enter poverty periodically. At times, a family's status can fluctuate between the two several times within a given year. This challenges the ideal of American upward mobility. On average during the 40 years following the Great Depression (roughly 1940 to 1980), children would eventually exceed the income of their parents and move between and among official economic classes. Yet in the last 30 years, the United States has become the most class-bound society among OECD nations (Isaacs, Sawhill, & Haskins, 2008). Although some children living in poverty or within low-income families might move to the middle class (26%) or even above (4%), they are much more likely to remain in the same economic class as their parents (70%) (Currier, 2012). That 51% figure (and 5-to-1 ratio) seems justified because low family income and lack of family wealth make them particularly vulnerable to unforeseen circumstances—household events (e.g., illness or accident), economic events (e.g., businesses moving or contracting in recession or rising prices during economic boom) or natural events (e.g., drought or catastrophic weather)—creating nearly continuous material and psychological stressors on their lives.

Rector and Sheffield (2011) argue that few Americans have "an inability to provide nutritious food, clothing and reasonable shelter for one's family" (p. 1) because federal assistance programs supplement their incomes if need be (e.g., National School Lunch Program, Social Security Disability benefits, Medicare, low-income housing assistance). According to the Pew Research Center (2015), most financially secure Americans believe "poor people today have it easy because they can get government benefits without doing anything in return" (as quoted in Blow, 2015). However, the new federal Supplemental Poverty Measure (2011) challenges these interpretations. The SPM calculations include direct federal assistance payments and tax credits as income and subtracts from that income certain out-of-pocket medical costs, work expenses, and taxes paid, then adjusts for cost of living difference by region. However, the SPM lowers the official poverty rates in less than half of the states and finds higher rates of poverty in 12 states (Short, 2014). Federal programs help poor families to be sure, but they do not make life "easy" for families, particularly for their children.

Consequences of Poverty on the Learning Lives of Children

During the Great Recession (2008–2009 officially; but still in progress for poor and low-income families, Greider, 2015), federal programs prevented more families from slipping below the poverty line. Earned Income Credits (eligible working families receive tax refunds), unemployment insurance (laid off workers received an income stipend), and Supplemental Nutritional Assistance programs (SNAP—formerly Food Stamps) were particularly effective, saving respectively 4, 5, and 3% of American children from being classified as poor. Yet, only SNAP served nearly all eligible families. The Affordable Care Act and Child Health Insurance Programs account for 85 to 95% of poor children, depending on families' state of residence. For lack of adequate funding, Head Start, the War on Poverty preschool program, enrolls 42% of eligible children. Temporary Assistance to Needy Families (Welfare before 1996) serves 40% of eligible families. Low-income housing assistance programs account for 25% of families who qualify. Despite federal services, many children in poor and low-income households are sick, hungry, and tired more often than their middle income and well-off peers, leaving the former with disadvantages that suppress their school performance.

Children living in low-income and poor households are diverse individuals who negotiate their lives in a variety of ways, and the effects of biological, psychological, and social characteristics associated with poverty and low income might not pertain to any individual child. Research on poverty and low-income effects provides general tendencies and not certainties. This being acknowledged, many scholars (see Duncan & Murnane, 2011) conclude that true disadvantage reduces children's opportunities and capacities to make the most of whatever happens at school. Statistically, poor and low-income children are more likely to have low birth weight, to be ill fed, to lack health care, to live in inadequate shelter, to feel unsafe and insecure, and to lack the expected dispositions and experiences for schooling. All arise from the economic realities of their daily lives and interfere with their learning.

Low birth weight is set at 5.5 pounds and is associated with prolonged and serious illness (asthma); infections (nose and throat); and motor (eye/hand coordination), social (externalizing aggression and/or internalizing anxiety) and cognitive (autism and lower intelligence) delays. Lower-income parents are twice as likely to have low-weight babies and four times as likely to have very low (3.3 pounds) or extremely low (2.2 pounds) weight babies (Kaiser Family State Health Facts, 2012). Lighter babies are likely to suffer multiple complications and to have those complications last through adolescence (Cheadle & Goode, 2010).

Food insecurity is a regular and sustained risk of experiencing an insufficient food supply at home to maintain one's health, development, and concentration. Over 16.7 million Americans experience food insecurity each month (Coleman-Jensen, Nord, Andrews, & Carlson, 2012). Hungry children are more likely to be ill, absent, lethargic, and inattentive. Chronic hunger among infants and toddlers is associated with slower cognitive development and lack of powers of concentration that last into adulthood (Wight, Thampi, & Briggs, 2010).

Lack of access to health care is directly and positively correlated with income (U.S. Census Bureau, 2011b). Despite the Affordable Care Act and CHIPs, 10% of children still lack insurance and/or easily available care (Kaiser Family Health Facts, 2012). Poor and low-income children are more likely to have lower rates of immunization, fewer preventive checkups for treatable illnesses, and vision and dental problems. Consequently, they are more likely to be sick when attending school or to be absent, causing "their educational achievement to suffer" (Bernstein, Chollet, & Peterson, 2010).

Inadequate housing is associated with greater chance of illness (colds and infections); exposure to toxins (lead and radon), damaged immune systems and cognitive functioning; sleep deprivation; and transience (Anatani, Chau, Wight, & Addy, 2011). Housing costs consume more than the HUD recommended 30% of family budgets, and therefore, poor and low-income children are more likely to live in older, drafty, poorly maintained buildings that are located in less safe neighborhoods.

Toxic stress is the continued activation of the genetically coded response system that prepares the body to engage temporal environmental challenges. Stress activates the nervous system and specific hormones that raise heart rate, breathing rate, blood pressure, and metabolism, enabling an individual to take on the challenge with enhanced focus, strength, and alertness until the challenge ends. Continued activation of the stress system, however, is toxic to the human body and disposition, leaving the individual feeling overwhelmed, weakening his or her immune system and causing long-term degradation of cognitive functioning. Children living in poverty are more likely to demonstrate the physiological symptoms of toxic stress daily, even when there is no apparent challenge in the immediate environment (Evans & Schamberg, 2009). As poverty and low income persists through childhood and adolescence, the symptoms become more acute, suppressing working memory (Farah et al. 2006; Nobel, Norman, & Farah, 2005), influencing the structure of the brain (Nelson & Sheridan, 2011), and limiting the genetic expression of individuals (Nisbett, 2009). These consequences disrupt logical thinking, behavioral control, language development and expression, and comprehension of oral and written messages.

In thoughtful (Payne, 2008) and not so thoughtful (Payne, 2005) ways, experts argue that *social factors* as well as biological factors inhibit poor and low-income students' learning. Segregated low-income communities have fewer institutional resources, fewer employment opportunities, greater concentrations of people suffering the biological effects on minds and bodies, and less social cohesion, which demoralize families and paralyze civic actions. Poor and low-income children are less likely to be supervised, to talk with adults, to engage in school-like literacy events, and to participate in academically enriching events and contexts inside and outside the home (Phillips, 2011). Parenting styles and uses of time inhibit readiness for typical school curricula and subsequent academic achievement (Lareau, 2003). However, as Heath (1983) and Taylor and Dorsey-Gaines (1988) demonstrated decades ago and Compton-Lilly, Rogers, and Lewis (2012) explained more recently, these limitations reflect as much on schooling and research epistemologies as they do on the potential of families and students.

Poverty and low income take a toll on children's bodies and minds and shape their behavior in ways that can interfere with their learning at school. This is not an excuse (G. W. Bush, 2000; Rhee, 2012; Tough, 2011), but rather, a research-based conclusion. Singly or more often in combination, these children are more likely to be in need of medical treatment, to be hungry and tired, to be absent, to suffer from cognitive and physical delays in development, to possess a smaller school vocabulary, to lack expected general and school experiences, to exhibit disruptive behavior/sullen dispositions, and to suffer a loss of working memory and lower genic expression because of toxic stress. Singular government programs (SNAP, CHIP, etc.) help, but cannot and do not address the complex disadvantage that poor and low-income children suffer. At the same time, advantaged families (the 49% not eligible for the NLSP) are pressing their advantage by providing opportunities for "educational related items and activities such as music and art lessons, children's books and toys, sports equipment and classes, and tutoring" (Kaushal, Magnuson, and Waldgogel, 2011, p. 187). Lareau (2011) maintains that these investments are intended to familiarize children with various social institutions and to prepare them to negotiate with adults in order to enhance their own positive outcomes.

If Ladd and Fiske were correct in the *New York Times*—that no one seriously disputes the fact—and if the United States is based on the propositions that all citizens are created equal with equal rights to opportunities for life, liberty, and the pursuit of happiness, then Americans should expect "What It Takes" approaches to eliminate the disadvantages of poverty and low income (Smyth & Schorr, 2009). What will it take to level the opportunities to learn between America's two school systems? The answer depends on how you represent the disadvantages, frame the issue of leveling, and explain the origin of the disadvantages in the first place. Those answers are influenced by the political ideologies currently popular in America and those currently most powerful. To be an American teacher who believes in fairness, you must engage these politics—otherwise, the realities of the "we're behind" blame continue.

Politics of Reading Education

In "Profiting From a Child's Illiteracy," *New York Times* columnist Nicholas Kristof (2012) provides a useful tool to investigate the relationship between the politics of poverty and reading education. Kristof assumes that poverty is a national problem and urges Americans to pay more attention to children. He points out that while anti-poverty programs—Social Security and Medicare, specifically—have reduced poverty rates for the elderly from 35% in 1959 to 8% today, they've left nearly a quarter of all children living in poverty. He attributes this imbalance to the fact that the elderly have been and remain organized and active in politics, while children do not have a political voice. However, speaking for poor children then, he advocates for early intervention programs—similar to the Collaborative for Poverty Research—that will teach poor and low-income parents to provide their children with oral and written language experiences that researchers have shown will prepare them to succeed at school and beyond. Further, instead of calling for full funding for Head Start after 50 years, Kristof promotes the work of Save the Children (2015), an international nonprofit non-government organization (NGO), to provide these services.

Kristof begins his argument with a story of rural Kentucky parents who withdrew their children from literacy programs because learning to read could disqualify the family later from federal financial assistance programs for disabled children. "Many people in hillside mobile homes here are poor and desperate, and a $698 monthly check per child from the Supplemental Security Income (SSI) program goes a long way – and those checks continue until the child turns 18" (p. 1). In 1972, the Nixon administration passed SSI, enabling parents to remain home in order to care for a child with severe physical and/or mental disabilities. Over time, Kristof alleges, the poor have subverted SSI to cover "fuzzier intellectual disabilities." "This is painful for a liberal to admit, but conservatives have a point when they suggest that America's safety net can sometimes entangle people in a soul-crushing dependency" (p. 1).

To describe the situation and the cure, Kristof followed Save the Children employees around Kentucky in order to see "a model of what does work" to break the cycle of generational poverty. "Almost anytime the question is poverty, the answer is children" (p. 9). These employees visited poor mothers in order to improve their parenting skills, demonstrating how to "read to their children, tell stories, talk to them, and hug them." Between visits, the employees left books and directions for activities the mothers could practice. Kristof reports that school personnel verified that after these interventions, targeted children entered school on par with their more well-to-do peers. Across the op-ed, Kristof is clear that poverty is not a natural condition; rather, it is a human artifact that could be remade one child at a time, if the political will exists. He ends, "I hope that the budget negotiations in Washington may offer us a chance to take money from SSI and invest in early childhood initiatives instead" (p. 9).

Kristof's piece set off a firestorm of responses that cut across political lines, including a Kentucky principal who denied the veracity of Kristof's tale of trailer park parents. (See for example: Kristof's blog, 2013; Marty Ford's response, 2012), and Harold Pollack's *The Incidental* Economist, 2012.) In his representation of poverty as a problem and his framing of the solution, Kristof illustrates the "real political hurdles" that CPR refers to. He jumps across liberal, conservative, neoliberal, and even radical democratic ideologies, and finally lands squarely on a neoliberal solution. For example, Kristof implies that he's a liberal, recognizing that some government interventions have been successful in reducing poverty. Note, however, that the two he mentioned directly—Social Security and Medicare—are not aimed at the poor per se, but are government benefits for all citizens that were passed during liberal highlights of 20th century politics—the New Deal and the Great Society. He supports his solution with research-based evidence and argues for shifts in federal funding from what he deems as a government crutch to a helping hand.

Perhaps reading educators identify the liberal principles in Kristof's argument: opportunity, caring, rationality, government intervention, and progress—and how they map onto the reading education policies and practices over the last 50 years. In order to overcome the unequal distribution of economic benefits, the government acts to ensure opportunities for all social groups to compete as equals for a good life. For example, Title 1 of the Elementary and Secondary Education Act (from 1965 to the present) provides low-income students with additional instructional support necessary to accelerate learning to read at school. Since its inception, policy makers have enlisted scientific rationality (e.g., Project Follow Through, the First Grade Studies, A Nation of Readers report, and the National Reading Panel report) in order to ensure best practices are available to all. Standardized reading tests were/are required to provide evidence to Title 1 parents that the funded services were rendered, to evaluate the relative effectiveness of competing interventions, and to demonstrate progress toward all high school graduates being able to compete on merit for the available high paying jobs. Kristof's solution would make poor preschool children ready to take full advantage of public schooling (Neuman & Celano, 2012).

But Kristof is not a liberal (at least not in this op ed). His representation of the Kentucky "cultural of poverty" is deeply based in conservative political ideology. First, he argues that the poor are not really destitute because they live in relative comfort with air conditioning, washing machines, and pick up trucks. Second, he implies that they are solely responsible for their condition because they lack intelligence, make poor choices, follow bad cultural habits, and practice moral relativism. With assistance programs like SSI, he claims that the federal government actually encourages these traits, providing the poor with alternatives to fending for themselves by accepting whatever work is available, joining the military, staying married, deferring material and emotional gratifications and attending church. Any of these steps, he suggests, would prove adults worthy of charity if and when it was needed (he's willing to "bet" on a young mother "with cracking intelligence," but not a pregnant-with-twins woman who walks two miles to work because her "$500 car" died).

Reading educators can hear the conservatism in Kristof's disciplinary tone when framing the problem—"soul crushing dependency"—and articulating the solution—"read to them," "talk to them," "hug them." Families are responsible for preserving "the organic moral order" (Buckley, 1955) by providing good models and structures for work, planning, and restraint. Such steps will organize poor children's time and space, provide examples and enforce acceptable moral choices, and demonstrate both how to accept responsibility for one's choices and persistence toward goals. Church serves as the primary means to support young families, and William Bennett (*Book of Virtues* series), Dolly Parton (Imagination Library) and others provide tools for parents to lead children's moral apprenticeships until they reach school. Once there when supplied with a firm moral compass, all students will to ready to engage a rich and rigorous liberal arts curriculum for as long as their intelligence will allow, learning to read deeply and to discuss the classic texts of each discipline (Ravitch 1987; 2010).

In the end, Kristof splits the difference between liberal and conservative ideologies on poverty and reading education. He claims liberal principles, but has lost faith in government directed solutions. Instead of recognizing legitimate uses of SSI or recommending full funding of Head Start, he proposes a market based solution to poverty in which governments fund a subcontractor to provide poor children with the early skills necessary for their success in school, and then, in the global economy. Save the Children is his subcontractor of choice, but other private firms could compete for these dollars too, and all, he implies, would be more effective and efficient than government run programs because the private ones must compete for consumers. This is a neoliberal view of poverty in which the poor simply lack the skills sufficient to compete for above poverty wage jobs. Reading is a necessary skill for those jobs that currently remain unfilled, and therefore, poor children being taught to read will end poverty within a generation and retain America's premier position in the world economy.

For 30 years, neoliberal principles have driven school reform rhetoric, if not reality—we are falling behind and only a free market is supple enough to match all the complexities of the United States' decentralized educational system in order to make it competitive with other nations. Reading educators know the latest version as the Common Core Standards for English language arts. If teachers will make three key shifts—reading increasingly complex texts; reading, writing and speaking from evidence found in texts; and building knowledge through nonfiction reading—all students will be career and college ready upon graduation. Newly produced tests will ensure this outcome. As Bill Gates (2009) explained, "When the tests are aligned with the common standards, the curriculum will line up as well, and it will unleash a powerful market of people providing services for better teaching. For the first time, there will be a large uniform base of customers looking at using products that can help every kid learn and every teacher get better." Kristof's solution names part of that market and brings it into the homes of poor and low-income children.

Missing What Works

These conflicting views of poverty, its causes and its cures construct the political hurdles that dissuade CRP, Kristof, and others from directly confronting poverty through social programs and actions. Each view has its constituents, and power has not been distributed equally among them over time. Think liberals' Great Society's War on Poverty; Reagan's welfare queens; Clinton's end of welfare as we know it; Obama's bail out of the auto industry, but not Detroit. Their solutions through reading education have been mixed at best. Consider the federal evaluation of the liberal Reading First initiative and its failed hypothesis that quick decoding automatically brings comprehension (Gamse, et al. 2011); the gap between state and national test scores within the conservative No Child Left Behind and its false positive positioning of poor and low-income students as proficient (Lee, 2009; Loveless, 2012); and the first employment of neoliberal, market produced, Common Core reading tests that simply confirmed the inequalities of the dual level school systems in New York and Kentucky. In the meantime, the numbers of poor and low-income children grow and the income achievement gap widens.

None of these ideologies approach Kristof's conclusion about how the elderly actually reduced their rate of poverty to less than a fourth of its size. Without much attention, Kristof writes that the elderly organized, raising consciousness about how power works, and then, they acted and continue to act as if they are human beings whose dignity and well-being should matter to all. Yet, Kristof doesn't entertain this possibility for the poor. Rather, he apes the ideological positions of liberals, conservatives, and neoliberals, thinking for the poor, speaking for them, and calling on powerful others to find solutions for them. His reading education intervention is designed to make the poor socially competent on his terms. This is not how the elderly worked as a group. They forced governments and society members to recognize their concerns as legitimate and to redistribute social, economic, and cultural benefits accordingly. Across the 20th century, labor organizations, racial and ethnic groups, women, and gays have acted similarly, raising their consciousness, organizing, and acting not to fit in according to others' plans for them, but to represent themselves, challenging and changing norms, practices, and laws for all in order to include their plans for themselves. Nancy Fraser (2009) labels this working for social justice.

These groups used their sociological imaginations (Mills, 1959; Lemert, 2011) to understand how their personal circumstances are parts of larger social/historical conditions and to imagine how those circumstances and conditions could change. Each group started with individuals recognizing how social biases kept them from participating fully in society, and then, these individuals found other like-minded people to form coalitions around their social (not personal) issues. They voted to be sure, but that was just one of the ways that they sought representation, recognition, and redistribution, challenging the ideologies that kept them at the margins of society and democratic power in the control of others. They engaged in and continue to engage in "what it takes" actions—discussions, marches, strikes, street theater, organizing, petitions, and letter campaigns—in order to disrupt the traditional flows of power and to make space for themselves in a democracy that would embrace difference and dissent.

Although coalition members didn't and don't always agree on every issue, they recognize that some specific personal troubles were and are social issues in need of remedies that would be impossible without collective actions. From a radical democratic point of view, poverty persists because power continues to circulate in the same historical ways that create and maintain disadvantages in the first place. To overcome poverty, the poor and low-income individuals (nearly half the population) must form coalitions and use the examples of other marginalized groups who have dismantled institutionalized barriers that prevent them from participating on a par with others as full partners in the "running" of communities, the nation, and the world. What could be reading educators' roles in addressing the radical democratic understanding of poverty and its solution?

Reading Education Against Poverty

Reading educators can take note of the coalitions already established (e.g., Home Defenders League, Witnesses to Hunger), and look for ways in which single-issue antipoverty groups could combine around a shared agenda (see Greg Kaufman's 2013 call for a common agenda for the antipoverty movement). Moreover, they can seek to develop fuller understandings of coalitions among educators who work to deinstitutionalize deficit models of curriculum, pedagogy, and assessment. (e.g., See Broader, Bolder Approach to Education, 2015, and Helen Ladd's *Education and Poverty: Confronting the Evidence*, – March 2014).

To ally with these groups and to support their future development, reading educators can engage their sociological imaginations around poverty and its possible relationships with reading. Despite the persistent claims in popular media, teachers and schools do not create or maintain poverty. These messages exist in order to maintain and increase the power among privileged groups. Liberal, conservative, and neoliberal ideologues use such messages to teach the public what we should know, who we should be, and what we should value about equity, civic society, and even reading. They work to divert attention from the fact that other developed nations have recognized all citizens' rights to food, shelter, clothing, health care, and even income, reducing greatly the effects of low income on their students' capacities and opportunities to learn. Public school experiences for poor and low-income children could be different in America, and reading educators can be agents in making that difference by dismantling institutional barriers that prevent poor and low-income children from participating in social, intellectual, and political interactions on par with others within the classroom, school, and community.

A first step in that direct would be to affirm that all students are of equal moral worth, and therefore, deserve social arrangements that permit all to participate as peers in classroom life. Perhaps this appears to be an easy undertaking, however much of American reading education is organized to sort students according to fixed understandings of learning to read that privileges some backgrounds over others. In the politicized name of "helping," schools screen students for differences, treat differences as deficits, and then assign students to ranked levels for participation within the curriculum accordingly. From such acts, poor and low-income students learn that the cultural, social, and human capital that they bring from home won't buy them much within the public institutions designed for social mobility. Kristof's well-intentioned intervention takes this lesson into homes, and the Common Core Standards extend the lesson to "white suburban moms who – all of sudden – find their child isn't as brilliant as they thought they were and their school isn't quite as good as they thought they were." (Arne Duncan as quoted in Strauss, 2013).

New social arrangements to invite full participation are based on the notion that "knowledge and learning are terms of relationship between an individual with both a mind and a body and an environment in which the individual thinks, feels, acts, and interacts" (Gee, 2008, p. 81). Just classroom environments, then, offer a curriculum with a variety of affordances to enable all students to identify their possibilities to act as productive members of communities of practice affiliated around common endeavors of inquiry (Larson & Marsh, 2015). Fortunately, reading educators have many examples of such communities of practice and the roles that reading takes. Winograd (2015) offers examples from preschools and primary grades in which students' differences are leveraged as differential resources. Pandya and Avila (2014) present voices from K–12 classrooms in which students share extensive knowledge of inquiry processes while developing intensive knowledge about the subject of investigation. Kinloch (2012) and Donehower, Hogg, & Schell (2011) explain how the literacy practices of inquiry are shared among communities within and across geographic boundaries. Brass and Webb (2015) assemble English language arts teacher educators who provide examples of how leaders might resource communities of practice in classrooms and might help reading educators extend the tacit knowledge gained through inquiry into explicit knowledge of academic registers.

A second step would be to adopt a What It Takes attitude toward reading education for poor and low-income students, taking a long-term view and pushing back against expedience and standardization of developmental expectations. None of the examples just named fit neatly into the evidence-based practices paradigm in which random control trials are considered the gold standard for decision making. As Berliner's, Carnoy and Rothstein's, and Reardon's analyses show, federally required evidence based practices have not served poor and low-income students and communities well. Rather, the examples above demonstrate the beginnings of practice-based evidence—bottom-up, field demonstrated effective approaches tested in the real, messy, and complicated worlds of students, classrooms, and communities. These approaches embrace complexities and differences, not simply try to control them as nuisance variables in order to isolate a single form of intervention. They view students through an ecological lens that encompasses challenges, strengths, relationships, and community contexts in order to make lasting changes in their lives. Smyth and Schorr (2009) would call such approaches What It Takes programs, if the reading educators work with an emphasis on building trusting relationships, collaboration with students, teachers' flexibility in decision-making, the importance of context linking community to global scales, and accountability to students and their parents.

What It Takes reading education takes the concept of life long learners seriously, troubling the assumption that learning to read happens in easily specified and tested yearly, monthly, or daily chunks. As the above examples demonstrate, to learn to read with sociological imagination can start in preschool with teachers helping students to see how texts work on and for them, what reading is for, and what writing can do in their lives, but it is neither a linear process of lockstep development across the grades (Johnston, 2012) nor ever mastered (Shannon, 2011). The social practices of inquiry—to name, to question, to enjoy, to learn, to explain, to believe and to argue—develop slowly and unevenly as students begin to trust themselves and each other in a variety of environments, with a variety of people, and on a variety of scales. Too early and misguided evaluations (not assessments) undercut each student's construction of their identities as human beings whose dignity and well-being should matter to all.

We are behind other developed nations recognizing and acting upon the rights of the poor and low-income people to live with dignity and to participate actively in the decisions that affect their lives. Reading educators can help to develop the sociological imaginations of the individuals (particularly the young ones) to help them see that their individual troubles are really social issues that require assertive social action to overcome. Because American reading educators teach inside the demands of liberal, conservative, and neoliberal ideologies at present, they must search within the cracks and contradictions among these demands as opportunities to do what it takes. They're out there. Conservatives' retreat from the Common Core cracks the neoliberal consensus. Liberals' demand for sophisticated school content in biology, physics, history, and English cleaves the conservative organic moral order. Neoliberals' promotion of innovation contradicts their enthusiasm for a single testing regime. These and other cracks and contradictions invite reading educators to step toward poor and low-income students with a what it takes attitude.

References

Anantani, Y., Chau, M., Wight, V., & Addy, S. (2011, November). *Rent burden. National Center for Children in Poverty*, Columbia University, New York. Retrieved Feb. 24, 2015 from www.nccp.org/publications/pub_1043.html

Berliner, D. (2009). *Poverty and potential.* Education Policy Research Unit. Boulder, CO. Retrieved February 24, 2015 from http://nepc.colorado.edu/publication/poverty-and-potential

Bernstein, J., Chollet, D., & Peterson, S. (2010, April). Does insurance coverage improve health outcomes? *Mathematica Policy Research, 1.* Retrieved February 24, 2015 from www.mathematica-,pr.com/publications/PDFs/health/reformhealthcare_IB1.pdf

Blow, C. (2015, January 18). How expensive is it to be poor. *New York Times.* Retrieved from http://www.nytimes.com/2015/01/19/opinion/charles-blow-how-expensive-it-is-to-be-poor.html?_r=0

Brass, J., & Webb, A. (Eds.). (2015). *Reclaiming English language arts methods courses.* New York: Routledge.

Broader, Bolder Approach to Education. (2015). Website. http://www.boldapproach.org

Buckley, W. F. (1955, November). Our mission statement. *National Review, 1.* Retrieved February 24, 2015 from www.nationalreview.come/articles/223549/our-mission-statement/william-f-buckley-jr

Burdkick-Will, J. Ludwig, J., Raudenbush, S., Sampson, R., Sanbonmatsu, L., & Sharkey, P. (2011). Converging evidence for neighborhood effects on children's test scores. In G. Duncan & R. Murnane (Eds.), *Whither Opportunity.* New York: Russell Sage.

Bush, G. W. (2000, July 10). *Speech to the NAACP 91st annual convention.* Retrieved February 24, 2015 from http://www.washingtonpost.com/wp-srv/onpolitics/elections/bushtext071000.htm

Carnoy, M., & Rothstein, R. (2013, January). *What do international tests really show about U. S. student performance?* Washington DC: Economic Policy Institute. Retrieved February 24, 2015 from www.epi.org/publication/us-student-performance-testing/

Cheadle, J., & Goosby, B. (2010). Birth weight, cognitive development, and life chances. *Social Science Research, 29,* 570–584.

Coleman-Jensen, A., Nord, M., Andrews, M., & Carlson, S. (2012 September). *Household food security in the United States in 2011.* Economic Research Service Report 141, U.S. Department of Agriculture. Retrieved February 24, 2015 from www.ers.usda.gov/media/884525/err141.pdf

Collaboration for Poverty Research. (2010). *Poverty and stress.* Retrieved February 24, 2015 from www.staford.edu/group/scspi/cpr/cpr_lab_poverty_and -stress.html

Compton-Lilly, C., Rogers, R., & Lewis, C. (2012). Analyzing epistemological considerations related to diversity: An integrated critical literature review of family literacy scholarship. *Reading Research Quarterly, 47,* 33–60.

Currier, E. (2012, July 9). *Pursuing the American dream: Economic mobility across generations.* Pew Charitable Trust Report. Retrieved February 24, 2015 from www.pewstates.org/research/reports/pursuing-the-american-dream-85899403228

Donehower, K., Hogg, C., & Schell, E. (Eds.). (2011). *Reclaiming the rural: Essay on literacy, rhetoric and pedagogy.* Carbondale, IL: Southern University Press.

Dorsey-Gaines, C., & Taylor, D. (1988). *Growing up literate: Learning from inner city families.* Portsmouth, NH: Heinemann.

Duncan, G., & Murname, R. (Eds.). (2011). *Whither Opportunity.* New York: Russell Sage.

Evans, G., & Schamberg, M. (2009). *Childhood poverty, chronic stress, and adult working memory.* Proceeding of the National Academy of Science (early edition). Retrieved February 24, 2015 from www.pnas.org/content/early/2009/03/27/27/0811910106.abstract

Farah, M., Shera, D., Savae, J., Betancourt, L., Giannetta, J., Brodsky, N., Malmud, E., & Hunt, H. (2006). Childhood poverty: Specific association with neurocognitive development. *Brain Research, 1110,* 166–174. Retrieved Feburary 24, 2015 from www.psych.upenn.edu/~mfarah/Development-povertyassociation.pdf

Federal Register/Vol. 79 No. 43/Notice 12467. (March 5, 2014). Eligibility Criteria for National School Lunch Program. Retrieved from http://www.fns.usda.gov/sites/default/files/2014-04788.pdf

Ford, M. (2012). *No profit in America's safety net for low income people with disabilities.* The Arc. Retrieved from http://blog.thearc.org/2012/12/21/no-profit-in-americas-safety-net-for-low-income-people-with-disabilities/

Fraser, N. (2009). *Scales of justice: Reimagining political space in a globalizing world*. New York: Columbia University Press.

Gamse, B., Bonlay, B., Fountain, A., Unlu, F., Maree, K., McCall, T., & McCormack, R. (2011). *Reading first implementation study 2008–2009*. U.S. Department of Education. Retrieved February 24, 2015 from www.ed.gov/about/offices/list/opepd/ppss/reports.html#reading

Gates, W. (2009, July 21). *Address to the national conference of state legislatures*. Retrieved February 24, 2015 from www.gatesfoundation.org/media-center/speeches/2009/07/bill-gates-national-conference-of-state-legislatures-ncsl

Gee, J. (2008). A sociocultural perspective on opportunity to learn. In P. Moss (Ed.), *Assessment, equity and opportunity*. New York: Cambridge University Press.

Greider, W. (2015, February 9). Obama is leading the way to economic catastrophe. *The Nation*. Retrieved February 24, 2015 from http://www.thenation.com/blogs/william-greider

Heath, S. B. (1983). *Ways with words*. New York: Cambridge University Press.

Isaacs, J. Sawhill, I., & Haskins, R. (2008). *Getting ahead or losing ground: Economic mobility in America*. Washington DC Brookings Institute.

Johnston, P. (2012). *Opening minds*. Portland, ME: Stenhouse.

Kaiser Family State Health Facts. (2012). Retrieved February 24, 2015 from http://kff.org/state/data/

Kaufman, G. (2013, November 25). This week in poverty: Anti-poverty leaders discuss the need for a shared agenda. *The Nation*. Retrieved from http://www.thenation.com/blog/177341/week-poverty-anti-poverty-leaders-discuss-need-shared-agenda

Kaushal, N., Magnuson, K., & Waldgogel, J. (2011). How is family income related to investments in children's learning. In G. Duncan & R. Murname (Eds.), *Whither Opportunity*. New York: Russell Sage.

Kinloch, V. (2012). *Closing boundaries: Teaching and learning with urban youth*. New York: Teachers College.

Kristof, N. (2012, December 7). Profiting from a child's illiteracy. *The New York Times*, 1, 9.

Kristof, N. (2013, January 23). Chipping away at poverty: An exchange. *The New York Times*. Retrieved from http://kristof.blogs.nytimes.com/2013/01/23/chipping-away-at-poverty-an-exchange/

Ladd, H. (2014). *Education and Poverty: Confronting the Evidence. Retrieved from* http://peabody.vanderbilt.edu/research/pri/VanderbiltMarch2014Ladd.pdf

Ladd, H., & Fiske, E. (2011, December 11). Class matters. Why won't we admit it. *The New York Times*. Retrieved February 24, 2015 from www.nytimes.com/2011/12/12/opinio/the-unaddressed-link-between-poverty-and-education.html?pagewanted=all&_r=0

Lareau, A. (2003). *Unequal childhoods: Class, race, and family life*. Berkeley, CA: University of California.

Lareau, A. (2011). *Unequal childhoods: Class, race, and family life* (2nd ed.). Berkeley: University of California Press.

Larson, J., & Marsh, J. (2015). *Making literacy real*. Los Angeles: Sage.

Lee, J. (2009). *Tracking achievement gaps and assessing the impact of NCLB on the gap*. Cambridge, MA: Civil Rights Project of Harvard University.

Lemert, C. (2011). *Social things* (5th ed.). Lanham, MD: Rowman & Littlefield.

Loveless, T. (2012). *How well are American students learning?* The Brown Center Report on American Education. Washington, DC Brookings Institute. Retrieved February 24, 2015 from www.brookings.edu/~/media/newsletter/0216_brown_education_loveless.pdf

Mills, C. W. (1959). *The sociological imagination*. Chicago: University of Chicago Press.

Nelson, C., & Sheridan, M. (2011). Lessons from neuroscience research for understanding causal links between family and neighborhood characteristics and educational outcomes. In G. Duncan & R. Murname (Eds.), *Whither Opportunity*. New York: Russell Sage.

Neumann, S., & Celano, D. (2012). *Giving our children a fighting chance: Poverty, literacy and development of informational capital*. New York: Teachers College.

Nisbet, R. (2009). *Intelligence and how to get it: Why schools and culture count*. New York: Norton.

Nobel, K., Norman, M., & Farrah, M. (2005). Neurocognitive correlates of socioeconomic status in kindergarten children. *Developmental Science, 8*, 74–87. Retrieved February 24, 2015 from www.cumc.columiba.edu/dept/sergievsky/fs/pulications/Nobel-et-el-2005-2.pdf

Obama, B. (2010, February 22). *Address to the National Governors Association*. Washington, DC. Retrieved February 24, 2015 from www.gpo.gov/fdsys/pkg/DCDPD-201000114/pdf/DCPD-201000114/pdf

Pandya, J., & Avila, J. (Eds.) (2014). *Moving critical literacies forward*. New York: Routledge.

Payne, C. (2008). *So much reform/so little change: The persistence of failure in urban schools*. Cambridge, MA: Harvard University Press.

Payne, R. (2005). *A framework for understanding poverty*. Highlands, TX: Aha.

Phillips, M. (2011). Parenting time use and disparities in academic outcomes. In G. Duncan & R. Murname (Eds.), *Whither Opportunity*. New York: Russell Sage.

Pollack, H. (2012). "Profiting from a child's illiteracy," Nicholas Kristof on the childhood SSI program. *The Incidental Economist*. Retrieved from http://theincidentaleconomist.com/wordpress/profiting-from-a-childs-illiteracy-nicholas-kristof-on-the-childhood-ssi-program-12/

Ravitch, D. (1987). *The schools we deserve*. New York: Basic.

Ravitch, D. (2010). *The death and life of the great American school system*. New York: Basic.

Reardon, S. (2011). The widening academic achievement gap between rich and poor. In G. Duncan & R. Murname (Eds.), *Whither Opportunity*. New York: Russell Sage.

Rector, R., & Sheffield, R. (2011). Understanding poverty in the United States: Surprising facts about America's poor. *Backgrounder, 2607*. Heritage Foundation. Retrieved February 24, 2015 from www.heritage.org/research/reports/2011/09/understanding-poverty-in-the-united-states-surprising-facts-about-america's-poor

Rhee, M. (2012, September 5). Poverty must be tackled, but never used as an excuse. *Huffington Post*. Retrieved February 24, 2015 from http://www.huffingtonpost.com/michelle-rhee/poverty-must-be-tackled-b_b_1857423.html

Rich, M. (2015, January 16). Percentage of poor students in public schools rises. *The New York Times*. Retrieved February 24, 2015 from http://www.nytimes.com/2015/01/17/us/school-poverty-study-southern-education-foundation.html

Rowan, B. (2011). Intervening to improve the educational outcomes of students in poverty. In G. Duncan & R. Murname (Eds.), *Whither Opportunity*. New York: Russell Sage.

Save the Children. (2015). https://sponsor.savethechildren.org/?pid=238

Shannon, P. (2011). *Reading wide awake*. New York: Teachers College.

Shannon, P. (2014). *Reading poverty in America*. New York: Routledge.

Short, K. (2012, November). *The research supplemental poverty measure. 2011*. Current Population Reports. The United States Bureau. Retrieved February 24, 2015 from www.census.gov/prod/2012pubs/p60-244.pdf

Smyth, K., & Schorr, L. (2009, January). *A lot to lose: A call to rethink what constitutes "evidence" in finding social interventions that work*. Working Paper Series. Malcolm Wiener Center for Social Policy, Harvard Kennedy School.

Southern Education Foundation. (2015). *A new majority research bulletin: Low income students on the majority in the nation's public schools*. Retrieved February 24, 2015 from http://www.southerneducation.org/Our-Strategies/Research-and-Publications/New-Majority-Diverse-Majority-Report-Series/A-New-Majority-2015-Update-Low-Income-Students-Now

Strauss, V. (2013, November 16). Arne Duncan: 'White suburban moms' upset that the common core shows that their kids aren't 'brilliant.' *Washington Post*. Retrieved February 24, 2015 from http://www.washingtonpost.com/blogs/answer-sheet/wp/2013/11/16/arne-duncan-white-suburban-moms-upset-that-common-core-shows-their-kids-arent-brilliant/

Swartz, A., & Stiefel, L. (2011). Immigrants and inequality in public schools. In G. Duncan & R. Murname (Eds.), *Whither Opportunity*. New York: Russell Sage.

Tough, P. (2011, July 7). No seriously: No excuses. *New York Times*. Sunday Magazine. Retrieved February 24, 2015 from http://www.nytimes.com/2011/07/10/magazine/reforming-the-school-reformers.html?pagewanted=all

U.S. Census. (2011, March). *Dynamics of economic well-being 2004–2006*. Retrieved February 24, 2015 from www.census.gov/prod/2011pubs/p70-123.pdf

U.S. Census. (2011b). *Poverty*. Retrieved February 24, 2015 from www.census.gov/hhes/www/poverty/data/threshold

Vigor, J. (2011). School desegregation and the black-white test score gap. In G. Duncan & R. Murname (Eds.), *Whither Opportunity*. New York: Russell Sage.

Wight, V., Thampi, K., & Briggs, J. (2010). *Who are America's poor children? Examining food insecurity among children in the United States*. National Center for Children in Poverty. Columbia University. New York. Retrieved February 24, 2015 from www.nokidhungry.org/sites/default/files/test_958.pdf

Winograd, K., (Ed.). (2015). *Critical literacies and young learners*. New York: Routledge.

ELEVEN

Counter-Narratives in State History: The 100 Years of State and Federal Policy Curriculum Project Educational Thought and Sociocultural Studies

Glenabah Martinez

Introduction

Indigenous youth in high schools in the Southwest are faced with daily challenges to their individual and collective existence as Indigenous Peoples.[1] While the argument is made that all youth and teachers face challenges to some degree in school settings by scholars such as Casanova (2010), Lee (1995, 2005), Lopez (2003), and Patel (2013), the challenges that Indigenous youth face in public school settings are different. In the Southwest, they are different because of the history of tense relations between Indigenous Peoples and the colonizing nations of Spain, Mexico, and the United States that precedes them as they enter high school for the first time. They are qualitatively different because of their cultural ties to their aboriginal homeland, which calls for them to fulfill community and cultural obligations throughout the year. They are unique, as Indigenous legal scholar David Wilkins (2002) reminds us, because Indigenous Peoples are the original inhabitants of the Americas. As descendents of the original inhabitants, Indigenous Peoples possess cultural distinctiveness, property rights, and political sovereignty. Oftentimes, however, the unique position that Indigenous Peoples occupy is not consistently recognized in public education. Instead, the interests of the colonizing state are dominant in determining, for example, what counts as knowledge.

The intensity of cultural hegemony in public institutions of learning is symptomatic of a larger educational crisis that has prevailed in the historical and contemporary experiences of Indigenous Peoples globally. Graham Hingangaroa Smith's (1990) historic examination of the crisis of Maori education is particularly useful in making this point. According to him, the crisis must be "analyzed within a theoretical framework of contested power relations" (p. 79). He continues:

> In New Zealand the state of education system embraces the social, political and cultural structures of Pakeha (white New Zealanders; non-Maori) dominant society....Pakeha cultural capital is firmly embedded in the structures of schooling and education....It is the dominant cultural group or selected members from within the group who are able to influence what is to count as valid, acceptable knowledge, culture, and language at every level, from the majority of teachers at the classroom level, to the majority of members on Boards of Trustees at the organization level. Acceptable knowledge is maintained and protected by a variety of visible and hidden gate-keeping strategies. (pp. 79–80)

Hingangaroa Smith (1990) explains the power of dominant interests in the public spheres at the state, district, and school levels where educational policies regarding curriculum, instruction, and assessment are developed and enforced. He also emphasizes the pivotal role of numeric advantage in justifying and confirming the power of dominant interests in curriculum, instruction, assessment, and policy.

Hingangaroa Smith's analysis of nonsynchronous power relations as it exists in New Zealand is similar to the disposition of Indigenous Peoples in the state of New Mexico. Indigenous Peoples have been forced to contend with three groups of colonizers—Spain (1598–1821), Mexico (1821–1847), and the United States (1847–present)—each with their own programs of deculturalization, land theft, and hoarding of the limited natural and mineral resources. The current regime that established itself through the Treaty of Guadalupe Hidalgo began the process of confirming its authority through the statehood process of Texas (1845), California (1850), New Mexico (1912), and Arizona (1912).[2]

The road to New Mexico statehood (1847–1912) and political events from 1912 to the present is marked with federal and state policies that serve the interests of the U.S. government and *Nuevo Mexicanos*.[3] Many of these policies challenged the sovereignty of the 22 Indigenous Nations of New Mexico through reduction of land holdings, religious persecution, and violation of aboriginal rights to natural resources. At the present time, we are living with the present-day manifestations of this history of turmoil. Yet, this history is largely absent from the official knowledge presented in state and national history textbooks. This chapter will focus on a movement by the 19 Pueblo Nations of New Mexico to challenge the hegemonic agenda embedded in the state's core curriculum (social studies, math, science, and language arts). In order to gain a deeper appreciation of the significance of the curriculum, the next section is an overview of the disposition of Indian education at the state level.

Diversity: What Counts as Knowledge?

> The diversity of cultures in New Mexico is one of its most unique features. **Diversity** means variety. Our diversity creates cultural depth and richness. Many tourists visit New Mexico to experience this richness. However, our diversity also causes conflict and can create political power struggles, discrimination, and negative stereotyping. Today, our government, schools, and various cultural groups work to understand, respect, and preserve the cultures and traditions that are New Mexico. (*The New Mexico Journey*, p. 213)

New Mexico is currently identified as a minority-majority state.[4] This designation is a political tool that can be employed in a variety of ways for political, economic, and social policy legislation. For example, in the executive summary of the *Tribal Education Status*

Report for the School Year 2011–2012 published by the New Mexico Public Education Department (2012) is the following passage:

> New Mexico is one of the most culturally linguistically diverse and rural states in the country with a population of 59.51% Hispanic, 26% Anglo, 10% Native American, and 2% are African American, and 1% are Asian or of other ethnicity. Inhabited by Native American populations for many centuries, New Mexico has also been part of the Imperial Spanish Viceroy Royalty of New Spain, part of Mexico, and a United States Territory. In the USA, New Mexico has the highest percentage of Hispanics including descendants of Spanish colonists and recent immigrants from Latin America. New Mexico also has the third-highest percentage of Native Americans, after Alaska and Oklahoma, and the fifth-highest total number of Native Americans. The tribes in the state consist of mostly Navajo, Apache and Pueblo peoples. *As a result, the demographics and culture of the state are unique for their strong Hispanic and Native American influences* [Italics added for emphasis]. (p. 6)

On the same page is a list of initiatives and projects that "comprise the Indian Education Division's current focus" (p. 6), which includes:

- State-Tribal Education Partnership (STEP)
- State Tribal Collaboration Report
- Navajo Nation Data Memorandum of Agreement (MoA)
- Rural Literacy Request for Proposal (RfP)
- Exemplary Grants
- Teacher Support Initiative RfP
- Tribal Language Grant Request for Application (RfA)
- Seat NMIEAC members
- Tribal Education Status Report (Statewide)
- Information Sessions
- Pueblo/Tribal visits
- Meetings on Indian Policies and Procedures (IPP) related to Impact Aid & Indian Add-On funds

Directly beneath this list is the following statement:

> We pledge to provide every Native American student with a valuable, worthwhile education and hold ourselves accountable for progress and results. Therefore, it is essential that our education system integrate continuous improvement within our regulations, policies, actions, and investments ensuring a strategic and coherent system. "If we're going to be in control of our destiny, we have to be in control of our education."—Everett Chavez, Governor, Pueblo of Kewa (p. 6).

A list appears on the next three pages of the 2012 Strategic Efforts and Achievements under the headings of Smarter Return on New Mexico's Investment; Real Accountability. Real Results; Ready for Success Initiative; and Rewarding Effective Educators and Leaders. A list of accomplishments that cover a wide spectrum of activities (64) or "elements" that impact the Indian Education Department is provided. A comparison of the list in the *Tribal Education Status Report* to the list of elements in the *2012 New Mexico Strategic Plan* (http://ped.state.nm.us/ped/PEDDocs/2012NMPEDStrategicPlan.pdf) yields a nearly identical list of elements. This calls into question the authenticity of the pledge to serve the educational needs of Indigenous youth in New Mexico and it demonstrates that the interests of the state continue to prevail.

Derrick Bell's (1980) theory of interest convergence is applicable here in that the state's Public Education Department may support social justice and equity-oriented policies and practices yet still believe that injustice can be "remedied effectively without altering the status of whites" (p. 522). Drawing on the work of Bell, G. R. Lopez (2003) argues that interest convergence centralizes the "belief that Whites will tolerate and advance the interests of people of color only when they promote the self-interests of Whites" (p. 84). Furthermore, the list of "educational programs targeting Native American students" in the *Tribal Status Report* does not address the hardcore curricular issue that Hingangaroa Smith cites as contested areas in places like New Zealand and New Mexico. The closest reference to curriculum is about operationalizing the Core Curriculum State Standards (CCSS).

A review of the website devoted to the New Mexico Common Core Standards (NMCCSS) (http://newmexicocommoncore.org/) yielded limited information on the role of Indigenous Peoples in the process of creating the standards. Like other states, New Mexico selected to adopt an additional 15% of local standards in the area of English Language Arts (ELA). The ELA/Literacy Launch Team included ELA educators and specialists, with Hispanic and Indian Education representatives. I returned to the Indian Education Division's website to locate information on the link between the NMCCSS and Indian education, but the search was unsuccessful.[5]

It appears that while diversity is recognized in the rhetoric of an executive summary and "Indian" participation on the ELA team is mentioned, there is no information on how the Core Standards will be aligned with the New Mexico Indian Education Act (NMIEA). The NMIEA was enacted as policy in 2003. The act is politically significant because of the potential power embedded in the 11-part statement of purpose.[6] Jojola, Lee, Alacantara, Belgarde, Bird, Lopez, and Singer (2010) provide a succinct description of the act:

> The *New Mexico Indian Education Act* (NMIEA) was passed in 2003 in an effort to ensure equitable and culturally relevant learning environments for Native students in public schools. The act sought to develop and implement positive educational systems; enhance the educational opportunities for students and aid in the development of culturally relevant materials for use in New Mexico schools; develop strategies for ensuring the maintenance of Native languages; increase tribal involvement and control; create formal government to government relationships between the tribes and state; and increase parental involvement in schools. The act also created an advisory council to oversee the Indian Education Act. The New Mexico Public Education Department, Indian Education Division contracted with the IESG to examine how well the schools were doing with regard to implementing the act. (p. 1)

New Mexico is one of a handful of states in the nation to legislate Indian Education in public education.[7] New Mexico governor Susanna Martinez and Secretary of Education Hannah Skandera have consistently disregarded the New Mexico Indian Education Act. In testimony before the Education Study Council in 2011, Acoma scholar Christine Sims stated: "Our concerns are about the current actions being taken with the Public Education Department that we see as undermining the intent and spirit of that law." She was referring to the disregard for parental involvement in reform measures and the siphoning of funds from the state's Indian Education office to Teach for America (TFA).[8]

Indeed, this may leave Indigenous Peoples with a less-than-optimistic view of educational reform. However, as scholars of color like San Miguel and Donato (2009) point out in their examination of the history of Latino education, that "while those in control of education used the schools or tried to use them for eliminating cultural differences and for promoting the subordination of ethnic and racial minority groups" people of color have "actively challenged, subverted, adapted, rejected, reinterpreted, co-opted, or contested these efforts" (p. 44). I believe this holds true for Indigenous Peoples. Furthermore, Hingangaroa Smith (2000) challenges Indigenous Peoples "to engage in positive, proactive initiatives rather than resorting to reactive modes of action" (p. 210) by setting "our own courses with respect to realizing our dreams and aspirations, and therefore we ought to be considering developing resistance initiatives around that kind of philosophy, initiatives that are positive and proactive. We must claim our own lives in order to put our destinies in our own hands" (p. 211).

Months preceding the 2012 state-wide celebration of a century of statehood, Pueblo leaders initiated a project to "claim our own lives" that would set the foundation for a special exhibit at the Indian Pueblo Cultural Center in Albuquerque called *100 Years of State & Federal Policy: The Impact on Pueblo Nations*.[9] Borne out of this project was the creation of a curriculum to provide K–12 educators with unit plans on the complex political, social, cultural, and economic history of the Pueblo Nations of New Mexico between 1912 and 2012.[10]

Description of the Curriculum

Exercising our right as Indigenous People to impart centuries-old knowledge and skills that predate European contact is critical to our survival in the 21st century and beyond. Indigenous People of New Mexico have routinely been engaged in the education of their youth since time immemorial. The curriculum served as a counter-narrative to the official presentation of the history of New Mexico presented in schools today. At the center of the curriculum were concepts and core values that have operated as vehicles for resistance, emancipation, and transformation for Pueblo People as they maintained cultural integrity and exercise sovereignty in the face of a sustained history of colonization.

The Leadership Institute at Santa Fe Indian School and a body of tribal leaders, educators, and scholars set the foundation for the curriculum. Regis Pecos of Cochiti Pueblo and Codirector of the Leadership Institute created a "Core Values Paradigm." The major components of the paradigm were Pueblo core values, gifts of the Creator, and the traditional calendar. Gifts of the Creator included land, language, way of life, laws and customs, governance, family, community, and natural resources. Core values included love, respect, compassion, faith, understanding, spirituality, and balance. The traditional calendar is comprised of the four seasons: spring, summer, fall, and winter. A timeline of federal and state policies set the chronology of historic events: 1912–2012. Collectively these components served as a framework for the curriculum project.

Pueblo educators were recruited to write the curriculum. They represented K–12 schools that served Pueblo youth across New Mexico.[11] With the support of facilitators from Taos, Acoma, and Zuni and staff from the Indian Pueblo Cultural Center, the writers designed a curriculum to be rich with instructional strategies, resources, and Pueblo-centered cultural knowledge. The main goal of the curriculum was for Indigenous students and their teachers to become intellectually aware of the critical roles of Pueblo People in exercising agency as they met (and continue to meet) the imposition and challenges of federal and state policies on our quality of life as sovereign entities. At the core of the curriculum is the belief that a critical sociopolitical-historical education is an effective avenue to strengthen home communities and to develop an increased awareness and examination of present-day manifestations of historic oppression.

From the first cycle of the curriculum development, three sets of curricula—elementary, middle, and high school—in four content areas (social studies, math, science, and language arts) were written, edited, and distributed at professional development sessions throughout the state. The sessions were designed for teachers to learn about the curriculum project, to review the curriculum, and to think critically about curriculum, instruction, and assessment. Five geographic areas—Zuni, Taos, Laguna, Santa Fe, and Albuquerque—were identified as sites for the workshops in 2013. Teachers were invited to participate in the workshop and in the pilot program.

The pilot program served as a means for classroom teachers to teach a lesson from the curriculum in their own classrooms, evaluate the effectiveness of the lesson plan (evaluation tool was provided), and to collect student work. Teachers who completed all of the conditions of the pilot program were compensated from a grant for their participation.[12] A total of 58 teachers participated in the five workshops. Twenty-three of the workshop participants completed the pilot program (39%). The lesson plan evaluations and student work provided important insight on the effectiveness of the curriculum in achieving the goals set for this project.

Religious Persecution of Pueblo People: A Lesson in Civil Rights

My role in the curriculum project began as a writer and moved to one of three facilitators of the project. I teamed up with Natalie Martinez, PhD, of Laguna who was the principal of Laguna Middle School and an experienced social studies teacher for close to 20 years. Together we developed a unit plan on the concept of civil rights. The rationale of the unit plan is below:

> Since 1912 the Pueblo People of New Mexico have been engaged in struggles to maintain the integrity of our cultural life, pre-Christian religious traditions and ceremonies, and political sovereignty. A key component that characterizes this struggle is the infringement on civil rights of Pueblo People as individuals and as sovereign entities. This unit plan will provide students with an opportunity to examine the concept of civil rights within the context of Pueblo history between 1912 and 2012. The emphasis is two-fold: one, to examine primary sources that represent multiple perspectives on:
>
> - Religious persecution of Pueblo People
> - Land tenure and water rights (Bursum Bill and Pueblo Lands Act)
> - Suffrage (Trujillo v. Garley, 1948)
> - Indian Civil Rights Act (1972)
> - American Indian Religious Freedom Act (1978)
> - Martinez Language Act (2006)

The second part of the two-fold emphasis is to illustrate how Pueblo People exercised sovereign powers to preserve cultural integrity and how we continue to not only address present day manifestations of infringements of our civil rights, but how we persevere and flourish as 19 sovereign nations.

One workshop participant who taught at a charter high school selected the lesson *Religious persecution of Pueblo People* to pilot in a humanities course.[13] The lesson was a primary source analysis of two documents from the 1920s: "Circular 1665: To All Indians" (February 24, 1923) written by Charles Burke, Commissioner of Indian Affairs, in 1923 and "Declaration to all Indians and to the People of the United States" (May 5, 1924) created by the Council of All the New Mexico Pueblos. See Appendix A to view the student packet. The packet consisted of four handouts:

- Handout #1: Formulate-Share-Listen-Create
- Handout #2: Transcription of "Circular 1665: To All Indians" (February 24, 1923)
- Handout #3: Council of All the New Mexico Pueblos, "Declaration to all Indians and to the People of the United States," May 5, 1924
- Handout #4: Questions for individual reflection and group discussion

The lesson was designed for students to critically analyze the concept of religious persecution as it was conceptualized and enforced in a period of anti-Indian, racist history in New Mexico.

The lesson was piloted at a charter high school in northern New Mexico. As directed, the teacher submitted his evaluation of the lesson along with student work. Student identifiers were removed from the worksheets so racial, ethnic, gender, and grade information was not included in the analysis of the responses. It should also be noted that the second set of questions in handout #4 that asked students to reflect on the primary sources was not complete. I did not ask the teacher why the worksheet was not complete, but it is highly probable that there was not enough time in the class period to complete the entire lesson. However, responses to the first set of questions in handout #1 provided insight on student perspectives of religious persecution.

The first set of questions in handout #1 consisted of "What is going to happen? Is this memo for real or is someone playing a cruel joke on us? If it is real, what can be done to challenge this order?" Below are the responses of eight students:

- Student A: I think the Natives would have to study up on their rights, make a case and take it to Washington, D.C.
- Student B: I think it's messed up. It's their land and we came to it. They shouldn't be able to do or take what's theirs! Dances, ceremonies, etc. just because it takes up time and money….The whole idea that no one can take our right and your religion even the government.
- Student C: Foolish, evil, the way the memo is. It's your way of looking at it. Everyone have the right to do something.
- Student D: The memo is someone playing a cruel joke. Native American people have the right to practice any religion or practices they want. This memo is denying the right of their people. Foolish, unreal. No right to do this. Reminds me of Christianizing Indians in Pueblo Revolt. No one can take away your religion or practices. Even the government!
- Student E: That's messed up for the people to say that your dances are foolish or evil or you can't do any cultural events during certain months.

- Student F: I would burn this in tonight's fire to stay warm. That's a whole lotta bullshit and that shit sucks. Shouldn't listen to out-of-towners. Just give them the finger and tell them to take a hike.
- Student G: Whether this memo is real or not, I believe that it is very wrong.
- Student H: I think the Natives would read their rights and rebel and take it to Washington, D.C.

The concept of "rights" is mentioned in five out of the eight responses. In this case, it refers to a claim, entitlement, or freedom to religious freedom. A second concept—government—is identified as the entity that is either persecuting Indigenous Peoples or it is the place where one can seek justice; e.g., "take it to Washington." Finally, the questions elicit emotive responses like the one written by student F: "I would burn this in tonight's fire to stay warm. That's a whole lotta bullshit and that shit sucks. Shouldn't listen to out-of-towners. Just give them the finger and tell them to take a hike" to a perspective that appears to be from the outside (non-Indigenous) but sensitive to the situation: "I think its messed up. It's their land and we came to it. They shouldn't be able to do or take what's theirs! Dances, ceremonies, etc. just because it takes up time and money....The whole idea that no one can take our right and your religion even the government." In the teacher's evaluation of the lesson was the comment: "Subject matter promotes engagement. Most people pay attention to injustice."

Student engagement with the past and making connections to the present was a major goal of the curriculum project. At one level, student engagement with an event in history—"Circular 1665: To All Indians" (February 24, 1923)—demonstrated how historical thinking can lead to the development of a historical consciousness. Drake and Nelson (2009) describe historical thinking and historical consciousness:

> Historical thinking involves historical consciousness, which requires thinking back and forth in time. It involves rational thinking about time and change and recognizing the interdependence, as well as the uniqueness, of the past, present, and future. Historical consciousness is more than "personal memory." It entails a willingness to look at the world through the "memories of others" and to contemplate the world through the filter of their thoughts. Historical thinking includes thinking about each era of the past in terms of its own values, perspectives, and context (called *historicism*), rather than imposing present values on the past. It compels a constant reviewing and thinking about a view of life. It requires a reflection on worldview…. Historical thinking is an antidote to self-centeredness. (p. 55)

The racial and ethnic composition of the class was diverse. For Indigenous youth in the class, the "message to all Indians" was a personal memory. It sparked a personal connection to a time when elders in their families had to contend with religious persecution. For others, the exercise moved them to reflect on a specific time in history—1924—when the religious and cultural rights of Indigenous Peoples were violated. Both groups were engaged in historical thinking.

Conclusion

Historical thinking as a means of developing a historical consciousness is a major thread that runs throughout the curriculum from the framework to the lesson plans. Three major goals were established for the curriculum project: (1) To help K–12 teachers educate their students about the factors and conditions—social, cultural, economic, and political—that shaped key relationships among the Pueblo Nations and between the Pueblo Nations and the United States throughout historical periods of turmoil and peaceful coexistence; (2) To guide instruction that enhanced self-esteem and cultural identity, encouraged guidance by ethical considerations, acknowledged concern for others, and incorporated an overall global perspective; and (3) To promote intellectual awareness among all students and their teachers of the critical roles of Pueblo Peoples in exercising agency as they addressed impositions and challenges of federal and state policies on their quality of life as sovereign nations. The envisioned outcome of the curriculum was to provide students with a strong foundation of knowledge for examining present-day manifestations of historical oppression. Ultimately, the question for Pueblo youth who will be leaders in the future is: What will be your contribution?

Envisioning the role of Pueblo youth in as leaders in the future requires a critical look at the sociocultural, political, and economic context of society. This form of reflection, according to Apple (2009) is relational analysis.

> It involves seeing social activity – with education as a particular form of that activity – as tied to a larger arrangement of institutions which apportion resources so that particular groups and classes have historically been helped while others have been less adequately treated. (p. 9)

In a relational analysis, the questions are formulated in such a way to probe the historical and contemporary underpinnings of how economic, political, and cultural processes operate. By asking questions that delve beneath the surface of what appears to be a *natural* outcome, educators and students can gain a deeper understanding of how and why certain perspectives are glorified and are at the center of public life while other narratives of history are marginalized or entirely absent from public view. The *100 Years of State and Federal Policy: The Impact on Pueblo Nations Curriculum* is one curricular challenge to the hegemony of official knowledge.

Appendix A: Student Packet

Handout #1: Formulate-Share-Listen-Create Read the passage below. Think about the questions raised at the end of the passage and complete step two on the back of this page.

Imagine that you are a Native youth who lives in one of the nineteen Indian pueblos in New Mexico. You attend the local high school in town. Your routine is take the school bus to your grandparents' house and help with chores until your parents pick you up after work. One day you find your grandmother crying at the kitchen table. Immediately, you drop your backpack on the floor and rush to her side. You ask, "Why are you crying grandma?" Unable to speak, she hands you a memo from the Department of Interior in Washington, D.C. The memo states:

TO ALL TRIBAL MEMBERS OF THE NINETEEN PUEBLOS OF NEW MEXICO:

Not long ago I held a meeting of federal officials in Washington, D.C., at which the feeling of those present was strong opposition to the enormous amount of time, money, and energy expended by the People of the Nineteen Pueblos on feast days, Indian dances, and other ceremonial activities held in your villages throughout the year. From the views of this meeting and information provided by non-Indian observers, I feel that something must be done to stop the neglect of your obligations at work and homes which are caused by these dances, celebrations, kiva activities, and gatherings of any kind that take the time of your people for many days.

Now, what I want you to think about very seriously is that you must first of all try to make your own living, which you cannot do unless you work faithfully and take care of what comes from your labor, and go to dances or other meetings only when your home work will not suffer by it. I do not want to deprive you of decent amusements or occasional feast days but you should not do evil or foolish things or take so much time for these occasions.

No good comes from your "give-away" custom at dances and it should be stopped. It is not right to torture your bodies in your ceremonies. All such extreme things are wrong and should be put aside and forgotten. You do yourselves and your families great injustice when at dances you give away money or other property and then after an absence of several days go home to find everything going to waste and yourselves with less to work with than you had before.

I could issue an order against these useless and harmful performances, but I would much rather have you give them up of your own free will and, therefore, I ask you now in this letter to do so. I urge you to come to an understanding and limit your cultural practices. Here are some suggestions:

1. That the Indian dances be limited to one in each month in the daylight hours of one day in the midweek, and at one center in each district;
2. That no dances or any other Indian religious activities take place during the months of March, April, June, July and August.
3. That no one take part in the dances or be present who are under 50 years of age.
4. That a careful propaganda be undertaken to educate public opinion against the dance and to provide a healthy substitute.

If at the end of one year the reports which I receive show that you are doing as requested, I shall be very glad for I will know that you are making progress in other and more important ways, but if the reports show that you reject this plea, then some other course will have to be taken.

With best wishes for your happiness and success,
Secretary of Interior

You try your best to console your grandmother. Meanwhile, a million thoughts and questions race through your mind. What is going to happen? Is this memo for real or is someone playing a cruel joke on us? If it is real, what can be done to challenge this order?

Formulate your answer to the questions: What is going to happen? Is this memo for real or is someone playing a cruel joke on us? If it is real, what can be done to challenge this order?
Listen carefully to your partner's answers and take notes.
With your partner, create new answers that incorporate the best of the ideas. Be prepared to present your answer if called upon.

Handout #2: Transcription of "Circular 1665: To All Indians" (February 24, 1923)
Carefully read the message written by Charles Burke, Commissioner of Indian Affairs, in 1923. Notice the similarities between this letter and the fictional memo that you read for the Formulate-Share-Listen-Create activity.

> Department of the Interior
> Office of Indian Affairs
> Washington
> A Message
>
> TO ALL INDIANS:
> Not long ago I held a meeting of Superintendents, Missionaries and Indians, at which the feeling of those present was strong against Indian dances, as they are usually given, and against so much time as is often spent by the Indians in a display of their old customs at public gatherings held by the whites. From the views of this meeting and from other information I feel that something must be done to stop the neglect of stock, crops, gardens, and home interests caused by these dances or by celebrations, pow-wows, and gatherings of any kind that take the time of the Indians for many days.
>
> Now, what I want you to think about very seriously is that you must first of all try to make your own living, which you cannot do unless you work faithfully and take care of what comes from your labor, and go to dances or other meetings only when your home work will not suffer by it. I do not want to deprive you of decent amusements or occasional feast days but you should not do evil or foolish things or take so much time for these occasions. No good comes from your "give-away" custom at dances and it should be stopped. It is not right to torture your bodies or to handle poisonous snakes in your ceremonies. All such extreme things are wrong and should be put aside and forgotten. You do yourselves and your families great injustice when at dances you give away money or other property, perhaps clothing, a cow, a horse or a team and wagon, and then after an absence of several days go home to find everything going to waste and yourselves with less to work with than you had before.
>
> I could issue an order against these useless and harmful performances, but I would much rather have you give them up of your own free will and, therefore, I ask you now in this letter to do so. I urge you to come to an understanding and an agreement with your Superintendent to hold no gatherings in the months when the seed-time, cultivation of crops and the harvest need your attention, and at other times to meet for only a short period and to have no drugs, intoxicants, or gambling, and no dancing that the Superintendent does not approve.

> If at the end of one year the reports which I receive show that you are doing as requested, I shall be very glad for I will know that you are making progress in other and more important ways, but if the reports show that you reject this plea, then some other course will have to be taken.
> With best wishes for your happiness and success, I am
> Sincerely yours,
> *Chas. H. Burke*
> February 24, 1923   Commissioner
> The Indian Print Shop, Chilacco, Oklahoma 2–17–1923

Handout #3: Council of All the New Mexico Pueblos, "Declaration to all Indians and to the People of the United States," May 5, 1924, Reel 40, Indian Rights Association Papers, Pennsylvania Historical Society, Philadelphia, Pennsylvania. Carefully read the response by the Pueblo Indian leaders to the message "To All Indians" from Charles Burke.

To all Pueblo People Indians, all Indians, and all the people of the U.S.:

We have met because our most fundamental right of religious liberty is threatened and is actually at this time being nullified. And we make as our first declaration the statement that our religion to us is sacred and is more important to us than anything else in our life. The religious beliefs and ceremonies and forms of prayer of each of our Pueblos are as old as the world, and they are holy. Our happiness, our moral behavior, our unity as a people and the peace and joyfulness of our homes, are all a part of our religion and are dependent on its continuation. To pass this religion, with its hidden sacred knowledge and its many forms of prayer, on to our children, is our supreme duty to our ancestors and to our own hearts and to the God whom we know. Our religion is a true religion and it is our way of life.

We must tell how our religious freedom is threatened and is denied to us. We specify first the order issued by the Commissioner of Indian Affairs to Superintendents, dated April 26, 1921. In that lengthy order, the Commissioner gives us a list of "Indian Offenses for which Corrective penalties are provided." He places upon local Superintendents the duty of determining whether Indian religious observances "cause the reckless giving away of property," are "excessive," promote "idleness, danger to health and shiftless indifference to family welfare." And one of our present Superintendents states his attitude in a printed Government report: "Until the old customs and Indian practices are broken up among this people we can not hope for a great amount of progress. The secret dance is perhaps one of the greatest evils. What goes on I will not attempt to say but I firmly believe that it is little less than a ribald system of debauchery." We denounce as untrue, shamefully untrue and without any basis of fact or appearance, and contrary to the abundant testimony of white scholars who have recorded our religious customs, this statement, and we point out the Commissioner's order, quoted here, to be interpreted and enforced by the local Superintendents, is an instrument of religious persecution. We next refer to the circular addressed "To All Indians," February 24, 1923. He states: "I could issue an order against these useless and harmful performances, but I would much rather have you give them up on your own free will and, therefore, I ask you now in this letter to do so. If at the end of one year the reports which I receive show that you are doing as requested, I shall be very glad, but if the reports show that you reject this plea, then some other course will have to be taken." And on February 14, 1923, the Commissioner addressed all Superintendents commending them to their attention the proposals of certain Christian missionaries stating that "the suggestions agreed in the main with his attitude." Among these suggestions were the following:

"That the Indian dances be limited to one each month in the daylight hours of one day in the midweek and at one center in each district; the months of March and April, June, July, and August being excepted (no dances these months)."

"That none take part in these dances or be present who are under 50 years of age."

"That a careful propaganda be undertaken to educate public opinion against the (Indian) dance."

We Pueblo Indians of course have not consented to abandon our religion. And now the Commissioner of Indian Affairs has just visited the Pueblos, and he went to Taos Pueblo and there he gave an order which will destroy the ancient good Indian religion of Taos if the order is enforced. He ordered that from this time on the boys could no longer be withdrawn temporarily from the government school to be given their religious instruction. These boys would stay longer in school to make up for the time lost, and there is no issue about the Indians not wanting their children to be educated in the Government schools. But if the right to withdraw the children for religious instruction be withdrawn, then the Indian religion will die. The two or three boys taken out of school each year are the boys who will learn all the religious system of the tribe, and they in turn will pass on this knowledge to the generation to come. When issuing this order to the Taos Pueblo, the Commissioner denounced the old customs and religions and he used harsh words about us who are faithful to the religious life of our race. He called us "half-animal."

And now we will call attention to the fact that when our children go to school, as they all must do and we want them to do, they are compelled to receive the teachings of the Christian religion no matter what the parents or the clan may desire. And the parents, the clans and the tribes are not even given the privilege of saying which branch or denomination of the Christian religion their children shall be taught. Thus a division is made between the parents and the children. And now if we are to be, according to the Commissioner's new order, forbidden to instruct our own children in the religion of their fathers, the Indian religions will quickly die and we shall be robbed of that which is most sacred and dear in our life.

We address the Indians and the people of the U.S. and we ask them to read the guarantees of religious liberty, which we have received. We came into the United States through the Treaty of Guadalupe Hidalgo, and that treaty guaranteed to all the inhabitants of the Southwest, that until such time as they were made citizens of the United States, "they should be maintained in the free enjoyment of their liberty and property, and secured in the free exercise of their religion without restriction." And we call attention to the covenant, which was a treaty, made between the United States and the People of New Mexico, whose words were embodied in the enabling act making New Mexico a State and in the Constitution of New Mexico:

"And said convention shall provide by an ordinance irrevocable without the consent of the United States and the people of the said State:

"First: – Perfect toleration of religious sentiment shall be secured, and no inhabitant of this state shall ever be molested in person or property on account of his or her mode of religious worship."

We conclude this statement by asking the citizens of the United States: shall the Commissioner of Indian Affairs be permitted to revoke these guarantees which the Congress of the United States itself could not revoke under the Constitution? We are but a few people, in the pueblos. We have inherited and kept pure from many ages ago a religion which, we are told, is full of beauty even to white persons. To ourselves at least, our religion is more precious than even our lives. The fair-play and generosity of the American People came to the rescue of the Pueblos when it was proposed to take away their lands. Will the American people not come to our rescue now, when it is proposed to take away our very souls?

We request and authorize the various organizations friendly to the Indians' cause, to act with and for us in this crisis. This appeal has been written with the help of representatives of these organizations though what it says is our own thought and our own plea.

Most of all we say to all Pueblos whom we represent – to all of the ten thousand Pueblo Indians, and likewise to the Hopi and Navajo Indians: This is the time of the great question. Shall we peacefully but strongly and deathlessly hold to the religions of our fathers, to our own religion, which binds us together and makes us the brothers and children of God? There is no future for the Race of the Indians if its religion is killed. We must be faithful to each other now.

This declaration was signed by leaders and members of these Pueblos: Taos, Picuris, San Juan, Santa Clara, San Ildefonso, Nambe, Acoma, Tesuque, Cochiti, Sandia, San Felipe, Santa Ana, Sia, Isleta, and twenty-two Santo Domingo Indians including the leaders.

Handout #4: Questions for individual reflection and group discussion, Drawing on information from the primary sources and your knowledge of this period of New Mexico history, write a three- to five-sentence response to each question. Be prepared to share your responses with your classmates.

1. What are the major differences between the letter from Commissioner Charles Burke and the Declaration from the Council of All the New Mexico Pueblos? In what ways are the differences significant?
2. What generalizations can be made about Charles Burke's perception of Pueblo Indian culture and religious life? What factors might have shaped his perception?
3. What generalizations can be made about the Pueblo leadership's perception of their cultural traditions, ceremonial life, and traditional religion?
4. In what ways are the points reflected in the statement by Cochiti elder Joseph Suina similar to the major points in the "Declaration to all Indians and to the People of the United States?"

Participation in the traditional practices is strong in all the communities, and many report that more and more young people have been taking part in recent years. There is greater pride in being a Pueblo than in earlier days. In the 1940s and 1950s, as the elders remind us, it was thought that living the good life meant being out in the wage-earning world of the white man. Today Pueblo youth are better educated about the past and have better employment, yet they come home – if they don't already live there – to participate in the religious activities of the Pueblo.

Unity and pride in the native culture and religion developed through silent resistance and made the Pueblo Revolt successful. The same unity and pride have undoubtedly kept the integrity and dignity of the Pueblo spirit alive and well over the years. From their ancestors, who struggled under the tyranny of outside rulers, they have learned to be masters of their own lives in their own way, provided they work together in the interest of all the people in the village.

Source: Suina, J. H. (2005). Underestimation of Pueblo Power. In *Po'Pay: Leader of the first American revolution* (pp. 80–81). Santa Fe, NM: Clear Light Publishing.

5. Pueblo people have consistently responded to challenges of colonizing powers—Spain, Mexico, and the United States—since first contact in the late 16th century. Why do you think Pueblo People continue to maintain a strong position on maintaining cultural integrity in the 21st century?

Notes

1. I use the term "peoples" in the plural form because it has a special connotation in international law. The term "peoples" signifies a right to self-determination and collective rights.
2. Officially known as the *Treaty of Peace, Friendship, Limits and Settlement between the United States of America and the Mexican Republic*, the treaty between the United States and Mexico brought an end to the war between the two nations. Negotiations began on January 2, 1848 and concluded on February 2, 1848. Mexico ceded the present-day states of Texas, New Mexico, and Alta California to the United States and Mexico received a payment of $15 million. The treaty was and continues to be politically significant for negotiating disputes over international boundaries, water and mineral rights, civil and property rights, citizenship, and land claims. There was opposition to New Mexico statehood by politicians in Congress who opposed statehood because of the large non-English speaking population and high illiteracy rates.
3. *Nuevo Mexicano* signifies a strong affinity with Spanish ancestry for some. Benjamin (1997) uses the term *Nuevo Mexicano* to refer "to those of Spanish-speaking descent who have lived continuously in New Mexico for several centuries and who, while sharing some cultural characteristics with those from Mexico, identify primarily with patria chica, *Nuevo* Mexico" (p. 40). Another term that is used in this state is Hispanic.
4. In 2000, New Mexico was officially designated a "minority majority" state, that is, a state in which the number of "minorities" (Hispanics, Native Americans, Asians, and African Americans) exceeds the number of non-Hispanic whites.
5. It should be noted that in 2010, a PowerPoint presentation, *New Mexico Adoption of Common Core Standards: Native American Input*, created by Dr. Anya Dozier Enos of Santa Clara Pueblo was available at the IED website. The presentation focuses on a strategy for Native Americans to contribute to the 15% allowance for local knowledge.
6. See the website http://www.ped.state.nm.us/indian.ed/dl08/ARTICLE.23A.pdf for the entire text of the act.
7. Montana Indian Education for All; South Dakota Indian Education Act; Arizona Indian Education Act; Wisconsin Educational Act 31; Washington State House Bill 1495; Maine Revised Statute 4706.
8. See article by Anthony Cody (March 18, 2013) "Native Americans Challenge Teach for America in New Mexico" at http://blogs.edweek.org/teachers/living-in-dialogue/2013/03/native_americans_challenge_tea.html for a critique of TFA in New Mexico.
9. History of this exhibit can be accessed at http://www.indianpueblo.org/100years/index.html.
10. New Mexico is the geographical site of 22 Indigenous nations of which 19 are the Pueblo nations: Taos, Picuris, Ohkay Owingeh, Santa Clara, San Ildefonso, Pojoaque, Nambe, Tesuque, Kewa, San Felipe, Santa Ana, Sandia, Isleta, Zia, Cochiti, Jemez, Acoma, Laguna, and Zuni. The non-Pueblo nations are the Diné, Mescalero Apache, and Jicarilla Apache. Each of the 22 nations operate as sovereign entities politically, culturally, and linguistically. However, it should be noted as late Jemez scholar Joe Sando (2005) writes: "[Pueblo nations] share a common traditional native religion, although rituals and observations may vary; a similar lifestyle and philosophy; and a common economy based on the same geographical region occupied by them for thousands of years. However, the Pueblos also have an independence similar to that of nations; although they are in close proximity to one another, and subject to the same natural forces, each maintains a unique identity" (pp. xv–xvi).
11. Fifteen curriculum writers representing elementary, middle, and high schools participated in the project. All writers were enrolled members of a Pueblo Nation.
12. A grant from the W. K. Kellogg Foundation provided funding for the curriculum project.
13. This was one of three lessons that I developed for the unit plan.

References

Apple, M. (2009). *Ideology and curriculum*. New York: RoutledgeFalmer.
Bell, D. (1980). *Brown v. Board of Education* and the interest-convergence dilemma. *Harvard Law Review, 93*(3), 518–533.
Benjamin, R. (1997). *Si hablas Espanol eres mojado*: Spanish as an identity marker in the lives of Mexicano children. *Social Justice, 24*(2), 26–44.
Casanova, U. (2012). *¡Sí Se Puede!* New York: Teachers College Press.

Cody, A. (2013) "Native Americans Challenge Teach for America in New Mexico." Retrieved from http://blogs.edweek.org/teachers/living-in-dialogue/2013/03/native_americans_challenge_tea.html

Drake, F. D., & Nelson, L. R. (2009). *Engagement in teaching history: Theory and practices for middle and secondary teachers.* Upper Saddle River, NJ: Pearson.

Gómez, L. (2005). Off-white in an age of white supremacy: Mexican elites and the rights of Indians and Blacks in nineteenth-century New Mexico. *Chicano – Latino Law Review, 25*(9), 9–59.

Jojola T., Lee, T. S., Alacantara, A., Belgarde, M., Bird, C., López, N., & Singer, B. (2010). *Indian Education in New Mexico, 2025.* Contracted by the New Mexico Public Education Department, Indian Education Division.

Lee, S. J. (1995). *Unraveling the "model minority" stereotype: Listening to Asian American youth.* New York: Teachers College Press.

Lee, S. J. (2005). *Up against whiteness: Race, school, and immigrant youth.* New York: Teachers College Press.

Lopez, G. R. (2003). The (racially neutral) politics of education: A critical race theory perspective. *Educational Administration Quarterly, 39*(1), 68–94.

Lopez, N. (2003). *Hopeful girls, troubled boys: Race and gender disparity in urban education.* New York: Routledge.

Martinez, G. (2010). *Native pride: The politics of curriculum and instruction in an urban public high school.* Cresskill, NJ: Hampton Press, Inc.

McCarthy, C. (1990). *Race and curriculum: Social inequality and the theories and politics of difference in contemporary research on schooling.* Bristol, PA: The Falmer Press.

Melzer, R., & Kerwin Reyes, C. (2012). *The New Mexico Journey.* Layton, UT: Gibbs Smith Education.

New Mexico Public Education Department Indian Education Division (2010). *Indian education in New Mexico, 2025.* Retrieved from http://www.unm.edu/~socdept/pdfs/NMIndianEdRpt2011Apr2411.pdf

Patel, L. (2013). *Youth held at the border: Immigration, education, and the politics of inclusion.* New York: Teachers College Press.

San Miguel, G. & Donato, R. (2009). Latino education in twentieth-century America: A brief history. In Murillo, Villenas, Trinidad Galvan, Munoz, & Martinez (Eds.), *Handbook of Latinos and Education: Theory, Research, and Practice* (pp. 27–62). New York: Taylor and Francis.

Smith, G. H. (1990). The politics of reforming Maori education: The transforming potential of Kura Kaupapa Maori. In Lauder & Wylie (Eds.), *Towards successful schooling* (pp. 73–87). London: Falmer Press.

Smith, G. H. (2000). Protecting and respecting indigenous knowledge. In Battiste, M. (Ed.), *Reclaiming indigenous voice and vision* (pp. 209–224). Vancouver: UBC Press.

Suina, J. H. (2005). Underestimation of pueblo power. In Sando, J., & Agoyo, H. (Eds.), *Po'Pay: Leader of the first American revolution* (pp. 72–81). Santa Fe, NM: Clear Light Publishing.

Wilkins, D. (2002). *American Indian politics and the American political system.* Lanham, MD: Rowman & Littlefield.

TWELVE

Broadening the Circle of Critical Pedagogy

E. Wayne Ross

Critical pedagogy is understood (and misunderstood) in myriad ways. Most often associated with Paulo Freire's (1970) problem-posing approach in opposition to the traditional banking method of education, it is also closely connected with neo-Marxist, critical theory-based analyses of education, schooling, and society. Despite popular perception, and the conceptualizations of critical pedagogy by some of its most well-known proponents, there is no single ideological perspective or particular social movement that defines critical pedagogy.

The dominant conceptualizations of critical pedagogy are unnecessarily narrow, both politically and philosophically. As a result, a pedagogical approach that is undeniably powerful has been undermined and its impact blunted. Critical pedagogy has become less a process of students investigating the world and constructing personally meaningful understandings that aid them in the struggle to overcome oppression and achieve freedom and more akin to an *a priori* set of beliefs about the world presented as maps to be followed. In other words, critical pedagogy has met the enemy and he is us, or at least includes us. If critical pedagogy, as a process of education, is to achieve its aims it cannot exempt itself from the same uprooting and examination of its own underlying assumptions, pronouncements, clichés, and received wisdom.

My aim here is to broaden the circle of critical pedagogy. I will illustrate how we might increase its uptake by teachers and its effects on individuals, schools, and society by adopting a less orthodox conception of what it means to practice critical pedagogy.

Broadening the Circle Philosophically

Critical pedagogy did not evolve from a single philosophical source and its core aims and methods can be tied to a variety of philosophical traditions.

Freire and Dewey

The core idea of critical pedagogy is to submit received understandings to critical analysis with the aim of increasing human knowledge and freedom. Ira Shor offers the most straightforward description of critical pedagogy:

> Habits of thought, reading, writing, and speaking which go beneath surface meaning, first impressions, dominant myths, official pronouncements, traditional clichés, received wisdom, and mere opinions, to understand the deep meaning, root causes, social context, ideology, and personal consequences of any action, event, object, process, organization, experience, text, subject matter, policy, mass media, or discourse. (Shor, 1992, p. 129)

Now consider philosopher John Dewey's description of "reflective" thinking.

> Active, persistent, and careful consideration of any belief or supposed form of knowledge in the light of the grounds that support and the further conclusions to which it tends…(p. 8)

While Dewey's philosophy falls outside the realm we know as critical theory, there is significant commonality between these two approaches to understanding and knowing the world. Critical pedagogy is a tool to expose and deconstruct cultural hegemony, the idea that the ruling elite manipulates social mores so that their view becomes the dominant worldview. While Dewey did not use the term hegemony, he recognized the problem and constructed his conception of education in response to it. In *Democracy and Education* (1916) Dewey wrote

> …the word education means just a process of leading or bringing up. When we have the outcome of the process in mind, we speak of education as shaping, forming, molding activity—that is, a shaping into the standard form of social activity….The required beliefs cannot be hammered in; the needed attitudes cannot be plastered on. But the particular medium in which an individual exists leads him to see and feel one thing rather than another; it leads him to have certain plans in order that he may act successfully with others; it strengthens some beliefs and weakens others as a condition of winning the approval of others. Thus it gradually produces in him a certain system of behavior, a certain disposition of action. (Chapter 2, paras. 1–2)

Dewey and Freire share the idea that education is not a neutral process. Dewey's *Democracy and Education* (1916) opens with a discussion of the way in which all societies use education as a means of social control by which adults consciously shape the dispositions of children. He goes on to argue that education as a social process and function has no definite meaning until we define the kind of society we have in mind. In other words, there is no "scientifically objective" answer to the question of the purposes of education, because those purposes are not things that can be discovered. Similarly, Freire (1970; 1974) described education as either an instrument that is used to integrate people into the logic of the present system and bring about conformity to it, or it becomes "the practice of freedom," that is the means by which people deal critically and creatively with reality and discover how to participate in the transformation of their world.

Dewey's radical reconceptualization of democracy has much to offer critical pedagogy (Bernstein, 2010). His notion of democracy cannot be found in the electoral democracies of capitalism. For Dewey, the primary responsibility of democratic citizens is concern with the development of shared interests that lead to sensitivity about repercussions of their actions on others. Dewey characterized democracy as a force that breaks down barriers that separate people and creates community. The more porous the boundaries of social groups the more they welcome participation from all individuals, and as the varied groupings enjoy multiple and flexible relations, society moves closer to fulfilling the democratic ideal.

From a Deweyan perspective, democracy is not merely a form of government nor is it an end in itself; it is the means by which people discover, extend, and manifest human nature and human rights. For Dewey, democracy has three roots: free individual existence; solidarity with others; and choice of work and other forms of participation in society. The aim of democratic education and thus a democratic society is the production of free human beings associated with one another on terms of equality.

For me, there is an easy connection to be made between Dewey and the more traditional roots of critical pedagogy in Freire's work. Additionally, I see threads in these Deweyan roots of democracy that are in sync with at least some strains of anarchist thought, particularly opposition to authority and hierarchical organization in human relations and mutual aid and respect. Dewey was not an anarchist; far from it. But, as Noam Chomsky (2000; Ross, 2014) has pointed out, Dewey's conceptualization of democracy and democratic education can be understood as supportive of social anarchist principles (something I come back to later). While Dewey's democratically informed education philosophy is quite familiar to folks in education, it has largely been influential only conceptually; its radical potential remains, in almost every respect, unrealized in schools and society and that is a challenge for critical pedagogues.

Dialectics and Critical Pedagogy

From Shor's defining of critical pedagogy we can see reality is more than appearances and focusing exclusively on appearances—on the evidence that strikes us immediately and directly—can be misleading. Basing an understanding of ourselves and our world on what we see, hear, or touch in our immediate surroundings can lead us to conclusions that are distorted or false.

> Understanding anything in our everyday experience requires that we know something about how it arose and developed and how it fits into the larger context or system of which it is a part. Just recognizing this, however, is not enough….After all, few would deny that everything in the world is changing and interacting at some pace and in one way or another, that history and systemic connections belong to the real world. The difficulty has always been how to think adequately about them, how not to distort them and how to give them the attention and weight that they deserve. (Ollman, 1993, p. 11)

Dialectics, Ollman explains, is an attempt to resolve this difficulty by expanding the notion of "anything" to include (as aspects of what is) both the process by which it has become that thing and the broader interactive context in which it is found. Dialectics restructures thinking about reality by replacing the commonsense notion of "thing," as something that has a history and has external connections to other things, with notions of "process" (which contains its history and possible futures) and "relation" (which contains as part of what it is its ties with other relations). Or, as Sciabarra puts it, dialectics is the "art of context-keeping":

> It counsels us to study the object of our inquiry from a variety of perspectives and levels of generality, so as to gain a more comprehensive picture of it. That study often requires that we grasp the object in terms of the larger system within which it is situated, as well as its development across time. Because human beings are not omniscient, because none of us can see the "whole" as if from a "synoptic" godlike perspective, it is only through selective abstraction that we are able to piece together a more integrated understanding of the phenomenon before us—an understanding of its antecedent conditions, interrelationships, and tendencies. (2005, para. 8)

Abstraction is like using camera lenses with different focal lengths: a zoom lens to bring a distant object into focus (what is the history of this?) or using a wide-angle lens to capture more of a scene (what is the social context of the issue now?) This raises important questions: Where does one start and what does one look for? The traditional approach to inquiry starts with small parts and attempts to establish connections with other parts leading to an understanding of the larger whole. Beginning with the whole, the system, or as much as we understand of it, and then inquiring into the part or parts of it to see how it fits and functions leads to a fuller understanding of the whole.

For example, many people of various political persuasions have pointed out the paradox of the growing wealth of the few and the increasing poverty of the many, as well as connections between the interests of corporations and the actions of governments and of being powerless and poor. As Ollman (1993) points out, despite awareness of these relations, most people do not take such observations seriously. Lacking a theory to make sense of what they are seeing, people don't know what importance to give it; forget what they have just seen, or exorcise the contradictions by labeling them a paradox. The problem is that the socialization we undergo (in and out of school) encourages us to focus on the particulars of our circumstances and to ignore interconnections. Thus, we miss the patterns that emerge from relations. Social studies education plays an important role in reinforcing this tendency. The social sciences break up human knowledge into various disciplines (history, anthropology, sociology, geography, etc.), each with its own distinctive language and ways of knowing, which encourages concentrating on bits and pieces of human experience. What existed before is usually taken as given and unchanging. As a result, political and economic upheavals (such as the revolutions of 1789, 1848, 1917, and 1989) are treated as anomalous events with discrete explanations.

Dialectical thinking, on the other hand, is an effort to understand the world in terms of interconnections—the ties among things as they are right now, their own preconditions, and future possibilities. The dialectical method takes change as the given and treats apparent stability as that which needs to be explained (and provides specialized concepts and frameworks to explain it). Dialectical thinking is an approach to understanding the world that requires not only a lot of facts that are usually hidden from view, but a more interconnected grasp of the facts we already know.

Dialectics is a core method of critical pedagogy. And while dialectics has been called "Marx's method" it should be noted that most of Marx's dialectic evolved from Georg Wilhelm Friedrich Hegel, who systematized a way of thinking that goes back to the ancient Greeks, Aristotle's *Topics*. Additionally, non-Marxist thinkers like Alfred North Whitehead and British Idealist F. H. Bradley developed their own versions of dialectics, while Chris Matthew

Sciabarra and John F. Welsh (2007) put dialects to use in the service of libertarian social theory. And as Sciabarra (2005) writes:

> What makes a dialectical approach into a *radical* approach is that the task of going to the root of a social problem, seeking to understand it and resolve it, often requires that we make transparent the relationships among social problems. Understanding the complexities at work within any given society is a prerequisite for changing it. It is simply mistaken to believe that Marx and Marxists have had a monopoly on this type of analysis. It is also mistaken to believe that this emphasis on grasping the full context is, somehow, a vestige of Marxism.

Priestcraft and Critical Pedagogy

Like mainstream liberal educators who believe in the culturally redemptive power of schooling, critical pedagogy has an educational messiah complex that too often turns critical educators into priests, whose aim is to mediate the everyday life of students and teachers. Too often critical pedagogy is conceptualized from above.

Paulo Freire is undoubtedly the key figure in the development of critical pedagogy. His focus on consciousness, critique, utopian vision (the need for imagining a better future before it can be achieved), the critical role of education for social justice, and the necessity of leadership unified with the people, should be seen as fundamental guidelines for movements for social change. Yet as Gibson (2007) points out, there are problems with Freire's work and he and his work have been reified in uncritical praise by prominent academics surrounding his work in the English-speaking world.

> As an icon, Freire indeed became a commodity. His work was purchased, rarely as a whole, but in selective pieces, which could further the career of an academic, propel the interests of a corporation or a state-capitalist "revolutionary" party. Many of his enthusiasts called his work "eclectic," and let it go at that. But Freire called himself a contradictory man. His politics were often seemingly at odds. (p. 180)

Gibson's analysis reveals two Freires. The Marxist Freire urged the analysis of labor and production, but was unable to resolve the incongruity of human liberation and capitalism's demand for inequality in order to motivate national economic development. The Catholic-humanist-postmodern Freire denied the centrality of class and focused on deconstructing culture and language. In both cases, Freire relied on the ethics of the educator-leader to mediate the tensions between middle-class teachers and profoundly exploited students.

It is impossible to imagine critical pedagogy without the profound contributions of Freire (e.g., his emphasis on the pivotal role of ideas as a material force, his critical method of analysis, his determination to engage in concrete social practice, his democratic and ethical pedagogy, and his insistence on non-hierarchical leadership), however, being true to his legacy requires us to critically re-examine his work and what it means for us today; avoiding reification of his texts; taking care not to strip them of their politics or overlook the contradictions to be found there.

There is no place for evangelists in critical pedagogy because the aim is not to convert people to *a priori* assumptions, beliefs, or knowledge. At the heart of Freire's interactive approach to education, and often overlooked or ignored, is observation, experience, and judgment (as opposed to knowledge that proceeds just from theoretical deduction).

Humans tend to construct beliefs based upon insufficient knowledge and understanding, then cling to them, rejecting evidence to the contrary, as a result, there is no place for "believers" in critical pedagogy. Critical pedagogy as a process rejects prejudices or prejudgements, that is, thought or belief that accepts superficial appearances. Tradition, instruction, and imitation all depend on authority in some form. A critical pedagogy thrives on scepticism, doubt, analysis, radical inquiry, thus no priests are necessary because the point is for people to think for themselves. Whether the promise of critical consciousness and liberation from oppression can be achieved by Freire's theoretical stance or his "see-judge-act" system of interactive education is an empirical question.

The Individual, Institutions, Social Change, and Critical Pedagogy

Critical pedagogy as a practice has been critiqued both internally and externally. For example, McLaren laments "the domestication of critical pedagogy," that is critical pedagogy efforts that have been accommodated to mainstream liberal humanism and progressivism and "marked by flirtation with but never full commitment to revolutionary praxis" (2000, p. 98). Identifying postmodernism and poststructuralism as the heart of this problem, McLaren quotes Carl Boggs to make his point:

> In politics as in the cultural and intellectual realm, a postmodern fascination with indeterminacy, ambiguity, and chaos easily supports a drift toward cynicism and passivity; the subject becomes powerless to change either itself or society. Further the pretentious, jargon-filled and often indecipherable discourse of postmodernism reinforces the most faddish tendencies in academia. Endless (and often pointless) attempts to deconstruct texts and narrative readily become a façade behind which professional scholars justify their own retreat from political commitment...the extreme postmodern assault on macro institutions severs the connections between critique and action. (1997, p. 767)

On the other hand postmodernist Elizabeth Ellsworth (1989) critiques the critical pedagogy literature as highly abstract, utopian, and out of touch with the everyday practice of teachers. Ellsworth maintains that the discourse of critical pedagogy gives rise to repressive myths that perpetuate relations of domination where "objects, nature, and 'Others' are seen to be known or ultimately knowable, in the sense of being 'defined, delineated, captured, understood, explained, and diagnosed' at a level of determination never accorded to the 'knower' herself or himself" (p. 321). In response to critical pedagogy Ellsworth offers her preferred version of classroom practice as a kind of communication across difference that is represented in this statement:

> If you can talk to me in ways that show you understand that your knowledge of me, the world, and 'the Right thing to do' will always be partial, interested, and potentially oppressive to others, and if I can do the same, then we can work together on shaping and reshaping alliances for constructing circumstances in which students of difference can thrive. (p. 324)

In this argument I tend to agree with McLaren (see, for example, Hill, McLaren, Cole, Ritkowski, 2002; Ross & Gibson, 2007), but Ellsworth's critique identifies an important blind spot within critical pedagogy regarding the individual, the personal, and identity.

In his excellent history of the free school movement of the 1960s, Ron Miller (2002) reassesses and revives the legacy of John Holt. Holt was not a scholar or a theorist, but rather a moralist and reformer, a thinker described as a social ecologist and constructive postmodernist, who became closely associated with the deschooling and homeschooling movements in North America.

As Miller points out, Holt, like John Dewey, was not an ideologue and endorsed no "-ism." Holt warned against the quest for ideological purity and "over-abstractness." He advocated an organic worldview, "an appreciation for the living, dynamic, evolving, interacting, and responsive nature of reality" (Miller, p. 83). Holt held several fundamental principles that should be taken seriously by critical educators:

- the dignity and value of human existence and faith in the human capacity to learn;
- concern for freedom and belief that it was being seriously eroded by the impersonality of large organizations and the forms of surveillance and control practiced in social institutions, particularly schools;
- opposing centralized political and economic power that rests on scientific-technological management of natural and human resources;
- the driving concern for the need of each person to find a meaningful, fulfilling sense of identity in a mass society that makes this difficult. (Miller, p. 83)

Holt "sought a thorough renewal of culture that would be as concerned with personal wholeness and authenticity as with social justice" (Miller, p. 85). In the tradition of Thoreau, he saw himself as a "decentralist" who "leaned in the direction of anarchism," he "did not so much seek to reform social institutions as to circumvent and thus deflate them" (Miller, p. 85). Holt was primarily concerned about human growth and learning, but he focused on the relationship between social institutions and human development. His emphasis on the personal dimension of social reality addresses a blind spot within critical pedagogy, which too often privileges the institutional analysis at the expense of existential authenticity, that is the individual person's concern that his or her life is meaningful and fulfilling. Holt described his deepest interest as, "how can we adults work to create a more decent, humane, conserving, peaceful, just, etc. community, nation, world, and how can we make it possible for children to join us in this work?" (Miller, p. 86).

> Holt emphasized the connection between the social and the individual, between the political and the existential. Human beings could not grow whole in a fragmented or violent culture, but at the same time a decent culture would only emerge when people personally experienced meaning and fulfillment. (Miller, p. 86)

Miller argues that what distinguishes Holt's position from "progressive" critiques was his insistence that reform of social institutions alone was not sufficient for cultural renewal. For Holt, the source of violence, racism, and exploitation was not in institutions as such, but in the psychological reality people experience as they live in society. The implication for critical pedagogy is that its focus on institutional transformation has neglected the existential dimension of meaning, too often ignoring personal desire for belonging, community, and moral commitment.

To be clear, neither Holt nor I am advocating a perspective that is merely personal or individualistic. Holt was very aware of political forces and expressed his concern that the worship of progress and growth was inevitably leading to fascism. In his 1970 book, *What Do I Do Monday?* Holt suggests that alienation bred by authoritarian education could "prepare the ground for some naïve American brand of Fascism, which now seems uncomfortably close." Miller quotes a letter Holt wrote to Paul Goodman, in 1970:

> I keep looking for and hoping to find evidence that [Americans] are not as callous and greedy and cruel and envious as I fear they are, and I keep getting disappointed....What scares me is the amount of Fascism in people's spirit. It is the government that so many of our fellow citizens would get if they could that scares me—and I fear we are moving in that direction. (p. 89)

Unfortunately, Holt was prescient about politics in the United States, as well as about institutional, particularly school, reform, as an effective path for social change. In 1971, Holt wrote in *New Schools Exchange Newsletter*,

> I do not believe that any movement for educational reform that addresses itself exclusively or even primarily to the problems or needs of children can progress very far. In short, in a society that is absurd, unworkable, wasteful, destructive, coercive, monopolistic, and generally anti-human, we could never have good education, no matter what kind of schools the powers that be permit, because it is not the educators or the schools but the whole society and the quality of life in it that really educate....More and more it seems to me, and this is a reversal of what I felt not long ago, that it makes very little sense to talk about education *for* social change, as if education was or could be a kind of getting ready. The best and perhaps only education for social change is action to bring about that change....There cannot be little worlds fit for children in a world not fit for anyone else. (Quoted in Miller, 2002, p. 90)

In his 1972 book, *Freedom and Beyond*, Holt grappled with the key concepts of critical pedagogy: social justice, racism, poverty, and class conflict, arguing, as Miller points out, that schools were contributing to these problems rather than helping to solve them. Unlike the social reconstructionists of mid-20th century (e.g, Counts, 1932), Holt came to see schools (even democratic free schools) not as potential sources for recreation of the social order, but rather obstacles to be overcome in the pursuit of social change. He wondered whether "we are trying to salve our consciences by asking our children to do what we can't and don't want to do" (1972, p. 232).

Holt concluded that schools "tend to take learning out of its living context and turn it into an abstraction, a commodity" (Miller, p. 95). Or as he once said, "I'm enough of an anarchist to feel that things are improved in general when they are improved in their particulars." And this is the principle that addresses, at least in part, the concerns Ellsworth famously raised in her critique of critical pedagogy.

The question becomes how can we create a better balance between the abstraction (a focus on the general nature of things) and authenticity (a focus on the particulars) within critical pedagogy. Holt argued that attempting to change society through schools was an evasion of personal responsibility because authentic meaning cannot be cultivated en masse. "People don't change their ideas, much less their lives, because someone comes along with a clever argument to show that they're wrong" (Holt, 1981, p. 66). So, critical educators are left with a conundrum.

The Future of Critical Pedagogy

Foucault argued that practicing criticism is a matter of making facile gestures difficult and his definition of critique has much in common with Shor's definition of critical pedagogy.

> A critique is not a matter of saying that things are not right as they are. It is a matter of pointing out on what kinds of assumptions, what kinds of familiar, unchallenged, unconsidered modes of thought the practices that we accept rest....Criticism is a matter of flushing out that thought and trying to change it: to show that things are not as self-evident as one believed, to see what is accepted as self-evident will no longer be accepted as such. (1988, pp. 154–155)

Critical pedagogy continues to evolve and it is up to us, as critical educators, to continually engage in self-critique and pedagogical renovation.

People who talk about transformational learning or educational revolution without referring explicitly to everyday life, without understanding what is subversive about learning, and love, and what is positive in the refusal of constraints, are trapped in a net of received ideas, the common-nonsense and false reality of technocrats (or worse).

Schools are alluring contradictions, harboring possibilities for liberation, emancipation, and social progress, but, as fundamentally authoritarian and hierarchical institutions, they produce myriad oppressive and inequitable by-products. The challenge, perhaps impossibility, is discovering ways in which schools can contribute to positive liberty. That is a society where individuals have the power and resources to realize and fulfill their own potential, free from the obstacles of classism, racism, sexism, and other inequalities encouraged by capitalism and its educational systems as well as the influence of the state and religious ideologies. A society where people have agency and capacity to make their own free choices and act independently based on reason, not authority, tradition, or dogma.

Education, as a whole, really is a critical knowledge of everyday life. Genuine community and genuine dialogue can exist only when each person has access to a direct experience of reality, when everyone has at his or her disposal the practical and intellectual means needed to solve problems. The question is not to determine what the students *are* at present, but rather what they *can become*, for only then is it possible to grasp what in truth they *already are*. (And the same applies to us, as critical educators.)

Studying how people (and things) change is the heart of social understanding and critical pedagogy. For me, perhaps the most compelling element of critical pedagogy is that active investigation of social and educational issues contributes to change. As Mao Zedong (1937) said,

> If you want to know the taste of a pear, you must change the pear by eating it yourself. If you want to know the theory and methods of revolution, you must take part in revolution. All genuine knowledge originates in direct experience.

Mao's position on the role of experience in learning is remarkably similar to those of John Dewey. Both of these philosophers, although poles apart ideologically, share what has been described as an activist conception of human beings, that is the view that people create themselves on the basis of their own self-interpretations. Although, as Marx points out, while people make their own history, they do not make it as they please, but under circumstances existing already, given and transmitted from the past.

Reduced to its most basic elements, critical pedagogy should seek to create conditions in which students (and educators) can develop personally meaningful understandings of the world and recognize they have agency to act on the world, to make change.

Critical pedagogy is not about showing life to people, but bringing them to life. The aim is not getting students to listen to convincing lectures by experts, but getting them to speak for themselves in order to achieve, or at least strive toward an equal degree of participation and a better future.

References

Bernstein, R. J. (2010). Dewey's vision of radical democracy. In M. Cochran, *The Cambridge companion to Dewey* (pp. 288–308). Cambridge, UK: America's Cambridge University Press.
Boggs, C. (1997). The great retreat: Decline of the public sphere in late twentieth century America. *Theory and Society, 26,* 741–780.
Chomsky, N., & Macedo, D. P. (2000). *Chomsky on miseducation.* Lanham, MD: Rowman & Littlefield.
Counts, G. S. (1932). *Dare the school build a new social order?* New York: John Day Company.
Dewey, J. (1916). *Democracy and education.* New York: Macmillan. Retrieved from http://xroads.virginia.edu/~HYPER2/dewey/ch02.html
Dewey, J. (1933). *How we think.* Lexington, MA: Heath.
Ellsworth, E. (1989). Why doesn't this feel empowering? Working through the repressive myths of critical pedagogy. *Harvard Educational Review, 59*(3), 297–324.
Foucault, M. (1988). Practicing criticism. In L. D. Kritzman (Ed.), *Politics, Philosophy, Culture: Interviews and Other Writings 1977–1984.* New York: Routledge.
Freire, P. (1970). *Pedagogy of the oppressed.* New York: Continuum.
Freire, P. (1974). *Education for critical consciousness.* New York: Continuum.
Freire, P. (1985). Reading the world and reading the word: An interview with Paulo Freire. *Language Arts, 62*(1), 15–21.
Gibson, R. (2007). Paulo Freire and revolutionary pedagogy for social justice. In E. W. Ross & R. Gibson (Eds.), *Neoliberalism and education reform* (pp. 177–215). Cresskill, NJ: Hampton Press.
Hill, D., McLaren, P., Cole, M., & Rikowski, G. (Eds.). (2002). *Marxism against postmodernism in educational theory.* Lanham, MD: Lexington Books.
Holt, J. (1981). *Teach your own.* New York: Dell.
Holt, J. (1995). *Freedom and beyond.* Portsmouth, NH: Boynton/Cook. (Originally published in 1972).
Holt, J. (1995). *What do I do Monday?* Portsmouth, NH: Boynton/Cook. (Originally published in 1970).
McLaren, P. (2000). *Che Guevara, Paulo Freire, and the pedagogy of revolution.* Lanham, MD: Rowman & Littlefield.
Miller, R. (2002). *Free schools, free people: Education and democracy after the 1960s.* Albany State University of New York Press.
Ollman, B. (1999). *Dance of the dialectic.* New York: Routledge.
Ross, E. W., & Gibson, G. (Eds.). (2007). *Neoliberalism and education reform.* Cresskill, NJ: Hampton Press.
Ross, E. W. (2014). Noam Chomsky. In D. C. Phillips (Ed.), *Encyclopedia of educational theory and philosophy* (pp. 126–127). Thousand Oaks, CA: Sage.
Sciabarra, C. M. (2005, September 1). Dialectics and liberty: A defense of dialectical method in the service of a libertarian social theory. *The Freeman.* Retrieved from http://fee.org/freeman/detail/dialectics-and-liberty
Shor, I. (1992). *Empowering education: Critical teaching for social change.* Chicago: University of Chicago Press.
Welsh, J. F. (2007). *After multiculturalism: The politics of race and dialectics of liberty.* Lanham, MD: Lexington Books.

PART IV

Social Justice Education Outside the Classroom

THIRTEEN

"Putting First Things First": Obligation and Affection in Ecological Agrarian Education

Leah Bayens

In a 2009 commencement address at Northern Kentucky University, farmer and writer Wendell Berry (2010) calls out higher education's "Upward Mobility major" as an instigator of "social instability, ecological oblivion, and economic insecurity" (pp. 32, 33). The upward mobility major, he argues, "has put our schools far too much at the service of what we have been calling overconfidently our *economy*" (p. 32). It has been preparing graduates for "expert servitude to the corporations" (p. 32) rather than for reciprocal community membership. Echoing his colleague Wes Jackson, Berry calls for an alternative: a major in "Homecoming," a curriculum that, rather than leading up and away from socio-ecological communities, brings students down to earth. A homecoming major, as Jackson (1996) puts it, educates "the young to return home, or to go some other place, and dig in" (p. 3).

To be sure, as access to postsecondary education expanded in the United States, it tended to separate students from the cultural and ecological contexts they inhabited. As a result, our colleges and universities generally fall short of Berry's exhortation to "draw succinct and tangible connections between education and communities and the land" (personal communication, January 12, 2012). Instead, college advertisements and curricula often construe education as job training, as a product to be traded in exchange for employment—wherever that happens to be—and as a gateway to supposedly liberatory affluence. On this matter, Berry (2014b) issues a cautionary note:

> Education is not properly an industry, and its proper use is not to serve industries, either by job-training or by industry-subsidized research. Its proper use is to enable citizens to live lives that are economically, politically, socially, and culturally responsible....A proper education enables young people to put their lives in order, which means knowing what things are more important than other things; it means putting first things first. (p. 21)

For students to learn to put first things first, our classes—and ultimately our institutions—must be rooted in a prime ecological reality: all human economies are ultimately accountable to nature's economy. Berry (2014b) deems this an agrarian economy, one that arises "from the fields, woods, and streams—from the complex of soils, slopes, weathers, connections, influences, and exchanges that we mean when we speak, for example, of the local community or the local watershed" (p. 116). This approach is not limited to farmers; an ecology-based agrarianism encompasses all of us as it fuses nature and culture: "the local community and the local watershed." It fits into the landscape human life lived "responsibly in a world of limits," and it "holds together a synoptic vision of the health of the land *and* culture" (Wirzba, 2003, pp. 4–5).

Teaching students why and how to live within ecological limits runs counter to the cultural paradigm that links progress and prestige to ever-expanding accumulation—of capital, of political power, of environmental goods. The prevailing approach to education duplicates the related illogical belief that the very economic and cultural values that have perpetuated gross disparities and despoilings will eventually bring parity and health to communities. We see this specious thinking at work, for instance, in efforts to invent a technological fix to mitigate catastrophic climate change and in a multinational curriculum that purports that fair trade can be had through "free" trade. Education informed by an ecological agrarian design, on the other hand, casts doubt on philosophies of human prosperity earned at the expense of ecological health. From this perspective, wealth that hinges on environmental degradation is unavoidably short-lived and tends to perpetuate social injustice.

Educators who embrace this ethos have begun the thorny process of redirecting the major in upward mobility back down to earth. This rerouting plays a pivotal part in ongoing work at St. Catharine College (SCC) to translate Berry's convictions into an interdisciplinary undergraduate sustainable agriculture and agrarian studies curriculum. The Berry Farming and Ecological Agrarianism[1] Program took shape three years after Berry's talk in Northern Kentucky when Berry, his daughter Mary, and I gathered in a 150-year-old farm house in Henry County, Kentucky, to envision an education that returns the "human household or economy" (*oeconomia*) toward its ancient membership in the "household of nature," ecology (*oikos*, dwelling place) (Berry, 2010a, p. 178).

Through that and other conversations, the Berry Center[2] established a partnership with SCC—a small, liberal arts, Dominican college in Central Kentucky—to institutionalize ecological agrarian thought by using nature as the standard for and measure of cultivation practice. As a result, we crafted a homecoming major through which students can suss out how monetary, domestic, political, economies might be guided by a true-cost accounting, one that takes into its purview the gamut of physical, civic, and ethical dimensions. We provide students the chance to cultivate indispensable connections to and affections for community and to understand obligation to others as the cornerstone of justice.

The Berry Farming Program (BFP) is guided by ethics of affection and obligation in our efforts to build and bolster healthy, thriving, equitable communities, a design that suggests an understanding of justice, of rights, as being rooted first in reciprocity. This chapter explores these ideas as they are reflected in and as they evolved through the Berry Farming Program's major in homecoming. This sketch provides a glimpse of the possibilities for transforming higher education, generally, and agricultural education, specifically, to a model that "shifts from the economy to the ecosphere as the basis of curriculum, teaching, and learning" (Berry, 2010b, p. 33).

Breathing Life Into a Major in Homecoming

Founded in August 2012, the Berry Farming Program (BFP) offers two interdisciplinary, experiential learning-based and community-centered undergraduate degrees and a minor. Students majoring in Farming and Ecological Agrarianism (FEA) select one of four areas of guided concentration: agroecology, plant and soil stewardship, community leadership, or environmental arts and humanities. We teach students in every concentration how to employ the range of sustainable agriculture[3] tenets, which are predicated on the goal of satisfying human food and fiber needs without compromising the ability of future generations to meet their needs. This communal objective requires a comprehensive fusion of science and culture: the science of agroecology[4] (practicing soil conservation, cultivating biodiversity, rotating crops, and avoiding synthetic inputs) as well as the social parity components of community food systems:

1. Promote conditions that are healthy and humane for workers, consumers, and animals.
2. Provide a fair wage for farmers and community partners.
3. Encourage local economic networks.
4. Enhance and support connections between rural and urban communities.
5. Satisfy human food and fiber needs without compromising future generations' needs.

At every possible turn, students in the BFP are reminded that in a sound, just, and mindful local economy, "nature will become the standard of work and production" (Berry, 2014b, p. 121). To understand and preserve nature's integrity, students and faculty alike foster deep affections for place and a responsibility to all the lives therein. In this way, the curriculum is geared toward expanding the base of engaged citizens who are committed to sustainability- and equitability-minded cultivation, economics, arts, leadership, and ultimately, ways of being. We are driven by the need not simply to populate the countryside with people who "have no economic or cultural ties to the land and are not a community," as Berry (1977) cautioned over three decades ago (p. 63). Rather, we aim to encourage people to settle into the nooks and crannies and hollers of places with a commitment to using nature as the measure for their land use.

The land-based curriculum requires that we get down to the ground and "Consult the genius of the place," as Alexander Pope recommends (as cited in Berry, 1990, p. 105). Doing so, Berry writes, will help us determine a *practical* harmony between the land and its human inhabitants" (1990, p. 105). This concept entails careful study of nature's processes—from microbial soil life to compost mucks. It also involves establishing meaningful relationships with the people who inhabit the landscape. Thus, the BFP takes interdisciplinarity seriously. The degrees do more than weave into an ecosystems-based curriculum a smattering of cultural studies courses. It entwines the arts, the sciences, and professional studies to foster in students a holistic understanding of their relationships to nature and each other.

We laid the cornerstones of this curriculum after taking up key questions about education:

- What causes people to learn in the first place?
- What can formal education add to that?

- What do we want our students to become? Not simply their professional statuses. Rather, what kinds of people do we hope they will be in the world?
- What kinds of experiences can we provide to advance that character?

As we mulled the human impetus to learn, we kept coming back to Berry's (2012b) proposal in his National Endowment for the Humanities Jefferson Lecture, "It All Turns on Affection." In that address, he intones:

> Affection is personal. If it is not personal it is nothing.... The word 'affection' and the terms of value that cluster around it—love, care, sympathy, mercy, forbearance, respect, reverence— have histories and meanings that raise the issue of worth. We should, as our culture has warned us over and over again, give our affection to things that are true, just, and beautiful. (p. 4)

Affection, then, formed the foundation of our understanding not only of the human motive for learning but also for our conceptualization of the kinds of people we hope our students become—people who cultivate affections for place and for each other and allow that to provoke a sense of wonder that compels their educations. It might also, according to Berry, engender "such love for a place and its life that they want to preserve it and remain in it" (2012, p. 2).

We filtered this concept into our specific goals for the curriculum:

1. Foster conversations between students and community members with an eye toward mutual production of knowledge.
2. Provide immersive experiences that allow students across the disciplinary spectrum to connect with people and land, with a place and all its intricacies.
3. Teach students to "read" specific places by using methods of inquiry and analysis that are place-transferrable so that they will dig in to the places they call home.
4. Show students the inseparable connections between disciplines and move toward forms of study in which "disciplinary boundaries begin to lose their efficacy," as Berry, calls for (personal communication, January 12, 2012).
5. Raise students who are dissatisfied with easy answers and who "feature questions that go beyond the available answers" (Jackson, personal communication, February 12, 2015).

Bringing Theory Into Practice

To fulfill these goals and bring these theories into practice, we developed a thorough liberal arts curriculum. As they settle in to their specific areas of interest, students majoring in FEA take a set of core courses that intersperse agroecology, food studies, environmental literature, agricultural history, whole farms design, and community development. The agroecology concentration is geared toward students who plan to farm. Coursework covers topics such as organic crop production, ethical issues in sustainable farms, developing local and sustainable food systems, livestock husbandry, biological inputs, and microbial farming. The plant and soil stewardship concentration is aimed at students interested in farm ecosystems. Coursework comprises botany, agricultural entomology, crop pathology and physiology, soil ecology, and plant genetics.

The community leadership concentration caters to students interested in transforming the food system through business, policy, and planning. Coursework includes study of livable and sustainable land use, local economies and small town trades, theories and practices of urban and rural relations, management, and environmental ethics. Finally, the environmental arts and humanities concentration is designed for students who, regardless of where they live or what their occupations, have a passion for learning about and contributing positively to issues of sustainability, stewardship, ecology, and agrarianism. The curriculum includes environmental writing to environmental justice theory, heritage arts and crafts, and ecospirituality. Each of these concentrations overlaps one another such that a farmer will make decisions informed by literary configurations of the land, and a student concentrating on environmental writing will have dug her hands in the dirt. The BFP grounds students in these tenets through internships, service learning, and community education programs.

The following writing excerpts illustrate how students in these courses are internalizing ecological agrarian tenets. In a Fall 2014 iteration of "The Measure of Nature in Literature" course, I invited students to write about the essays in Berry's (1990) collection *What Are People For?*, which presents a range of thoughts about agriculture, ethics, ecology, economy, and rural-urban interdependence. The prompt compelled students to explore Berry's visions for healthy, sustainable, and just food systems and to consider the roles of eaters and farmers alike in fulfilling this design.

Rachel Cox, an FEA community leadership major from Louisville, Kentucky, explores the intersection of economy, history, and rural-urban relations in food systems development:

> Providing that a food system respects our involvement in the environment, it should create healthy cultural and social food connections. Currently, we should restore systems in rural communities. Healthy rural systems based on local structures can educate and more sustainably work alongside urban communities. Berry understands the necessity of culture in agriculture. Berry explains in "Damage" that the cultural role of a society is to protect a community's histories, practices, and customs. This serves as a guide to our future (Berry 8). On a cultural and social level, food systems should learn from our past and apply this to our future. Systems in the past were reliant on local levels of contact. Berry would suggest that lying in the small and medium scale farms of the past are the only solution for our future. These systems created community and protected rural culture. They provided good income for many families rather than a large conglomerate. They protected the local trade and sales of goods and services…. Social sustainability of community holds rural communities together. (Cox, 2014, p. 2)

Cox seamlessly connects a multiplicity of factors necessary for revitalizing rural communities and, in the process, invigorating living wage- and ecology-minded farming. For a student who plans to work extensively in urban agriculture development, this respect for the pivotal role rural communities play in the broader food system is essential.

Her colleague Alexander Knowles, an English major from Huntington Beach, California, demonstrates a profound understanding of our responsibility to remedy the damages wrought through the bifurcation of nature and culture:

> Wendell Berry's work as a whole shows the complex relationship between humanity and nature through multiple texts that illustrate why society must practice harmony with all living organisms to create sustainability. Berry's work suggests that these relationships that have been damaged between people and nature must be resurrected in the name of responsibility, health, and ultimately, the economy as well. Berry suggests that this work is not for farmers only, as all

consumers are participants in agriculture whether they realize it or not. Every decision that humanity makes, economically specifically, affects nature, and the recent wave of decisions have been detrimental to the landscape. As Berry's collection of essays *What Are People For?* makes clear, once a sense of community is revived between people and nature, then society can begin to heal through understanding. (Knowles, 2014, p. 1)

Throughout the semester, Knowles was repeatedly drawn to the monetary economics of "cheap" food. He struggled with the quandary of how to change the negative human health effects, especially borne by the poor, of highly-processed products made from federally-subsidized, industrially-produced commodity crops. Knowles recognized the difficulty of going up against an economic and social structure that perpetuates these inequalities. In his essay, he works through this frustration by honing in on examples of common trust between neighbors. "Through this trust," he writes, "agricultural ideals that are both practical and wholesome can regain control on health, prosperity, and community" (p. 3).

These two writing samples represent a typical strain of thought emerging in students' conversations with each other and with our neighbors. The BFP facilitates conversations about environmental stewardship and cultivation across the curriculum and across the community through such tools as internships, service learning, and collaborative research. FEA majors complete 9 to 12 credit hours of experiential learning—some of it devoted to farming work and some devoted to learning about the spectrum of community components that make agriculture possible (e.g., with policy-makers, environmental organizations, sustainability-oriented businesses, and the like). Students acquire skills in crop and livestock planning and propagation, soil systems management, marketing and budgeting, farm infrastructure development, food systems policy and planning, and arts and culture components.

One student's internship particularly illustrates how immersive learning with a community partner expands the classroom parameters beyond campus and, in the process, forges in all parties strong ties of affection for place and people. From May through August 2014, community leadership major Winifred Cheuvront served as an intern at Foxhollow Farm in Crestwood, Kentucky, and worked extensively with the farm's fourth generation owner, Maggie Keith. Foxhollow employs organic and biodynamic methods to produce a variety of fruits and vegetables and grass-fed and -finished beef. The farm markets through direct retail sales and farmers' markets, and it serves as an incubator site for a young farm family's Community Supported Agriculture (CSA) operation. Keith and her mother, Janey Newton, conceive of their farm as being "less about the dominance of the farmer, and more about the harmony between the farmer and the wisdom of the natural world" (2014).

Foxhollow Farm's methods and philosophies correspond to the Berry Farming Program's, and Cheuvront proved to be an excellent match for the farm. She hails from Taylor County, Kentucky, where her family has a 70 acre farm on which they raise a variety of small livestock, grow hay, maintain a kitchen garden, and run a country store. When her internship began, Cheuvront brought a good working knowledge of farm equipment, basic horticulture and livestock management familiarity, and some experience with planning and marketing. By summer's end, she had not only honed these skills, but she had also gained a broader sense of the possibilities for diversified production. As this excerpt from her reflective essay shows, she also emerged with a profound commitment to sharing what she learned with others:

> I truly believe that what I learned on this farm will help me in my job or on my own farm. I learned/grew as I was tending to the earth and picking the fruits (vegetables) of my labor. I have a new respect for all gardeners; I never knew how much work it really was, but how rewarding it is as well. …Education is important in trying to change the way of the old and to influence the younger generation of farmers or future farmers. (2014, p. 2)

Cheuvront's summer education site became her home, and she internalized a loyalty to that place—returning there for events in the fall and testifying about her experience in numerous venues. At the same time, she was exposed to a model in which nature's economy holds an important place in conceptualizing monetary economics. She has a conviction about sharing that approach with her Taylor County neighbors, which is evidence of her sense of responsibility to her home community.

The farmers who worked with Cheuvront were similarly enthusiastic about the experience, in part because they found it invigorating to witness a young person's learning process but also because they encountered new ideas with their student. Pavel Ovechkin, who leases Foxhollow land for his CSA operation, noted that because Cheuvront's agricultural background was different from those of other interns with whom he had worked, it served to improve his approach to mentoring. Jenn Smith, Foxhollow's administrator, encapsulated the farm staff's interest in Cheuvront's calling:

> It's a gift at such a young age to know what one is "called" to do, it is wisdom to accept and pursue that calling, and it's bravery and dedication that allows one to carry on after discovering that their calling is actually very hard work. Winnie is to be admired for demonstrating all of the above. (2014, p. 3)

In sum, this internship demonstrates how the Berry Farming Program is attempting to blur the lines between campus and community through occasions that invite mutual production of knowledge.

The BFP also provides important opportunities for students to serve and educate our community. The Fall 2013 "Introduction to Agroecology and Food Studies" cohort connected with the youngest residents in our community by implementing a composting education project for the Washington County preschool program. The Spring 2014 cohort of that course took this idea a step further and set up a Kentucky Wonder Bean planting station at the Springfield Green Festival. Students in the "Historical Perspectives on Agrarianism" class have hosted documentary screenings and reflection sessions that bring to light women's roles in sustainable agriculture. Most recently, students in "The Measure of Nature in Literature" course helped winterize the St. Catharine Motherhouse gardens, an act FEA agroecology major Patricia Moyer related to herself, Berry's work, and the Dominican Sisters of Peace's mission:

> I was able to hear my inner voice more clearly and "feel the attraction of [my] most intimate sources" (Berry, "Healing" 11). Not only did working in the garden help me focus on myself and alleviate my loneliness, but in doing that I was able to reconnect with the people and community around me. In doing the work for the Sisters, I inserted myself in their community and became a part of their mission.

In these few lines, Moyer articulates precisely why the BFP invests so much energy in bridging gaps between education in and out of classrooms.

Moyer's words also reflect our deep-seated hope that our students' affections for individual places and people will reveal their obligation to care and to act. We want them to promote and maintain robust communities and agricultural economies by using nature as a measure and guide. We hope their decisions will be based on an understanding of the economy as "the making of the human household upon the earth: the *arts* of adapting kindly the many human households to the earth's many ecosystems and human neighborhoods" (Berry, 2012, p. 16). If our students embrace and breathe life into this concept, then they will surpass the leading economists and enter into an understanding of economy that is "the primary vocation and responsibility of every one of us" (p. 16).

Prospects for Ecological Agrarianism

In the long view we are calling on education as a resource for cultural change, a resource that is, as Berry points out, itself in need of transformation. The incarnation of ecological agrarianism we are using to initiate and inform this transformation provides an apt model for imagining how our scholarship and pedagogy might diminish the boundaries between colleges and land-communities. Without this merger, our prospects for stopping the damages caused by the dominant economy, much less for achieving ecological justice or social parity, are weak. We cannot, Berry writes, use "'liberal' or 'conservative' tweaking of corporate industrialism" to stymie the inequities wrought by the industrial mindset, "against which the ancient imperatives of good care, homemaking, and frugality can have no standing" (2012, p. 13). We might reach an "authentic correction" from one of two causes: "scarcity and other serious problems arising from industrial abuses of the land-community" or by building "local economies, starting with the economies of food" and efforts to "connect cities with their surrounding landscapes" (p. 13).

Surely the latter is just as preferable as it is necessary. Every time my colleagues and I send our students out into the world, the prospects for spreading an ecological agrarian perspective mount. We are heartened by their actions, our attachments to one another, and their words. A handful of student reflections on the November 2014 Slow Money National Gathering in Louisville, Kentucky, shed light on the prospects. These statements embody the spirit of our work. Toussaint Shaak Rose, a freshman FEA major from Houston, Texas, contextualizes local-global power structures: "I learned the best way to fight global power is by building a strong local community." Lusekelo Nkuwi, a sophomore from Singida, Tanzania, "formed relationships not networks." And sophomore Sié Tioyé, of Ouagadougou, Burkina Faso, illuminates the marvel of cultivation:

> Farming is a way of life, not just a job that people take who are too dumb to become doctors and engineers. A good farmer's livelihood and involvement in food production is full of miracles: germination, nurturing and healing. In return, the farmer acquires wisdom, more knowledge than a library, or the cloud, can hold.

These homecoming majors offer hope, and we have a responsibility to provide them authentic experiences that will inform and shape their capacities for putting first things first.

Notes

1. Ecological agrarianism is roughly defined as a faith in the liberatory potential of citizen-directed and equity-driven agricultural economies, practices, and cultures. This worldview folds together a belief in cultivation as a potential path to fair social organization and a belief in the principles of ecological democracy, which encourages citizens' "direct, hands-on involvement" in environmental decision making (Hester, 2006, p. 4). Ecological agrarianism is a helpful addition to social justice pedagogy because it recognizes that environmental impoverishment is inextricable from socio-economic marginalization. In fact, the "land and people have suffered together," Berry writes, and under "the rule of industrial economics, the land, our country, has been pillaged for the enrichment, supposedly, of those humans who have claimed the right to own or exploit it to the limit" (2012b, p. 17). In this light, ecological justice- and social justice pedagogies are inextricable: "[T]he movement to preserve the environment...[is] not a digression from the civil rights and peace movements, but the logical culmination of those movements" (Berry, 2012a, p. 70).
2. The Berry Center (TBC) is a nonprofit organization in New Castle, Kentucky, founded by Executive Director Mary Berry. TBC works to improve farm policy and economies as well as farmer education.
3. FEA curricula rely on an amalgam of sources to define sustainable agriculture, including more recent sources such as the edited collection *Meeting the Expectations of the Land: Essays in Sustainable Agriculture and Stewardship* (Jackson, Berry, & Colman, 1984), the 1990 Farm Bill, Stephen Gliessman's *Agroecology: The Ecology of Sustainable Food Systems* (2006), and University of California, Davis's "Sustainable Community Food Systems" publication (2014) as well as germinal texts like Liberty Hyde Bailey's *The Holy Earth* (1916) and Sir Albert Howard's *An Agricultural Testament* (1943). In short, these sources merge ecology, economy, and community in sustainable agriculture practice.
4. Stephen Gliessman (2006) defines *agroecology* as "the application of ecological concepts and principles to the design and management of sustainable food systems" (18).

References

Bailey, L. H. (1916). *The holy earth*. New York: Charles Scribner's Sons.
Berry, W. E. (1977). *The unsettling of America: Culture and agriculture*. New York: Sierra Club.
Berry, W. E. (1990). A practical harmony. *What are people for? Essays by Wendell Berry*. San Francisco, CA: North Point Press. (Original work published 1988).
Berry, W. E. (2010). A major in homecoming. *What matters? Economics for a renewed commonwealth*. Berkeley, CA: Counterpoint Press. (Original work published 2000).
Berry, W. E. (2010). The total economy. *What matters? Economics for a renewed commonwealth*. Berkeley, CA: Counterpoint Press. (Original work published 2000).
Berry, W. E. (2012). It all turns on affection. *National endowment for the humanities*. Retrieved from http://www.neh.gov/about/awards/jefferson-lecture/wendell-e-berry-lecture
Berry, W. E. (2012). Think little. *A continuous harmony: Essays cultural and agricultural*. Berkeley, CA: Counterpoint Press. (Original work published 1969 in *Whole Earth Catalog*).
Berry, W. E. (2014). Thoughts in the presence of fear. *Citizenship papers*. Berkeley, CA: Counterpoint Press. (Original work published 2001).
Berry, W. E. (2014). The whole horse. *Citizenship papers*. Berkeley, CA: Counterpoint Press. (Original work published 1996).
Berry, W. E., Jackson, W., & Colman, B. (Eds.). (1984). *Meeting the expectations of the land: Essays in sustainable agriculture and stewardship*. San Francisco, CA: North Point Press.
Cheuvront, W. (2014). *Foxhollow internship report*. Unpublished manuscript, Berry Farming and Ecological Agrarianism Program, St. Catharine College, St. Catharine, KY.
Cox, R. (2014). *Locality in food*. Unpublished manuscript, Berry Farming and Ecological Agrarianism Program, St. Catharine College, St. Catharine, KY.
Foxhollow Farm. (2014). About Foxhollow farm. *Foxhollow farm*. Retrieved from http://www.foxhollow.com/
Gliessman, S. (2006). *Agroecology: The ecology of sustainable food systems* (2nd ed.). Boca Raton, FL: CRC Press, Taylor and Francis Group.
Hester, R. (2006). *Design for ecological democracy*. Cambridge, MA: MIT Press.
Howard, A. (1943). *An agricultural testament*. New York: Oxford University Press.
Jackson, W. (1996). *Becoming native to this place*. Berkeley, CA: Counterpoint Press.
Knowles, A. (2014). *Community in nature*. Unpublished manuscript, Berry Farming and Ecological Agrarianism Program, St. Catharine College, St. Catharine, KY.

Moyer, P. (2014). *Community service project reflection.* Unpublished manuscript, Berry Farming and Ecological Agrarianism Program, St. Catharine College, St. Catharine, KY.

Nkuwi, L. (2014). *Slow money national gathering reflection.* Unpublished statement, Berry Farming and Ecological Agrarianism Program, St. Catharine College, St. Catharine, KY.

Rose, T. S. (2014). *Slow money national gathering reflection.* Unpublished statement, Berry Farming and Ecological Agrarianism Program, St. Catharine College, St. Catharine, KY.

Smith, J. (Ed.). (2014). *Berry farming program: Assessment of student internship performance.* Unpublished report for Berry Farming and Ecological Agrarianism Program. Crestwood, KY: Foxhollow Farm.

St. Catharine College. (n.d.) *Mission statement, vision statement, and core values.* Retrieved from http://www.sccky.edu/aboutus/mission.php

Tioyé, S. (2014). *Slow money national gathering reflection.* Unpublished manuscript, Berry Farming and Ecological Agrarianism Program, St. Catharine College, St. Catharine, KY.

U.S. Department of Agriculture, *Food Agriculture Conservation and Trade Act of 1990.* (USDA Publication No. 101–624, 104 Stat. 3359). Washington, DC: U.S. Government Printing Office.

University of California, Davis, Agricultural Sustainability Institute. (2014). Sustainable community food systems. Retrieved from http://sarep.ucdavis.edu/sfs/def

Wirzba, N. (2003). Why agrarianism matters—even to urbanites. In E. Freyfogle (Ed.), *The essential agrarian reader: The future of culture, community, and the land* (pp. 1–22). Washington, DC Shoemaker and Hoard.

FOURTEEN

"Barely in the Front Door" but Beyond the Ivory Tower: Women's and Gender Studies Pedagogy Outside the Classroom

Tara M. Tuttle

The value of community engagement promoted in countless university mission statements may be most readily accomplished by a discipline that may be absent or among the least prominent on their campuses: Women's and Gender Studies. In "Education Beyond Institutionalization: Learning Outside the Formal Curriculum," Nicole Harper (2011) asserts, "Focusing attention on learning beyond the formal curriculum will result in a perpetual transformative process" (p. 12). This is particularly crucial to disciplines promoting social justice. The ultimate goal of much Women's and Gender Studies academic labor is not only the transformation of learning and learners but also the transformation of society. We want not only more egalitarian classrooms but a more egalitarian world. Students' educations about gender occur mostly outside of the classroom and formal curriculum, and outside of the classroom are the inevitable spaces wherein students put their educations into practice. In this essay, I argue that the pedagogical aims and practices of the interdiscipline of Women's and Gender Studies are particularly suited for the successful translation of course objectives from the formal curriculum into outside-the-classroom applications. I demonstrate how the four strands of liberatory pedagogies of Women's and Gender Studies programs, outlined by Tisdell (1995), are implemented in the many beyond-the-curriculum activities fostered by these programs. In its devotion to creating transgressive pedagogical spaces of possibility that resist uncritical replication of the hierarchical norms of power, privilege, and patriarchy permeating traditional structures of formal education, Women's and Gender Studies higher education often extends beyond the classroom and traverses conventional course boundaries to create a direct link between theory and action (praxis), directing students toward engagement in activism, advocacy, and other forms of social justice work both on campus and in the community.

Though lacking a vocabulary of pedagogical praxis at the time, from my initial encounter with Women's and Gender Studies (WGS) as a graduate student, I clearly detected a difference from other disciplines that had been part of my studies. As I might have phrased it at that time, the clearest difference was that as students of WGS, we were fully expected to do something with what we learned out in the world. Liberal arts college academics often speak of this as the promotion of civic engagement; we want our students to become involved in the improvement of their communities. Though the term itself may be problematic with regard to both historic and contemporary exclusion of certain segments of society from citizenship and what is considered the civic realm, this concept of civic engagement has become common in university mission and value statements. How does WGS translate this named ideal to reality? What is it that WGS does that facilitates this extension of its pedagogy past the steps of the ivory tower?

According to Catherine Orr (2011) of the Teagle Working Group on Women's Studies and Civic Engagement, "Women's Studies produces...some of the 'most innovative thinking and programmatic activity on civic and democratic engagement' in higher education" (p. 19). One reason WGS is well suited to promoting civic engagement is its acknowledgement and confrontation with Paolo Freire and I. Shor's (1987) observation that "no pedagogy is neutral" (p. 13). Women's and Gender Studies is one of the few fields which from its early stages grappled with the ways in which "Pedagogy is always related to power" (Giroux, 1992, p. 15). Because of this acknowledgement and its commitment to challenging oppressive hierarchies of power, practitioners of Women's and Gender Studies (WGS) have taken as a central concern ways of validating, empowering, affirming, and including students in the educational experience both inside and outside of the classroom. Orr (2011) explains, "Civic engagement in Women's Studies draws on histories of radical politics to make both connections and distinctions between service and struggle, provides perspectives on deep democracy and informed reciprocity, counteracts both consumer and missionary models of community-based learning, examines the possibilities of dissident citizenship" (p. 10). Moreover, she concludes, "Civic engagement in Women's Studies brings intersectional approaches to power, privilege, and inequality, examines local/global connections, acknowledges sexism and its relationship to other forms of oppression, [and] produces life-long learners and critical inquiry toward social transformation" (Orr, 2011, p. 11). Few disciplines attempt such radical goals, and fewer succeed.

A CUNY Hunter College student explained, "women's studies goes beyond the classroom, this paper, and just touches everything else I'm involved in because it gives me a way to see, a way to think, a way to question everything, so it's applicable everywhere for me" (Musil, 1992, p. 199). WGS pedagogy does this on four fronts outlined by Elizabeth Tisdell (1998) in her article "Poststructural Feminist Pedagogies." Tisdell explains, "the four interrelated themes of poststructural feminist pedagogy [are] knowledge construction, voice, authority, and positionality." Through these four approaches, WGS academics help students transform themselves from passive learners in classrooms to change agents outside them.

Knowledge Construction

Feminist theorists and WGS educators examine relations between knowledge and power, considering who produces what is constituted as knowledge. The first of the themes articulated by Tisdell (1998) perhaps most easily lends itself to classroom accomplishment; research of historical representations of women, scrutiny of cultural myths and metanarratives, and analyses of power structures in the dissemination of texts and knowledge in the classroom help students understand how their knowledge and the knowledge of others has been shaped, directed, and limited. However, activities outside of class contribute to this understanding. If students embrace the label "feminist," they must contend with its connotations and the misunderstandings of others outside of the classroom and both inside and outside academe who may equate feminism with male-bashing and reverse sexism or who may narrowly associate it with only abortion activism. They must confront first hand the misshaping of this term and potentially help reshape others' knowledge of it as members of a feminist minority up against a hegemonic false or ambivalent narrative. If WGS students engage in feminist activism, they may experience media silences or misrepresentations of their actions that demonstrate the knowledge constructions of feminisms. They may be required to confront race-, class-, and gender-based stereotypes and bigotry if involved in advocacy or activist work. Handling these stereotypes requires contention with historical and social forces, which have contributed to this "knowledge" that prevents others from seeing the myriad and often overlapping inequities activist WGS students work to eliminate. More positively, as part of agencies that use or conduct research, WGS student activists may help in the kinds of knowledge construction that motivate others to act. By compiling reports, publishing pamphlets, issuing evidence-packed mailings, and disseminating data via social media, WGS students participate firsthand in knowledge production on a variety of issues including but not limited to affordable housing, bullying of LGBTQQI individuals, domestic violence, media bias, sexual harassment, women and children in poverty, contraceptive access, campus rape, shelter shortages, and environmental concerns.

I remember thinking that the expectation of student participation in knowledge construction, which is underpinned by the premise that students possess or are able to discover knowledge to contribute, was startlingly high in the WGS courses in my graduate educational formation. While my experience is anecdotal, I see the same initial shock from many of my own undergraduates now. Though it is not the only field to encourage such, it felt radically different in its acknowledgement and inclusion of students as agents of knowledge production. Another key difference is its examination of historically constituted knowledges and how many groups have been denied inclusion in the authorship of traditionally and academically validated bodies of knowledge. Susan Acker (1994) explains, "Asking feminist questions opens up the possibility of radical alterations in prevailing paradigms" (p. 133).

Elizabeth Tisdell (1998) describes this as helping students to develop a third eye capable of a new kind of sight:

> To see with a third eye is to recognize that the self (or the author) constructs knowledge in relation to others, and both the self and others are situated and positioned within social structure where they are multiply and simultaneously privileged and oppressed. These social structures and power relations affect not only how knowledge has been produced and disseminated in the society but how what has counted as 'knowledge' has been determined, and by whom. They also affect how individuals construct knowledge and come to voice, which again foregrounds the connection between the individual and the social context.

This new vision is not obscured when students leave the classroom. It helps them identify issues in other contexts with which they may grapple. According to Orr (2011), "By theorizing power relations that encompass embodiment, sexuality, and oppressive structures that permeate everyday life whether they gain their purchase from culture, from tradition, or from changing local, national, transnational, and global practices, feminist scholarship renders the politics of difference and the politics of knowledge intelligible and actionable" (p. 12). "Actionable" is a key word here. Knowing is not doing; learning does not necessarily result in change or action. WGS pedagogy first problematizes the concept of knowledge, but activists and educators know that knowledge is usually not enough to prompt change or action. Tisdell names four approaches for this reason, and they often occur in tandem. The three additional (often overlapping) approaches of WGS pedagogy combine to make this knowledge (or meta-knowledge) actionable.

Voice

The nontraditional structure of WGS courses, that realization of the transgressive pedagogical space, allows for normally taciturn students to interact verbally in more comfortable ways. In Caryn Musil's 1992 in-depth analysis of case studies of 10 well-established WGS programs, *The Courage to Question: Women's Studies and Student Learning*, she notes, "No single refrain was heard more clearly in the reports [from the scrutinized institutions] than that women's studies courses gave students a voice and empowered them" (p. 201). WGS pedagogy creates a better environment for using one's voice, and students who gain confidence in WGS classrooms may transition from speaking up in class to speaking out in advocacy beyond the perimeter of campus. What does a WGS classroom look like? It is "a non-hierarchical place where personal narrative is both validated and integrated into the curriculum" (Tsemo, 2011, p. 701) because "To include the personal as part of the course's subject matter is to move to the surface what previously has been dismissed or forced underground" (Musil, 1992, p. 200). Students find their personal experience is validated, so they may enter into the course's concepts feeling that they speak from a position of personal, embodied expertise rather than expected to behave as detached strangers to the content; this allows them to understand as well their positionality and how that affects their interpretations of knowledges.

In addition to the complexities of knowledge construction, Tisdell (1998) asserts, these

> "pedagogies help learners to examine the connection between…how sociostructural systems of privilege and oppression such as race, ethnicity, gender, sexual orientation, and religion have affected the development of their 'constantly shifting identities';…who easily speaks and who tends to remain silent in 'coming to voice' in the learning environment, and who consciously or unconsciously is recognized as 'smart' or 'leaders' in light of these same systems of privilege and oppression."

As they critique knowledge production and their position within a knowledge-creating framework, students may also take notice of whose voices and experiences are represented and whose are neglected both in the learning environment and outside it in social structures, media representations, and hierarchies of power.

Positionality and Authority

The third and fourth concerns of WGS pedagogy that have clear out-of-the-classroom applications are authority and positionality, which I will address together for the ways in which these two concepts overlap. Authority refers to the right to make decisions and the right to control, and this depends upon both individual and social recognition. Dr. Ryan Smith (2002) of Rutgers University explains, "The important difference between power and authority consists in the fact that whereas power is essentially tied to the personality of individuals, authority is always associated with social positions or roles….Authority is a legitimate relation of domination and subjection" (p. 511). One fundamental premise of WGS pedagogy is that we cannot train students to obedience and passivity in the classroom and expect engagement and activity in their communities outside it. We must create an environment for active, participatory learning if we hope for activism and engagement after graduation.

We must grant students authority in the classroom if we desire they act with agency outside it. Professors of Women's and Gender Studies, particularly female ones, have to walk a tightrope in class that requires they teeter between recognizing their empowered positions as professors in hierarchical institutions of higher learning despite the lingering legacy of the historic denial of authority to women (which has contributed to a degree of denial of the authority of the interdiscipline of Women's and Gender Studies in academe) and achieving the goal of flattening hierarchies of power in the classroom to establish a sense of authority and equity among students. Classroom authority in WGS pedagogy is not modeled on a teacher/student binary opposition but is constructed through constantly evolving negotiations in which the classroom is transformed in such a way that professors use their empowered positions to empower students to see themselves not as mere recipients but contributors. By acknowledging that each student is capable of contributing efforts to problem solving and knowledge production and then demanding that they do so, by allowing them to be first authorities of their own experiences, and by conveying that they become authorities on other topics of inquiry only via participation, not memorization and regurgitation, WGS pedagogy models a process that fosters activism or engagement outside of the classroom in response to social and personal issues in ways that traditional pedagogies that locate sole authority in the instructor may not.

This is directly related to the concept of positionality. This term comes from Linda Alcoff's (1988) assertion that certain markers such as race, class, and gender often associated with identity are not essences of who we are but are indicators of relational positions in particular contexts that carry social meanings. According to Maher and Tetreaux (1993), "knowledge is valid when it includes an acknowledgement of the knower's specific position in any context, because changing contextual and relational factors are crucial for defining identities and our knowledge in any given situation. The fashioning of one's voice in the classroom is largely constituted by one's position there" (p. 118). WGS educators demand this not only of students but also draw attention to their own position within this pedagogical framework. Carmen Luke (2005) points out "our labor as academic teachers is unthinkable without acknowledging our institutionally sanctioned authority and power" (p. 174). Though this may feel threatening to a professor's own authority in the classroom, it offers an alternative view of power that is not power *over* others but is power via participation in collaborative inquiry and discovery.

By modeling this in the classroom, students may then apply this process of discernment outside of it in their varieties of roles and contexts. This positionality "recognizes that multiple communities determine both the context and content of student learning, and that students locate themselves and their identities, wittingly or unwittingly, in relation to these communities based on gender, race, class, culture, family, friends, politics, religion, inter/national citizenship, and so on" (Carbine, 2010, p. 321). This focus upon issues of authority and positionality seeks to stimulate "students to move beyond their own experiences, to see life from other points of view in order to gain a critical perspective on how they have understood their own lives" (Carbine, 2010, p. 330). Jenna Niece, a student of Women's and Gender Studies at St. Catharine College, explains that prior to her involvement in WGS courses,

I had no idea what it meant to have agency. I was oblivious to the inequality of daily life. I was entirely ignorant of the power I could hold as a woman who was aware of herself, and for that matter, what that even looked like. I have never found myself so academically and personally challenged as when I sit in a gender studies course and contemplate what I will do with my womanhood, what I am capable of doing with it. For me, what it boils down to, is that women's studies makes us aware of ourselves, not just as women, but as autonomous human beings, and the world around us in way that we never realized we were unconscious of in the first place. (personal communication, September 15, 2014)

Rhodes Scholar Ryan Thoreson verifies this emphasis on the "real world," out-of-class applications: "In my government courses I learned about political theory, but I found the political theory I learned in my women's studies curriculum to be much more broadly applicable" (Stewart, 2007).

This anecdotal evidence is affirmed in larger studies. Musil's (1992) report from Wellesley College included "startling statistics on how much women's studies students continue their discussion outside the classroom in contrast to the amount of out of class discussion generated in non-women studies classes. Nearly 84% of women's studies students versus 63% of non-women's studies students reported talking 'constantly' or 'usually' about the content of their courses" (p. 206). From this data, Musil concludes, "Since the overwhelming part of an undergraduate student's life is spent outside the classroom rather than inside it, the Wellesley report has broad implications for women studies and for education as a whole" (p. 206). This is the endeavor of all fields of study in institutions of higher learning, that what we teach them proves useful and meaningful in their lives beyond the ivory tower, and solid evidence suggests that the pedagogical praxis of Women's and Gender Studies successfully accomplishes this.

Through a pedagogical approach that combines strategies of critiquing knowledge production, fostering the development of voice, critically examining authority, modeling collaborative power, and addressing positionality, WGS students acquire new ways of seeing, new knowledges that include the contributions of previously excluded and marginalized groups, and new modes of inquiry useful far beyond the perimeters of their campuses. In their study of *Women's Studies Graduates: The First Generation,* Luebke and Reilly (1995) documented "a unique set of skills learned through women's studies programs: empowerment, self-confidence, critical thinking, building community, and understanding differences and intersections among racism, homophobia, sexism, classism, ableism, anti-Semitism and other types of oppression" (Stewart, 2007). This unique set of skills proves invaluable in a variety of contexts, in personal and professional lives, in advocacy and activism, and in leadership and collaborative efforts in communities of any size.

All of our labor in the classroom should work toward the achievement of these same out-of-the-classroom applications, and Women's and Gender Studies may serve as a paradigm for other disciplines in this regard. Carol Schneider, president of AAC&U, asserts,

For too long, our campuses have made civic engagement and social responsibility an extracurricular activity, the realm of student affairs and off-campus life…[when] successful integration of learning is surely the key to success. The more students transfer knowledge and skill from the classroom to the community and then back again, the better prepared they will be to take responsibility for their lifelong roles as citizens and human beings. (Orr, 2011, p. 9)

Though Women's and Gender Studies has become a recognized and established field, social justice educators who have long applied these pedagogical tenets must be wary of assuming that WGS pedagogy has permeated the mainstream of academia. Despite its successes, only approximately 23% of colleges and universities offer a Women's and Gender Studies major or minor. A 2007 census of Women's and Gender Studies program identified only 650 programs in the nearly 3,000 4-year undergraduate institutions in the United States with just over 4,000 students majoring in the field (Reynolds et al., 2007, p. 3). Feminist historian Beverly Guy-Sheftall (1995) writes, "We must debunk the myth that women's studies has taken over the academy…women's studies is barely in the front door on hundreds of campuses" (p. 27).

Though this status is insufficient for those of us in the field, the precarious position of Women's and Gender Studies on the margins of academe may be partly why it proves readily applicable outside the academic realm. Its transgressions of conventions of pedagogy are fruitful in increasingly verifiable ways. Borne from a crusade for women's liberation and developing alongside and intersecting with a variety of social justice movements since its birth, it is precisely because WGS pedagogy never had mere knowledge acquisition as its "learning outcome" that WGS pedagogy is not confined to classrooms. The primary objective of WGS educators is nothing less than transforming students into agents of change working toward a more gender egalitarian world. S. Jackson (1997) asserts, "above all feminist pedagogy rests on a vision of 'social transformation.'" Orr (2011) echoes this sentiment: "Much more than a gender equity project, the discipline of Women's Studies investigates issues of power, privilege, and difference at the course level and helps students connect those investigations to various means of social transformation" (p. 7). Moreover, the data suggests the achievements of WGS pedagogy are neither anecdotal nor merely theoretical. Musil's multiple-institution study found that for students, "women's studies…contributed to students, gradual progression from voice to self empowerment to social engagement (1992, p. 203). Many of us in the field have witnessed this firsthand in some of our students' lives as they enter into a broad range of professions and endeavors; many of us have experienced the same progression ourselves. Beverly Guy-Sheftall comments, "In the early years, women's studies graduates tended to work on gender-specific issues, getting jobs in battered-women's shelters and rape crisis centers. But more and more we have students going into public health, international policy, journalism, electoral politics, film-making, K–12 education and other careers that allow them to effect large-scale change" (Stewart, 2014). While the field's practitioners are sensitive to charges of being too academic by those outside of academe and not academic enough by those in more traditional disciplines inside it, what WGS pedagogy accomplishes is not to be discounted. Ample evidence demonstrates that Women's and Gender Studies pedagogy increases students' likelihood of engaging in community activism outside of the classroom because of what they experience in it.

References

Acker, S. (1994). *Gendered education*. Buckingham, UK and Philadelphia: Milton Keynes, Open University Press.
Alcoff, L. (1988). Cultural feminism versus post-structuralism: The identity crisis in feminist theory. *Signs, 13*(3), 405–436.
Bauer, M. (2000). Implementing a liberatory feminist pedagogy: bell hooks's strategies for transforming the classroom. *MELUS 25*(3/4), 265–274.
Carbine, R. P. (2010). Erotic education: Elaborating a feminist and faith-based pedagogy for experiential learning in religious studies. *Teaching Theology and Religion 13*(4), 320–338.

Corson, D. J. (1992). Language, gender and education: A critical review linking social justice and power. *Gender & Education 4*(3), 229–255.
Freire, P., & Shor, I. (1987). *A pedagogy for liberation.* Basingstoke, UK: Macmillan.
Gallagher, K. (2000). The everyday classroom as problematic: A feminist pedagogy. *Curriculum Inquiry 30*(1), 71–81.
Giroux, H. (1992). *Border crossings: Cultural workers and the politics of education.* New York: Routledge.
Grace, A. P., & Gouthro, P. A. (2000). Using models of feminist pedagogies to think about issues and directions in graduate education for women students. *Studies in Continuing Education, 22*(1), 5–28.
Guy-Sheftall, B. (1995). *Women's studies: A retrospective,* a report to the Ford Foundation. Naugatuck, CT: Ford Foundation.
Harper, N. R. (2011). Education beyond institutionalization: Learning outside of the formal curriculum. *Critical Education,* (4) 2–17.
Hobgood, M. E. (2012). Feminist classrooms as counter public spaces: Notes on the education they provide and the challenges they face. *Journal of Feminist Studies in Religion, 28*(1), 189–195.
Jackson, S. (1997). Crossing borders and changing pedagogies: From Giroux and Freire to feminist theories of education. *Gender & Education 9*(4), 457–467.
Levin, A. K. (2007). Questions for a new century: Women's studies and integrative learning. A report to the *National Women's Studies Association.* College Park, MD: NWSA.
Luke, C. (2005). Feminist pedagogy theory in higher education: Reflections on power and authority. In C. Marshall (Ed.), *Feminist Critical Policy Analysis II: A Perspective from Post-Secondary Education* (pp. 283–302). London: Taylor & Francis.
Maher, F. A. (1999). Progressive education and feminist pedagogies: Issues in gender, power, and authority. *Teachers College Record 101*(1), 35–59.
Maher, S., & Tetreault, M. K. (1993). Frames of positionality: Constructing meaningful dialogue about gender and race. *Anthropological Quarterly 66*(3), 118–126.
Motta, S. C. (2013). Teaching global and social justice as transgressive spaces of possibility. *Antipode 45*(1), 80–100.
Musil, C. (1992). *The courage to question: Women's studies and student learning.* Washington, DC Association of American Colleges and the National Women's Studies Association.
Odegard, M. A., & Vereen, L. G. (2010). A grounded theory of counselor educators integrating social justice into their pedagogy. *Counselor Education and Supervision 50,* 130–149.
Orr, C. M. (2011). Women's studies as civic engagement: Research and recommendations. *The Teagle Working Group on Women's Studies and Civic Engagement and the National Women's Studies Association.* Retrieved from http://www.teaglefoundation.org/teagle/media/library/documents/learning/2011_nwsa.pdf?ext=.pdf
Reynolds, M., Shagle, S., and Venkataraman, L. (2007). *A national census of women's and gender studies programs in U.S. institutions of higher education.* Chicago: National Opinion Research Center.
Smith, R. (2002). Race, gender, and authority in the workplace: Theory and research. *Annual Review of Sociology 28,* 509–542.
Stewart, N. (2007). Transform the world. *Ms. Magazine.* Retrieved from http://www.msmagazine.com/spring2007/womensstudies.asp
Tisdell, E. J. (1998). Poststructural feminist pedagogies: The possibilities and limitations of feminist emancipatory adult learning theory and practice. *Adult Education Quarterly 48*(3) 139–156.
Tsemo, B. H. (2011). Decentering power in pedagogy: From "Feminism" to "Feminisms." *Feminist Studies 37*(3), 696–708.
U.S. Department of Education, National Center for Educational Statistics. (2014). Retrieved from http://nces.ed.gov/fastfacts/display.asp?id=84
William, T., & McKenna, E. (2002). Negotiating subject positions in a service-learning context: Toward a feminist critique of experiential learning. In A. A. Macdonald & S. Sánchez-Casal (Eds.), *Twenty-first century feminist classrooms: Pedagogies of identity and difference* (pp. 135–154). New York: Palgrave Macmillan.

FIFTEEN

Our Pass-Fail Moment: Livable Ecology, Capitalism, Occupy, and What Is to Be Done[1]

Paul Street

I guess I'm here to put a little green in your rouge. The title of my talk (I hope you all appreciate the education-related wording) is "Our Pass-Fail Moment: Livable Ecology, Capitalism, Occupy, and What Is to Be Done."

Pissing in the Wind

Let me start with a quotation from a brilliant radical philosopher named John Sonbanmatsu. The quotation comes from a personal e-mail in which John was responding to something I'd said last year about progress I'd seen on the left with the labor uprising in Wisconsin and the emergence of Occupy Wall Street. The response from Sonbanmatsu was so profound I printed it off and taped it onto a bookshelf next to my desk.

"What's striking to me, though," John wrote,

> "is how much extraordinary social progress has been made in some corners of the globe, toward sexual equality for gays and lesbians and liberal rights for women, while at the same time there has been zero progress–zero–toward challenging wage slavery, the power of monopoly capital, or the national security state. Nor…is there any meaningful progress being made toward the #1 issue of our or any time, which is the ecological crisis (including mass species extinctions and global warming)…to me the Left is just pissing in the wind. Remember the late-1980s, when the most important issue for the American left was freeing Mumia Abu Jamal? There is a psychotic element to the way we focus our energies, or rather dissociate from the fundamental problems confronting humanity and the other living creatures."

There's no small truth in that statement.

The Last Half Century

Lately I've been talking to a number of my fellow middle-aged leftists about the biggest underlying changes we've seen in American life and society during our lifetimes. My portside cohorts tend to sort the changes they mention into three basic categories: good, bad, and neutral or ambiguous. The *good changes* mentioned generally relate to civil rights and identity, to historic defeats of bigotry and discrimination won by the Civil Rights, women's and gay rights movements. Other good things get mentioned—consumer safety laws, clean air and water laws, abolition of the death penalty in most states, the rise and spread of organic foods.

The *neutral or ambiguous* stuff that gets mentioned include globalization, the rise of the personal computer and the Internet, and the end of the Cold War. Lefties I know tend to be split or neutral on whether these developments are ultimately liberating or oppressive from a Marxist perspective. Many seem to think they are neither good nor bad and that it's up to social and political action to harness the Internet and globalization for positive, democratic purposes.

The *bad stuff* comes in a long list. The highlights, perhaps I should say the low-lights, include:

- The rise of a deeply racist mass incarceration and criminal branding and surveillance complex that puts more than 3 million Americans behind bars each day and saddles more than 1 in 3 black adult males with the crippling lifelong mark of a felony record.
- The permanent, structural nature of unemployment for millions of Americans—a livable wage employment vacuum so deep that the current economic crisis can seem worse than the Great Depression of the 1930s because this time we sense—all too correctly—that most of the jobs that have been shredded are never coming back.
- A concentration of wealth and power so great that the top 1% now owns more than 40% of the nation's net worth, more than 57% of the nation's financial wealth, and a probably larger share of the nation's elected officials—this in a country where the bottom 40% owns just 0.3% of the wealth, essentially nothing.
- A concentration of wealth so great that six inheritors of the Walmart fortune, six Walton heirs, together possess as much wealth as the bottom 30% of the country.
- A de-unionization of the American working class so steep that the percentage of workers enrolled in unions has fallen from more than 40 in the early 1960s to less than 10% today.
- The eclipse of democracy in a neoliberal state where business power has not merely the dominant political shadow cast across society (as John Dewey put it nearly a century ago) but a dark cloud that envelops society and pushes both of the reigning political organizations (hardly even real parties anymore) so far to the right of the populace that it becomes hard to see the United States as anything but a corporate plutocracy.
- The disappearance of any single credible military deterrent to U.S. global military power and the spread of American and Western imperialism to parts of the world previously considered off limits.

- The deepening exhaustion of the once easily accessible natural resources that fed the long industrial era and whose exploitation underpinned the remarkable expansion of Western and global economic activity after 1945.

Now, for some reason, in these discussions, it's always left to me to mention the biggest negative development of all. I am referring of course to the emergence of catastrophic anthropogenic global warming and a related broader environmental apocalypse that threatens a decent livable future for humanity and other sentient beings. According to new research released three weeks ago by the science journal *Nature,* humanity is now facing an imminent threat of extinction—a threat caused by its reckless exploitation of the natural environment. The report reveals that our planet's biosphere is steadily and ever more rapidly approaching a tipping point meaning that all of the planet's ecosystems are nearing sudden and irreversible change that will not be conducive to human life. "The data suggests that there will be a reduction in biodiversity and severe impacts on much of what we depend on to sustain our quality of life, including…fisheries, agriculture, forest products and clean water. This could happen within just a few generations." So says lead author Anthony Barnosky, a professor of integrative biology at the University of California, Berkeley. "My colleagues who study climate-induced changes through the Earth's history are more than pretty worried," Barnosky said in a press release. "In fact, some are terrified."[2]

It's the Capitalism, Stupid

Going through the list of negative and neutral developments I just gave, I am struck by two basic observations. One is that all of these changes are strongly and dialectically linked to each other. They are all connected one to the rest in a kind of simultaneous equations system of death and decline reflecting their common grounding in the imperatives of capital and the profits system.

Look, for example, at the problem of structural unemployment. It is obviously all bound up with globalization in an era when multinational corporations have largely shut down manufacturing in the United States and out-sourced production to China and other cheap labor developing world nations. That export of jobs is of course source of the monstrous fortune enjoyed by the Walton heirs, for Walmart excels above all in selling cheap items made in China.

Globalization and structural unemployment are intimately related to mass incarceration. Most the nation's substantial and growing army of prisoners and felons come from communities where real jobs long ago disappeared. That army functions as the essential human raw material for an industry that has emerged to provide employment communities where manufacturing and farming no longer absorb much surplus labor. That industry is the prison industrial complex and the related ongoing permanent so-called War on Drugs.

Staying on this theme of interconnectivity, look at American Empire's lethal neo-colonial presence in the Middle East and Southwest Asia. Behold its presence and pressure in the provocative underbelly of nuclear Russia, and look at the Empire's growing focus on East Asia and particularly on the oil-rich South China Sea. That dangerous and unbound presence is obviously related to the end of the Cold War = to the capitalist defeat and collapse of the Soviet Union. It also reflects inter-imperial rivalry over what's left of the world's declining stock of easily accessible fossil fuels.[3]

One interconnection that particularly deserves mention here given my topic today is the intimate relationship between inequality and ecological collapse. The promise of growth has long been Western capitalism's answer for the inequality that the profits system creates. "A rising tide lifts all boats," longstanding Western "growth ideology" proclaims, supposedly rendering irrelevant popular anger over the fact that an opulent minority sails in luxurious yachts while others struggle in rickety dinghies and leaking rowboats. "Governments love growth," the British environmental writer George Monbiot notes, "because it excuses them from dealing with inequality….Growth is a political sedative, snuffing out protest, permitting governments to avoid confrontation with the rich…" The problem, of course, is that the false, conflict-avoiding solution called growth is tipping the environment past the point where it can support life in a decent fashion. [4]

"Everything Else We're Talking About Won't Matter"

The other thing that strikes me about all those big and interrelated half-century changes I listed above is that for all their dialectical inseparability and common capitalist connectivity they are not equal. Sonbanmatsu is right when he says that the ecological crisis is "the #1 issue of *our or any time.*" *Or any time.* Think about that. Climate change isn't just the biggest development of the last 50 years. It is, as the environmental writer and activist Bill McKibben notes, *the biggest thing that has ever happened in human history*. As the great American left intellectual Noam Chomsky said in a widely read essay last year, "if the [environmental] catastrophe isn't… averted – [then] in a generation or two, everything else we're talking about won't matter."[5]

And that is why I always say that I don't want to choose between being a red and being a green, but that if you told me I absolutely had to decide between being a socialist or being an environmentalist, I'd go with the latter. Who wants to turn the world upside down only to find that it is irredeemably riddled with disease and decay? What good is it to inherit a poisoned Earth from the bourgeoisie? What's the point of more equally sharing out a poison pie?

Now, as it happens, I don't think we have to—or should—select between green and red. I think we can and in fact must be both.

A Distinctive Triage Patient

When I cite data on environmental collapse and argue that ecology is the top issue of our time, I sometimes get accused of advocating a politics of triage—a politics of putting forward only what I think is the single most urgent problem and thereby unduly neglecting other issues that rightly concern us on the left.

Well, okay, let's go with the triage analogy for a moment. Think of all the issues that concern radicals as newly arrived patients in an over-ridden, disaster-burdened emergency room. On one gurney you've got institutional racism, with numerous complications including racial profiling, hiring discrimination, residential segregation, and more. On another gurney there's workers' rights, with numerous different wounds relating to labor law, overtime abuse, state-capitalist union officialdom and bureaucracy, out-sourcing, immigrant rights, and more. You've got another gurney carrying imperialism, with numerous and different fractures relating to Iraq, Libya, Yemen, Afghanistan, Pakistan, Colombia, Honduras, the influence of "defense" contractors. and much more. You've got yet another gurney with the problem of democracy and here again we have multiple fractures and wounds including campaign finance law, Citizens United, corporate personhood, political advertising, corporate media, ballot access, spoiled ballots, winner-take-all elections, the national security state, and much more. And then there's the gurney carrying this mess called the ecological crisis, with various wounds and breaks and complications including not just global warming but also ocean acidification, stratospheric ozone depletion, the nitrogen and phosphorous cycles, global freshwater use, changes in land use, biodiversity loss, atmospheric aerosol loading, and chemical pollution.

We all know what triage means in the battlefield operating room. You forget about the patients that can't survive, you sort out the rest by level of urgency, and you offer first treatment to those closest to death. If livable ecology is the triage choice in this scenario, and it might be, I think it's a very distinctive sort of triage choice in four key ways. First and most terribly of all, I'd have to admit that it's not 100% clear that it isn't already too far gone. Some experts already put it in the category of un-savable. I don't agree but there you are.

Second, and also pretty terrible, it's not entirely clear to me that livable ecology is any closer to death than other issues we care about. I don't know for a fact if the time window for meaningful action on democracy or on worker rights or on economic equality is any bigger or longer than the window for saving a livable natural environment.

Third, however, if livable ecology is a save-able triage patient—and I think it is—then it's a triage patient of a very odd sort in that if it dies so do all other patients in the emergency room. To repeat the Chomsky line, "if the [environmental] catastrophe isn't...averted – [then] in a generation or two, everything else we're talking about won't matter."

Green Work

Fourth, if livable ecology is the top triage patient it's a distinctive sort of triage patient in the different sense and that the serious and effective treatment of its wounds and fractures provides much of the healing required by other patients in the ER. Take structural unemployment, imperialism, and corporate globalization. Tackling climate change and other environmental ills in a meaningful way means putting many millions of people to work at all skill levels to design and implement and coordinate and construct the environmental retro-fitting of economy and society—the ecological re-conversion of production, transportation, office space, homes, agriculture, and public space. What kind of work? To start, hundreds of thousands of so-called green collar jobs involved in weatherizing and energy-retrofitting every building in the United States There will be plenty of work for college-educated environmental engineers and architects and planners but even more work for people without college degrees. Here's a decent passage from Van Jones' bestselling 2007 book *The Green Collar Economy*:

> When you think about the...green economy, don't think of George Jetson with a jet pack. Think of Joe Sixpack with a hard hat and a lunch bucket, sleeves rolled up, going off to fix America. Think of Rosie the Riveter, manufacturing parts for hybrid buses or wind turbines.... If we are going to beat global warming [Jones wrote] we are going to have to weatherize millions of buildings. Install millions of solar panels, manufacture millions of wind turbine parts, plant and care for millions of trees, build millions of plug-in hybrid vehicles, and construct thousands of solar farms, wind farms, and wave farms. This will require...millions of jobs.... And don't think of green collar workers as laboring only in the energy sector...we will also need

[well-paid] workers in a range of green industries: materials reuse and recycling, water management, local and organic food production, mass transportation and more.[6]

As demand goes up for labor thanks to an imagined boom of "green collar" jobs rights and union power improve. The vicious circle of arrest, felony-branding, and incarceration recedes as millions of inner city and suburban ring blacks and Latinos and rural whites are employed in the ecological retrofitting of ghettoes and barrios and the broader society. Former prison guards and ex-cops join ex-auto-workers in the making and maintenance of local and regional and national high-speed solar- and wind-powered light rail systems and wind towers and wind turbines. The Pentagon's global petroleum protection service loses some of its imperial sting as distant and declining oil and gas reserves cease to hold the keys to development. As an added benefit, much the work involved in greening the economy and society can't be out-sourced since, as Jones notes, "it involves making over the sites where we work and live and altering how we move around. That sort of work is difficult or impossible to send abroad." You can't pick up an office building, send it to China to have solar panels installed, and have it shipped back.

Van Jones' Great Mistake

For comrades who worry that privileging the environmental issue means giving up on the socialist revolution and the struggle against the 1%, let me give you my 100% guarantee that the Green Revolution will also be bright rouge. With its inherent privileging of private profit and exchange value over the common good and social use value, with its intrinsic insistence on private management, with its inbuilt privileging of the short-term bottom line over the long-term fate of the species, with its deep sunk cost investment in the old carbon-addicted way of life and death, and with its attachment to the division of the world into competing nations and empires that are incapable of common action for the global good, capitalism is incapable of bringing about and surviving the deep environmental changes required for human survival. "Green capitalism" is an oxymoron.[7] Not getting that is the great flaw of Van Jones' book and career. He seems to think that the green transformation can take place without undertaking an epic confrontation with concentrated wealth and ridding ourselves of the bourgeoisie.

From Letter Grades to Pass-Fail

He's wrong about that. Saving ourselves from environmental ruin poses what Dr. Martin Luther King Jr. referred to in 1968 as "the real question to be faced…the radical reconstruction of society itself." And it poses that question with a strong emphasis on what Dr. King used to call "the fierce urgency of now." As the Marxist writer Ricardo Levins-Morales noted a few years ago, the cautious "one small step at a time" approach to progressive change loses credibility when the existing order is posing imminent radical threats to survival. "If the road we are on leads to a precipice," Levins-Morales wrote:

> …then a shift in…orientation is overdue.…If we envision ourselves…advancing across an expanse of open field, then we can measure our progress in terms of yardage gained and be

satisfied that we are least moving in the right direction. If, instead, a chasm has opened up which we must leap across to survive, then the difference between getting twenty percent versus forty percent of the way across is meaningless. It means we have transitioned from a system of political letter grades to one of 'pass/fail.' We either make the leap or not....Too late for Van Jones (dropped under fire)...[8]

As the environmental tipping point chasm looms ever closer, we are coming, comrades, to our pass-fail moment. Centrist incremental-ism won't do the job. It's either the revolutionary reconstitution of society or what Marx and Engels called in 1848 the only alternative: "the common ruin of the contending classes."[9] Physics and chemistry don't negotiate. To prioritize ecology and green issues is not to demote or delay the socialist revolution. It means the elevation and escalation of the red project.[10]

The Obvious Demand, the Obvious Analogy

I don't have time to say everything I wanted to about Occupy—about my simultaneous love for and discomfort with the Occupy Movement. I loved the Occupy Movement—maybe I should say the Occupy moment—for putting the focus of popular anger on the real perpetrators, the real ruling class—the corporate and financial elite. I loved it for bringing back to American political culture the essential language of class, the language of us and them, of the struggling many and the privileged few, of the fat cats versus the ordinary people, of the plutocrats versus the citizenry, of the haves and the have-nots. I loved Occupy for learning from the revolting and predictable (and predicted) Obama experience to act on the wisdom of Howard Zinn's counsel that it's not about "who's sitting in the White House, it's about who's sitting in," who's sitting in the streets, who's taking direct action, who's occupying factories, and offices, and cafeterias, and public squares and legislative halls when it comes to bringing about progressive change. I loved Occupy for getting it that it's about grassroots rank and file social movements beneath and beyond these big-money-big-media-major-party-narrow-spectrum-candidate-centered electoral extravaganzas the masters stage for us every 4 years, telling us "that's politics"—the only politics that matters. I loved Occupy for daring to prefigure what a democratic community beyond class rule might look like.

At the same time, Occupy drove me nuts with its fetishization of space, its fetishization of process, its fetishization of expression over strategy, its reluctance to name and offer a serious critique of capitalism as a system, and its over-reluctance to make specific demands for real world changes desired by the working class majority of people it claimed to represent. What would have been so terrible about demanding from the beginning a financial transactions tax to pay for universal health care and the restoration of basic public family cash assistance and transitional jobs and treatment programs to end the "new Jim Crow"[11] of mass imprisonment and felony marking? What would have been wrong about talking from the beginning about the right to work at a livable wage and (more radically) about workers' control and about the right to a free public education?

I put Lenin's phrase "what is to be done" in the title of my talk. It might have been better for me to say "what is to be demanded?" With respect to the ecological crisis, "the #1 issue of our or any time," the demand is so basic and simple and the historical analogy is so clear that it's almost embarrassing to note. *The demand,* informed by deep rage over the scandalous absurdity of mass unemployment in a world of hugely unmet social need, and by rage and fear over the imminent capitalist extermination of our species and other species, is *the right to socially useful and environmentally necessary work*. The policy expression of the demand is to tax the rich with extreme prejudice to pay for public works programs dedicated to the ecological retrofitting of the American and global economy along post-carbon, post-nuclear, and post eco-cidal lines. The historical analogy is staring us in the face. I mentioned Rosie the Riveter above. The analogy is World War II, when the United States, still reeling from the Great Depression, taxed its rich like never before and reconverted its economy and put millions to socially useful work producing what the world needed at the time: weapons and other goods to defeat fascism. Crippled now by another systemic depression, the so-called Great Recession, the first true crisis of capitalism in its neoliberal phase, America can and must do it again. We can and must reconvert our economy and reorient our society to produce what humanity requires if we are to have any chance for a decent and democratic future. This time, however, there's an added benefit—the re-conversion required will take us once and for all beyond the world the 1% made and into a world both saved and turned upside down. Let the rouge-verde revolution begin. Soon. Thank you very much.

Notes

1. This article was originally delivered as a Keynote Address at The Rouge Forum 2012 Occupy Education! Class Conscious Pedagogies and Social Change at Miami University in Oxford, OH.
2. Common Dreams Staff, "Earth Facing Imminent Environmental Tipping Point: Report," *Common Dreams* (June 7, 2012) at https://www.commondreams.org/headline/2012/06/07-3 On the current grave and deepening environmental crisis, see John Bellamy Foster, Brett Clark, and Richard York, *The Ecological Rift: Capitalism's War on the Planet* (New York: Monthly Review, 2010); Massachusetts Institute of Technology, "Climate Change Odds Much Worse Than Thought: New Analysis Shows Warming Could Be Double Previous Estimates," *MIT News*, May 19, 2009, at http://web.mit.edu/newsoffice/2009/roulette-0519.html#.; Bill McKibben, *Eaarth: Making Life on a Tough New Planet* (New York: Times Books, 2010); Mark Lynas, *Six Degrees: Our Future on a Hotter Planet* (London: Fourth Estate, 2007); Chris Williams, *Ecology and Socialism: Solutions to Capitalist Ecological Crisis* (Chicago: Haymarket, 2010); James Gustav Speth, *The Bridge at the End of the World: Capitalism, the Environment, and Crossing from Crisis to Sustainability* (New Haven, CT: Yale University Press, 2008); Herve Kempf, *How the Rich Are Destroying the Earth* (White River Junction, VT: Chelsea Green, 2007).
3. See Michael Klare, *The Race for What's Left: The Global Scramble for the World's Last Resources* (New York: Metropolitan, 2012).
4. For useful discussions of the growth ideology, see Kempf, *How the Rich Are Destroying the Earth*; 69–74; William Greider, *Come Home America: The Rise and Fall (and Redeeming Promise) of Our Country* (New York: Rodale, 2009), 192–217; Speth, *The Bridge*, 46–66. Monbiot is quoted in Greider.
5. Noam Chomsky, "Plutonomy and the Precariat," *Huffington Post* (May 8, 2012), read online at http://www.huffingtonpost.com/noam-chomsky/plutonomy-and-the-precari_b_1499246.html
6. Van Jones, *The Green Collar Economy: How One Solution Can Fix Our Two Biggest Problems* (New York: Harper, 2009), 10–11.
7. For useful perspectives from a Marxist, red-green perspective, see Foster et al. *The Ecological Rift*; Williams, *Ecology and Socialism*.
8. Ricardo Levins-Morales, "Revolution in the Time of Hamsters," *ZNet Magazine*, September 1, 2009, read at http://www.zcommunications.org/revolution-in-the-time-of-the-hamsters-by-ricardo-levins-morales. "Dropped under fire" refers to the fact that Van Jones served briefly as the Obama administration's "green jobs czar" but was quickly fired (without complaint from Jones) when the Republican right raised objections to his supposed radicalism.
9. Karl Marx and Frederich Engels, *The Communist Manifesto* (1848), first page, second paragraph of the first section.
10. In the sixth chapter of their important volume *The Ecological Rift*, titled "The Planetary Moment of Truth," Marxist academicians Foster, Clark, and York observe that "Overcoming the ecological rift (and the social rift that lies beneath it)…demands the transcendence of capitalism and the development of a genuine socialist alternative associated with substantive equality and socioeconomic-ecological planning.…Given the limitless ecological crisis emanating from today's business as usual, all hope for the future of humanity and the earth must lie in this direction."
11. Michelle Alexander, *The New Jim Crow Mass Incarceration in the Age of Colorblindness* (New York: Metropolitan, 2010).

SIXTEEN

Youth-Led Organizations, the Arts and the 411 Initiative for Change in Canada: Critical Pedagogy for the 21st Century

Brad J. Porfilio and Michael Watz

The implementation of commercialized and militaristic policies within K–12 schools across North America have made it arduous for even the most committed, transformative school leaders and educators to guide their students to reflect critically upon the nature of their social world and to gain the courage and skills necessary to join other cultural workers in the struggle to eliminate social inequalities in schools and in the wider society. Many schoolteachers, especially social actors who mentor and educate students in urban contexts, are situated in debilitated, unsafe, and unsanitary educational environments, where their students are criminalized and demonized through an array of surveillance equipment, armed security guards, military recruitment stations, and draconian "get tough on youth" zero-tolerance policies. They also educate youth amid overcrowded educational structures where they must implement "teacher proof" drill and kill forms of instruction and assessment in order to ensure their students perform adequately on a battery of corporately-produced examinations (Casella, 2008; Kozol, 2006; Porfilio & Carr, 2008; Ross & Gibson, 2007; Saltman & Gabbard, 2010). Among an array of reprisals, failing to perform well on the exams can result in teachers losing their jobs, closing of schools, corporate or state takeover of underperforming schools, as well as the confiscation of vital resources from already cash-strapped educational structures.

Fortunately, some youth artists and activists are cognizant of commercialized and dehumanizing forms of schooling afforded to them and other "border" youth fail to spark their intellectual desire to understand the relationship between self and Other, knowledge and power, or the constitutive forces giving rise to institutional forms of oppression, such as racism, sexism, classism, and homophobia. Moreover, they realize schools fail to include the pedagogical outlets necessary to formulate intercultural alliances that question what is responsible for the world's unjust conditions and advocate for building a society on the ideals of justice, equity, and democracy (Lund & Nabvi, 2010; McLaren & Kincheloe, 2007; Prier, 2010). Consequently, critically aware youth have collectively formulated a burgeoning emancipatory pedagogical movement, which is geared to filling the pedagogical hole generated by most educational institutions. Through multimedia presentations, workshops, and student-developed artistic projects, they set out to garner resistant students' attention and interest in understanding what gives rise to human suffering in their communities and other social contexts, gives students space to vocalize their concerns and apprehensions with challenging the structures and social actors who impact their personal and social development, and provide unfamiliar information in ways that aid youth in making sense of unfamiliar concepts and connecting this knowledge to their own lived experiences (Ginwright, Noguera, & Cammarota, 2006; Prier, 2010).

The purpose of this essay is to document a group of Canadian youth activists' and artists' perceptions and experiences with developing and sustaining an arts-based educational initiative that "undertakes public education and the promotion of civic participation of young people on social issues that frame their development within their communities" (http://www.whatsthe411.ca/). Through the youth activists' and artists' narratives, we highlight their motivation to establish or to be active in this organization; the methods they use to engage their audience in social commentary and activism; how they confront and overcome barriers in schools when implementing their pedagogical initiatives; and the challenges they face in keeping their project intellectually vibrant and culturally relevant to youth. Moreover, we argue that critical pedagogues must take seriously the cultural work proffered by youth-led social justice initiatives if current and future teachers are to have the emancipatory vision and courage to find fissures amid commercialized and militarized schooling structures so as to "provide students the knowledge and skills they need to learn how to deliberate, make judgments, and choices about participating in and shaping decisions that affect everyday life, institutional reform and government policy" (Giroux, 2008, p. 3). Or if schoolteachers and the general public are to move beyond the debilitating portraits of youth in media culture, which characterize them as aberrant, violent, and anti-intellectual creatures who must be blamed for the social and economic problems created by adult economic and political "leaders."

The essay is organized as follows. In the first section, we provide a brief overview of the social and cultural conditions that are affecting the aims and scope of socially transformative youth-led initiatives, which have been implemented across North America over the past decade. In the second section, we highlight several of the 411 members' narratives in order to capture their motivation for organizing or being a part of the initiative; document the methods they employ to captivate students' attention and spark their awareness vis-à-vis the constitutive forces generating injustice and human suffering; document how they overcome obstacles in the educational arena that often make it arduous for teachers, youth, and scholars to sustain youth-led, transformative projects; and detail the challenges they may encounter in sustaining their youth-led initiative. We conclude the essay with a brief summary of the value of the 411 Initiative as it relates to promoting culturally-responsive teaching in K–12 schools, fostering critically engaged citizenship, and providing schoolteachers alternative visions of how to conceptualize teaching, youth, and activism.

Youth-Led Resistance and Transformation in the Age of Neoliberalism

The ruling elite's push to commodify all elements of social life, to eliminate social entitlements for citizens, and to outsource labor from First World to the so-called Third World regions, is having a deleterious impact on many citizens in North America. Working-class citizens are frequently facing job loss, home foreclosures, living out of tents, boxcars, caves, and cars, are without medical assistance or adequate transportation, and are working several dead-end service-orientated jobs in order to feed and clothe their families. The neoliberal ordering of our social world has been particularly devastating to our youth. It has generated a political, cultural, and economic context that is "unforgivable and intolerable for youth" on numerous levels (Grossberg, 2007). For instance, more and more youth, particularly youth of color, at a young age are grappling with police harassment, living in debilitated, blighted communities, living without adequate food and shelter, and living without adequate public facilities. Echoing Giroux (2008), "the cultural of cruelty and inequality" present in the age of "bootstrap capitalism" is also spawning an "epidemic of violence," which is causing pain, suffering, and alienation for many youth. As Grossberg suggests (2007):

> The U.S. infant mortality rate is higher than that of any industrialized nation in the world. More importantly, 75% of all violent deaths (including homicide, suicide, and firearms-related deaths) of children in the industrialized world occur in the United States. The suicide rate for kids under the age of fourteen is double the rate of the industrialized world....And while it is hard to get statistics, it appears that for every violent and sexual offense committed by kids, there are three such crimes committed by adults against kids. (p. 97)

Today's youth are also often preyed upon by political leaders in economically depressed communities in the United States. These communities often turn to the elite leaders, the very individuals responsible for the lack of adequate jobs, resources, and social provisions in North America, to build juvenile detention centers and prisons. In essence, securing jobs for its citizens often comes at the expense of minoritized youth of color and impoverished youth of the dominant culture, who are, ultimately, forced to live, at an increasingly younger age, life in confinement (Giroux, 2009).

Youths' quality of life has also been denigrated by the implementation of commercialized and militarized practices in K–12 educational structures. For instance, many urban schools in the United States and Canada, plagued by the state contracting its economic support of education, are unsafe, unsanitary, dilapidated, racially segregated, and overcrowded institutions, where ill-equipped educators implement "drill and kill" methods of instruction (Kozol, 2006; McLaren & Kincheloe, 2007; Porfilio & Malott, 2008; Ross & Gibson, 2007; Saltman & Gabbard, 2010). Minoritized students must also grapple with military recruiters' continual attempts to cajole them to join the U.S. imperial forces. When NCLB (No Child Left Behind) was implemented in 2001, the U.S. military was granted the power to enter school settings and, not coincidentally, have preyed upon the most socially and economically vulnerable student populations.

In response to the child-hating culture offered by the ruling elite, youth have increasingly banded together over the past decade to raise their doubts, concerns, and oppositions to the policies, practices, and structures imperiling their life chances as well as affecting the quality of life of working-class peoples across the globe. Unlike youth in previous generations, however, today's youth are starting to organize around local, community, and international concerns in high school settings, rather than remaining idle until they attend college or university (Fine as cited in Verderame, 2009). Fortunately, compared to youth in previous decades, today's youth have an easier time unearthing where they can turn to work with others who have encountered similar debilitating situations or are critically aware about the urgent need to dismantle structures, policies, and practices that cause oppression. They also have an easier time locating additional informational sources so as to understand the nature of social and economic problems impacting global citizens. The growth of mass media and social networking have provided outlets for youth to connect with marginalized populations, build globalized intergenerational networks that are designed to highlight what causes oppression, and find political sites and other "free spaces" where they can lobby for fundamental change in schools and in the wider society (Kippenbrock & Thornburgh, 2009; Verderame, 2009). According to Fine (2009), mass media and social networking have also broadened the scope and sophistication of youth activism:

> People are working both locally and in some cases globally. So it's operating at multiple levels, and that's really exciting. It's powerful for young people to feel like they're part of national and sometime international movement of youth trying to create change. (Fine as cited in Verderame, 2009)

In some cases, new forms of youth activism have emanated from preexisting youth movements that have challenged unjust social and economic formations on a local, national, or international level. For instance, over the past several years, numerous minoritized and impoverished youth from dominant cultures across the globe have been inspired by the cultural work and alternative narratives of hip-hop and punk pedagogues who banded against many of the unjust conditions influencing their lives in North America during the 1980s and 1990s. Their narrative reflected working-class youth and communities dealing with joblessness, homelessness, over policing, police brutality, and overcrowded and unfunded schools (Malott & Porfilio, 2007; Porfilio & Carr, 2010; Prier, 2010). Youth have now merged the two alternative cultures, analyzing their music, art, and activism, in order to reflect critically on how neoliberal globalization, deindustrialization, speed technology, and Western militarism are spawning social and economic problems in localized contexts as well as fueling economic and environmental devastation across the globe.

The hip-hop and punk pedagogues' activism also functions as emancipatory guideposts for many of today's disaffected youth. They learn what steps to take in building a collectivist, worldwide, intergenerational movement to subvert the social relations responsible for today's morally bankrupt world. For example, hip-hop artists, punk pedagogues, activists, and other intellectuals have created a virtual community called Rap Conscient (www.rap-conscient.com). Community members generate blogs, essays, and share their music to confront the policy makers, business leaders, and politicians responsible for marginalizing youth socially, emotionally, and economically. Artists who frequent the website also invite calls to action, highlight worldwide protests, and publicize events and concerts designed to challenge the neoliberal status quo. Furthermore, the website provides community members with links to the following categories of social justice organizations and groups: anti-publicity organizations, hip-hop artists, militant groups, libertarian groups, media alternatives, and political prisoner organizations (Porfilio & Porfilio, 2010).

Other youth have developed an online presence to bring awareness to their grassroots efforts, which are designed to confront social injustice in their schools and in their communities. For instance, Seattle's Young People's Project is typical of how many youth-led organizations, which are supported financially by non profit organizations and socially by adults, employ the Internet to showcase how their groups empower youth "to express themselves and to take action on the issues that affect their lives" (http://www.sypp.org/about-us). Youth showcase a range of activities on the Internet, such as workshops, participatory action research projects, conferences, and speaker series, in which they partake to make sense of the hegemonic forces causing racism, classism, homophobia, sexism, and environmental degradation. Finally, some youth artists not only employ technology and generate cultural activities to educate other youth about social problems impacting the globe, but also use the same pedagogical forms to engage educators and activists about the salience of implementing their messages, cultural work, and art directly within schools and their surrounding communities. It is here that we pinpoint how one particular youth-led initiative, the 411 Initiative for Change, uses the virtual world to get its social commentary and instructional materials to youth and educators, as well as to showcase how art, music, and technology can be fused to generate culturally-relevant forms of instruction. Their artistic and pedagogical work has the potency to captivate youths' attention and interest in understanding their social world and in joining their peers and other socially-committed actors in the ongoing global struggle to eliminate injustice, hate, and hostility.

The 411 Initiative for Change and Research Methods

More than 10 years ago the 411 Initiative for Change launched in Toronto, Canada in an effort to offer a pathway for young people to analyze and resist unacceptable patterns of human corruption. Tamara Dawit, Patrick McCormick, and Anita Wong founded the organization; they realized that the growing intensification of violence, poverty, pollution, racism, and other social maladies, permeating life across the globe, can only be ameliorated if youth are prepared to be agents of social transformation, individuals who hold the civic imagination to be "self-reflective about public issues and the world in which they live" (Giroux, 2010). The founders also believed it was imperative to provide youth opportunities to network with other "border" youth, activists, and socially-committed artists. By building these connections, they hope the participants generate collectivist movements "on common global issues, in their domestic and international contexts" ("The 411 Initiative for Change"). Thus far, they have reached over 100,000 youth with their multimedia presentations, music, workshops, and art in schools and communities across Canada, and have given inspiration and hope to numerous young adults who frequently seek advice and guidance in relation to solving pressing problems in their lives, problems within their communities, and understanding social issues impacting peoples across the globe. They have also inspired countless educators and activists to implement culturally relevant curricula in K–12 classrooms and other social sites. The curricula are intended to guide youth to be socially aware, empathetic individuals who are dedicated to transforming society. Educators and activists have found invaluable information on the organization's website in their pursuit to transform students' lives, such as instructional designs, youth-led organizations' cultural work, and strategies for developing youth-led organizations within often-hostile educational communities.

Employing qualitative research methods, a uniform set of interview questions was compiled and distributed through e-mail to the participants. The participants include two of the organization's founders and two of the organization's current artists. A qualitative framework was employed because it allows researchers to capture the experiences and subjective experiences and interpretations of social phenomena as well as establishes the participants rather than researchers as the experts in the study (Creswell, 2006; Denzin & Lincoln, 2007). The interview method employed in this study allowed the participants to share their experiences with creating or taking part in youth-led organizations and being situated in oppressive contexts during their childhood. This method also allowed the participants to share their insights in terms of the impact the initiative has had on youth, educators, and other community members, of the social forces that cause young people to become disaffected and oppressed, and of the challenges that may make it difficult to sustain the 411 initiative.

The researchers also engaged in telephone exchanges with the participants. This allowed the researchers to clarify any ambiguous information from the transcripts and the participants to provide further information on their experiences with youth, schools, and social activism (see Appendixes A and B). Then, the authors combed through the transcripts to find common themes within the participants' narratives. The data collection process was completed when the authors examined the youth-led organization's website for additional information that focused on the organization's pedagogical and cultural work.

The participants' narratives provide teacher-educators, administrators, schoolteachers, and activists key insight in developing sustained informal educative initiatives inside and outside of K–12 classrooms, which have the potency to develop students' self-confidence, critical-thinking skills, imagination, and engagement in social and political issues impacting life across the globe. Within the scope of their interviews, the 411 members focused their attention on their *communication* with youth across Canada; the *reaction* from students and administrators to their messages, workshops, multimedia presentations, and community work; and what the *future* looks like for the organization.

Communication With Youth Across Canada

The artists and founders of the 411 Initiative for Change are quite cognizant that classroom practices typically generated by schoolteachers in North America to spark, echoing Freire (2005), a "passion to know" within students are generally a failure. For instance, most students find little relevance in social studies teachers continually spewing disconnected facts about "dead White" men and their military conquests for the purpose of having them regurgitate this information on corporately-sponsored, high-stakes examinations (Kornfeld, 1998). Instead, the 411 team recognizes that most of today's "border" youth express themselves, communicate with each other and their family members, and learn about their social world through various "teaching machines," such as televisions, videogames, cell phones, zines, music, and other art forms[1]. The founders of the organization have much experience engaging youth with technology and culturally relevant artistic forms. For instance, Tamara Dawit, a founder of the organization and currently the executive director, has formulated educational programs that impact social issues around the world, has led initiatives that focus on youth and AIDS, and also has employed the media and advertising to capture social commentary proffered by young people. Tamara has also worked with the National Youth Anti-Racism Network, the 2006

International Aids Conference, and the United Nations Association. Here she speaks about how technology is fused with art to give socially-conscious artists an outlet to express their ideas around issues impacting youth and society as well as to grab the attention of youth who are exposed to their school or community-based presentations.

> *411 is a Canadian arts-based organization founded by a group of young people interested in using art to engage young people in social commentary and advocacy. 411 has worked with members of the Canadian arts, music, and film industry to produce quality arts programming fusing the content of Canadian NGOs and charities working on international development issues affecting young people both in Canada and around the world. 411 aims to provide a platform using the arts as a medium for the voices and ideas of young people to be heard on the world stage.*[2]

Patrick McCormack, program director of the 411 Initiative for Change, is also deeply familiar with how to incorporate music, technology, and art to gain youths' attention and interest in social issues impacting their lives. With a love for hip-hop and a talent for organization and music, Patrick formed the successful group Boogaloo Trybe, which gained popularity from its roots in urban Ottawa. As Mantes, one of the group members, stated, "Boogaloo is not just about a crew, it's about a force, it's about building business, it's about recognizing our roles, it's about stepping up and becoming leaders" (Dj Alive, 2003). Patrick has worked and studied in many areas dealing with music creation, production, and engineering. He has also participated in numerous speaking engagements pertaining to music, black history, and conflict resolution.

In addition to the particular platform that is used to communicate with youth, the 411 organization is cognizant that in order to forge a critical dialogue among youth and to generate a mutual point to embark upon the process of peaceful and transformative social change, its members must illustrate to youth that young people are the social actors who have been the most exploited and have experienced the most social and economic oppression with the rise of neoliberal capitalism (Grossberg, 2007; Author & Carr, 2010; Author & Malott, 2008). Below, Tamara addresses some of the societal issues that the 411 foregrounds to its audience to give a more personalized perspective of why they must become educated about what causes oppression and why they must be active in the struggle to build a more socially just world.

> *Some of the most critical issues impacting young people, both in Canada and internationally, relate back to the basic rights of young people as set out in the UN Convention on the Rights of the Child. In Canada and other countries youth play a very tokenistic role in policy making (if they play any role at all)—especially in the formation of policy that directly impacts young people. Other critical issues including HIV/AIDS (infection and stigma) which is further impacted by poverty—both which are real issues affecting young people even in a "developed" country like Canada. The final issue which 411 has noted through our programming in Canada and overseas relates to integration and belonging (faced by immigrant and refugee populations) and discrimination and exclusion faced by indigenous populations.*

The artists and administrators of the 411 team also create a deep connection with their audience because their cultural work is often a product of struggles they have confronted living in this unjust society, as well as a reflection of a deep commitment to improving the human condition through critical awareness, collectivist movements, and pro-social values, such as freedom, respect, and empathy. Here Patrick notes some of the issues of focus for the 411. Several of the issues he confronted when growing up in Ottawa, Canada, where racism, violence, and encountering whitewashed curricula in schools.

> *Key issues of focus for the 411 Initiative have been HIV/AIDS, Human Rights, Black History Education, Asian Heritage Education, Anti-Violence and Conflict Resolution, Diversity and the Canadian Identity, Girls' Rights, Women's Rights, Anti-Racism, Diversity Appreciation, and various aspects of the music business.*

It can be noted that some aspects seem to be significant to all administrators and artists, while other categories are personal and unique. Tamara, for example, has extensive experience dealing with AIDS awareness and social stigma for those who have the disease. Patrick has dedicated much of his time drawing attention to the importance of black history and eliminating youth violence. The administrators seem to look at the concepts and goals from a macro perspective. They outline the total impact of the 411 organization and highlight all the artists and the topics that the artists cover. The artists, however, have more focused issues emphasized by the nature of their performances and backgrounds. Here Eternia, one of the many artists involved in the 411 Initiative for Change, discusses some of the issues most critical to her work.

> *We have a number of initiatives that we work on including AIDS Awareness, Global Women's Issues, Gun Violence, Black History Month, and more. I've had the privilege of touring with the 411 for AIDS awareness in Canadian high schools, and am about to embark on a tour creating awareness for Women's issues globally.*

Eternia was raised in a poor multicultural Canadian neighborhood. She sought her own path by leaving her household at age fifteen. Despite dealing the social, emotional, and physical costs associated with being impoverished for most her life, she completed high school and college with outstanding grades. Strongly influenced by the wonderful women in her family, Eternia has been active in the Canadian hip-hop industry for more than a decade. She is also deeply committed to learning more about what causes social injustice because she recognizes, unlike the mass media conglomerates and political leaders that demonize, criminalize, and trivialize youth, that young people are "smart and empathetic and aware."

Below, Dwayne Morgan, another artist from the 411 organization, reflects upon how some artists' interests in solving specific social problems motivate motivate thousands of young people to learn more about what causes injustices and how they can formulate their own youth-led initiatives or join other social collectives to eradicate human misery.

> *Through the tours that we've done, we've managed to reach thousands of young people, some who have gone on to start chapters of Amnesty International in their schools. Recently, one of the artists, Rochester, went to Africa with the organization. That experience led to his desire to do more. As a result, he is now actively fundraising and encouraging young people to join him to raise funds for African AIDS orphans. Personally, I hope to help others to understand sexism and misogyny in pop culture.*

A distinguished musician who lives in Toronto, Dwayne has spent his life attempting to better the world in many ways. Dwayne has toured numerous countries and, in appreciation for his music and writing, has been awarded with the African Canadian Achievement Award for Youth Achievement and the Harry Jerome Award for Excellence in the Arts. Frustrated with racial inequity and inspired to help youth across the globe, Dwayne encourages youth to become educated and empower themselves to change the world. A family man and college graduate, he has published chapbooks[3] and volumes of his work.

Each of the administrators and artists brings strength to the organization and, as has been observed, their communication with youth varies. However, as their narratives illustrate, they are cognizant that many youth will only be open to the ideas they proffer during their presentations if they use the technological modalities that youth harness to communicate and to understand themselves and their social world on a daily basis. Their narratives also indicate that the artists must have a deep connection with the issues they highlight during their presentations if youth are to open to the messages generated during their presentations. Finally, the artists and organizers realize that most youth will only connect with their cultural work if they demonstrate how specific social and economic problems impact them and other youth across the globe.

Although the organization's first priority is to develop its workshops and multimedia presentations to make young people engage in social commentary and advocacy, it also must try to package its presentations to at least be palatable to the educators, media outlets, administrators, and citizens who have the power to thwart the organization from engaging young people in the struggle to transform the world. Despite the organizations' and artists' attempts to position the various constituents surrounding the education of youth in Canada to be open to the 411's activists' agenda, the reaction to the organization's agenda and presentations is not unified. Ultimately, there are many social processes involved in how an audience responds to any texts, such as the audience members' subject position, the social context of the act of consumption, and the form in which the text is packaged and presented (Dover, 2007).[4] Below, we document the 411 members' perceptions and experiences with how youth, teachers, and administrators react to the multimedia theatrical presentations, workshops, and other online social-justice initiatives generated by this organization.

Reaction to the 411

Two major audiences seemed to emerge in the communications with the 411 organization. According to the participants, each group held different perceptions and reactions to the messages of the 411 Initiative for Change. The first audience, and primary recipients of the work of the organization, is comprised of students. The second audience includes those individuals and organizations who are related to the target audience, but who are not the chief benefactors of the presentations. These members include media, parents, teachers, and administrators.

The reaction from students has been overwhelmingly positive. This is not surprising because, as demonstrated above, the organization packages its messages in ways to spark students' interest in unearthing what causes injustices and how to work collectively to eliminate oppressive conditions within their schools, communities, and the wider society. The 411 organization serves as a catalyst for social transformation: its members spread a message of hope and they serve as positive role models whom youth can relate to, whom youth can believe in, whom youth can understand, and whom youth can harness to examine the socially-mediated nature of their own experiences. Administrators and artists alike highlighted numerous instances where students responded eagerly and genuinely to the organization's cultural work.

Really, just watching how the youth get into our presentations is very positive. The interaction and engagement is truly inspiring. Young people are smart and empathetic and aware. Everyday it inspires me to learn more, know more, and be a better example. Young people are looking to me for answers. I know many women and girls have approached me and reached out to me, expressing how my music mirrors many of their experiences, such as pain, sadness, joy, and others. They say, "It's like you wrote my life story in your songs." That happens a lot. I think people crave authenticity and genuineness. I provide that for a lot of people. I'm just me.

Eternia discussed the energy, inspiration, and responsibility that modeling for youth entails. The artists draw in this strength and fortitude and use them to instill the need for fundamental personal and societal change. Students can then guide their friends and family members to reflect upon what causes oppression, generate youth-led initiatives that challenge social inequalities, and procure funding for critical global issues themselves, which have the potency to fuel an ever-expanding epicenter of progress. Many students have discussed the organization's initiatives long after the artists moved on. Not consequently, some of these students joined youth-led organizations; some students fundraised to meet personal and collective goals; and some students even created their own youth-led groups, which are designed to challenge injustice, remove unjust policies, and to implement pro-social institutions.

The accepting and positive reaction of students has not necessarily been the conventional reaction of parents, teachers, and administrators. For those individuals in power in the educational arena, there have been some instances, albeit rarely, where reaction to the presentations was negative. Some individuals hold negative perceptions and uninformed opinions of youth, minorities, and hip-hop music and artists. They appear to have internalized pernicious stereotypes often associated with youth in general and hip-hop and minoritized youth in particular, such as being criminals, lazy, gang bangers, drug users, and anti-intellectual social actors.

The organization felt that some of the audiences' initial perceptions of youth and their presentation also emanated from the privileged racial class status of the audience, who may never have dealt with institutional forms of oppression. Other adults also may have failed to connect with the groups' messages because the form of the presentations employed music and technology that were unfamiliar to them. Most often, the initial misunderstanding or skepticism about the organization was replaced with acceptance and encouragement.

Teachers are often wary of us when we arrive. For example they find out the project is being run by a group of young people or, in some all-white parts of Canada, people of color (we actually had a teacher in Nova Scotia tell a presenter that the school had never had a black person come and talk to the students). These things make the principals and administers look visually worried before the show starts. However, after the show, they are always happy with the project and many of those schools have invited us back. Basically our group defies the stereotype of what guest speakers to high school are supposed to look like.

Tamara noted that some teachers and administrators from white middle-class communities hold stereotypical views of minoritzed youth and hip-hop culture and look "visually worried" before the 411 artists perform. Patrick, who wisely observed that the organization had the ability to "smash stereotypes," also shared comments about the need for the organization to build credibility with multiple institutions, particularly schools. Many times adults questioned the motives of the group, most likely because they wonder whether the group has the understanding or ability to make a difference in the lives of students, and doubted that the 411 organization could accomplish its goals.

However, the participants do not mention the numerous educators, administrators, and teachers, and youth across Canada who never got beyond their resistance to the 411 organization, its messages, and its members. They are the individuals who were exposed to the artists' messages and the organizers' lesson plans on the Internet or learned about the organization from students in their learning communities. Beyond this shallow contact with the 411, they never plan to have any additional contact with the youth-led initiative. They never got beyond the negative stereotypes associated with the artists, beyond seeing the artists' messages as irrelevant because they believe the Canadian society supports multiculturalism and diversity, and beyond blaming youth for the social and economic problems resonating within and outside of Canada. In the end, most schoolteachers and adults realized that the 411 organization felt positively about the impact the presentation had on their academic communities. It remains questionable, however, whether some audience members believe in the organization's message of guiding students to become self-reflective about the nature of their world, and whether they build upon the organization's cultural work in the attempt to leave youth better prepared and more motivated to become involved in promoting social justice and equity in schools and in society.

The Future of the 411

Accompanying the themes of communication and reaction, there was a realistic and hopeful message concerning the future of the 411 Initiative for Change. Each member of the organization had her or his own concerns and hopes about the future of the organization. Much of the concern was stated in the repeated comments that considered future funding. Because the organization deals with arts and youth, it falls outside many traditional charitable funding categories that are recognized by the Canadian government. With the assistance of numerous artists, organizations, and corporations, the 411 organization has been able to flourish, at least in the short term.

Another potential challenge for the organization is the need to keep youth focused. As every organization grows and ages, there is a distinct possibility that the original energy and focus strays, changes, or loses touch with the initial excitement and direction that brought the organization to life in the first place. Here Dwayne makes it clear that the organization's impact may wane if it fails to address how the social world is altering what is important to Canadian youth:

> *The major challenge that faces the organization is the fact that it isn't run by young people. With that said, the organization has to keep in tune with the speed with which youth culture changes, so that it can always stay relevant. Just like the organization, I need to stay relevant. The older I get, the further removed I am from the heart of youth culture. The difficult thing is finding an "in," so that I can always know what issues are on the minds of youth.*

Dwayne and the remaining participants all recognize the importance of how their age may eventually disconnect them from the culture that impacts their current audience. Addressing this challenge is necessary to keep the organization relevant to its current audience and to bring new youth into its programs.

Not coincidently, the participants mentioned they think it is vital to be open to the ideas put forth by youth in terms of making the 411 more culturally-relevant and youth-centered. Over the past decade, the organization has, in several cases, acted upon the suggestions put forth by youth. It now incorporates contemporary issues impacting youth in Canada as well as the cultural forms consumed and produced by young adults. For example, based on youths' feedback, the organization generated a "video commentary with girls in countries around the world, theater, music performance and audience participation" for the purpose of giving girls across the globe a space to highlight "both their struggles and successes in impacting change as local heroes" (http://www.whatsthe411.ca/). Also, based on youths' suggestions, the organization is contemplating reaching out to punk artists who are committed to fostering youth consciousness and activism. By continually acknowledging and respecting world issues significant to youth, as well as listening to the concerns and ideas generated by its audience, the 411 organization believes it will stay relevant, young, and positive for many years to come.

Eternia provided the researchers some lyrics that summarized her thoughts and desires for the future:

> *The story isn't over, my friends, it's the beginning.*
> *Some things I can't explain in words, it takes a stronger vision.*
> *But still – listen to the story, God forgive him for me,*
> *Have mercy on my father's soul when he's to meet your glory.*
> *'Cause every man's a sinner right? Some will take a life…*
> *Some will beat their wife, repenting for sins in afterlife.*
> *Nobody deserves the life you led – my mother, you bled for me,*
> *Fought tooth and nail just to be there for me.*
> *In the trunk of the car, were you scared for me?*
> *Knowing that he'd pull the trigger on you, in a second you'd be dead for me?!*
> *And that's the funny part of matrimony –*
> *Feeling that you got a duty to the church, u'd sacrifice your own body.*
> *I love my life, I love my mother, and I love myself.*
> *I love my family, I'd sacrifice to no one else.*
> *And if you taught me one thing, Mother you taught me well: this is just another survival story to tell.*
> *And if you taught me one thing, Mother you taught me this:*
> *Always have Faith, Live Strong, and Resist!* ("Its called life," 2005)

As the song described, invoking positive change in a society predicated on greed, materialism, and individualism is a struggle. It is not an easy road, but there is tremendous significance in those who lead the way as well as in the journey itself. The selfless and talented individuals in the 411 Initiative for Change exemplify such leadership.

Through the participants' narratives, we learned several key insights in relation to promoting culturally-relevant and youth-centered pedagogies within schools and other social contexts. Teachers, activists and other citizens would be best served to have a personal connection to the social and cultural issues they highlight for their audience, employ technological mediums familiar to contemporary youth, and capture how current social and economic issues directly impact youth across the globe. They ought to be prepared to confront resistant educators, parents, administrators and youth who have been inculcated to believe that the problems confronting global citizens are a result of individual deficiencies, the toxic values embraced by minoritized groups, or today's socially generative youth, rather than connecting how neoliberal policies, practices, and structures are behind the intense suffering and misery experienced by most globalized citizens. Finally, they ought to be responsive to the social and economic forces that alter what youth find socially relevant, be open to the ideas put forth by youth, and recognize if their way of thinking and doing are out of sync with youth.

The Value of Youth-Led Organizations and Arts to Engendering a Transformative Pedagogy for the 21st Century

The clarion call generated by Joe Kincheloe, (2007, p. 10) before his untimely death, to reinvigorate critical pedagogy "as we move toward the second decade of the twenty century," so that it "is to be more than a historical blip on the educational landscape" can be answered, in part, by schoolteachers, administrators, critical scholars, and other activists taking seriously the artistic forms and cultural work produced by youth-led organizations, such as the 411 Initiative for Change. The directors of the 411 Initiative for Change place at the forefront the experiences and ideas of youth who are dedicated to understanding what causes oppression in their world and how they can engage other youth in the same reflexive examination of uncovering the policies, practices, and structures making the world miserable for youth and the vast majority of global citizens. Unlike some critical pedagogues who fail to think about how to make their messages of critique and hope assessable to youth and other citizens, the activists and artists from the 411 are dedicated, like Kincheloe, to developing methods that broaden the scope of transformative work in schools, on the Internet, and in other social contexts. As we have demonstrated, they design multimedia presentations that attract youths' interests and attention, reflect upon how their own lived experiences can be used as a bridge to help youth and adults reflect upon what is responsible for injustice inside and outside of schools, and structure workshops, instructional designs, and highlight other resources that can help educators and school leaders develop additional forms of critical pedagogies inside and outside of their learning communities.

Therefore, we call on critical pedagogues to examine the cultural manifestations and cultural work generated by youth. For instance, the Ya-Ya network is a youth-led organization that uses multimedia presentations and workshops, and engages in critical dialogue with anti-racist, anti-sexist, and other allies in order to eliminate the recruitment of disempowered youth into the U.S. military (http://www.yayanetwork.org/). There are also critical elements of youth culture, such as those possessed by anarchists, queer youth, and female punks, that capture what factors cause oppression in youths' lives, provide guidance in building collective movements that challenge the structures breeding social inequalities, and lend vision for structuring schools and the wider society on democratic rather than on asymmetrical power relationships (Driver, 2008; Leblanc, 1999; Haworth, 2010). If critical pedagogues take seriously the cultural manifestations and cultural work generated by socially aware and critically engaged youth, critical pedagogy will move beyond being an 'ivory tower' phenomenon that merely stirs discussion and debate among academics and students in graduate seminars, in coffeehouses, in journal articles, or at academic conferences. Critical pedagogy will become an inclusive social force that pinpoints how today's globalized, technological, electronic-based era impacts youth as well as highlights subjugated knowledge generated by youth and other oppressed social groups. Therefore, critical pedagogy will have the potency to meet its major challenge of the second decade of the 21st century—how to engaging youth and other concerned social actors in a reflexive process to critically understand and transform the world.

Notes

1. We are very cognizant that corporate giants also win from youths' use of multimedia and attraction to media culture, as they not only inculcate youth to embrace such hegemonic ideologies of consumerism, individualism, and intolerance, but also propagate a lucrative market to sell goods and services to children and their caregivers. The 411 Initiative for Change does attempt to get beyond how youth typically use technology and their interaction with media culture. The artists guide youth to develop their own alterative stories and poems with technology. They showcase their intellectual work online and perform their work in schools and in their communities.
2. To help center the participants' voices in this center, we chose to italicize their narratives and lyrics.
3. A chapbook is recognized by Dictionary.com as "A small book or pamphlet containing poems, ballads, stories, or religious tracts." Modern chapbooks frequently appear as online publications of poetry that circulate within specific spheres of content.
4. There is much to offer critical pedagogues by taking a more in-depth examination of the social process behind youth and teachers' consumption of media texts produced by student-led organizations such the 411 Initiative for Change. This form of investigation is beyond the scope of our project, since our focus was centered on understanding the youth artists and leaders' motivation for creating this youth-led initiative, how they spark youths' interest in understanding the nature of their social worlds, their experiences with interacting with youth and teachers who were exposed to their cultural work, and the strategies they implemented to overcome barriers to enacting youth-based initiatives in K–12 schools.

References

Casella, R. (2008). Security, pedagogy, and the free-market approach to "troubled youth." In B. J. Porfilio & C. Malott (Eds.), *The destructive path of neo-liberalism: An international examination of urban education* (pp. 63–80). Rotterdam, Netherlands: Sense Publishers.

Chapbook. (2009). *Dictionary.com*. Retrieved December 23, 2009 from http://dictionary.reference.com/browse/chapbook.

Creswell, J. W. (2006). *Qualitative inquiry and research design: Choosing among five approaches*. New York: Sage Publishers.

Denzin, N. K., & Lincoln, Y. S. (2007). *Collecting and interpreting qualitative materials*. New York: Sage Publications.

Dj Alive. (2003, August 31). Interview with Boogaloo Trybe. In *Hip Hop Canada: Interviews*. Retrieved December 23, 2009 from http://www.hiphopcanada.com/_site/entertainment/interviews/ent_int089.php

Dover, C. (2007). Everyday talk: Investigating media consumption and identity amongst school children. *Particip@tions, 4*(1). Retrieved June 13, 2009 from http://www.participations.org/Volume%204/Issue%201/4_01_dover.htm

Drive, S. (2008). *Queer youth cultures*. Albany, NY: SUNY Press.

Eternia. (2005). Love. On *It's called life* [CD]. Toronto: Urbnet Records.

The 411 initiative for change. (n.d.). Retrieved June 13, 2008 from http://www.whatsthe411.ca

Freire, P. (2005). *Teachers as cultural workers: Letters to those who dare teach*. New York: Westview Press.

Ginwright, S., Noguera, P., & Cammarota, J. (Eds.). (2006). *Beyond resistance! Youth activism and community change: New democratic possibilities for practice and polices for America's youth*. New York: Routledge.

Giroux, H. A. (2007). Democracy, education and the politics of critical pedagogy. In P. McLaren & J. Kincheloe (Eds.), *Critical pedagogy: Where are they now?* (pp. 1–8). New York: Peter Lang.

Giroux, H. A. (2009). *Youth in a suspect society: Democracy or disposability?* New York: Palgrave Macmillan.

Giroux, H. A. (2010). Rethinking education as a practice of freedom: Paulo Freire and the promise of critical pedagogy. *Truthout*. Retrieved January 8, 2010 from http://www.truthout.org/10309_Giroux_Freire

Grossberg, L. (2007). Cultural studies, the war against kids, and the re-becoming of U.S. modernity. In N. K. Denzin & M. D. Giardina (Eds.), *Contesting empire globalizing dissent: Cultural studies after 9/11* (pp. 231–249). New York: Paradigm Publishers.

Haworth, R. (2010). Anarcho-punk: Radical experimentations in informal learning spaces. In B. J. Porfilio & P. R. Carr (Eds.), *Youth culture, education and resistance: Subverting the commercial ordering of life* (pp. 183–196). Rotterdam, Netherlands: Sense Publishers.

Kincheloe, J. (2007). Critical pedagogy for the 21st century: Evolution for survival. In P. McLaren & J. Kincheloe's *Critical pedagogy: Where are they now?* (pp. 9–42). New York: Peter Lang.

Kippenbrock, J., & Thornburgh, J. (2009). Having a say: Youth and educational activism. Retrieved January 3, 2010 from http://www.whatkidscando.org/featurestories/2009/07_having_a_say/index.html\

Kornfeld, J. (1998). Melting the glaze: Exploring student responses to liberatory social studies. *Theory into Practice, 37*(4), 306–313.

Kozol, J. (2006). *The Shame of the Nation: The restoration of apartheid schooling in North America*. Pittsburgh: Three Rivers Press.

Leblanc, L. (1999). *Pretty in punk: Girl's gender resistance in a boy's subculture*. Rutgers, NJ Rutgers University Press.
Lund, D., & Nabavi, M. (2010). Renewing youth engagement in social justice activism. In B. J. Porfilio & P. R. Carr (Eds.), *Youth culture, education and resistance: Subverting the commercial ordering of life* (pp. 91–110). Rotterdam, Netherlands: Sense Publishers.
Malott, C., & Porfilio, B. (2007). Punk rock, hip-hop and the politics of human resistance: Reconstituting the social studies through critical media literacy. In D. Macedo & S. Steinberg's *Media Literacy: A reader* (pp. 582–592). New York: Peter Lang.
McLaren, P. L., & Kincheloe, J. L. (Eds.) (2007). *Critical pedagogy: Where are they now?* New York: Peter Lang.
Porfilio, B. J., & Carr, P. R. (Eds.) (2010). *Youth culture, education and resistance: Subverting the commercial ordering of life*. Rotterdam, Netherlands: Sense Publishers.
Porfilio, B. J., & Malott, C. (Eds.). (2008). *The destructive path of neo-liberalism: An international examination of urban education*. Rotterdam, Netherlands: Sense Publishers.
Porfilio, B. J., & Porfilio, S. M. (2010). Hip-hop pedagogues: Youth as a site of critique, resistance and transformation in France and in the neo-liberal social world (pp. 129–148). In B. J. Porfilio & P. R. Carr (Eds.), *Youth culture, education and resistance: Subverting the commercial ordering of life. Rotterdam,* Netherlands: Sense Publishers.
Prier, D. (2010). Hip-hop as a counter-public space of resistance for Black male youth. In B. J. Porfilio & P. R. Carr (Eds.), *Youth culture, education and resistance: Subverting the commercial ordering of life* (pp. 111–128). Rotterdam, Netherlands: Sense Publishers.
Ross, E. W., & Gibson, R. (Eds.). (2007). *Neoliberalism and education reform*. Cresskill, NJ: Hampton Press.
Rap conscient. (n.d) Retrieved June 13, 2008 from www.rap-conscient.com
Saltman, K. J., & Gabbard, D. (2010). *Education as enforcement: The militarization and corporatization of schools (2nd ed.)*. New York: Routledge.
Seattle young people project. (n.d.) Retrieved January 8, 2010 from http://www.sypp.org/about-us
Verderame, T. (2009). Breaking the silence: Youth and social justice. Retrieved January 2, 2010 from http://www.whatkidscando.org/featurestories/2009/11_breaking_the_silence/index.html
Ya-Ya Network. (n.d.). Retrieved July 1, 2010 from http://www.yayanetwork.org/

Appendix A

Questions for the directors:

1. In your own words, tell us about the 411 project.
2. When did the 411 movement begin?
3. What was the motivation for the 411 project?
4. What are some of the most critical issues facing contemporary youth in Canada and across the globe?
5. Does the 411 organization focus on specific issues? Please list those issues, explain what they are, and elaborate on 411's methods to impact the issues.
6. Specifically, how have individuals and organizations responded to the 411 project?
7. What are some of the implementation challenges that occurred during the formulation and continuance of the 411 project?
8. What are some of the most positive aspects of the 411 project?
9. How could the 411 project be improved?
10. Where is the 411 organization going in the future?

Appendix B

Questions for the artists:

1. In your own words, tell us about the 411 project.
2. What are the most positive aspects of the 411 project?
3. Can you provide some examples that show how the 411 project has influenced youths in Canada and across the globe?
4. What challenges does the 411 organization face?
5. How could the 411 project be improved?
6. Please tell us some personal history (such as your age, the location of your birth, the location of your childhood, etc.).
7. What were some key struggles that you faced when growing up?
8. When and why did you begin in the 411 organization (what was your motivation)?
9. What specific issue(s) do you hope to bring to the forefront of public knowledge? Please list and explain those issue(s).
10. Please list some figures that influence(d) your life/art.
11. Can you provide some examples that show how your music/art has influenced youths in Canada and across the globe?
12. What things have you done, do you do, and do you plan on doing that positively impact social justice issues?
13. How have individuals and organizations responded to you as an artist?
14. What challenges do you face?
15. Can you provide some lyrics that summarize your thoughts and desires for change?
16. Where do you see the 411 project going in the future?

Editors

NANCYE MCCRARY is associate professor of Education and Chair of the Department of Professional Studies at St. Catharine College. She has published on issues of social justice in *Critical Education*, *Educational Technology Research & Development*, *Journal of Postsecondary Education and Disabilities*, *Social Education*, and *Theory & Research in Social Education*, as well as a several book chapters. She is also an instructional designer and visual artist, employing aesthetic mediation and narrative forms of instruction to move learners toward embracing social justice in education.

E. WAYNE ROSS is professor in the Department of Curriculum and Pedagogy and co director of the Institute for Critical Education Studies at the University of British Columbia. Prior to joining the UBC faculty in 2004, he was Distinguished University Scholar at the University of Louisville. He has also taught social studies education and curriculum studies at the State University of New York campuses at Albany and Binghamton and was a secondary social studies and day care teacher in North Carolina and Georgia. His most recent books include *The Social Studies Curriculum: Purposes, Problems, and Possibilities* (4th Edition) and *Critical Theories, Radical Pedagogies, and Social Education* (with Abraham P. DeLeon). He edits three journals: *Critical Education* (criticaleducation.org), *Workplace: A Journal for Academic Labor* (workplace-gsc.com), and *Cultural Logic* (clogic.eserver.org) and is co founder of the Rouge Forum (rougeforum.org). Find him on the web at ewayneross.net and follow him @ewayneross.

Contributors

FAITH AGOSTINONE-WILSON is associate professor of Education at Aurora University in Aurora, Illinois. She is the author of *Dialectical Research Methods in the Classical Marxist Tradition* and *Marxism and Education Beyond Identity: Sexuality and Schooling*, and has several articles published in *Journal for Critical Education Policy Studies, Critical Education, SoJo Journal: Education Foundations and Social Justice Education,* and *Public Resistance*. A member of the Rouge Forum educational collective, Faith lives in Waukegan, Illinois and her research interests include education policy, sexuality, and counter-hegemonic research methodologies. Currently she is editing a group authored book for advisors who work with undergraduates conducting research.

LEAH BAYENS is the developer and coordinator of the Berry Farming and Ecological Agrarianism Program at St. Catharine College. This program translates Wendell Berry's visions for thriving farming communities into interdisciplinary, experiential learning-oriented and ecology-based sustainable agriculture bachelor's degrees. She earned her PhD from the University of Kentucky in 19th-century American and environmental literature in 2011 and serves as assistant professor of English and chair of the Department of Earth Studies.

FOUR ARROWS (Wahinkpe Topa), aka Don Trent Jacobs, earned a doctorate in Curriculum and Instruction with a cognate in Indigenous Worldviews from Boise State University. Formerly dean of Education at Oglala Lakota College and a tenured associate professor at Northern Arizona University, he is currently on the faculty at the College of Educational Leadership and Change at Fielding Graduate University. Of Cherokee/Irish ancestry, he is also a "made relative" of the Oglala and has fulfilled his Sun Dance vows with them. He currently lives with his artist wife in a small fishing village in Mexico where he is working on his 20th book, *Reoccupying Education*. His previous publications can be reviewed at http://www.teachingvirtues.net

RICH GIBSON is an emeritus professor at San Diego State University and a part-time community college history professor. He has worked as a pot and pan washer, ambulance driver, Ford Rouge Plant iron foundry worker, classroom teacher, organizer, arbitration specialist, and bargaining agent for the National Education Association and the Director of Organizing for a federal workers' union. He was a professor of labor relations and history at Wayne State University in Detroit, and a social studies professor at SDSU. With perhaps 10 others, he founded what is now the largest local in the UAW–Local 6000, state employees, not auto workers. He is saddened, but not surprised, that the local became what it is—just another dues collection machine and protection racket. For seven years, he actively served on the Steering Committee of the Historians Against the War, until they could no longer handle his insistence on the reality of class war and empire in their midst. He'll run again. He is a co founder of the Rouge Forum. He can be reached at rg@richgibson.com

DAVE HILL is research professor of Education at Anglia Ruskin University in Chlemsford, England and visiting professor of Education at the National University of Athens (Greece); Middlesex University, (London); and The University of Limerick (Ireland).

STAUGHTON LYND is an American conscientious objector, peace and civil rights activist, historian, professor, author, and lawyer.

GLENABAH MARTINEZ (Taos/Dine), an associate professor in the Department of Language, Literacy, and Sociocultural Studies at the University of New Mexico, was raised in Taos Pueblo. At UNM she teaches graduate and undergraduate courses in education theory, policy, and praxis and teaches Native American Studies to Indigenous youth at the Youth Diagnostic Development Center in Albuquerque. Dr. Martinez's research focuses on Indigeneity, youth, and education, with a particular emphasis on Indigenous youth, critical pedagogy, and the politics of social studies curriculum. She captures these research areas in her 2010 book, *Native Pride: The Politics of Curriculum and Instruction in an Urban, Public High School*. She continues this scholarship today in a narrative ethnographic study titled, *An Examination of Educational Experiences of Indigenous Youth in a New Mexico Bordertown*. Dr. Martinez is a contributing editor to the *Wicazo Sa Review* and is a co-coordinator of the K–12 curriculum project: *100 Years of State and Federal Policy: The Impact on Pueblo Nations Curriculum*. Prior to earning her PhD from the University of Wisconsin at Madison, she taught high school social studies for 14 years.

DARCIA NARVAEZ is professor of psychology at the University of Notre Dame and studies moral development and well-being. Her most recent books are *Neurobiology and the Development of Human Morality: Evolution, Culture and Wisdom* (2014); *Ancestral Landscapes in Human Evolution: Culture, Childrearing and Social Wellbeing* (co edited with Valentino, Fuentes, McKenna, & Gray, 2014).

SUSAN OHANIAN is National Resistance Editor for *Substance* newspaper and Fellow of the New England Society for the Study of Education. She is a long time teacher and author of more than 300 essays and 25 books, including *Why Is Corporate America Bashing Our Public Schools?* (with Kathy Emery). She can be found on the web at susanohanian.org

BRAD J. PORFILIO is the director of Doctorate in Educational Leadership for Social Justice at California State University, East Bay. He has published numerous peer-reviewed articles, edited volumes, book chapters, and conference papers on the topics of urban education, youth culture, critical social studies education, neoliberalism and schooling, transformative education, teacher education, and gender and technology. He teaches courses on critical pedagogy, qualitative research, globalization and education, multicultural education, foundations of education, and curriculum theory.

DOUG SELWYN is a professor of education at the State University of New York at Plattsburgh. He taught for 14 years in the Seattle public schools and was Washington State social studies teacher of the year in 1990–1991. His most recent book is *Following the Threads: Bringing Inquiry Research Into the Classroom*, published by Peter Lang. He is a cofounder of the North Country Alliance for Public Education, a parent and educator group working toward supporting a public education system that truly serves the students and the public.

PATRICK SHANNON has taught, worked with teachers, and conducted research across North America. A former preschool and primary grade teacher, he is the author, co author, or editor of nine books. Most recent titles: *Reading Poverty* and *Education and Cultural Studies*. He is the chair of the Research Foundation for the National Council of Teachers of English.

ALAN J. SINGER is a social studies educator in the Department of Teacher Education Programs at Hofstra University in Long Island, New York and the editor of *Social Science Docket* (a joint publication of the New York and New Jersey Councils for Social Studies). Dr. Singer is a graduate of the City College of New York and has a PhD in American history from Rutgers University. He taught at a number of secondary schools in New York City. Dr. Singer is the author of *Education Flashpoints* (Routledge, 2014), *Teaching to Learn, Learning to Teach: A Handbook for Secondary School Teachers, (2nd ed.)* (Routledge, 2013), *Social Studies for Secondary Schools (4th ed.)*, (Routledge, 2014), *Teaching Global History* (Routledge, 2011), and *New York and Slavery, Time to Teach the Truth* (SUNY, 2008). He has a regular blog on educational issues on *Huffington Post*.

PAUL STREET (www.paulstreet.org) is the author of numerous books, including *Empire and Inequality: America and the World Since 9/11* (Paradigm, 2004), *Segregated Schools: Educational Apartheid in the Post-Civil Rights Era* (Routledge, 2005); *Racial Oppression in the Global Metropolis* (Rowman & Littlefield, 2007), *The Empire's New Clothes: Barack Obama in the Real World of Power* (Paradigm, 2010), and (co authored with Anthony DiMaggio) *Crashing the Tea Party: Mass Media and the Campaign to Remake American Politics* (Paradigm, 2011). Street can be reached at paulstreet99@yahoo.com

EUSTACE THOMPSON is an associate professor of Teacher Education and chair of the Department of Teacher Education Programs in the Hofstra University School of Education. Dr. Thompson earned his BA from the City College of New York in political science and secondary education, a MS from Long Island University in social science, and a MA and PhD from New York University in educational administration. He has 37 years of experience in urban and suburban public schools as a social studies teacher, middle school and high school principal, and as a district-level administrator.

TARA M. TUTTLE is the director of the Honors Program and an associate professor of English and Gender Studies at Saint Catharine College, a private Dominican college in rural

Kentucky. Her research examines the effects of religious belief on expressions of female sexuality in contemporary American popular culture and the ways in which contested groups use discourse from the dominant paradigm to challenge oppressive practices.

MICHAEL WATZ is a lecturer in the Educational Foundations program at Buffalo State College, SUNY. He teaches courses on the psychological and social foundations of education. He has published several peer-reviewed articles and given numerous conference presentations on the topics of character education, critical social studies education, and youth culture.

sj Miller & Leslie David Burns
GENERAL EDITORS

Social Justice Across Contexts in Education addresses how teaching for social justice, broadly defined, mediates and disrupts systemic and structural inequities across early childhood, K–12 and postsecondary disciplinary, interdisciplinary and/or transdisciplinary educational contexts. This series includes books exploring how theory informs sustainable pedagogies for social justice curriculum and instruction, and how research, methodology, and assessment can inform equitable and responsive teaching. The series constructs, advances, and supports socially just policies and practices for all individuals and groups across the spectrum of our society's education system.

Books in this series provide sustainable models for generating theories, research, practices, and tools for social justice across contexts as a means to leverage the psychological, emotional, and cognitive growth for learners and professionals. They position social justice as a fundamental aspect of schooling, and prepare readers to advocate for and prevent social justice from becoming marginalized by reform movements in favor of the corporatization and deprofessionalization of education. The over-arching aim is to establish a true field of social justice education that offers theory, knowledge, and resources for those who seek to help all learners succeed. It speaks for, about, and to classroom teachers, administrators, teacher educators, education researchers, students, and other key constituents who are committed to transforming the landscape of schools and communities.

Send proposals and manuscripts to the general editors at:

sj Miller sj.Miller@colorado.edu
Leslie David Burns L.Burns@uky.edu

To order other books in this series, please contact our Customer Service Department at:

(800) 770-LANG (within the U.S.)
(212) 647-7706 (outside the U.S.)
(212) 647-7707 FAX

or browse online by series at:

WWW.PETERLANG.COM

www.ingramcontent.com/pod-product-compliance
Lightning Source LLC
LaVergne TN
LVHW081449060526
838201LV00050BA/1743